KNOWLEDGE-BASED DESIGN: DEVELOPING URBAN & REGIONAL DESIGN INTO A SCIENCE

Faculty of Architecture
Delft University of Technology

KNOWLEDGE-BASED DESIGN: DEVELOPING URBAN & REGIONAL DESIGN INTO A SCIENCE

Ina T. Klaasen

DUP Science / 2004

Colophon

Design **Science** Planning

Series editor:
Dr. I.T.Klaasen, Faculty of Architecture (Spatial Planning), Delft University of Technology (Neth.)
(i.t.klaasen@bk.tudelft.nl)

Published and distributed by:
Delft University Press
P.O. Box 98
2600 MG Delft
The Netherlands
Telephone: +31 15 278 5121
Telefax: +31 15 278 16 61
E-mail: info@library.tudelft.nl

Printed in the Netherlands

Knowledge-based Design: Developing Urban & Regional Design into a Science; dissertation
Keywords: urban design, regional planning, spatial activity patterns, practical science, research by design, theoretical models

ISBN 90-407-2479-2

Translation: Victor Joseph (Amsterdam)
Lay out: Damen en de Wit (Delft)
Cover photograph: Sinai (I.T.Klaasen/D+dW)

This publication is the result of the research programme Sustainable Urban Areas, carried out and financed by Delft University of Technology

I.M. **ARNOLD DIRK KLAASEN 1919-1992**

Contents

Notes on the translation from Dutch into English

The Dutch term *stedebouw* can be translated literally as 'town building'. *Stedebouwkunde*, which accordingly means the 'discipline of town building', is normally translated at Delft University of Technology as 'urbanism', but a more accurate translation would be 'urban planning and design' (*planning and ontwerpen*). The Polish scientist W.W. Gasparski noted (1993) that in some languages, the terms for 'planning' and 'design' have more or less the same meaning, for instance in English, while in others - in particular, Dutch - they do not. The word 'design' has as Gasparkski put it, an 'aesthetical flavour' in many languages, including English (ibid.: 168). This flavour is absent from the Dutch word ontwerpen (conventionally translated as 'design').

In English, the designers of towns have traditionally been called 'town planners' or 'town and country planners'. 'Planning' is still often used interchangeably with more modern terms such as 'urban design', particularly in the United Kingdom. Dutch, however, maintains distinctions between 1. *planologie* ('urban/regional planning'), which has strong connections with economics and politics but only secondary ones with aesthetics, 2. *ontwerpen* ('design'), which is design in the functional or technical sense and does not necessarily include an aesthetic element, 3. *vormgeven* ('visual design'), which has functional motives but a relatively strong aesthetic component and 4. the loan word design, which refers largely to visual design in its most commercial, fashionable and superficial sense: design for design's sake.

The Dutch stedebouwkundige (or *stedebouwkundig ontwerper*) is a designer, not a planner in the strict sense; there are considerable differences between the training of urban designers and that of urban planners in the Netherlands. For the discipline of stedebouwkundig ontwerpen, I have opted for the translation 'urban & regional design', since 'urban design' alone might give the impression that only the lower levels of scale are involved. The urban designer Kevin Lynch preferred the term 'city planning' for the same reason, but few followed him in this, as Banerjee & Southward note in their introduction to the book *Writings and Projects of Kevin Lynch* (Lynch 1990) which they edited. For design in which there is an aesthetic flavour (*vormgeving*), I use the term 'visual design'.

Not surprisingly, these are only a few of the translation problems that affect the field of urban & regional design. Wherever a new term is introduced in the English text, I have inserted the equivalent Dutch term afterwards in brackets, for the benefit of Dutch readers.

1 Motivation, problem statement and research approach

1.1 Motivation: problem statement

"A city can not be a work of art."

(Jane Jacobs 1961,
The Death and Life of Great American Cities: 372)

An implemented design of an urban area imposes long-term conditions on societal processes, such as the opportunities people have to organize their lives in temporospatial respects in a healthy and safe living environment, and the way social, cultural and economic institutions can function. "Cities are the largest and most complex objects that human beings can make" state Hillier and Penn (1991: 2).
In a world like ours, laden with scientific knowledge and its applications, one would expect the construction of these 'objects' to be scientifically based. That is however only indirectly true. The design of urban space is based scarcely, if at all, on substantive scientific knowledge in the area of urban & regional design (*stedebouwkundig ontwerpen*[1]). The spatial functioning of people and institutions in our society is certainly not without problems, however. They include monotonous housing estates with inadequate public transport, poor access to public transport stops and stations, inattention to the requirements of mobility chains, the spreading of regional facilities resulting in increasing traffic congestion (Klaasen & Jacobs 1999), the underutilization of economic location values, the ill-planned siting of city functions (Boer 1989) etc. Besides these spatial conditions being bad in themselves, some of them also contribute to the inequality of opportunity between individuals and between social groups (Klaasen & Radema 1985: 722). Surprisingly, there is hardly any pressure from society to develop more knowledge and understanding about the way our urban areas are designed. It is mainly government officials, and rarely the urban & regional designers, who hear complaints about the difficulty of getting to work, the time it takes to visit someone in hospital without a car, hazardous traffic situations, public spaces that are difficult to keep clean, windswept crossroads, daunting cycle routes, and the impossibility of finding one's way in an unfamiliar part of town. Ivan Nio and Arnold Reijndorp (1997: 234) have observed, on the basis of many interviews with known persons involved in Dutch urban & regional design, that this area of design seems to ignore societal problems.

As to the professional field, there has been very little concern to develop a scientific foundation for urban & regional design, particularly during the last few decades. Widely held notions, such as the uniqueness of each design and each design situation, or such as urban design being an artistic activity based on individual creativity or focussed on conserving cultural heritage, have hitherto left little room for thinking about urban design as a science. The same goes for learning the design craft in a studio in an apprentice and master relationship, with the concomitant test of mastery in the form of a graduation project.

One of the explanations for urban & regional design not being regarded as a science may be the immense complexity of the 'object', the urban area, although the considerable biological adaptability of the human kind undoubtedly plays a part too (Huisman 1996). Another factor is certainly that people tend to regard urban & regional design as a special case of architecture, albeit on a different scale, or concerned with public space as opposed to architecture which is concerned with buildings (Meyer, Heeling, Westrik & Sauren 2000). Not surprisingly, then, the aspect of experiential value (or 'beauty'), which is possibly but not necessarily related to cultural history, receives as much attention in urban & regional design as it does in architecture. For example, urban design is one of the artistic categories of the Dutch *Prix de Rome* competition. This conception of urban & regional design obviously does not leave much room for a scientific approach to the discipline.

As far as designers take any interest in science, that interest concentrates on the process of design, i.e. on developing a theory of design. Such substantive scientific knowledge as there is mainly concerns the context surrounding urban & regional design, e.g. the formulation of present and future societal needs, the project realization process, and the evaluation of historically interesting (realized) designs. Apart from collections of historical examples and certain checklists, one can hardly speak of the existence of a systematically accumulated body of knowledge for urban & regional design, a theory in design, which will support designers in their work. The emphasis is on the realization of concrete projects, and the development of knowledge is therefore attuned to those projects. What people build up that way is experience, Nio and Reijndorp state. Research into the 'city' phenomenon and into the development of this concept actually takes place in other disciplines such as geography, sociology and history (Nio & Reijndorp 1997: 244 ff.).

1.2 Objectives and research approach

> "The notion that one can begin anything at all from scratch, free from the past, or unindebted to others, could not conceivably be more wrong."
>
> (Bryan Magee 1973, *Popper*: 69)

The objectives of the research described in this book are:

- **to lend theoretical support to the assertion that a substantive scientific approach to the discipline of urban & regional design is valid and recommendable; and**
- **to give concrete substance to this substantive scientific approach to the discipline of urban & regional design.**

An assumption underlying this research is that urban & regional design is capable of being developed as a societal relevant science. I base this assumption on the knowledge and insights acquired during the last fifteen years, to an extent through the efforts of students, the first 10 years within the Chair of Urban & Regional Design, after that within the Chair of Spatial Planning of the Faculty of Architecture of the Delft University of Technology. This statement of objectives also carries the implication that this assumption is not universally shared.

The research may be characterized as an intellectual quest, based partly on research results obtained by myself and others in the above-mentioned university subdepartments and partly on literature study. The research approach is cognate to what the methodologist A.D. de Groot, who is highly reputed in the Netherlands, calls an 'interpretative-theoretical study'. This is a form of research that meets the following criteria:

- it establishes connections, if necessary tentative, within a certain body of data;
- it must be impossible to solve the problem directly by experimental tests, and
- the interpretation arrived at is not the only possible one. (Groot (1961) 1968: 325 ff.).

"In fact," De Groot states, 'it is often the case in interpretative studies that the researcher has set down the main outline of his structural and explanatory scheme at a relatively early stage, and then, with this idea in mind, starts probing the subject matter more deeply - reading one study after another and extracting whatever he 'finds useful'." (ibid.: 328).

The present quest is 'structured' by (1) the thinking described above under 'motivation', (2) work carried out within the Chair of Urban & Regional Design based on the growing conviction that a certain research method supported the development of generally applicable, i.e. scientific, urban & regional design knowledge, and (3) the expectation that treating or not treating urban & regional design as a science would prove to be related to the opinion on the significance of urban & regional design for society.

Some important questions that need answering are:

- What position could urban & regional design potentially take in relation to the sciences as a whole?

- How far is this position connected with opinions on the significance of urban & regional design for society, and on the consequent definition of the object of urban & regional design?

- Does the actualization or non-actualization of this potential position of urban & regional design within the field of sciences, or the manner of such actualization, depend on the view held about the definition of the object of urban & regional design?

- What avenue or avenues may be followed, starting from the view that usefulness (including future usefulness) to society is a central aspect of urban & regional design, in order to build up a scientific body of knowledge? What contribution has already been made during recent years to the development of such a body of knowledge?

A research project of this kind is inevitably coloured by the researcher's outlook on the world. I therefore start in Chapter 2, 'Reality, System and Model', by giving an explicit account of my ontological and epistemological standpoints, and a broad definition of the object of the discipline based on these standpoints (see Huisman 1996: 276 ff.) Then, in Chapter 3, 'Science', I explore the field of sciences in general and the potential position of urban & regional design within that field, and sketch a perspective for a scientific approach to this discipline. These chapters supply the foundation for those that follow.

Chapter 4, 'Urban & regional design, physical urban system and society', analyses the significance of the built (*gebouwd en aangelegd*) environment for society, whether views differ on that subject, and what this implies for the definition of the object of urban & regional design. It establishes that the scientific perspective differs according to what one considers the essence of the significance of urban & regional design. Chapter 5, 'Urban & regional design and science', concretizes these perspectives by distinguishing research into what is or was the real situation ('design research'; *ontwerponderzoek*) from research into which real situations are 'possible' and what these possible future real situations in their turn would make possible given the contextual circumstances ('research by design'; *ontwerpend onderzoeken*). I thus involve myself in the ongoing discussion on how 'research by design' must be interpreted if it is to contribute to the development of a substantial theory of urban & regional design.

Examples of results achieved in research by design within the Chair of Urban & Regional Design and subsequently the Chair of Spatial Planning of the Delft University of Technology, are the subject of Chapter 6, 'Developing a practical-scientific body of knowledge'. Some of this material comes from earlier publications.

In the final Chapter, I return to the objectives and research questions stated above and to the answers formulated during my 'quest' and I draw my conclusions. My thesis ends with recommendations based on these conclusions for university training and research in urban & regional design.

2 Reality, system and model

2.1 Reality

"Demandez à un Indien pourquoi le monde reste suspendu dans les airs, il vous répondra qu'il est porté sur le dos d'un éléphant; et l'éléphant sur quoi l'appuiera-t-il? Sur une tortue; et la tortue, qui la soutiendra?.... Cet Indien vous fait pitié; et l'on pourrait vous dire comme à lui: Monsieur Holmes mon ami, confessez d'abord votre ignorance, et faites-moi grâce de l'éléphant et de la tortue." [a]

(Denis Diderot (1749) 1951,
Lettre sur les Aveugles à l'usage de ceux qui voient)

Although the real world is knowable only by approximation - a question of epistemology - that is not to say that the real world does not exist as an object of knowledge, independently of the knowing subject - a question of ontology. The 'object' here refers to a thing, a process, a phenomenon etc., all of which are governed by the spatial coordinates x, y and z and the time coordinate t. Problems in areas such as environmental pollution or vandalism do not simply disappear if we deny knowledge of them; and remedies for problems do not solve them simply because people agree they ought to work.

The real world that exists independently of us as knowing subjects is only knowable by approximation, for there are limits to the cognitive power of human beings. Epistemological questions have biological, sociological and psychological aspects. What we perceive, with or without the aid of instruments, as reality and how we interpret our perceptions is 'filtered' by our human capacities, i.e 'nature', and is influenced by our cultural environment and our individual experiences, i.e. 'nurture' (Huisman 1996).

People perceive the world selectively, using the general organization principles of simplification, categorization and generalization. We also make causal connections, so forming a picture of how reality 'fits together'. The neurologist Oliver Sachs explains some forms of autism as an incapacity to use pragmatic systems to make sense of a chaos of perceptions (1995: 253 ff.).

Not only are our perceptions are matched to our frame of reference, but we perceive what we expect to see (Huisman 1996: 162/163). "Perceptual similarity is the basis of all expectation, all learning, all habit formation. It operates through our propensity to expect perceptually similar stimulations to have sequels perceptually similar to each other. This is primitive

---

a "Ask an Indian why the world remains suspended in the air, he will tell you it is carried on the back of an elephant. What supports the elephant? A tortoise; and who will support the tortoise?.... The Indian pities you; and one could say the same to him as to you: Mr. Holmes, my friend, confess your ignorance from the start and be thankful for the elephant and the tortoise."

induction." (Quine 1995: 19). We anticipate repetitions of events, perceptions and so on, and then we do indeed see them. We impose these regularities on the real world (Popper (1962) 1968: 44) because this has increased our survival prospects in the past - as it still does, for example in complex traffic situations (Huisman 1996: 163). Frames of reference are partly determined by social and cultural factors, with language playing a part because it has an ordering and creative function in thinking (Huisman 1996: 145). Psychologically, we can moreover be motivated to perceive some phenomena more readily than others.

Besides the present reality (that 'which is the case'), we have to deal with a historic reality (that 'which was the case') and a future reality (that 'which will possibly and/or probably be the case'). From the viewpoint of the present, the future is uncertain, just as what is now the present was uncertain in the past. Uncertainty is, of course, a form of non-knowing but it is not the same as an epistemological unknowability[2].

Someone who was born blind and whose eyesight has just been restored by an operation will be overwhelmed by a plethora of visual impulses. That person is still effectively blind, because his or her sensations are unstructured; perception 'drowns' as it were in a deluge of information. (Sachs 1995: 114 ff.; Diderot 1749). As Sachs writes, "We are not given the world; we make our world through incessant experience, categorization, memory, reconnection." (ibid.: 114).
Research by Robberts and Suppes, by Piaget and Inhelder (cited in Harvey 1973: 192/193) shows that children learn to perceive space in a Euclidian sense, by the perception of topological attributes such as proximity and separation, but that innate spatial perception is Riemannian.

Some peoples, despite an excellent capacity for spatial orientation, are unfamiliar with the interpretation and drawing of topographical maps. The urban designer Kevin Lynch illustrates this with an account by the Everest climber Shipton. "Approaching Everest from a new direction, Shipton immediately recognized the main peaks and saddles that he knew from the north side. but the Sherpa guide accompanying him, to whom both sides were long familiar, had never realized that these were the same features, and he greeted the revelation with surprise and delight." (Lynch 1960: 11). The comparative linguist F.H.H. Kortlandt (1997) reports that the language of the Wakashan people of Western Canada has 46 different classes of numerals. People standing still are counted differently from people running, and boats floating alongside one another are counted differently from boats floating in a row. The Nijmegen linguist Stephen Levinson (1999) offers another example. When, in our culture, we wish to indicate (in speech or thought) how objects are spatially disposed relative to one another, we do so from a relative-egocentric perspective: the car is parked to the left of the house, for example. If we go to the other side of the house, and decide that the car is on the left of the house, it means the car has been moved to the other side. Speakers of the Australian aboriginal tongue GuuguYimithirr, by contrast, use an absolute designation of position: the car is on the 'west' of the house, for example.

We systematize and simplify the real world within a given culture in order to comprehend it. We 'see' parts, relationships, patterns and structures. In doing so, we may adopt various viewpoints - literally and figuratively. As a football spectator, you see different patterns of play from the grandstand and from the sidelines respectively. A football connoisseur will observe defensive and attacking patterns, while novice might simply see 22 players running about or standing still as the case may be. Similarly, an advanced chess player will notice significant patterns in the position on the board which would be invisible to a beginner.
These differing viewpoints result in different interpretations of the real world. People with similar frames of reference will have interpretations that overlap to a significant extent (thus forming subcultures). There will always be individual differences, however. Besides, a given individual's interpretation may vary at different times.

A striking example of people seeing what they expect to see (or, rather, not seeing what they do not expect to see) is provided by the 5,300 year old 'ice man' found on the Austrian/Italian border. After remaining unnoticed despite 10 years of detailed scientific study, an arrow head was discovered in the mummified flesh of Ötzi's back in 1991. Yet the arrow head is plainly visible in X-ray photographs such as those published in the newspapers - now that we know it is there (Fig.2-1).

source:
http://www.angelfire.com/me/ij/oetzi.html
(04-2003)

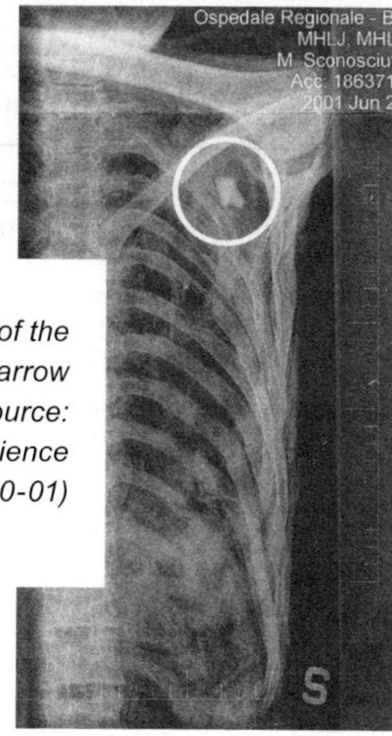

Fig.2-1 Part of an X-ray picture of the chest of the ice man Ötzi. An arrow head is visible inside the circle.(source: NRC-Handelsblad, Science Supplement, 27-10-01)

2.2 System

"Though this be madness, yet there is method in 't."

(William Shakespeare (1564-1616),
Hamlet : Act 2, Scene 2 - 208)

The fact that we perceive reality as a composite of parts with spatial and temporal dimensions means we can consider reality as a system. Many specific definitions have been produced over the years for the term system, which derives from the Greek *systèma* meaning an 'organized whole'. Here I cite that of the urban planner Alan Steiss: '... any entity, physical or conceptual ... which is composed of interrelated parts' (Steiss 1974: 194). Steiss is referring here to closed systems. An open system - and in the real world all systems are open - also has relations to its environment (e.g. a hydrological system, a central heating system, a business enterprise, a school or a language) (Fig.2-2). This environment is in principle unbounded.

Reasoning from the standpoint of systems theory, a system operates according to automatic control and communication mechanisms. If a system consists of conditional relations, that system has a social component (or is a social system), and the term 'system' is strictly speaking being used metaphorically (Huisman 1996: 268 ff.).

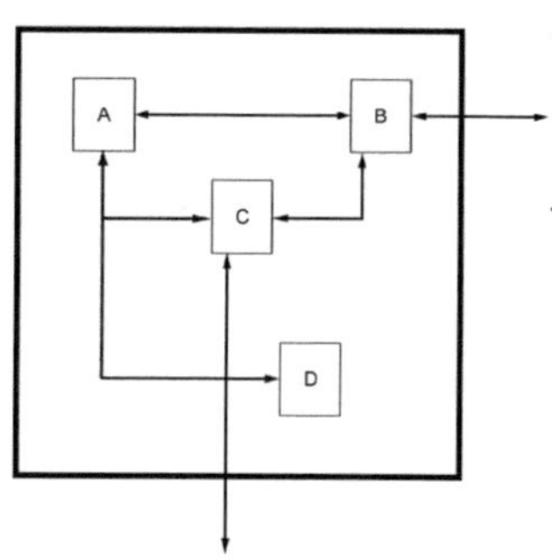

Fig.2-2 Abstract depiction of a system; processes occur within this system under the influence of the environment, causing changes in elements (and/or their attributes) and the relations between elements.

A more precise definition of a system would be that it exists of:

- a set of elements with certain variable characteristics (attributes), plus
- a set of relations between these element-attributes (structure), plus
- a set of relations between these element-attributes and the environment of the distinguished system (Harvey 1973: 451).

This is a verbal formulation of the mathematical definition 'every set S = {A,R} is a system' where A stands for a set of elements and R for a set of relations; stated by Klir and Valach in *Cybernetic Modelling*, 1967 (in Harvey 1973: 451).
If the elements do not possess attributes, then the system is termed 'formal'[3] cf. the dimensionless entity, the mathematical point.

"An element of a system is what it is, only in, and by virtue of, the system of which it forms part." (Roozenburg & Eekels 1991: 39). A positional value (or location-value: *plaatswaarde*) is attributed to an element according to the position it occupies in a system. "The members of a system,...., do not become constituents of the system by means of their immanent qualities, but by means of their distribution or arrangement within the system. The object does not participate in the system by an inherent quality but by its positional value in the system." (Angyal (1941) 1969: 20). This means that merely adding elements-with-attributes to a system (aggregation) does not amount to enlargement of the systems contents: "In aggregates it is significant that the parts are added; in a system it is significant that the parts are arranged."(ibid.: 26).

A set of element-attributes is termed a class. Examples include the class of cities with over 100,000 inhabitants, or the class of plot division forms (*verkavelingsvormen*) occurring within a city.

Relations within systems may be of varying complexity, and either causal or conditional in nature. "Causal thinking ... is almost generally considered as *the* scientific thinking, although it may well be only a subvariety of it." (Angyal (1941) 1969: 29).

People are naturally inclined to perceive wholes or organizations, and by preference we see as little as possible differentiation in those wholes. The internal coherence of a system is exaggerated, as is the demarcation of the system from its environment. "Perception strives, as it were, either to detect no differences or to detect 'exaggerated' differences. As soon as an organization exceeds a certain level of differentiation (or is broken up into parts), we preferentially see as many differences as possible." This can be related psychologically to the law of assimilation-contrast, Vroon proposes (1995: 251), citing Krech and Crutchfield, *Elements of Psychology*, 1961.

The environment of a system is understood to be

- the larger system within which the first-mentioned system is embedded: similar and hierarchical (Fig.2-3) or similar and of the same order (Fig.2-4)
- dissimilar systems that occupy the same space (and time) (Fig.2-5).

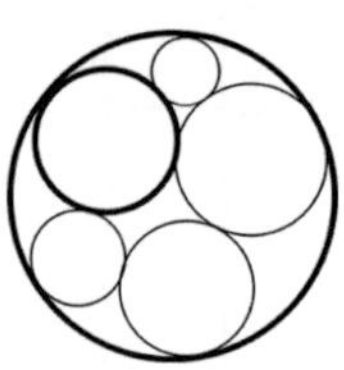

Fig.2-3 System and system environment: similar and hierarchical.

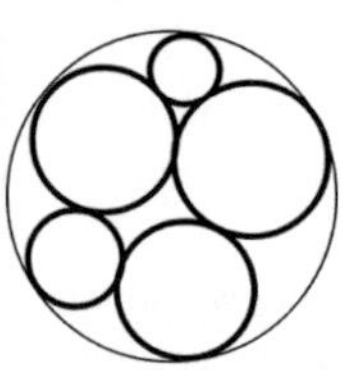

Fig.2-4 System and system environment: similar and equivalent.

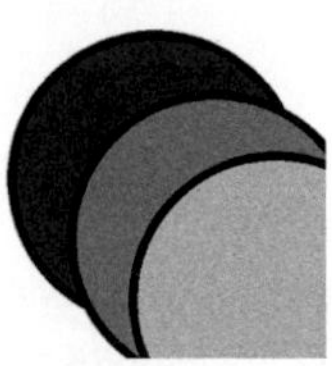

Fig.2-5 System and system environment: dissimilar and equivalent (e.g. natural system, economic system, cultural system).

Systems can be conceived as being linked for modelling purposes in two different ways. Fig.2-6a shows relations existing between the elements of a system only within that system, with a single relation existing between the two systems. Fig.2-6b shows relations existing between the elements of two systems (after Harvey 1973: 453).

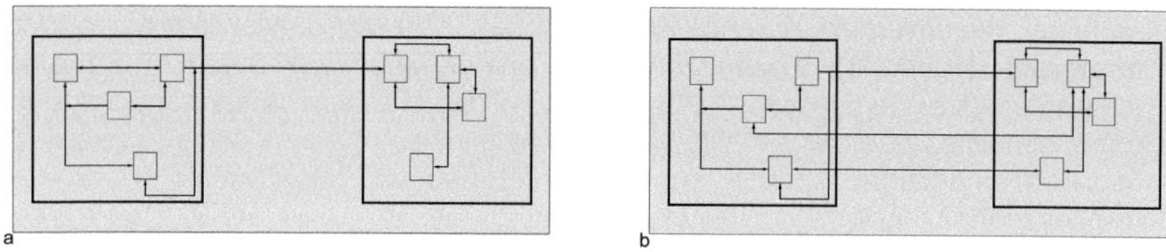

Fig.2-6 Systems can be linked together in two different ways (after Harvey 1973: 453).
In Fig.2-6a relations exist only between the elements of a system within that system, and there is a single same-order or higher-order relation between the two systems.
In Fig.2-6b mutual relations exist between the elements of the two systems.
The way the systems are related to one another in Fig.2-6a is a simplification of the relationship shown in Fig.2-6b.

Similarly, an element (subsystem) may be placed inside a system in two ways. In the system of Fig.2-2, the element 'subsystem D' has only one relation with another element of the system, but the element 'subsystem C' has multiple relations to other system elements.

The user and/or experiencer of a physical system like a chair, a house or a neighbourhood could be regarded as the environment of the physical system, but the object and the user also form a system together. A car is a system in its own right, but a car with a driver (and perhaps passengers) is also a system. The latter system can in turn be an element of a traffic and transportation system.

In order to grasp the world we think of systems in terms of subsystems, and these subsystems may vary widely in size, content and complexity. Systems may thus always be regarded as elements of a higher-order system (Fig.2-7).

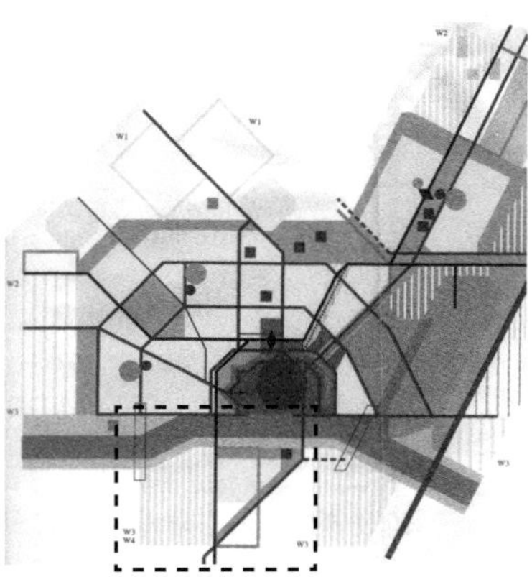

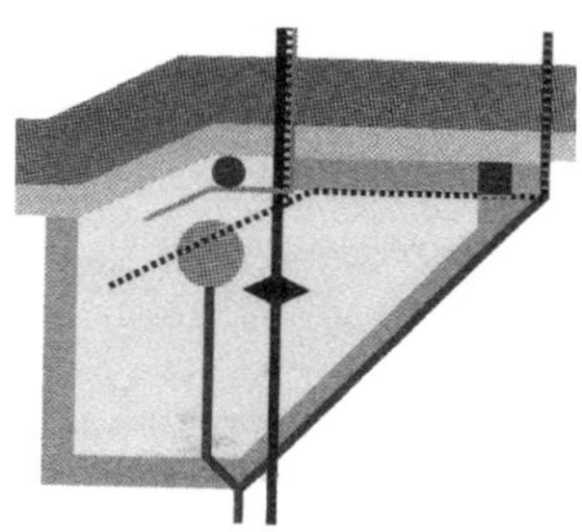

Fig.2-7 The image on the left shows part of a design for the city of Deventer (Neth.). Residential area W4 (see zone with dotted boundary) is an element of the 'Deventer' system but is itself also a system. See the representation of this residential area on the right. The legend has been omitted here. (Source: Niek de Boer, Amsterdam, in collaboration with Urbis Rotterdam; 1989).

We moreover simplify a system by taking a distinct viewpoint of it. This simplification of reality, often deliberate, involves emphasizing certain aspects of reality considered essential and/or omitting aspects considered irrelevant. In other words, it entails systematic incompleteness.

Reality can be past reality, present reality or a probable, desirable and/or possible future reality. "If you try to understand everything at the same time, you will end up understanding nothing", the physicist Lawrence Krauss stated; "The two keywords are abstraction and irrelevant." (1994: 28). "The mind needs in one act to have an overview of the essential characteristics of a domain ..." (Apostel 1961: 15). The environment of a system is also very often simplified. We can simplify a system by thinking of it as a closed system. The system is isolated, as an approximation, from its environment and our attention is focussed on internal processes[4].

Both open and closed systems necessarily have a spatial and/or temporal dimension, because it would otherwise be impossible to imagine more than one separate element. This, in turn, is a precondition for the existence of relations (Angyal (1941)1969: 21; Jong 1992: 17). Elements and their attributes, such as their position with regard to one another, change in time owing to relations (interactions) between the elements and their attributes and to relations between the system and its environment: flows of information, energy, material and living beings - in other words, processes. If a system has an internal structure with only spatial dimensions or only a temporal one (e.g. a piece of music), we can term this a composition.

> "Once her mother has left the room, she opens the score and studies the notes with pencil in hand. She turns the pages upside down and sees that this, too, is fantastic. It is not simply that she "hears" what she sees, but she realizes what an audience would hear when listening to the piece: a structural beauty, which exists as sheet music in space, but as heard music only in time." (Harry Mulisch, *De ontdekking van de hemel* (The Discovery of Heaven) 1992: 76).

A process is said to exist in the case of a prolonged, regular action or succession of actions that takes place or is carried out in a certain manner. Processes too can be subject to change. Processes may be distinguished into cyclic and linear processes (Fig.2-8). Cyclic processes may themselves have a linear component (Fig.2-9). Processes can be reversible or irreversible and rhythmic or stationary; they can be distinguished according to duration and spatial extensiveness (after Otto Lehovec, in Klaasen 1974: 38).

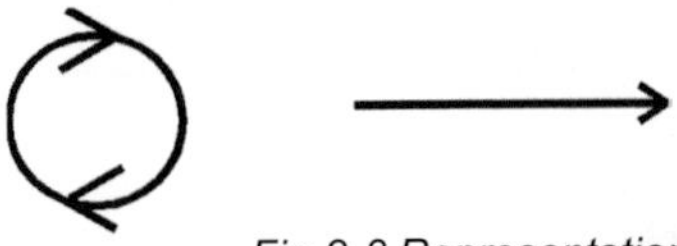

Fig.2-8 Representations of a cyclic process (left) and a linear process (right).

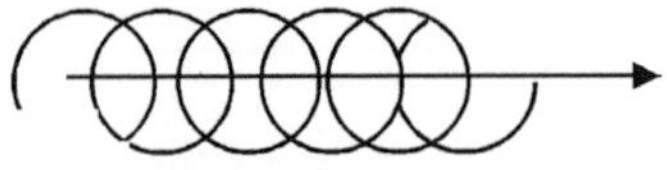

Fig.2-9 Representation of a cyclic process with linear component.

Whether we register spatial or temporal changes depends on the spatial or temporal grain of the observation. "The smallest difference that we wish to or are able to perceive, conceive or represent while not yet designating it as 'equality' is ... the 'grain' of the perception, concept or representation," states De Jong (1992: 16). Registering may relate to the concrete size of an element, but also to its visual or functional sphere of influence.
The concept 'spatial grain' is related to the concept 'spatial scale', and the 'temporal grain' to the 'timescale'. Spatial compositions can be characterized as regular, varied, differentiated, concentrated etc. - but not independently of the spatial 'grain' of the perception (Fig.2-10). In a similar way, the timescale of a mayfly has a different inherent grain to that of a human life, to the Christian era or to the process of mountain formation.

Fig.2-10 According to the grain size chosen, the grains are either different or identical in character (Jong 1992: 17; Jong & Rosemann 2002: 37)

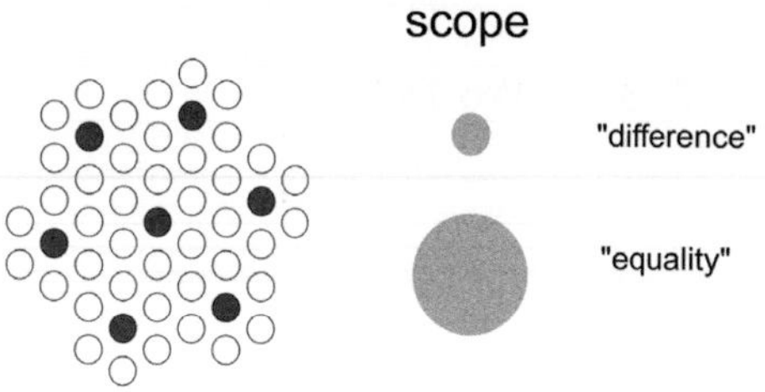

A temporal composition, too, can be regular, varied etc. Minimal music, for example, has a very regular pattern with a low level of variation.

Ik droomde dat ik langzaam leefde... langzamer dan de oudste steen. Het was verschriklijk: om mij heen schoot alles op, schokte of beefde, wat stil lijkt. 'k Zag de drang waarmee de bomen zich uit de aarde wrongen.	I dreamed I lived slowly...slower than the oldest stone. It was awesome: everything that seems still shot up, shook and trembled around me. I saw the urgency with which the trees wrung themselves out of the ground.

M.Vasalis, begin van het gedicht 'Tijd' (The first lines of the poem 'Time'). Uit: Parken en woestijnen (Parks and Deserts), 1940.

According to the timescale chosen, and the temporal grain appropriate to that timescale, a process may be characterized as linear or cyclic. Cycles of mountain formation and mountain erosion take place on a linear geological timescale. The development of mankind is a linear process, the succession of generations is a cyclic one, the life of a human being is linear, and an individual's daily and yearly activities are again cyclic in character.

A relation exists between the order of magnitude of temporal grain and spatial grain, and thus between spatial scale and temporal scale. The changes in shape and position of a desert sand-dune (a relatively small spatial grain) may be observed from week to week (a relatively small temporal grain by geological standards). The development of a desert as an element of the system 'Earth' requires a considerably larger temporal grain if one is to attempt to understand this development.

2.3 Model

> "The model does not originate spontaneously in the human mind, but requires creative activity. Thus senses and intellect both play an active part in our shaping of the model ...."
>
> (A.Kuipers 1961, Model and Insight: 132)

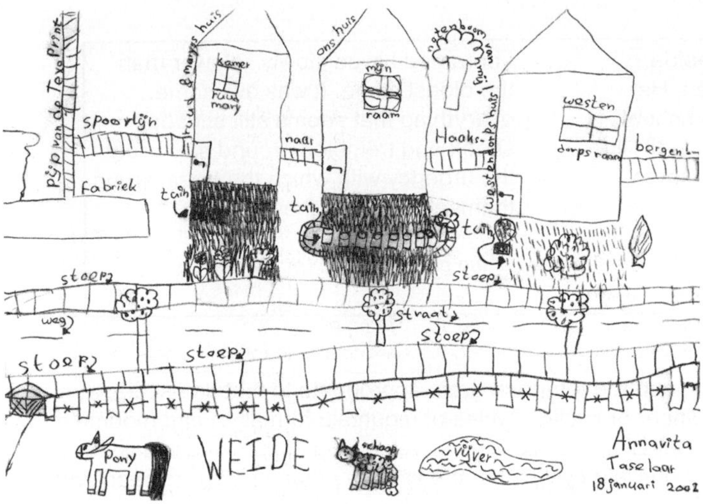

Fig.2-11 We make models even as children. A model of her neighbourhood by Anna Vita Taselaar (11 jaar).

In order to communicate about and/or reflect on the real world (past, present or future), we have to represent the simplified systems we have distinguished using information carriers: models (discussion models, consultation models, action models, research models etc.) (Fig.2-12).

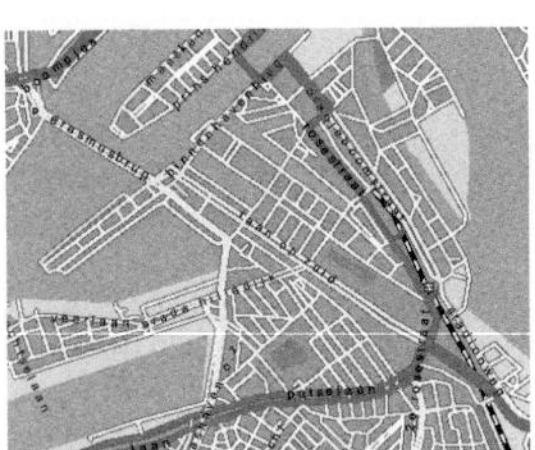

extract of street plan

Gedetailleerde reistijden

Station	Tijd	Spoor
Amsterdam CS	V 07:24	14a
Den Haag HS	A 08:04	
Den Haag HS	V 08:14	3
Delft	A 08:25	
Reisdetails		
Amsterdam CS	V 07:41	1
Delft	A 08:36	
Reisdetails		
Amsterdam CS	V 07:42	13a/b
Leiden Centraal	A 08:20	
Leiden Centraal	V 08:23	8b
Delft	A 08:55	
Reisdetails		
Amsterdam CS	V 08:11	1
Delft	A 09:06	

(part of) railway timetable

-Tijdens het practicum "ruim
Zuidvleugel van de Randstad
-Vervolgens worden hiervan
TU-gebied en voor de aard e
Stedenbouw- en Bouwtechni
de haltes en de omgeving va

(part of) teaching module specification

'This is not a plane.'

Fig.2-12 Models we use in everyday life.

A simplified representation of the real world conceived as system is a model of reality (or a past or future reality) only if it has a certain structural kinship with that reality, and only if the model is the result of a conscious interpretation of that reality[5].

"If we use system A, which is not in a state of either direct or indirect interaction with system B, to obtain information about system B, then we are using A as a model of B." (Apostel 1961: 36).

A system extracted from the (past, present or future) reality can be deliberately reduced by a selective simplification process in one of the following forms:

- omitting elements considered irrelevant;
- omitting element-attributes considered irrelevant;
- categorizing attributes of elements.

These three forms of reduction often occur in combination.

The original meaning of the term 'model' is, surprisingly, an architectural one. Medieval authors took the term 'modulus' from Vitruvius. In the last century, the architect Le Corbusier developed a system of proportions which he called *le Modulor*, and the Greek urban designer Doxiadis used the term modulus to designate the units from which a settlement is made up (in which the constituents differ per level or per scale).
Modulus was Italianized into *modello* and used for the standard measurement (the radius of a column) for expressing all the proportions of a building. Compare *modello* with the French *moule* and the English *mould*. In the 16th century, the term acquired the meaning of 'exemplar' under influence of the Italian *modello*(French *modèle*, English *model*). It gained the additional attributes of being smaller that the object it exemplified and of being made of a different material (Frey 1961; Bertels & Nauta 1969: 20). The word *module* also derives from *modulus* and has retained the secondary meaning of a standard or unit of measurement.

In contemporary common usage, the term 'model' has two different meanings relevant for present purposes. Firstly, it is used in the sense of 'a model of' something, a simplified representation of part of the real world such as a model aeroplane or an architectural model of a building. Secondly, it is used in the sense of 'a model for' something (a meaning derived from Platonic thinking), i.e. an example to be imitated (cf. mould) (Bertels & Nauta 1969: 22). In discussions about the term model, it is important to verify which of these meanings is being applied. Many urban and regional designers use the term 'model' in the latter sense: "For our purpose, a model is a picture of how the environment ought to be made, a description of a form or a process which is a prototype to follow." (Lynch 1981: 277). "Only if a design can be realized is it a model," state De Jong and Van der Voordt as editors of *Ways to Study and Research* (2002a: 87), to distinguish the terms 'model' and 'type' (see Section 5.3).
My use of the term 'model' is in the former sense and corresponds to Apostel's formulation as a 'bridge between the theoretical and observational levels, ...' (1961: 3).

This distinction between 'model' and 'type' dates from the 18th century, when the French rationalist architectural theorist Quatremère de Quincy defined the term 'type' by opposing it to the then current meaning of 'model' (Broadbent 1990: 90 ff.; Leupen 2002: 113). If there were any truth to the statement "the type is not a model. It can not be copied in reality" (Jong & Van der Voordt 2002a: 87), then many models, ranging from a model of DNA to a model of a hydrological system, could not correctly be called models. An 'exploratory model' would be a fatal contradiction.

Fig.2-13 illustrates the relation between reality and model.

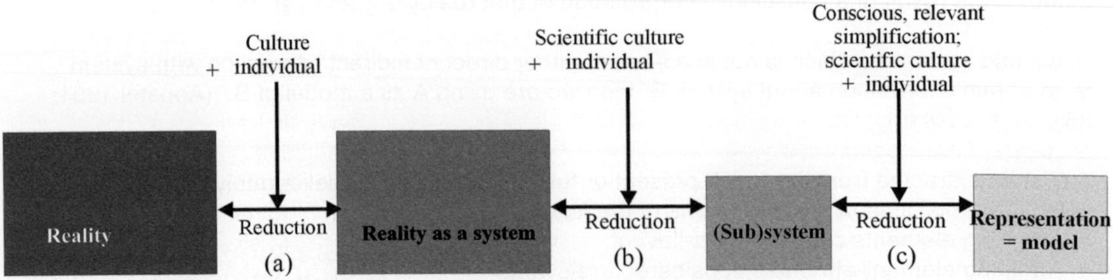

Fig.2-13 We can conceive of reality as a system or a complex of systems (a). This simplification (reduction) of reality is partly unconscious, and is based both on the scope of the natural human powers of perception and thinking and on cultural assumptions (which may also affected by individual differences). We can extract selected systems and/or subsystems (b) from this reality on the basis of intentional considerations and scientific assumptions (which may also differ per individual), and then represent these as models (c).

An urban designer makes a different kind of model of a neighbourhood to a social geographer. Models are thus neither value-free, nor should one try to make them so (see also Bailer-Jones 1999: 29; Giere 1999: 46).

Reality can be expressed in words or numbers, depicted to scale and imitated (with both the spatial and temporal grain of course always being relevant) (Fig.2-14):

- verbal models
- mathematical models
- spatial models
- mechanical models.

In de door ons gehanteerde werkwijz
modelmatige weergaven van de
wensmodellen.
Konfrontatie van beide modellen - th
een synthese-, een ontwikkelingsm
omschrijven als een ruimtelijk ka
richting geeft aan verdere ontwikkelir

A verbal model and a visualized verbal model: method of working for a graduation project (Frijlink & Leferink 1991)

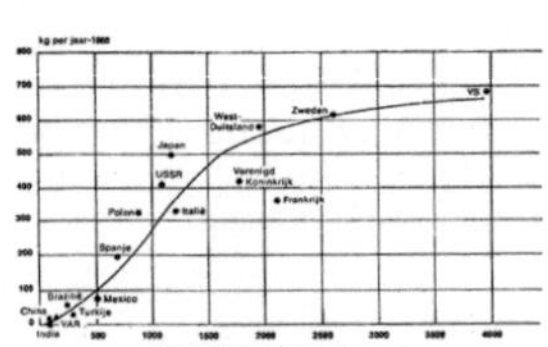

Graphically represented mathematical model (diagram). (Meadows 1972: 114)

Spatial scale model: a (possible future) plot division plan (Thüsh 1993: 140)

Illustration of a mechanical model (source *Miniatuurbanen* (model railway magazine) 1963 (6): 170)

Fig.2-14 The four types of model.

In order to understand a verbal model, you have to know the language in which it is couched. Mathematical models, on the other hand, employ a universal 'language', except for the verbal components. Computer models of architectural or spatial designs are also mathematical models, even though they are presented as spatial models.
A spatial model is a 2 or 3 dimensional spatial representation of the 3 dimensional world, normally to scale. The use of symbols in visual language is similar to that of words in normal language. Unlike words, however, their meaning is not universal. Symbols have to be explained (in a legend or key). "Graphic images have tremendous cognitive compactness. You can incorporate mountains of information in them, information that is not so easy to grasp in words. Just consider how much effort it takes to get computers to recognize faces. Graphic images are gauged to what the human brain is good at. We could all draw before we could write, and we have a fabulous memory for images - better than for text." (quote from an interview with Douwe Draaisma in the Scientific Supplement of *NRC Handelsblad*, 10 May 1997)

A spatial model may have an underlying formal metaphor. A well-chosen metaphor activates two association processes at the same time, verbal and visual. This improves the chance that the relevant information will indeed be communicated: the communicative value is high (Draaisma 1995: 26). The vague, evocative quality of a metaphor, Bertels and Nauta hold (1969: 38), can moreover have a high artistic value and can elicit aesthetic pleasure.

A mechanical model is a model that functions in the same way as the thing represented. It is a spatial model with real time as a fourth dimension. The reality of a mechanical model can only be depicted as a spatial model. Computers can be used to simulate a mechanical model: cf. a film, a rapid succession of static images.

Models may be specific as well as generic. I refer to the latter as 'theoretical models' (*principemodellen*). The term 'type' is sometimes also used (see Section 5.3).

These four types of models may be categorized as to their relation to reality as follows.

- Concrete, corresponding to 'thing'.
  A concrete model has spatial dimensions. Realistic experiments may be conducted using it: e.g. a planetarium.
- Conceptual, corresponding to 'notion'.
  A conceptual model is a mental construction that refers to reality (past, present or future). The only experiments than can be carried out using it are thought experiments. "Much as though concrete definitions of initial situations and plans (e.g. in sketches and reports) may appear similar, they remain in the final instance mental constructions or models ...." (Kleefmann 1984: 100). Nancy Nersessian (1999: 14) holds that mental modelling is a fundamental form of human reasoning. It originally developed as a survival mechanism and was subsequently extended to cope with special situations such as the construction of prescriptive scientific procedures for seeking creative solutions to problems. Spatial models prove particularly useful as conceptual models, for they miss certain specific constraints that characterize verbal and mathematical models (ibid.: 17).

A classic example: "Galileo considered an imaginary experiment involving perfectly spherical balls in motion on a perfectly smooth plane. It would be impossible to achieve these ideal conditions in any actual experiment because of the intervention of friction and imperfections on the spheres. However, this ability to abstract from the conditions of the real world played an essential part in Galileo's formulation of a new science of motion." (Commentary on Galileo's Dialogue concerning the Two Principal Systems of the World, Florence 1629; Open University 1974: 117).

- Formal, corresponding to 'abstraction'.
  A formal model is an uninterpreted syntactic symbol system (calculus). An element of a formal model may be compared to the (dimensionless) concept 'point' (Harvey 1973: 452). Only the structure is important, not the reference.

Examples of formal models include uninterpreted mathematical models (consistent systems of mathematical equations) of e.g. a concrete hydrological system (reality condensed into a series of equations) and Euclid's formalized axiomatic system of the conceptual system 'Euclidian space' (see Fig.3-2).

The literature dealing with the subject of models distinguishes formalistic models (set-theoretical entities), also known as interpretative or instantial models, from pragmatic (analogue) models (e.g. Bertels & Nauta 1969; Bailer-Jones 1999; Giere 1999; Suárez 1999).

A model may indeed possess the same structure as the depicted system-in-(past, present or future) reality, be it in the global sense, abstract sense or partial sense (Bertels & Nauta 1969: 107/108), but given the 'reductional limitations' that every model has with regard to reality, we can make no assertions on the basis of a model other than within these limitations: what you put into a model determines what comes out. Assertions may be made on the basis of a model only within the field of applicability. The testing of an aircraft model in a wind tunnel, for example, does not allow us to deduce that the plane will continue to fly in reality, because the pilot's behaviour is not taken into account in the model (Soest et al. 1988). We must make allowance for this when we take the 'return trip' from the model to (past, present or future) reality (Fig.2-15).

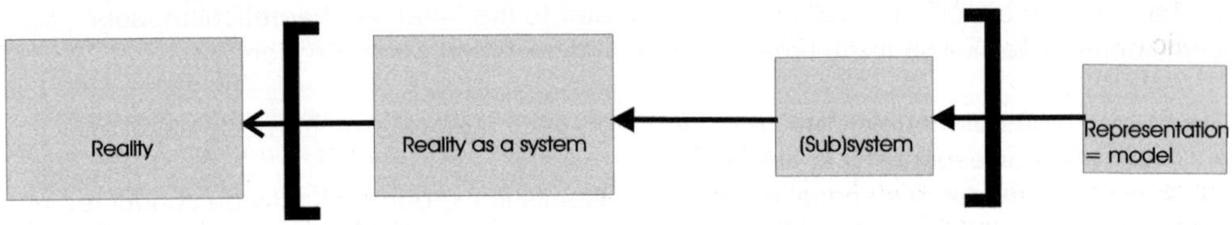

Fig.2-15 Interpretation of the model in (past, present or future) reality: 'the return trip'; 'reductional' limitations. Cf. Fig.2-13.

This implies that before we start using a model, we have to think about its area of applicability. Our assumptions in this respect must moreover be tested (Bertels & Nauta 1969; Soest et al. 1988). Venturing outside the area of applicability is known as overextension of the model. Examples of model overextension are:

- no distinction is made between the model and reality;
- the area of applicability is undefined
- due to misunderstanding of the nature of the reduction that has taken place, we are insufficiently acquainted with the area of applicability or have failed to test it sufficiently (Klaasen 2000a).

"The characteristics of models imply the existence of many dangers to which the model builder may fall prey. Simplification might lead to 'throwing the baby out with the bath water'; structuring to spurious correlation; suggestiveness to improper prediction; approximation to unreality, and analogy to unjustifiable leaps into different domains." (Chorley & Haggett 1969: 26).

2.4 Urban systems and models: 'town building'

"Wat is een stad? Een plaats op de kaart die in werkelijkheid een grote hoeveelheid plekken is, en nog een grotere hoeveelheid mensen die op die plekken bedrijvig zijn. Naarmate er meer van die plekken zijn is de stad groter, naarmate er langer mensen op dezelfde plekken bedrijvig blijven is ze grootser en naar mate ze die plekken vaker met elkaar verbinden door zich van de ene plek naar de andere te verplaatsen is ze steedser. Als veel mensen in zo'n stad zich vaak van de ene plek naar de andere verplaatsen en elkaar op allerlei verschillende manieren vertellen dat dat leuk is, spreken we van cultuur." [a]

(Michael Zeeman, quoted by Bob Frommé in *Het Parool*, 20-4-96)

A part of reality is the system 'Earth'. We can think of this system as divided into a natural (ecological) system and a cultivated system (see also Kleefmann 1984).

Since human beings, unlike animals, lack a fixed repertoire of reactions to circumstances (an 'organically laid-down stimulus-response model'), they must work out their 'own solutions', and thus no longer form part of the natural system (Huisman 1996: 149). I interpret a 'cultivated' system as being a system developed by thinking humans. Besides comprising e.g. an economic subsystem, it includes a cultural subsystem.

The natural system fulfils a carrying function, a productive function, an information function and a regulation function on behalf of the cultivated system[6]. The natural system (abiotic and biotic elements, natural processes) is hence a *conditio sine qua non* for the cultivated system. The starting point for the rise of the cultivated system can be traced back to about one million years ago, when human ancestors started using tools (Jong, Moens & Van de Akker 2002: 294-295). Whereas animals adapt to their environment by 'survival of the fittest', humans who have a relatively high adaptability, moreover adapt their environment to the needs of their species: accommodation. Mankind 'occupied' the earth, in particular the surface, which is why some authors use the term 'occupation system' for the cultivated system. Increasingly (both in space and in time), physical interventions have taken place from the cultivated system into the natural system. The cultivated system was initially solely rural, i.e. directly related to the productive function of the natural system. At various times in various places in the world, it became worthwhile to distinguish an urban system, only indirectly dependent on the productive function, within this rural occupation system: centres of trade, crafts, administration, finance, science, culture[7] etc.

I classify as urban systems not only cities and urbanised regions but also parts of cities, such as neighbourhoods and districts, and villages: entities of socio-cultural, spatial-ecological, economic-technical and administrative-organizational elements (including people), relations and processes. Urban systems are extremely complicated open systems (Doxiadis 1968: 189; Peursen 1986: 57) and they moreover interfere with abiotic, biotic and rural systems. These systems are mutually connected as illustrated in fig.2-6b. The complexity of urban systems

---

[a] "What is a city? A place on the map which is in actuality a large number of places and an even larger number of people who are active in those places. The more of those places there are, the bigger the city, the longer people remain industriously active in those places the more metropolitan the city is, and the more they link those places together by moving from one spot to another the more urban the city is. If many people in the city often move from one place to another and tell one another in all kinds of ways how much fun that is, we refer to it as culture."

is moreover 'organized complexity': "They present situations in which a half-dozen or even several dozen quantities are all varying simultaneously and in subtly interconnected ways." (J.Jacobs 1961: 433, citing from a report of Dr.Warren Weaver for the Rockefeller Foundation (1958)). Christopher Alexander too points to inter-variable linkage ((1964) 1973: 42; see also Fig.4-12).

"Organized complexity as opposed to the disorganized complexity of for instance telephone exchanges" (J.Jacobs 1961: 431).

The natural system has a spatial and temporal organizing influence on the rural and urban systems; the rural and urban systems have a destructive effect on the natural system.

It is also possible to take a 'cross section' through the system 'Earth' without distinguishing the natural and cultivation systems. The system thus 'extracted' may be called a 'human ecosystem' - or, in situations where only the natural system is considered relevant, an ecosystem. The 'human ecosystem' approach has been adopted in e.g. Stearns & Montag 1974.

Within these open urban systems, we can distinguish physical systems made up of spatial elements (objects) such as buildings, streets, parks, sewers, stations, and physical systems made up of configurations of spatial elements (of buildings, streets etc.)
(see e.g Fig.2-7). These physical urban systems, urban spatial elements/objects in mutually coherent combinations and in coherent combinations with natural (and possibly rural) spatial elements/objects, have been and are constructed or reconstructed in order to produce a certain effect, to fulfil functions, on behalf of the urban society. These physical urban systems fulfil a carrying function and an information function for society in a way similar to that of natural systems for the cultivated system (see note 6).

We customarily call the visual manifestation at a certain moment (the spatial pattern or the synchronous structure of a system) the urban landscape or townscape, or the composition of the urban area (see Section 4.6.1). Besides the urban spatial objects, this manifestation comprises natural objects and (in some cases) rural spatial objects, and remains of both these.

Urban society, consisting of individuals who, in a group connection or otherwise, must and/or wish to embark on social, economic and cultural activities, requires these spatial objects to allow those processes to develop, and to accommodate social, economic and cultural processes. The physical urban system has not only a spatial-ecological dimension, but also a socio-cultural, an economic-technological and an administrative-organizational dimension, both in a conditional sense and in the sense that it is also generated by socio-cultural, spatial-ecological, economic-technological and administrative-organizational activities/processes[8] (Fig.2-16).

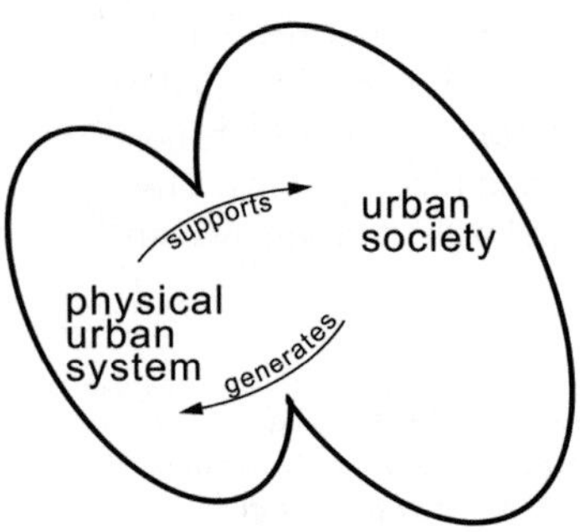

Fig.2-16 The physical urban system makes societal processes possible in a conditional sense. Conversely, societal processes lead to changes in and extensions to this system, and provide control over it.

The above-mentioned dimensions are interwoven. There exist socio-culturally determined needs that imply spatial interventions, which have to be carried out in a certain way. Both the needs and the manner of execution are codetermined by the spatial circumstances. Desirable and expected economic yield is always an issue in this connection, as are technical feasibility, laws and regulations, financial possibilities etc. (Boer 1990: 16, 17): Fig.2-17.

CATEGORIES – ASPECTS IN SPATIAL PLANNING		
activities	aspects	Categories
I life and survival	A social-cultural conditions B spatial conditions C socio-economic conditions D organizational conditions	1 natural environment
II protected activities	A social-cultural conditions B spatial conditions C socio-economic conditions D organizational conditions	2 spatial protection
III integration of activities	A social-cultural conditions B spatial conditions C socio-economic conditions D organizational conditions	3 spatial patterns
IV dwelling	A social-cultural conditions B spatial conditions C socio-economic conditions D organizational conditions	4 housing
V use of amenities	A social-cultural conditions B spatial conditions C socio-economic conditions D organizational conditions	5 amenities
VI work	A social-cultural conditions B spatial conditions C socio-economic conditions D organizational conditions	6 employment
VII transport	A social-cultural conditions B spatial conditions C socio-economic conditions D organizational conditions	7 transport links

Fig.2-17 The relation between urban activities (in the broadest sense, related to space-requiring human needs), the conditions that influence these activities and the spatial elements (spatial objects) of the physical urban system which 'carry' these activities. The categorization refers to policy sectors[9]. The sequence of the diverse activities is a (partly subjective) conditional one: if the circumstances are 'unliveable', people cannot dwell, work etc. De Boer sees category III as the essence of urban design. See Section 4.6.2. (Boer 1990: 68 ff.).

Elements of a physical urban system can be located both above and below the ground, and not only dry land but also bodies of water contribute to urban activities and supply information. A physical urban system, be it a neighbourhood, housing estate, district etc., is, in the words of Niek de Boer "... a contiguous mass of building and enclosed open spaces, on behalf of differentiated housing, differentiated amenities, differentiated employment and differentiated transport accommodation. (- - -) The open spaces will generally be landscaped (*aangelegd en ingericht*)" (1996: 113).

The spatial objects (and configurations of them) have certain formal attributes (e.g. height, width, straight, curved, spread), certain physical-state attributes (quality of maintenance, made of wood or masonry, Gothic or Baroque in style) and functional attributes (e.g.

residential function, transport function, public or semi-public). Relations (=structure) exist between these objects/configurations. These attributes are perceived by visual, auditive, olfactory and/or tactile means, or result from interpretation of perceptions on the basis of - implicit or explicit - (culturally related) assumptions. Relations between elements (structure) are sensory and/or physical in character. A physical relation presupposes an element with a functional attribute (footpath, air link). The boundaries of the physical component of an urban system may be self-evident, e.g. an island, a housing estate, but this is far from always the case.

As long as the social, cultural and economic process remain restricted to a single building or comparable object and its immediate environment, the accommodation of these processes belongs to the domain of architecture, civil engineering etc. If these processes are accompanied by movements of people, goods, energy etc. between buildings and similar spatial objects, we enter the domain of 'town building', the practice and discipline of urban & regional design. In the general sense, this physical urban system is the object of urban & regional design.

The creation and modification of physical urban systems is of public importance and therefore a political-administrative affair (e.g. Boer 1990). Private parties may play a part of varying significance in this connection.

An urban or regional design is a proposal for a coherent package of spatial interventions in a certain urban or urbanescent area, and always affects more than one sector (see note 9). "... only from the point of view of the connection ... can one understand how the individual parts or elements have their significance." (Peursen 86: 30).

Urban designers are not just concerned with making proposals for the expansion, or reorganization of physical urban systems of various scales, ranging from a detailed layout of a public space to planning a metropolitan region, they also study present and past urban systems and prepare spatial policies.

site analysis

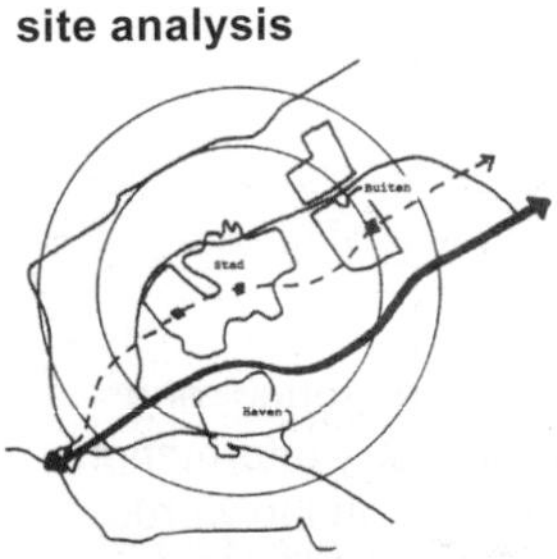

analysis of access to the main train station in Almere (Neth.) (Thüsh 1993: 90)

theoretical model

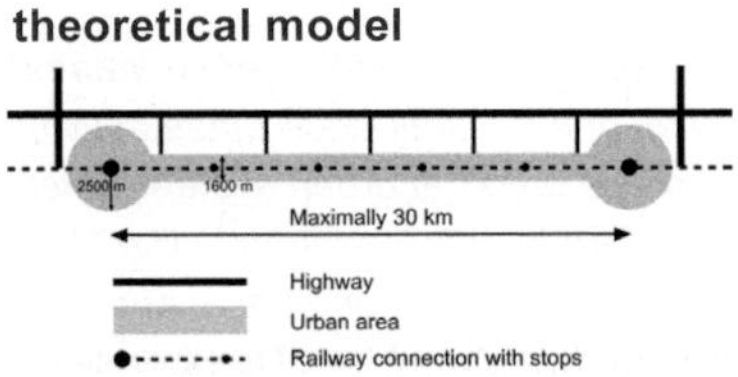

theoretical model of a lineair urban region (see also Fig.5-24/6-15.7)

exploratory model

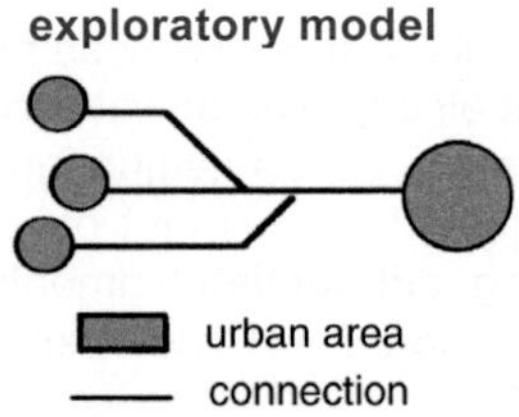

reducing the cost of constructing connections

design

spatial scale model, a (possible future) plot division plan (Thüsh 1993: 140)

Fig.2-18 Examples of spatial models in urban & regional design.

An urban design is a spatial model. Site analyses, capacity analyses, pilot plans, implementation plans and exploratory studies for all these are all spatial models (Fig.2-18).

In contrast to what for instance is stated in e.g. the urban planning and design research programme of the Delft University Faculty of Architecture (Faculteit Bouwkunde TU Delft 1994a), these models are never a goal in their own right but a means of reflecting and communicating about ideas, wishes etc. for a possible and/or desirable 'spatial future'. "Design is not an end in itself. The whole point of the design process is that it will result in some action to change the environment in some way." (Lawson 1990: 92)[10]. "Architecture is not architecture until it has been built." (Verheyen 2002: 9).

Non-spatial models also have a place in urban & regional design. When we construct a model of a past, present or future spatial situation and the modelled space is subject to differentiation (this depends on the spatial grain adopted), it makes sense to use a spatial model. This applies equally to differentiated qualitative properties and to quantitative ones. In cases where differentiation is not relevant to a given space, we can represent this space using a verbal model to indicate qualitative properties. A verbal model might for example describe the present state (or predict the future state) of maintenance of a house or housing estate. Where spatial differentiation is irrelevant within a given space, we can use a mathematical model to represent this space quantitatively (Fig.2-19).

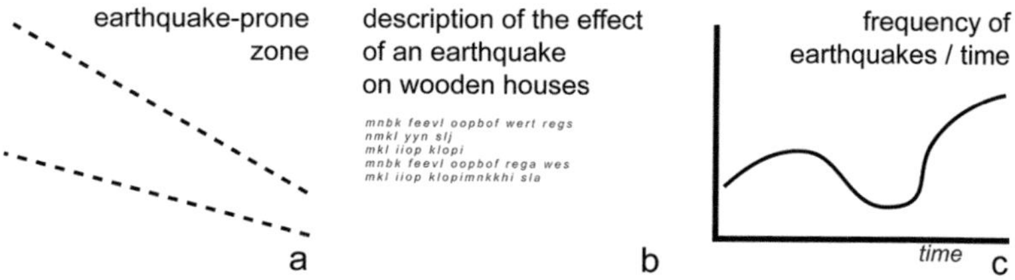

Fig.2-19 Models relevant in urban & regional design:
a. spatial differentiation → spatial model;
b. spatially undifferentiated qualitative guidelines → verbal model
c. spatially undifferentiated quantitative description → mathematical model

Personal preferences can moreover play a part in the choice of a type of model. For example, Geoffrey Broadbent states, "Every time we describe a concept we do so in one of these model forms; we decide what the model is for but ... we actually make the model verbally, numerically, spatially or mechanically, according to our personal abilities. Other things being equal, I tend to use words because I have a certain verbal fluency, but you may tend to use drawings, because you are high in spatial ability, to make (iconic) 'models' because you possess mechanical skills or to formulate mathematical models because you are high in numerical ability." (1988: 92).

3 Science

3.1 Science and reality

"The real is not exhausted by the actual"

(Hans Radder 1996, *In and about the world: philosophical studies of science and technology*: 86)

Science supplies a knowledge about the real world (past, present and future) which is more reliable than knowledge gathered by commonsense means or handed down by tradition (Vries 1984: 9). The description or explanation of nonrecurrent phenomena, such as a phenomenon associated with a single place in the spatial sciences or a unique historical event, without any relation to a general framework of scientific knowledge, is not a scientific activity. Knowledge is scientific only when there is a generalization (or some measure of generalization). For this purpose we must 'dare' to simplify/reduce systems in the real world (past, present or future) with a focus on similarities rather than differences. Concrete (by definition 'unique') phenomena are then explained (in more than just causal respects) from the viewpoint of this generalization process, and future unique 'phenomena' are predicted and/or made plausible. Science restricts 'chance' to the sense of 'random events'[11].

Scientific knowledge is distinct from everyday knowledge in that it is based on rational considerations, i.e. considerations that are based on a explicit, conscious and deliberate thought process, in which logically coherent relations are established and logical conclusions are drawn (Huisman 1996: 57). "Rationality is related to an open, critical attitude, to a willingness to argue the point." (Wilde 1987b: 154, referring to Stephen Toulmin).

Rationality and creativity are by no means mutually exclusive. According to the French philosopher Bergson, every scientific discovery has a (non-analysable) moment of 'creative intuition' (Vries 1984: 55). The urban designer Taeke de Jong expressed the same point as follows: "... science's main task is to query accepted implied assumptions. This factor alone has resulted in scientific breakthroughs in the history of science (Copernicus, Newton, Einstein). Creativity also assumes the non-inclusion of at least one widely accepted, but maybe infertile, assumption ..." (Jong 2002a: 67). C.A. van Peursen (1994: 107) offers the illustrative example of Riemann's and Lobachevski's abandonment of the belief that the angles of a triangle must add up to 180 degrees. Scientific creativity is however unlike artistic creativity in that it is governed by internal scientific criteria.

Nor are rationality and emotion mutually exclusive, according to Huisman. Emotion motivates. "Rational thinking is indeed fostered by a certain degree of emotional involvement. It boosts the alertness, acuteness and creativity which are needed for a satisfactory analysis [and synthesis - itk]." (Huisman 1996: 59). Thagard and Croft also make this point (1999: 129).

Given the fact that, as an object of knowledge, the real world is independent of the knowing subject, scientific knowledge is, in the context of human cognitive capacities, in principle objective - or, more accurately, intersubjective[12] - in the sense of open, unprejudiced and unbiased (Huisman 1996: 36). Scientific knowledge is in essence value-free (or alethic, from Greek *alètheia*: truth)[13]. Science does not prescribe, nor does it give answers about what is desirable. The fact that science deliberately selectively reduces reality does not change anything as long as the reduction is a conscious one (ibid.: 34). In Stephen Toulmin's words: "... selective attention is one thing, blinders are another." (2002: 42). Reality-reflecting knowledge is a biological necessity for the survival of humanity, and thus a necessary precondition for human action (Huisman 1996: 45; see also Hillier, Musgrove & O'Sullivan 1972: 29-3-4). That is not to say that those who conduct science go about their work in a value-free way. Bias may be personal, social or both (Huisman 1996: 161). Patricia Huisman distinguishes three forms of personal bias: cognitive style bias, attitude-dependant bias and cognitive concordance bias (ibid.: 175). These categories of bias refer, respectively, to how far one is prepared to tolerate uncertainty, to how far one is hindered by prejudices, and to the (emotionally driven) need to harmonize knowledge about reality with what one already knows. Social bias may be divided into interest-related (social integration, security) and discipline-related (obtrusive preconceptions that are not themselves open to discussion) (ibid.: 165 ff.).

Nor are scientific institutions, protocols or disciplinary boundaries value-free: "The sciences are like maps and the concrete world is like the landscape. ... just as there are many maps possible for the same landscape, so can different sciences give a [different - itk] interpretation of a single event ..." (Peursen 1986: 14). The attachment of importance to science in its own right or to its relevance to society, your choice of what to study, how you reduce reality, what your opinion is of scientific findings (peer review), what you do with the knowledge you acquire, etc. - all those things are value-bound (deontic, from the Greek *deon*: that which is binding) (Huisman 1996: 41 ff.).

The view I hold, that objective/intersubjective knowledge is possible in principle, is known as the correspondence theory of truth: a belief is true provided there exists a fact to which it corresponds. This realistic outlook on science is characterized by various movements and/or variants. Some well-known ones are 'logical positivism' (the Vienna Circle) and the 'critical rationalism' founded by Popper; but there are also less familiar currents such as 'scientific realism', 'metaphysical realism', 'naive realism', 'critical realism', 'instrumental realism', 'referential realism' and 'constructive empiricism'[14].

There exist not only objectivists but also subjectivists (idealists and relativists). Subjectivists consider the external world (the knowable object) to be an artefact of the human mind. They take the fundamental standpoint that there is no strict distinction between the knowable object and the knowing subject, and that the subject creates his own, internal, coherent reality - the coherence theory of truth (i.e. a theory is true if consistent with other ideas and theories within the branch of learning). Postmodernists such as Kuhn, Toulmin, Rorty and Latour hold that truth is relative (a view which is of course self-contradictory). For structuralists such as Derrida and Foucault, even the knowing subject disappears (Huisman 1996: 107). The world is a meaningful entity, in their view, by virtue of systems to which people must conform. Pragmatists from the school of C.S. Peirce and J. Dewey hold that the pursuit of scientific knowledge should not focus on the object but "on an objectivity that is not independent of human action, but is on the contrary bound up with it." (Peursen 1986: 68). The truth about the external world is not relevant: what matters is whether you can work with the theories, i.e. whether they are reliable (e.g. Freudian psychoanalysis) (Ende 2000: 129)[15].

Sceptical movements include the 'avowed irrationalism', which holds that all theories are equally valid (and is thus counterintuitive) and 'theoretic instrumentalism', which denies that theories have anything to do with truth. Lakatos cites as an example the attitude of the Roman Catholic church towards the view of Copernicus: "These people opted for instrumentalism: they came to regard theories as neither true nor false but merely as 'instruments' for prediction." (Lakatos 1978: 106).

As mentioned, languages, including visual languages, have on the one hand an organizational function in thinking, and on the other hand form a means of communicating ideas, including scientific ones (in verbal, mathematical and spatial models). Without language there can be no communication and thus no science. Language does not, however, mirror the structure of reality and truth (Toulmin 2001: 69; 72). "Language is an instrument, and what matters is what is done with it - in this case its use is to formulate and discuss theories about the world." (Magee 1973: 50 - see also Popper 1959: Preface).

Although reality is language-independent, language can have an effect on our conception and hence perception of the real world. Language limits thought, the urban designer Kevin Lynch argues, "While most professionals are aware of what is not conveyed, they may be less aware of how their thinking is channeled by the language they use. Zoning is a natural and obvious way of controlling changes in buildings and use, to anyone who is habituated to seeing cities represented as patches of landuse, in which use and form are combined. (---) Changes in ways of describing cities will not only follow on a better understanding of the city phenomenon, but could also lead to better understanding." (1981: 350). The close relation between language and culture/subculture-based ideas about the real world sometimes leads to an irreconcilable confusion of terms and in turn to blind-alley debates, both in and outside science. This does not imply, however, that there is more than one reality.

> "An interesting example of the subjective nature of models in town planning is the fact that in the US such models tend to be aggregated while in England they tend to be more unitary. This reflects real differences in the two cultures. These find expression in the reality of political and other systems which in the US are an aggregate of contending choices and decisions of many individuals and groups to a greater extent than in England. In France there is much more concern with the symbolic, visual, and hierarchic elements of the city which are largely ignored in the American preoccupation with process and information handling." (Amos Rapoport 1969: 139).

3.2 Types of science

> "Science is an essentially anarchic enterprise."
>
> (Paul Feyerabend (1975) 1993, *Against Method* : 9)

3.2.1 Introduction

Sciences may be divided into

- fundamental sciences (in some cases with an implicit action - or application - oriented character) such as mathematics, physics, astronomy, sociology; in these, progress is governed by intrascientific considerations[16]; and
- explicitly action - or application - oriented sciences: practical sciences such as the engineering sciences (and also e.g. environmental science, clinical psychology, medical science, law, business science), whose progress is governed by extrascientific considerations.

Among the fundamental sciences, a distinction is made between formal sciences (e.g. mathematics, logic) and empirical sciences. Formal, empirical and practical sciences stimulate one another in a non-hierarchical manner. The empirical sciences influence the practical and formal sciences, but the practical sciences also influence the empirical, both by raising questions to be answered and by supplying means of and aids to research (Ihde 1991; Drenth 1995). Within a given scientific field, we may encounter both a fundamental empirical component and a practical component. Geology is an example.

3.2.2 Formal sciences

Logic and mathematics are sciences without any empirical content and are termed 'formal'. I would argue with Van Peursen (1986: 44 ff.) that their systems of reasoning and calculation primarily aim to exclude internal contradictions. For the 'landscape of the concrete world', they develop networks that indicate ways of dealing with the real world. It is no coincidence that logical and mathematical systems are applicable to the real world, Van Peursen argues, referring to Piaget, because "our mind ... [is] necessarily attuned to everyday reality by a long process of evolution." (ibid.: 48).

3.2.3 Empirical sciences

The object of the empirical sciences is 'that which is (or was) the case' and 'that which will probably be the case'. The ultimate (critical) question is 'is it (always) true'. This question has belonged since ancient times (Plato, Aristotle) to the domain of *epistèmè*, while *theoria* was the term for knowledge/skill. It is useful to draw a distinction between (a) those sciences whose object is lifeless (natural or anthropogenic), (b) those whose object is alive - especially when it has a mental capacity and its own will, and (c) historical and spatial sciences.

An alternative broad division may be made into natural sciences and social sciences, given for example that the sciences mentioned under c. embrace both these types (e.g. historical geology and social history, or social geography and physical geography). The epistemological process is admittedly fundamentally independent of the nature of the object of knowledge, but objects in the social sciences are associated with more complications in the knowledge acquisition process than those in the natural sciences (Huisman 1996: 14). Some differences between natural-scientific objects and social-scientific objects are:
- respectively, the commonsense or non-commonsense interpretation of the object under investigation;
- the degree of ambiguity and complexity (double hermeneutics);
- the extent to which corrective feedback can occur (this is connected to human adaptability);
- the degree of subjective involvement to which the object invites. (Vries 1984: 124; Huisman 1996: 15).

Unlike the sciences that focus on general regularities, the historical and spatial sciences clearly have no choice but to address the unique and the unrepeatable, and even then often only in a descriptive fashion: ideografic science, as the German philosopher Windelband named it, as opposed to nomothetic science.
The circumstances that lead up to certain events in time and/or phenomena in space are, after all, never the same. I share the opinion of the historian Von der Dunk (1994: 43), the philosopher Van Peursen (1986: 43) and others that there is actually only a difference of degree. Unique entities - temporal and spatial patterns - are built up from repeatable units. This does indeed presuppose a certain measure of generalization.

In descriptive science, certain phenomena in present or past reality are described systematically, with a greater or lesser degree of generalization. In explanatory science, causal or conditional relations are established between phenomena (necessary conditions, causal analysis): the 'how' question (*waardoor*) in the natural sciences and the 'why' question (*waarom*) in the social sciences, respectively. In predictive science, hypotheses are formulated on the basis of the system of relations. The more complex the system extracted from the real world, the more difficult it is to make predictions.
Causal analysis is associated with contingency: there was/is no logically compelling necessity that *that* particular thing happened. But neither was/is it the outcome of chance/randomness : the circumstances were/are such that it could/can happen (Wilde 1987a: 126). Water will always flow downhill, but people can choose any route they like. Physical determinism is not involved.

3.2.4 Practical sciences

Practical sciences are those sciences that have the application of science as their object of scientific research (Peursen 1986: 61). That is not the same as applying science in a concrete case. Neither is a practical science (such as applied psychology) the same thing as knowledge acquired in practice (Drenth 1995: 157; Gunsteren 2001). Practice generates questions, not knowledge. The same scientific rules and standards apply in empirical and practical science: “both types of research lead to generalizable insights and laws. The difference concerns only the origin of the research question and the intention of the research.” (Drenth 1995: 152). Or, as Thagard and Croft put it: “Despite the differences in the form of the questions asked ... there is no reason to believe that the cognitive processes underlying questioning ... are fundamentally different.” (1999: 134).

The object of a practical science can be both a process, such as an agricultural technique, and a product. In general, the application will be a societal one, but the product could also be a scientific instrument: technical developments contribute to the advance of empirical scientific knowledge (Ihde 1991). Given the extrascientific problem statement a monodisciplinary approach is unlikely to succeed. The physical geographer Arthur Veen proposed in his inaugural address that a practical science is a task-oriented combination of two or more (empirical and/or formal) sciences: “A conglomeration of disciplines stuck together by an extrascientific function” (1976: 19)[17]. As an illustration he states that if we ignore the task of healing, medical science decomposes into biology, chemistry, psychology etc. (ibid.). The extrascientific problem statement and the consequent multidisciplinary character of a practical science make it unnecessary and moreover impossible for a practical scientist to have the same level of knowledge of the disciplines involved as the practitioners of those disciplines. Thomas Kuhn is certainly correct in stating:”... it seems likely ... that the applied scientist, to whose problems no scientific paradigm need be fully relevant, may profit by a far broader and less rigid education than that to which the pure scientist has characteristically been exposed.” ((1959) 1991: 147). “The application of relativistic mechanics does not lead to new information relevant to airplane designs.” (Sarlemijn 1993: 198).

> This view dates back to Vitruvius: “Again, although [an architect] may be no Hippocrates, he should have working knowledge of medicine, nor may he be learned to an outstanding degree in the other individual disciplines - still, in all of them he should have some expertise. No one, after all, can possibly master the fine points of each individual subject, because it can scarcely be in his power to master and grasp their reasoning.” (1999a: I.1.13).

Since ancient times practical science belongs to the realm of *poièsis*, that of productive action, with techné as accompagnying knowledge/skill. *Poièsis* and *techné* have a bearing on both art and technology[18]. *Techné* relates to cognitive activities; it means knowledge in a general sense about ‘the possible’. To quote Aristotle: ‘‘Now art arises when from many notions gained by experience one universal judgement about a class of objects is produced. (- - -) ... that it has done good to all persons of a certain conditions, marked off in one class, when they were ill of this disease, ... this is a matter of art.’’ (Metaphysics 1.1- translation W.D.Ross (1958: 109)). Although we nowadays see ‘art’ and ‘technology’ as separate domains, many European languages still bear traces of their former relatedness: the expression ‘the state of the art’[19] and the word ‘artificial’ bear little relation to art in its usual modern sense. Out of the many views of what ‘art’ is[20], the ones that are relevant in connection with both the term *techné* and architecture are those that hold that art must be linked to reality (a view of the author/philosopher Iris Murdoch (cited in Burg 1999: 69), that an artist must possess a ‘trained sense of general fittingness or balance’ (Popper 1976: 68), and that beauty can only be judged ‘by virtue of the function of the object to which it is ascribed’ (a view of Immanuel Kant, cited in Burg 1999: 72).

The ultimate (critical) question for the practical sciences is 'does it work?'; or more precisely "is effective action in specific situations possible on the basis of this knowledge?" - regardless of whether that action is desirable or not (yet) desirable. Essential in this connection are knowledge of the conditions under which the action (leading to a product or process) is purposeful, and insight into what effects the action will have - intended/unintended and/or desirable/undesirable. The term 'possible' is ambiguous. A distinction must be maintained between on the one hand the set of constructive options and on the other hand the set of utilitarian options. What is possible (or impossible) may moreover change in the course of time.

Not all effects of an action are theoretically predictable. "A theory has ... a certain autonomy with regard to the person who formulated it. It always comprises more than its producer could possibly have foreseen or 'planned'. (- - -) Every theory has unpredicted ''consequences'." (Vries 1984: 61). This applies equally of course to experimental actions, both in the empirical and practical sciences.

Since the practical sciences generally have a direct relation to society, the question 'does it work?' has to be considered in an ethical context.

Empirical science and practical science compared:

empirical science	*epistèmè:* (intersubjective) knowledge	what will probably be the case	progress generated by intrascientific considerations	characteristic: explicative and predictive models
practical science	*technè:* (intersubjective) knowledge	what can be the case	progress generated by extrascientific considerations	characteristic: descriptive, intentional and exploratory-projective models

Taeke de Jong has related these two modalities to one another as shown in Fig.3-1. The French political economist Bernard de Jouvenel introduced the neologism 'futuribles' for futures that are both possible and desirable (Toulmin 2001: 93).

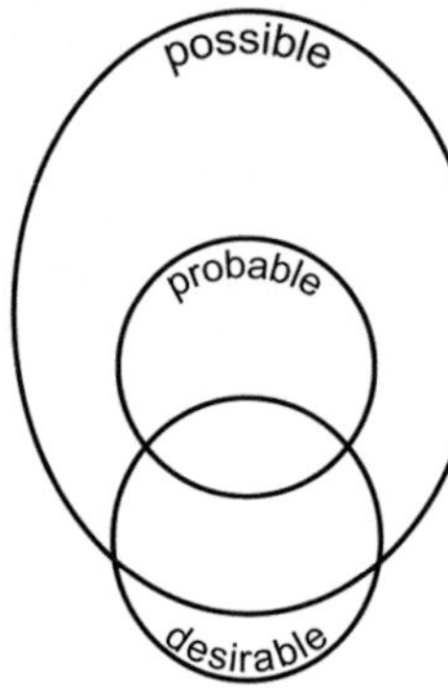

Fig 3-1. In this model, the probable futures form a subset of the possible futures, and the set of desirable futures includes parts of the set of possible futures and the set of probable futures. (Jong 1992: 9). The meaning of 'desirable futures' depends of course on the actor concerned.

Not everything that actually can be (the possible) is however realizable in all times and places (Peursen 1986: 97). This is because knowledge is generalized, and the peculiarities of specific situations have been disregarded (Radder 1996: 2/3). Generalized knowledge is not necessarily universally valid, but may also relate to a specific part of space or of time. Radder refers in this connection to non-localized knowledge (ibid.: 3).

In a concrete application, (subjective) value judgements are involved, made partly on the grounds of an interpretation of the specific case or situation, in the sense of the conditions that apply (or do not apply) and the effects to be expected as a result. “All the estimates of (say) the environmental impact of large-scale technological projects must be qualified by estimates of their intrinsic uncertainty; and, before making collective political decisions about such projects, we need realistic estimates of the unplanned but calculable side-effects of their execution, so that our decisions have some claim to human wisdom.” (Toulmin 2001: 81). Decisions in specific cases are supposed to be based on practical commonsense. Aristotle used the term *phronesis* for this. In diagrammatic form:

practical science	*technè* = (intersubjective) knowledge	what generally could be the case (under which conditions, and with what effects)
application of knowledge	*phronèsis* = reasoned decision	what is concretizable in a specific situation, given the applicable conditions and expected effects (predictions, empirically grounded as far as possible)

A doctor applies her knowledge in treating a patient. In doing so she takes advantage of the body of knowledge of the practical science of ‘medicine’. Whether the chosen treatment is appropriate depends not only on the diagnosis (problem definition) but also on the patient’s personal circumstances (e.g. character traits, existing medication, financial constraints).

Within the practical sciences, a distinction is made between ‘finalized’ and ‘functionalized’ research (Vries 1984: 139). Finalized research concerns the development of theories to bridge the gap between fundamental theory and its application. Examples of this are the design of aircraft wings, or the application of the law of entropy to urban systems. Functionalized research is based on trial and error, i.e. systematic experiments without recourse to a scientific theory. In pharmaceutical research, for example, various combinations of substances are tested for effectiveness in a systematic way. Luyten and Hoefnagel (1995: 124 ff.) give an example of investigating the effect of modifying one variable at a time in the production process of poultry farming.

Starting from the concepts of *epistèmè* and *technè*, we can trace the ancestry of the present conventional universities and the universities of technology. Broadly speaking, at the former universities one studies what there is (or was) and extrapolates the observations to the future, while at the latter one designs and constructs new things, i.e. explores new possibilities[21].

3.3 Models in science

"Thus, it was established thousands of years ago that
the universe as a whole, in its full complexity, can not be
represented by any simulation smaller than itself."

(Isaac Asimov 1988, *Prelude to Foundation*, Grafton Books: 163)

As stated in Section 2.3, we cannot ponder and communicate about reality (past, present or future) without models, which implies that scientific knowledge and insights cannot be developed without models. It must be observed that the literature concerned with the general concept of the model largely restricts consideration of the science-model relation to the formal and empirical sciences; little reference is made to the possible future realities that are relevant in the practical sciences (Apostel 1961; Frey 1961; Kuipers 1961; Chorley & Hagget 1967; Bertels & Nauta 1969; Soest et al. 1988). It is precisely in the practical sciences, and not in the last place in urban & regional design, that the use (or misuse) of models has direct societal consequences.

Below, models are classified by function from a scientific angle.

<table>
<tr><th>FUNCTION</th><th>FOCUS</th><th>EXAMPLE</th></tr>
<tr><td>descriptive model: model of a current or former situation or process</td><td>what (probably) is (was) the case</td><td>
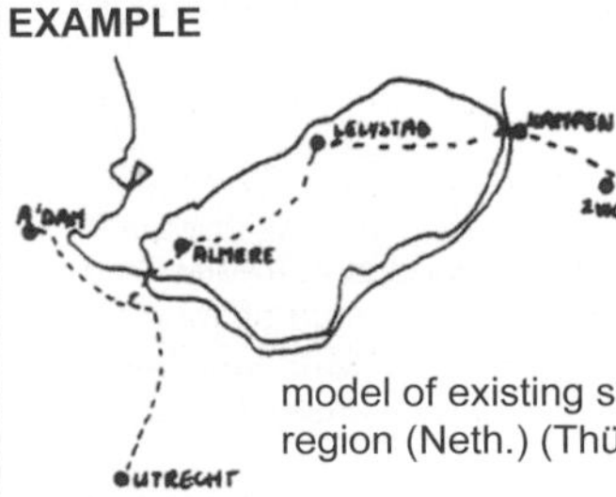

model of existing situation: Almere region (Neth.) (Thüsh 1993: 82).</td></tr>
<tr><td>explanatory model: based on insight into the operation of processes, seen from the point of view of causal thinking but also from that of conditional thinking</td><td>how or why that (probably) is (was) the case</td><td>
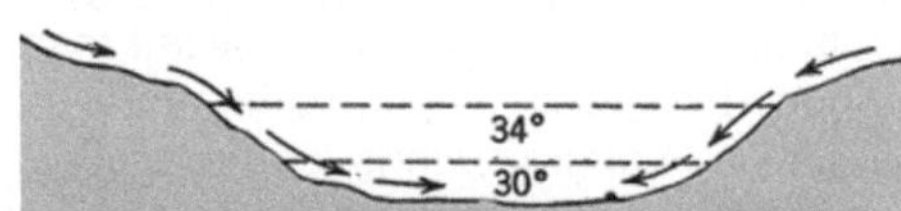

"Cold air, because it is denser, tends to settle in lower places. This drainage of the cold, dense air into depressions is the reason why frost and fog are more common in low places than on adjacent slopes." (Finch, Trewartha, Robinson & Hammond 1957: 38)</td></tr>
<tr><td>predictive model (probable-projective model = trend scenario): model clarifying what, given a certain situation, on the basis of insight into the operation of processes, will (probably) happen.</td><td>what will probably be the case (probable future)</td><td>Graphic representation of a mathematical model.
Given: the population of generation 0 and the average no. children per person e.g: population$_0$: = 2
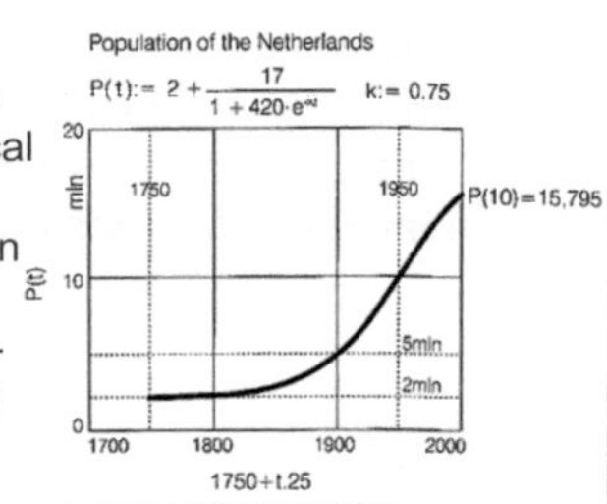

Solution by the following mathematical model:
population$_{generation}$:= population$_{generation-1}$+ children.population$_{generation-1}$ –population$_{generation-2}$</td></tr>
</table>

intentional-projective model = planning model[22] a model (design) of a not yet existing but desired situation, which, if it is to be achieved, will require one or more specific actions ('goal-oriented' design, desired scenario). Planning models are action models.	what we intend be the case	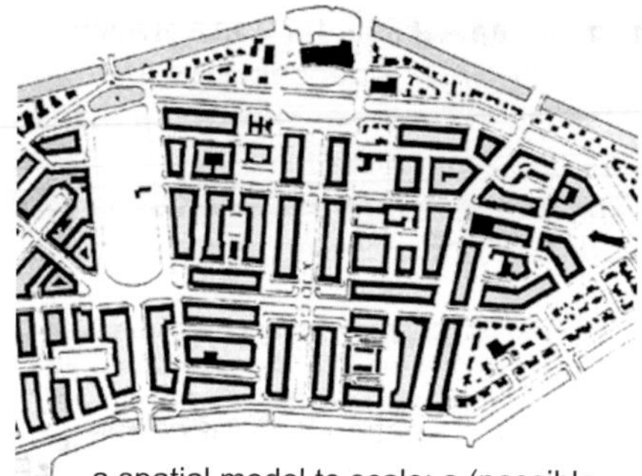 a spatial model to scale: a (possible, future) plot allotment plan (Thüsh 1993: 140).(Without a key to the symbols used, this model is incomprehensible to lay persons.)
exploratory model = research instrument: theoretical model in aid of developing a descriptive, explanatory, predictive or projective model.	what, how, why was/is/will be/could be the case	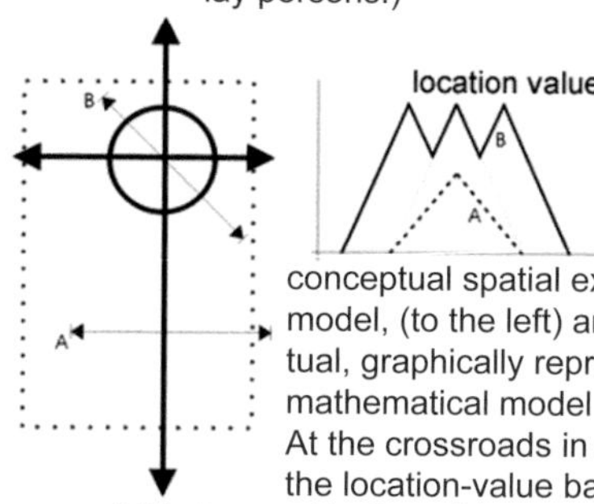 conceptual spatial exploratory model, (to the left) and conceptual, graphically represented mathematical model (to the right). At the crossroads in a ring road, the location-value based on accessibility is equal to that of the central intersection. It may even become equal to it or greater, depending on the quality of the ring road compared with that of the radial roads inside its perimeter (Klaasen & Jacobs 1999: 27).
exploratory-projective model (design or exploratory scenario): model representing a possible future situation, desirable and/or (still) undesirable.	what could possibly be the case (possible future)	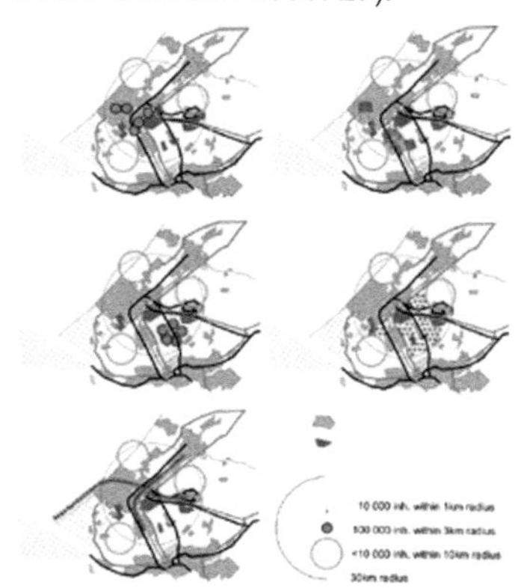 five scenarios for the way in which the region of the Hague could accommodate a population increase of 50.000 inhabitants in 2005. (Source: Klaasen 2002: 185).
FUNCTION	**FOCUS**	**EXAMPLE**

This table establishes a relation to the modality scheme of Taeke de Jong (Fig.3-1).

Descriptive, explanatory and predictive models are closely related and belong to the domain of the empirical sciences. Descriptive, explanatory and predictive models are based on established theories. They are *a posteriori* models. Exploratory models explore possibilities. They are *a priori* models.
Exploratory models are also used in the preliminary stages of descriptive, explanatory, predictive and planning models and designs (see Section 3.4.3).

In urban & regional design there are very few explanatory and predictive models. Next to descriptive models (analyses existing situations) and of course projective models (designs), exploratory models play an important role.

3.4 The conduct of science

"If there are any persons who contest a received opinion... let us thank them for it, open our minds to listen to them, and rejoice that there is some one to do for us what we otherwise ought ... to do with much greater labour for ourselves."

(John Stuart Mill (1859) 1991, *On Liberty*: 51)

3.4.1 Introduction

According to scientific outlook and the type of science, there are various views on how scientific knowledge has been and is acquired.

The methodology used in the formal sciences of mathematics and logic is traditionally an intuitive-deductive one. Practitioners of these systems of calculation and reasoning arrive at assertions by means of deduction, with the aid of formal models, and on the basis of axioms and rational rules such as the exclusion of internal contradiction (Peursen 1986: 45).

In the empirical and practical sciences, the term 'science' may be defined as the entirety of
1 systematically ordered, reality-adequate knowledge on past, present and probable and/or possible future reality,
2 hypotheses, laws and rules and
3 methods for obtaining further knowledge.

The equivalent to a proof in the formal science is an explanation in the empirical and practical sciences. Philosophers of science, especially in the last century, pondered deeply about how empirical science should be conducted, particularly from the viewpoint of the natural sciences. This resulted in the development of various types of 'game rules' (methodologies) for acquiring knowledge that could justifiably be termed 'scientific'. Methodologies[23] may be descriptive or prescriptive, or may be couched as theories. The expression 'game rules' is used here to accentuate the value-dependent character of methodologies. Incidental references were made to the application of science, but 'practical science' received scarcely any attention as an independent type of science. Aspects of the application of empirical knowledge were regarded as mainly the province of ethical philosophers.

The most important exponents of the two mainstreams mentioned in Section 3.1, the 'objectivists' and the 'subjectivists', were respectively, members of the Vienna Circle and Karl Popper, and Thomas Kuhn. Considering the significance of the views of the objectivist (and Popperian) Imre Lakatos for the practical sciences, and certainly, as we shall see, for urban & regional design, I add his name to this list. Below, I will examine a number of essentials of their thinking about the conduct of empirical science, and I shall take a standpoint of my own. Then I will comment, from the viewpoint of among other things the practical sciences, on the game-rules relating to context of discovery and context of justification, and I will introduce the term 'context of application'.

3.4.2 Vienna Circle, Popper, Kuhn, Lakatos

Vienna Circle

Hans Reichenbach (1891-1953), one of the logical positivists of the Vienna Circle (1922-1938) introduced the important distinction between context of discovery and context of justification. The context of discovery, which belonged to the domain of psychology and sociology, related to the formulation of hypotheses about reality; the context of justification referred to their verification. Scientific knowledge is acquired by what is known as the hypothetical-deductive method: from an explanatory hypothesis (based on inductive reasoning or not), given certain conditions, testable consequences are formulated (deduction), and these are confirmed (with high probability) by repeated verification (induction). Regularities are then embedded into a theory, a system of logically coherent (in particular non-contradictory) assertions, views and concepts regarding an area of reality, on the basis of which new hypotheses may be developed (Groot (1961) 1968: 42).

Popper

The inventiveness of the critical rationalist Karl Popper (1902-1993) turned the context of justification on its head by interpreting justification as non-falsifiability In a hypothesis, the real world supplies us with information (feedback) with regard to our assumptions about reality, but natural though the inclination may be to seek and find confirmation of our assumptions about reality, it is no more than inductive reasoning, which proves nothing. Falsifying feedback is much more useful than confirmative feedback; it can prove something, by refuting a hypothesis. An essential component of this outlook is a prohibition on immunization strategies (Popper (1959) 1968: 82 ff.)[25]. The falsification of a hypothesis gives food for thought, and challenges the scientist to formulate a better one.

In logical notation, where H stands for a hypothesis, A for a statement of initial conditions and O for one of the testable consequences of (H.A), the verification of hypotheses may be represented as follows:

$$\frac{\begin{array}{l}(H.A)\\ \rightarrow O\\ \quad O\end{array}}{(H.A)}$$

This is not a valid syllogism. What is logically valid is drawing a conclusion from the falsification of testable consequences:

$$\frac{(H.A) \rightarrow O \quad \text{not-}O}{\text{not-}(H.A)}$$

The higher the informative content of a hypothesis, the easier it is to test. The lower the probability that testing it will support the associated theory, the more significance may be attached to the corroboration[26] of the theory if the hypothesis is not refuted (Magee 1973: 36). Scientific knowledge, Popper states, is a set of expectations about the truth. The distinguishing feature of scientific knowledge is that, unlike other forms of knowledge, it is open to 'improvement' (e.g. Popper (1959) 1968: 273 ff.).

In science it is the context of justification that matters whereas the context of discovery is irrelevant, Popper holds (in this instance agreeing with the logical positivists of the Vienna Circle) in his book *The Logic of Scientific Discovery* (1959). It is a book whose title is misleading, as Jong & Schipper (1987: 145) rightly comment. Certainly, one cannot rely on observation to arrive by a process of induction at a hypothesis or theory, because observation is itself theory-dependent.

Scientific activity begins with the analysis of the problem (P_1) and a good formulation of it. Only then can one start seeking possible solutions: $P_1 \rightarrow TT \rightarrow EE \rightarrow P_2$ (TT = tentative theory, EE = evaluative error elimination) (e.g. Popper 1972: 144). "The evaluation is always *critical*, and its aim is the discovery and *elimination of error*.' (ibid.). In Popper's view, one can only speak of a scientific hypothesis if it has consequences which are in principle falsifiable, through 'crucial experiments'. A crucial experiment may also be a thought-experiment (Popper (1959) 1968: Appendix XI). A critical attitude, Popper argues, is essential for the conduct of science. Theories must always be open to debate. (Popper (1959) 1968: 16). Rival theories are necessary for this purpose. In other words, proliferation and pluriformity must be stimulated (see Feyerabend 1978: 168).

Critique of Popper's ideas came from two directions. On the one hand, it came from the subjectivists/relativists led by Thomas Kuhn (1922-1996). On the other hand, there was criticism from within Popper's own circle, in particular from Lakatos (1922-1974).

A milestone in the scientific philosophy debate between the two movements was undoubtedly the symposium that took place in July 1965 on *Criticism and the Growth of Knowledge*, part of the International Colloquium in the Philosophy of Science held at Bedford College, London University, and organized by Lakatos. This symposium brought Karl Popper, Thomas Kuhn and Imre Lakatos together, as well as Paul Feyerabend, Stephen Toulmin, John Watkins and others. The similarly titled *Proceedings*, edited by Lakatos and Musgrave, appeared in 1970 and was reprinted in 1972.

Kuhn

The essence of Kuhn's critique of Popper is that Kuhn holds that science is conducted in scientific communities, within which the research is not so much directed at the falsification of theories as at supporting and thinking them ('convergent thinking') (Kuhn (1959) 1991: 140). Theories must not be continually open to dispute. Feedback which conflicts with a theory holding within the community is ascribed to the inadequacy of the researcher and not that of the theory. This, Kuhn states, is the normal manner of conducting science which continues until, at a certain moment, on irrational grounds, the scientific community 'swings around' and adopts a new, better theory. This change is termed a paradigm shift (from the Greek *paradeigma* = example). Kuhn defines paradigms as 'models from which spring particular coherent traditions of scientific research' ((1962) 1970: 10). The irrational character of the revolution expresses itself in (among other things) the incommensurable ways the world is seen from the respective perspectives of the two theories (ibid.: 4).

Not only does historical research demonstrate, according to Kuhn, that natural and other sciences have developed in this manner (Kuhn (1962) 1970; 1970), but also that a 'closed' scientific community is a necessary precondition for the development of a sound theory, if only because people are unwilling to invest much time, energy and money into the paradigm unless everyone is convinced of its correctness (Kuhn (1962) 1970: 18; 25/26)[27]. A closed scientific community is characterized by shared values and by belief in and commitment to 'exemplars' ('representative examples'). "A scientific community consists ... of the practitioners of a scientific speciality. An apparently arbitrary element, compounded of personal and historical accident, is always a formative ingredient of the beliefs espoused by a given scientific community at a given time" (ibid.: 4). "To an extent unparalleled in other fields, they have undergone similar educations and professional initiations" (ibid.: 177). "He cannot ... solve problems at all unless he has first learned the theory and some rules for applying it." (ibid.: 187). Kuhn initially applied the term 'paradigm' also to this closed community with its values, game rules etc., but from 1969 onwards used the term 'disciplinary matrix' (1970: 271). Kuhn was moreover one of the first to express dissatisfaction with the strict distinction between the contexts of discovery and justification (Kuhn (1962) 1970: 9).

Lakatos

After fleeing Hungary in 1956, Imre Lakatos met Popper at the London School of Economics in 1959. A considerable proportion of his publications appeared posthumously. Lakatos, an objectivist, agrees with Thomas Kuhn that Popper's exclusive emphasis on falsification is 'unnatural': people have an inherent tendency to perceive whatever supports their ideas and opinions. Interestingly, it is a consideration that Lakatos shares with Popper, the anticipation that events will repeat themselves, that prompted him to reject the latter's conclusion. Falsification does, however, also play an important part in Lakatos' views on scientific practice.

> Lakatos distinguishes three forms of falsificationism: dogmatic, methodological and sophisticated methodological (Lakatos 1970). He rejects dogmatic falsificationism as untenable. To the methodological falsificationism backed by Popper, Lakatos adds a new element: "for the sophisticated falsificationist a theory is 'acceptable' or ''scientific' only if it has corroborated excess empirical content over its predecessor (or rival), that is only if it leads to the discovery of novel facts." (Lakatos 1970: 116). Dogmatic falsificationism is untenable, Lakatos argues, because no psychological, natural boundary can be drawn between theoretical propositions and observational propositions: assertions can not be proved by facts. "Scientific theories are not only equally unprovable, and equally improbable, but they are also equally undisprovable." (ibid: 103). With regard to methodological falsificationism, he adduces that 'basic statements' (Popper (1962) 1968: 267) can indeed be falsified (e.g. by instrumental innovations). A probabilistic theory is also capable of being falsified on the grounds of agreed rules.

Lakatos replaces the term 'theory' with the hypothesis as a falsifiable statement of it, by the term 'research programme', which may comprise both chains of theories and methodologies. 'Science is not simply trial and error, a series of conjectures and refutations.' (Lakatos 1978: 4). Lakatos further makes a distinction between 'mature' science and 'immature' science (ibid.: 87). Only a mature science, in Lakatos' view, has heuristic potential. A research programme moreover makes it possible to evaluate developments in a certain scientific field (Lakatos 1999: 108). A research programme consists of a 'hard core' and a 'protective belt around the hard core' (ibid.: 104). He follows Kuhn to the extent that he states the hard core should be temporarily immune to criticism (ibid.: 104). He shows himself to be a follower of Popper however in his stress on seeking counterexamples ('monsters' - Lakatos 1976), by the refutation of which hypotheses and theories may be strengthened (ibid.)[28]. Lakatos distinguishes two types of counterexample, local and global. The first type helps improve the quality of the proof; the second refutes the hypothesis or theory. This refutation is then used as a basis for seeking out hidden assumptions and making them explicit, for they are possibly false. He illustrates his methodology with the aid of thought experiments with polyhedra (Fig.3-2). Contrary to widely held beliefs, he shows that deduction can lead to an increase of content. "If a deduction does not increase content I would *not* call it deduction, but 'verification'. (ibid.: 81).

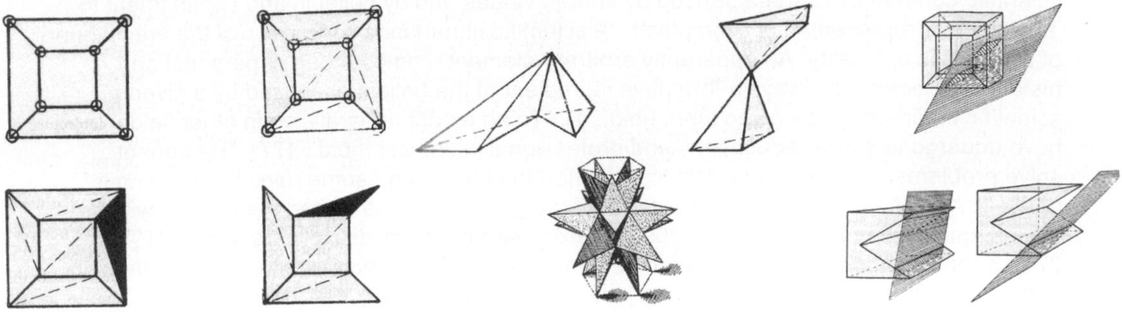

Fig.3-2 Some of the spatial models used by Imre Lakatos in Proofs and Refutations to explain his heuristic methodology (1976: 8, 15, 20, 61).

Lakatos calls this 'deductive guessing', a form of heuristics (from the Greek *heuriskein*: to find): the step by step exploration of a domain on the basis of an idea, while ignoring certain factual aspects. Like Kuhn, Lakatos supports his methodology partly with arguments based on historical examples.

The following example originates from Lakatos himself:
"... the hard core of Newton's research programme [was] formed by his three laws of motion together with his principle of universal gravity. But it was not possible to draw concrete conclusions until auxiliary hypotheses were formulated. Newton's purpose with these auxiliary hypotheses was to introduce diverse simplifications and alternative approaches in order to solve his equations. For example, Newton originally tried to calculate the elliptical planetary orbits by applying his laws of motion on the assumption that the sun is stationary and orbited by only one planet, attracted by gravitational force. But the sun would be reciprocally attracted by the planet's gravitational pull, in accordance with his own principle of universal gravitation; and this implied that the sun could not possibly remain stationary. He therefore abandoned the approximating assumption of a stationary sun, and succeeded in solving his motion equations in that case too. He went on to take into consideration the effect of other planets on the orbit of the planet under consideration, and showed that due to the influence of the other planets the orbit would in fact not be an *exact* ellipse." (Zandvoort 1987: 44).

In this heuristic approach, he distances himself from the view of Popper (and the Vienna Circle) that the context of discovery is scientifically irrelevant (see also Lakatos 1970: footnote 143/4). Critical debate is naturally a *sine qua non* in Lakatos' view of the conduct of science. The formerly convinced communist Lakatos agrees with Popper and explicitly opposes Kuhn in holding that scientific communities must be open and that the simultaneous existence of diverse theories (research programmes) should be stimulated. Although, unlike the views stated by Popper, he believes that psychological and social processes do play a part in the business of science, the evaluation of a scientific theory must not in his view be allowed to depend on power relations and 'groupthink' (Lakatos 1978: 9/10)

"Groupthink refers to a deterioration of mental efficiency, reality testing, and moral judgement that results from in-group pressures." (Janis 1972: 9). The members of a cohesive group are not normally aware of these in-group pressures (ibid.: 177).

In the field of opinions described above, I choose the following standpoint. Kuhn's model of the conduct of science as a largely irrational affair, avoiding critical debate, based partly on power, focussed on consensus but in practice successful, is undoubtedly valid in a descriptive respect. It is true that 'social bias' is one of the forms of bias that does affect science, as noted in Section 3.1. Kuhn's conclusion that science must therefore necessarily be conducted in this way is obviously something that I cannot accept considering my objectivist, rational, critical view of the acquisition of knowledge: an 'is' cannot imply an 'ought'. Kuhn's argument is an inductive one, and like all inductive arguments it proves nothing and excludes any possibility of improvement. I certainly cannot agree with his views from the perspective of practical sciences. Any successful, result-oriented action on the basis of knowledge obtained by consensus under the influence of power relations, is likely to be more good luck than good judgement. Finally, the conduct of science affects and involves people and therefore has an ethical aspect. And even if irrational behaviour and an uncritical attitude were to benefit the efficiency of the business of science, the submission of the individual to group processes would be as undesirable in scientific circles as elsewhere - in the same way as it would be undesirable to boost the armaments industry for the sake of its positive effect on the progress of science.

Interestingly, Kuhn's concept of a scientific community shows some points of resemblance to a medieval guild (see Section 4.2.2).

'Natural' though the inductive verification of hypotheses/theories may be (see Section 2.1), we are not obliged to follow this natural inclinations, any more than the inclination to prefer 'certainty' over 'doubt'. I side with the critical, rationalist views of Popper and Lakatos on the acquisition of knowledge. I regard the approach favoured by Lakatos (prescriptive methodology) - a research programme rather than the discrete theories/hypotheses of Popper, attaching significance not only to falsification but also to corroboration, no strict boundary between the context of discovery and the context of justification - as a more 'realistic' approach than Popper's. But I would concur with the qualification of Patricia Huisman, who argues that, due to their focus on the natural sciences, critical-rationalists tend to jump to the conclusion that a confrontation with empiricism would necessarily also unveil the constitution of the real world in other sciences (Huisman 1996: 135). The guarantee that rational thinking will always 'unravel' subjectivity is not one that can be given (ibid.: 72).

3.4.3 Context of discovery : heuristic approach

Having already been drawn into doubt, the distinction between the context of discovery and the context of justification introduced by members of the Vienna Circle and by Popper, where the former context was considered not to belong to the domain of science but to that of psychology, met increasing resistance in the nineteen seventies. Kuhn had admitted to having problems with the separation of those contexts as long ago as 1962: "Yet my attempts to apply them [i.e. distinctions like those as context of discovery versus context of justification - itk], even *grosso modo*, to the actual situations in which knowledge is gained, accepted and assimilated, have made them seem extraordinarily problematic" (Kuhn (1962) 1970: 9). Hilary Putnam expressed himself in more forceful terms: "... the idea that correct ideas just come from the sky, while the methods for testing them are highly rigid and predetermined, is one of the worst legacies of the Vienna Circle." (Putnam (1974) 1991: 134). Peter Urbach (1978) supported him, stating that theories have to be assessed even before they are tested, because otherwise money will not be spent on testing them: "I shall argue ... that new scientific theories have, as a matter of historical fact, often been obtained from older ones by the application of certain rules; and even (*pace* both Popper and Polanyi) by the deliberate application of articulated rules." (ibid.: 104), and "... that the power of a heuristic provides a suitable measure for the objective promise of the research programme in which it is embedded." (ibid.: 107).

More recently, David Gooding (1996) has argued on the basis of historical examples from the natural sciences that rationality and creativity (cf. Bergson's 'creative intuition', see Section 3.1) do indeed meet in the context of discovery, when the inspiration of anomalies (unexplained deviations from current theory) leads to 'abductive inference'. New hypotheses, he states, develop on the basis of complex cognitive processes. He concludes that "the abductive scheme [see below - itk] shows where a novel insight or interpretation fits into a larger framework of mental, physical and social activity, it allows us to characterise a rationale that is not restricted to a particular logical form." (ibid.: 97). This is not to say that standard 'recipes' for generating hypotheses exist or could be developed. There is no 'algorithmic method', fixed procedures for gaining new scientific knowledge. But neither is the generation of new knowledge based on arbitrary choices: "... the search has turned to looking for 'logic' in some weaker sense. Heuristic procedures, strategies for discovery and the like are explored."(Audi 1995, entry on 'abduction').

Radnitsky argued as long ago as the nineteen seventies that Lakatos' heuristics was a methodology that related to the context of discovery. "The structural study of hypothesis generation is not only compatible with but is suggested and guided by the Popperian approach." (1979: footnote 251). Boyd too stresses the importance of the 'explanatory power' of theories ((1985) 1991: 350). In 'armchair investigation', a term used by Radnitzky for this manner of logical information-theoretical investigations, not only 'heuristics' but the (also mutually) connected concepts of 'plausible reasoning', 'abduction' and 'exploratory models' play a part.

Heuristics also play a crucial part in the formal sciences (Lakatos 1976; Magnani 2001: 48).

Heuristics

Heuristics is the art of 'discovery'. Van Koningsveld (1976: 201) defines heuristics as 'the entirety of suggestions, hints and unformulated rules that point out certain avenues of research as potentially fruitful and block others'. Heuristics can also be synonymous with 'heuretic', which the Shorter Oxford English Dictionary (1997) defines as 'the branch of logic which treats of [-the art of] discovery or invention.' It is a classical concept which may be found in various forms in the work of such thinkers and philosophers as Cicero (1st century BC) Agricola (15th century), Leibniz (1646-1716), Whewell (1794-1866) and Peirce (1839-1914) (Peursen 1987; Jong & Schipper 1987: 147).
Heuristic rules are rules of behaviour that promote finding within the context of discovery (Roozenburg & Eekels 1991: 42). In heuristic strategies, in the context of 'abduction', 'plausible reasoning' and 'exploratory models', use is made of analogies, metaphors, 'tacit knowledge', i.e. of non-empirical considerations (Radder 1997: 46; Jong & Schipper 1987: 146).

'Tacit knowledge' is a concept introduced by the philosopher Polanyi in the last century to refer to a component part of scientific knowledge, which contributes to the discovery of new solutions and theories (Peursen 1986: 35).

Knowledge of existing theories is essential, as are the capacity to raise questions about solutions that are taken for granted, the capacity to integrate information from various sources and the capacity to make implicit assumptions explicit (Peursen 1986: 76; Magnani 2001).

Gooding (1990: 79) cites the example of Gallileo's challenge to Aristotle's claim with regard to falling bodies[29]. If the heavy stone (H) falls faster than the light stone (L), the combination H+L should fall less quickly than H alone. But since their joint weight is greater than that of H alone, they should fall more quickly. The paradox vanishes if we abandon the belief that the speed of falling is proportional to weight. Then H=L=H+L. Neither deduction nor induction operate here, but it is nonetheless a rational argument.

Positive heuristics are involved when assumptions are confirmed by examples, when counterexamples lead to the improvement of these assumptions, and when this improvement generates new predictions/applications. Research programmes may be either empirically or theoretically progressive. Zandvoort (1987: 44) gives the example of the research programme of Newton. The mental models used by Newton were underlain by a certain plan that set a direction for the elaboration of the programme.

Abduction

The term 'abduction' (also known as 'retroduction') was introduced by the pragmatic philosopher Charles S. Peirce (1839-1941). Peirce holds that this is the logic by which hypotheses are formed in the context of discovery (Roozenburg & Eekels 1991: 69). In induction, a hypothesis is inferred from the repetition of a certain phenomenon; in abduction, a hypothesis is inferred from a single, unique phenomenon. "Abduction merely suggests that something may be." (Hanson 1958: 85). "The form of the inference is this: some surprising phenomenon P is observed; P would be explicable as a matter of course if H were true; hence there is reason to think that H is true." (ibid.: 86).

Abduction plays an important part in classic detective stories as pioneered by Edgar Allan Poe and Sir Arthur Conan Doyle. The Finnish philosopher Ilkka Niiniluoto has examined Poe's The Murders in the Rue Morgue from this viewpoint in an analysis which is both instructive and fascinating for devotees of the genre (1999). It is believed that Poe was one of Peirce's favourite authors.

Abduction my be represented in logical notation as follows:

given $p \rightarrow q$
q

---

conclusion: p

The above conclusion is of course logically invalid.

In the practical sciences, the reasoning is as follows (Thagard & Croft 1999: 134):

how to do X
Y might do

---

so maybe try Y

Lorenzo Magnani (2001: 20 ff.) distinguishes (Fig.3-3):

- creative abduction: abduction that generates a new hypothesis (generally by focussing on certain aspects and ignoring others);
- selective abduction: abduction that generates a number of provisional hypotheses which could explain a certain case; rational selection on the basis of knowledge;
- evaluative abduction: abduction that 'corroborates' a hypothesis; 'inference to the best explanation', reducing uncertainty on the basis of consequences of the hypotheses.

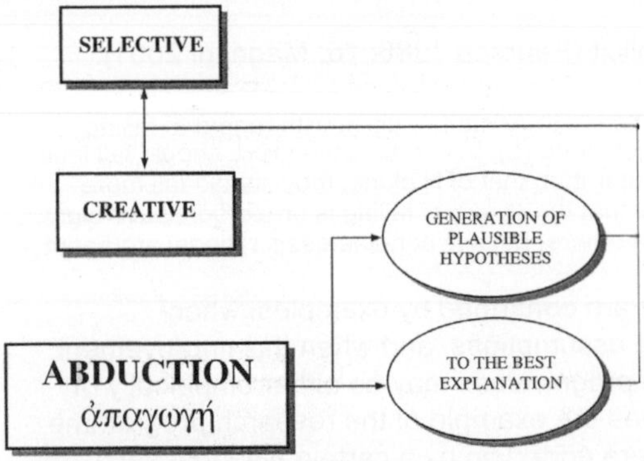

Fig.3-3 Types of abduction (Magnani 2001: 20).

Magnani (2001) refers to the views of Peirce and others in stating that creative (theoretical) abductive reasoning is generally based on conceptual spatial models. He also cites the relationship between cognitive and motor development in children demonstrated by Piaget. Manipulative abduction, both concrete and conceptual, forms a basis for useful inductive generalizations (ibid.: 60). The manipulation of (spatial) models is, in this outlook, a form of experimentation, but in a conceptual respect (Magnani 1999: 236). Magnani incorporates his ideas on selective and evaluative abduction into a medical diagnostic model (ibid.: 23). The psychologist Drenth concretizes Magnani's concept of 'creative abduction' for his own field, although without giving a comparable theoretical foundation (Drenth 1995: 150).

Creative abduction is related to the concept of 'serendipity', the discovery of something you aren't looking for.

Plausible reasoning

Argumentation theory offers a set of tools for justifying what one discovers in the context of discovery. Hypotheses may be justified on the basis of plausible arguments (Schomberg 1991: 58). Citing the similarly-titled publication of Rescher (1976), Von Schomberg defines 'plausible reasoning' as the derivation of a defensible standpoint from partly inconsistent and/or deficient data. The term 'ill-defined problems' is sometimes used in this situation (Meheus 1999: 204). Von Schomberg states that this could have the implication for the scientific context of discovery that "from partly inconsistent data, there can be derived by means of plausible reasoning a plausible hypothesis" which is worth the effort of investigating (1991: 59). The deficiency of data, Von Schomberg states, can also relate to the lack of opportunity for empirical testing due to the impracticability of experiments - questions of a type he calls 'transscientific'.

'Plausible reasoning' is sometimes also referred to as 'inference to the best explanation', i.e. "a pattern of reasoning by which one infers that a hypothesis is true from the fact that the hypothesis offers the most plausible or satisfactory explanation of the evidence." (Boyd, Gasper & Trout 1997: Glossary). Weak logic may also be employed in conjunction with this form of reasoning.

Nicolas Rescher (1976) developed a theory of plausibility which is non-probabilistic but which is based on the principle that the conclusion of an argument owes its status to the weakest premiss. By construing inductive arguments as enthymematic [i.e. based on probable premisses - itk] deductive arguments, he shows that considerations of plausibility may support our intuitions about strength of proof.
Applicable rules in this connection include:
- "in cases of conflict, never make the more plausible give way to what is less so" (Fig.3-4);
- "in the context of hypothetical reasoning, a generalization carries more weight than a specific 'datum'";
- "in the context of inductive reasoning, the converse is true (abduction)" (ibid.: 14).

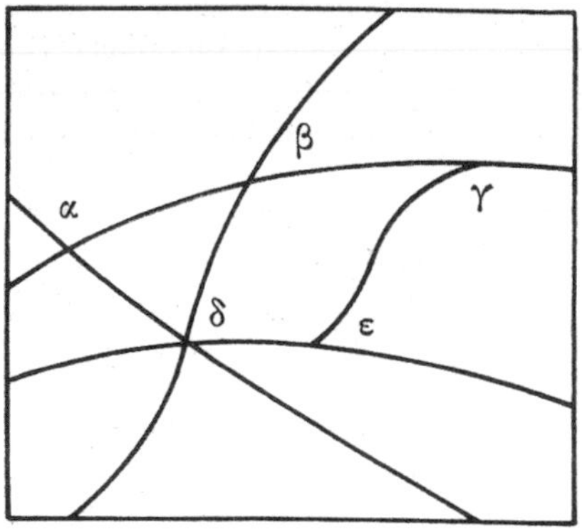

Fig.3-4 Two parachutists are to meet someone in the terrain depicted on the indicated map, of which each knows the other to have a copy. The time of the meeting has been fixed, but the place has not been revealed. Where is each parachutist to go? (Rescher 1976: 14).

Exploratory models

Models are gaining increasing importance in science, Daniela Bailer-Jones stated at a 1999 congress titled 'Model-Based Reasoning in Scientific Discovery' (1999: 23). In particular, Nersessian proposed at the same congress, "visual representation is a powerful tool for science when sufficient constraints are incorporated into the reasoning process." (Nersessian 1999: 20). In the context of discovery, exploratory conceptual models are a means of extending knowledge and forming theories, as a way of substantiating hypotheses and as preliminary sketches for the idea "couldn't it be true that..." (Bertels & Nauta 1969: 29). A model, Van Peursen states, "generally has an intermediate position between abstract theory and the sensory reality. And it is precisely this interaction of science and the concrete world that makes models suitable for heuristic purposes." (1986: 77). In Lakatos' words "A 'model' is a set of initial conditions (possibly together with some observational theories) which one knows is *bound* to be replaced during further development of the programme, and one even knows, more or less, how. This shows once more how irrelevant 'refutations' of any specific variant are in a research programme: their existence is fully expected, the positive heuristic is there as a strategy both for predicting (producing) and digesting them." (1978: 51).

3.4.4 Context of justification and context of application

The point that hypotheses and theories may have rational foundations in the context of discovery as well as in the context of justification is particularly important to the practical sciences. The concepts of context of justification and its associated 'falsification' and 'verification', developed in connection with the empirical sciences, must be seen in a different light in the practical sciences. As in the empirical sciences, the aim is to test hypotheses/ theories (empirically) under controllable, repeatable conditions (a 'laboratory situation'). In the practical sciences, however, one is less likely to seek a context in which the hypothesis/ theory can be falsified than a context in which the hypothesis/theory can be corroborated. A series of applications can then provide the basis for drawing probable conclusions with regard to necessary conditions and occurrent effects. Hilary Putnam already recognized this about 30 years ago: "Since the application of scientific laws does involve the anticipation of future successes, Popper is not right in maintaining that induction is unnecessary. Even if scientists do not inductively anticipate the future (and, of course, they do), men who apply scientific laws and theories do so. And 'don't make inductions' is hardly reasonable advice to give to these men." (Putnam (1974) 1991: 122).

A number of factors may stand in the way of creating such a laboratory situation.

- Ethical considerations may sometimes make it impossible to test a practical science hypothesis experimentally. This is particularly true when people are involved as experimental objects. Familiar examples are the ethical committees required to judge whether medical experiments may or may not be carried out. Animal experiments are also ethically controversial, as are experiments involving genetic modification.
- Experimental trials are sometimes impossibly expensive. This is particularly true for large-scale objects. Scale models may in some cases provide an alternative, but care must always be taken to avoid model overextension (Klaasen 2000a).
- The time factor can interfere in various ways.
  - Experiments may take time which can be ill afforded because of the need for prompt action;
  - Conditions that change in the course of time cannot always be artificially accelerated (temporal scale models, unlike spatial ones, cannot be made);
  - Conditions may change in the course of time in a highly unpredictable way, and this, especially in connection with processes and/or products with a large temporal grain, may form a considerable handicap to corroborating assumptions about longer term effects.

In cases such as these, one either abandons the application, or one has to rely on feedback supplied by applications of hypotheses in situations marked by different, unique, conditions in each case (see also Radnitzky 1979: 232). A series of applications can thus lead to (cautious) conclusions, in the spirit of 'under such and such conditions, it is not unlikely that such and such effects will occur', but only if the conditions have a certain degree of similarity. If a certain assumption proves false in practice, there are two possible explanations: either the *techné* is inadequate, or the specific conditions under which application took place were misinterpreted. Toulmin describes an irrigation project on Bali (Indonesia) that failed because no account was taken of the part played by water in Balinese culture (Toulmin 2001: 60 ff.).

Because laboratory-type experiments, when possible, merely supply corroboration, and because when only practical applications are possible, these take place under variable conditions which are only approximately similar in each case, the need for a scientific or at least rationally defensible grounding for hypotheses and theories (the context of discovery) is greater in the practical sciences than in the empirical sciences. This is also true for ethical reasons[30].

The term 'context of justification' thus loses considerable force in the practical sciences. Instead of this term, I propose using the term 'context of application' (*Anwendungszusammenhang*: Drewe undated, about 1975). This context - a diversity of spatial-ecological, socio-cultural, economic-technical and administrative-organizational conditions - does not supply the justification of hypotheses/theories so much as supply feedback to a heuristic approach in the context of discovery. Practical-scientific research can correspondingly be referred to as 'applied research'.

3.4.5 Demarcation between science and non-science

Determining the demarcation between scientific and non-scientific knowledge is not an aim in its own right, but is worthwhile for the sake of restricting the role of chance (see Section 3.1). Possessing knowledge that is adequately matched to reality is a biological necessity (Huisman 1996: 45); realistic knowledge has a direct and indirect bearing on both individual and societal interests - not only in positive but also in negative respects.

'Game rules' for the conduct of science must at the least imply that:

- the process of knowledge acquisition is rational, communicable, checkable and debatable;
- conclusions are consistent, generic in nature and, at least in principle, testable (verification/falsification);
- there is a dynamic "in the sense that it [science] is continually stretching out to extend its frontiers ..." (Hodgson 1979: 135).

In other words, if within a scientific community it is impossible to conduct a rational, critical, open debate, if 'truth is what the victor believes' (Lakatos 1999: 27), and if a theory permits any situation to pertain, with or without the aid of ad hoc auxiliary hypotheses, and thus does not deliver any testable consequences or predictions (Bertels & Nauta 1969: 58) then the term science is inapplicable.

> Communicating about scientific findings can be done in words, but also in images or formulas. All that matters is the comprehensibility of the verbal or visual language (see Section 2.3).

It is not the fact that predictions prove false that makes a theory unscientific, but the way people deal with such refutations. In the words of Lakatos: "... we do not demarcate scientific theories from pseudoscientific ones, but rather scientific method from non scientific method." (1978: 3).

3.5 Perspectives for urban design as a practical science

"Scientia non est individuorum"

(Anonymous)

When I combine the matter of Section 3.2.4. 'practical sciences' with that of Section 2.4 'urban systems', I must conclude that urban design is at least in principle a practical science, a conclusion already drawn earlier by Jelle Rijpma (1991). 'Urban & regional design' occupies a special place within the practical - and technical - sciences, because the above mentioned limitations that can affect the context of justification (context of application) apply in a cumulative manner.

A laboratory situation[31] cannot be created for the following reasons:

- the high capital outlay before testing can be started;
- the long time required for the implementation of proposals;
- the long period over which usability would have to be tested (the *longue durée* of implemented designs);
- ethical complications.

The context of application is subject to the following complications:

- the conditions under which proposals are implemented in practice show few similarities to one another;
- the conditions cannot be manipulated, not even partially (see also Jong 2002a);
- in practice there are only restricted opportunities for experiment for ethical reasons.

On the grounds of the above, the emphasis in the practical-scientific approach to urban & regional design lies on the context of discovery - what is presumed to be possible, and what effects will probably occur under which conditions. Empirical and formal scientific knowledge, in part derived from the context of application, should provide the necessary constraints.

Leaving aside whether the methodology of Lakatos is not only prescriptive but also descriptive, the game rules seem promising for scientific theorization in urban & regional design, considering the importance attached in that methodology to heuristics, creative abduction and the manipulation of spatial conceptual models designed to provide insight. Not that his rules have to be followed to the letter, but they should serve as a guideline. After all, design processes too are heuristic in nature (Roozenburg & Eekels 1991: 5; Spillers & Newsome 1993: 106; Vries 1993: 4).
I shall go into this subject in more detail in the chapters on ‘urban & regional design and science’ and ‘developing a practical-scientific body of knowledge for urban & regional design’. First, in the next Chapter, I intend to analyse the significance of urban & regional design for society, and what implications this analysis has for the object of research.

4. Urban & regional design, physical urban system and society

4.1 Introduction

"Cities are the largest and most complex objects that human beings make."

(Hillier & Penn 1991, *Is dense civilisation possible? Or the shape of cities in the 21st century* : 2)

A small library could be filled with all that has been written in Dutch alone during the last few dozen years about the structuring and design of urban regions and the siting of urban functions - not to mention all that has been published about 'the city' as a phenomenon. Not only urban & regional designers, but architects, sociologists, cultural theorists, politicians, government departments, project developers, industry organizations, environmental agencies, residents' associations and journalists all over the world hold varying opinions about how physical urban systems should be designed. Views similarly differ on the relevance of cultural history in urban & regional design, on relations between urban design and urban society, on the possibility of planning physical urban systems, on the respective roles in this field of government, the private sector, and urban & regional designers and/or architects. These are all views that have evolved along with changing social, economic and technical conditions, politically/culturally determined priorities, and by the actors involved in design[32].

As Maarten Hajer said in his interview in *Groeten uit Zoetermeer*, "The problem in the Netherlands is not a lack of reflection, but on the contrary the insanely huge amount of reflection." (Nio & Reijndorp 1997: 119).

The point of view I take in this study is that reality, and therefore urban reality, may be regarded as a system. The concern in this respect is to argue the thesis that urban & regional design is a practical science or is capable of developing into a practical science.

In Section 2.4, I defined urban systems as entities of socio-cultural, spatial-ecological, economic-technical and administrative-organizational elements (including people), relations and processes. Within such an urban system, we can distinguish a built physical system. This physical urban system, I proposed, fulfils a carrying function and an information function within the urban system. Physical urban systems are built by people, and are hence 'makeable'. This is not true for the urban system or for society, but it is true for the spatial conditions for the functioning of people (in group connection or as individuals) and of institutions (in the broadest sense). The construction or reconstruction of that system is a goal-oriented action, and, considering its social implications, has certain ethical aspects. These systems are in a general sense the object of a diversity of disciplines, among them the discipline of urban & regional design. Urban & regional designers make proposals for building or rebuilding in the form of designs. In doing so they use models, particularly spatial models.

I defined an urban design in Section 2.4 as a proposal for a coherent package of spatial interventions in a certain urban or urbanescent area which always affects more than one sector[33].

In the present Chapter, I will first examine the relevance of system thinking to urban & regional design (Section 4.2) and the constraints that are inherent to working with spatial models (Section 4.3). I will then go further into the concepts of the 'carrying function' and 'information function'. On the basis of these three viewpoints, I position the discipline of urban & regional design in relation to the discipline of spatial planning and the discipline of architecture. Establishing this position will make it clear that the general description of the physical urban system as the object of urban & regional design is capable of interpretation in two different ways, and is in practice dually interpreted. This is connected with the distinction that may be drawn between, on the one hand, linear processes within urban systems which are characterized by a relatively large temporal grain, and, on the other hand, cyclic processes which are characterize by a relatively small temporal grain. A distinction may be made within urban & regional design on these grounds with regard to views about what is the essence of the discipline of urban & regional design: respectively, *the pattern-oriented* approach and the *process-oriented* approach. These distinct views imply different perspectives for a scientific approach to urban & regional design.

4.2 Implications of the systems approach to reality

"The only people who see the whole picture .... are the ones who step out of the frame."

(Salman Rushdie 1999, *The Ground Beneath Her Feet* : Ch.2 Melodies and Silences)

4.2.1 Systems of equal and unequal order

The size and boundaries of urban systems and hence of physical urban systems are not fixed, and are generally not self-evident as they are, for example, in architecture. A given configuration may be regarded as a system if its internal cohesion is greater than the cohesion of the individual elements of the system with its environments (Section 2.2). As Niek de Boer puts it, "A plan covers a coherent unified area within which the consequences of 'separate' developments can be weighed up against those of others." (1990: 94). On the grounds of this outlook, urban districts are quite often regarded as physical urban systems - systems of equal order which may be but are not necessarily have a common boundary. These district-systems may even have neighbourhood-systems - systems of a lower order - as elements, and themselves constitute the elements of the city-system, which is a system of higher order (a higher level of scale) (see Fig.2-7). The considerations underlying this are generally implicit: assumed social coherence, similarities in the use of certain amenities, administrative-organizational unity, visual forms, historical origins (within the cultivated system). Natural systems and patterns are also sometimes used as a basis for the size and boundaries of (physical) urban systems. Greater importance is in this case attached to natural processes than to urban ones, often without any account being taken of the considerable differences in temporal grain (Klaasen 1993: 87 ff.).

In the course of the last century, different angles led to differing scale series being formulated as relevant. A few examples are given below. In the Netherlands, with a tradition of spatial policymaking, a scale series of relevant plan areas was coordinated with the administrative instrumentation, which was largely related to the administrative-organizational subsystem of the urban system. This has led to a series such as *region *city *borough/town *district/village *neighbourhood/hamlet. The urban designer Thomas Schurch, originating from the USA where an entirely different administrative-organization system exists, recently proposed the following (not very consistent) variant of that series: (1) the site-specific scale of an individual land parcel; (2) neighbourhood or district; (3) an entire city; (4) the region in which a city lies; (5) corridors (1999:18).

The Greek urban & regional designer Constantinos Doxiadis (1968: 29; 134) developed a logarithmic system with the factor 2.64, based on a hexagonal organizational principle and on time/distance considerations (Fig.4-1). The Dutch urban & regional designer Niek de Boer (1978) starts mainly from the potential user base (*draagvlak*) required for various public facilities, and, observing that the current administrative-organizational units and boundaries do not correspond with them, proposed changes to the administrative organization. In the late nineteen seventies, Taeke de Jong (1978) developed a semi-logarithmic series, now in use within the Faculty of Architecture of Delft University of Technology. It was based on the empirical observation that the characterization of the spatial pattern in urbanized areas of the Netherlands differs strongly according to the reduction factor used. On the basis of his findings, he proposes demarcating areas with an (indicative) radius of (respectively) 100 m, 300 m, 1.000 m etc., rising to 100 km (Figs.4-2 and 4-3). This classification of scales is also applied in the discipline of traffic and transport. The factor 3 used there is derived from Christaller's theory of spatial layout (Goeverden, Schrijver & Van den Broeke 1988: 866)[34]. The British architect Lawson (1990: 39) presented the pragmatic list illustrated in Fig.4-4.

Ekistic Logarithmic Scale of terrestrial space and Ekistic units

	elementary units of human settlements			communities of human settlements											
settlements	micro-shells			micro-settlements				meso-settlements				macro-settlements			
	micro-micro-space			micro-space				meso-space				macro-space			
	micro-micro-scale			micro-scale				meso-scale				macro-scale			
community scale	I	II	III	I	II	III	IV	V	VI	VII	VIII	IX	X	XI	XII
level scale	1	2	3	4	5	6	7	8	9	10	11	12	13	14	15
	Man	room	dwelling	dwelling group	small neigh/hood	neighbourhood	small town	town	large city	metropolis	conurbation	megalopolis	urban region	urban continent	Ecumenopolis

ELS documentation grid

Fig.4-1 The scale series developed by Doxiadis (1968: 31). He uses a ratio which is in principle equal to √ 7 =2.64, but in practice varies between 2.5 and 5. The factor √ 7 is based on a hexagonal division of space. This division leaves no space between the units, unlike circles or other polygons, while the distances of points on the polygon from its centre are nonetheless more or less equal.

scale	radius in km
National	300
Sub-national	100
Regional	30
Sub-regional	10
Local | Town | Borough	3
District | Village	1
Neighbourhood | Hamlet	0,3
Ensemble	0,1
Building complex	0,03
Building	0, 01

Fig.4-2 Levels of scale: semi-logarithmic classification (Jong 1978; Jong & Rosemann 2002: 37) based on the 'scale paradox': Fig.4-3.

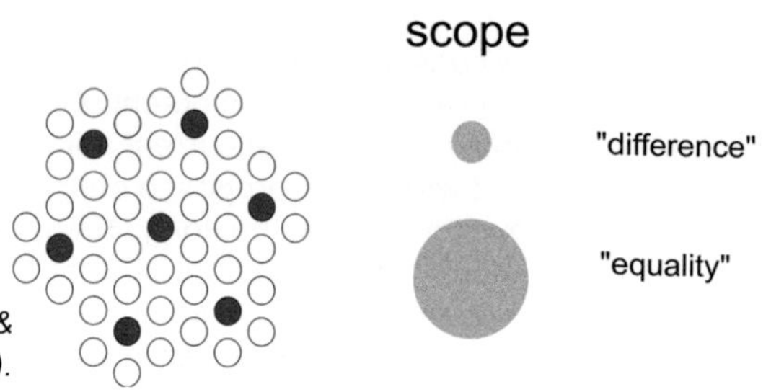

Fig.4-3 Scale paradox (Jong & Rosemann 2002: 37).

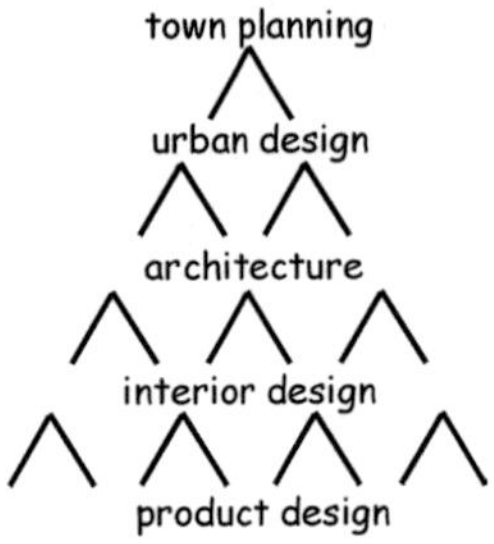

Fig.4-4 The hierarchy of environmental design fields according to Lawson (1990: 39).

All of them agree on one point: "... without the notion of scale the phenomenon we study and the conclusions we reach are of little value and can even be misleading." (Doxiadis 1968: 18). "The fact that all communities tend to be connected in a hierarchical manner does not mean that this connection is an exclusive one. Many other connections at the same level or at different ones are equally possible, but for organisational purposes the connections are hierarchical." (ibid.: 307). Consider the content of legend units and terms such as 'fsi' (floor space index), 'functional mixing', 'accessibility', 'variation', 'spreading' and 'concentration'.

The term 'scale' as used here must not be confused with the 'scale of presentation' (see Section 4.3).

4.2.2 Relations within a system: system versus set

Treating reality as a system means that the physical urban system consists of elements with certain attributes, which have mutual relations and relations with the environment of the system. This imposes constraints on the way urban & regional designers intervene in the physical urban system, at the same time raising the question of what these relations and their characteristics are. In proposals for spatial interventions, i.e. in urban & regional designs, attention must be paid both to relations within a system (this Section) and relations with the environment (see for instance Vogelij 1984: 21 ff.). As to the latter, I restrict my attention to relations with physical urban systems of a higher order (Section 4.2.3).

The addition of elements to an existing system (aggregation) does not automatically mean that the system expands or becomes more coherent or more complex (see Section 2.2). On the one hand, in a spatial system, places are created with a diversity of location (or positional) values for a diversity of functions that are related to spatial elements (Angyal 1941; Klaasen & Jacobs 1999). On the other hand, every spatial intervention affects the character of the spatial system concerned in its entirety, and hence the spatial conditions (both carrying and informative conditions, and, of course, future conditions) which this system offers for societal functions and processes. Or doesn't offer.

Fig.4-5 The office district surrounding Sloterdijk station in Amsterdam (photo left) is illustrative of a set of office blocks and other buildings, including the station, which were designed without concern for the experience of the zone as a whole. More importantly, no consideration was given to the fact that this district is part of the city. The open space is a kind of no-man's land where people venture at their peril (public safety!). That it can be done better is demonstrated by the urban development 'La Defense' in Paris (photo right). (Photography by the author)

When urban development takes place by the addition of independent 'pieces of city' to an existing urban area, or the addition of a detached element to a 'piece of city', the physical urban system becomes 'fragmented' in both functional and sensorily perceptible respects (Fig.4-5). Elements with given attributes (activity carriers with given attributes of form, function and physical state) are then added without sufficient attention being paid to the formal and functional structure of the affected physical systems of differing orders. This means that insufficient account is taken of e.g. the time/space budgets of the users of the physical systems and with the manner of experiencing them. Problems mentioned in Section 1.1 such as residential estates with inadequate transport links, insufficient utilization of location values, suboptimal mobility chains, poor access to hospitals and ill-defined traffic routes (of which examples are illustrated in Figs.4-7, 4-14 and 4-15) are connected to this. Urban sprawl, a particularly familiar problem in the USA, is actually a set of spatial elements with insufficient structure to be considered as an (urban) system. The destructive effect on the natural system is considerable (Klaasen 1993: 27).

" Industry sites are the most miserable places in the Netherlands. The collections of detached industrial buildings, often surrounded by private car parks, form depressing environments all over the country. The narrow strips of greenery you sometimes still find are too insubstantial for any plausible use. In any case, there are no possible users. Nobody would walk these streets for the pleasure of it, let alone go and sit on one of those little lawns."

source: Bernard Hulsman in NRC-Handelsblad, 19-02-03.

Examples of urban sprawl in the Netherlands include *Het Wilde Wonen* ('wild housebuilding' or the deregulated siting of new houses) as propagated by the architect Carel Weeber (Weeber & Vanstiphout 1998) and the 'Carpet Metropolis' (*Tapijtmetropool*) of the architect Willem Jan Neutelings (Heynen 1990) (Fig.4-6). Frank van der Hoeven (1999: 44) qualifies the carpet metropolis as 'anti-urban'. "The city consists solely of architectural interventions, with infrastructure serving to give a direction to the development." (ibid.: 44).

Ethics come to the fore when, in tensions between private and public interest, the question arises, if a spatial object (and/or the function attached to it) which profits from an existing spatial situation, may be required conversely to make a positive contribution to that situation (Klaasen & Van der Want 1988).

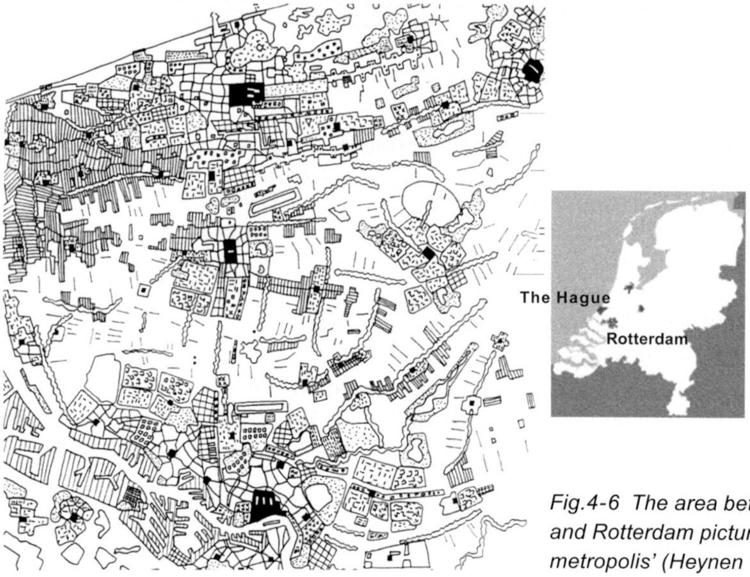

Fig.4-6 The area between The Hague and Rotterdam pictured as a 'carpet metropolis' (Heynen 1990).

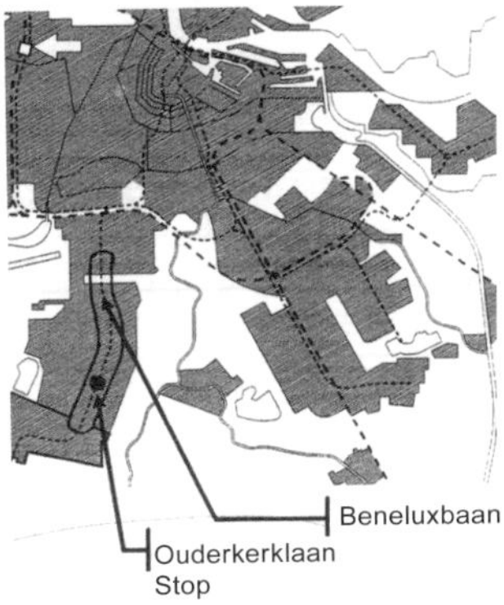

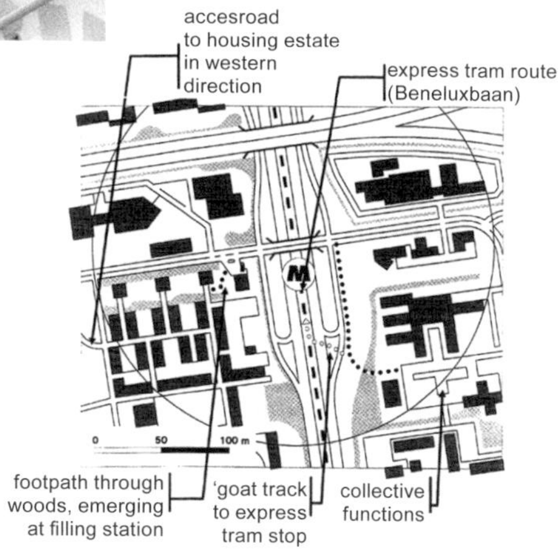

Fig.4-7a This express tram route in Amstelveen (part of the Amsterdam agglomeration - map above to the left) was built through an urban area dedicated entirely to the car. This area has a grid plot division with a mesh appropriate to the wishes of the car driver. Housing estates disposed along the feeder roads were designed to have minimum contact with these roads: wide, densely planted green strips containing large areas of water, and in some places car parking areas, are provided as noise barriers between the housing and the busy main road (map to the right and photo above). The tram stop (symbol M) is officially accessible only via routes designed for cars, which has prompted the development of relatively hazardous unofficial pedestrian routes (Fig.4-7b). Scarcely any passenger-generating activities are present within a circle of radius 400 m around a stop. The low utilization intensity of the tram stop area has so far remained a wasted opportunity to raise the economic efficiency of the rail link, and hence, by increasing the demand frequency of the service, in principle raising the quality of the transport link (Klaasen & Scholten 1998).

Fig.4-7b An unofficial pedestrian route to this bus stop has developed from the housing estate on the west side of the stop, which is officially accessible only from a westward direction (see map Fig.4-7a to the right). The unofficial route starts in a car park (photo left, background) and ends in the filling station on the corner of Beneluxbaan with the flyover to which the stop is linked. (Photography by the author)

4.2.3 Relations between systems

The need to establish relations between an urban area, and additions to and renovations of that urban area, raises the question of how urban systems are connected or should be connected, for both same-order and different-order systems (Figs.4-8a and 4-8b - cf. Figs.2-3 and 2-4.)

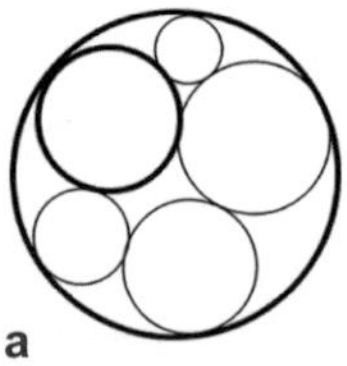

a

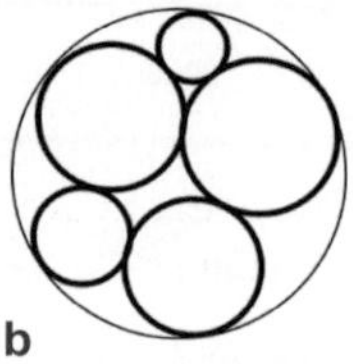

b

Fig.4-8a District as a component of a town
Fig.4-8b Various districts in a town

Extensive literature exists on the relations between urban systems. In connection with his doctoral thesis research on multinodal cities, Marc Jacobs (2000: 45 ff.) cites, among others, Geddes (*Cities in Evolution*, 1949), Pred (*City Systems in Advanced Economies*, 1977), Berry (*Growth Centers in the American Urban System*, 1973) and Friedman and Alonso (*Regional Policy*, 1975). All these authors base their books on empirical research which focuses chiefly on economic processes and hence on levels of scale relevant to economic processes: cities and urban regions. This research relates to the ways systems both of the same and of different orders affect one another. Marc Jacobs himself distinguishes 'interaction' between more or less same-order urban systems (systems may exchange people, goods and information), 'interference' (the functional structure of one or both of the systems starts to change) and 'system formation' (the two original systems develop into a single, larger system) (M.Jacobs 2000). In relation to the present thesis, focussed as it is on urban & regional design, i.e. on manipulation by spatial intervention in physical urban systems, I will restrict myself to the way people, goods and information may be 'exchanged' via physical elements[35].

In principle there are two ways of linking systems together or a system to its environment: single and multiple (Figs.4-9a/b and 4-10a/b). The system environment clearly consists not only of other physical urban systems, but also systems of other kinds: non-physical urban systems, rural and natural systems of various orders (see also sections 2.2 and 2.4).

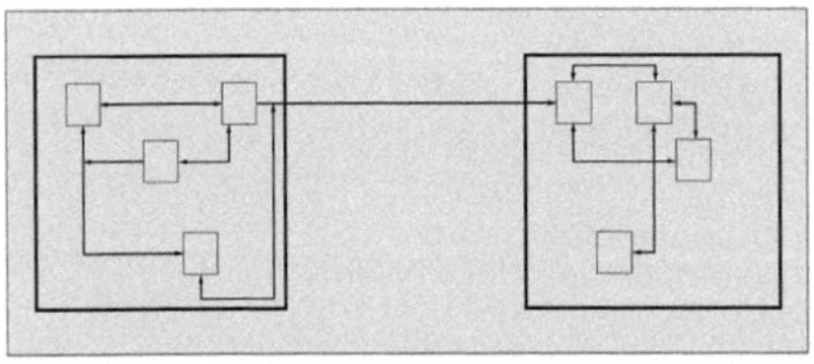

a

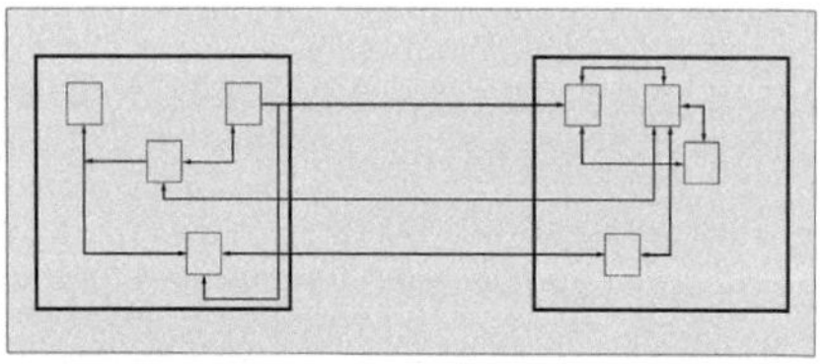

b

Fig.4-9 Systems can be connected in two ways, by single (Fig.4-9a) and multiple (Fig.4-9b) relations. (See also Fig.2-6)

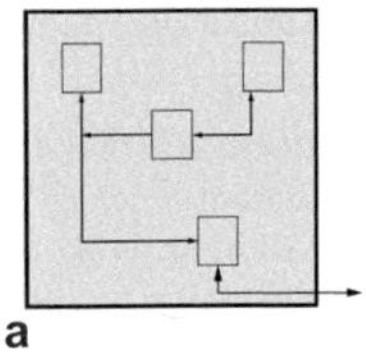

a

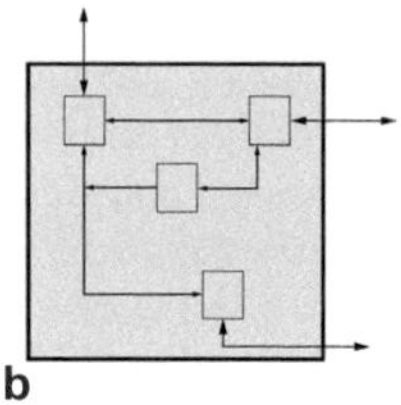

b

Fig.4-10a and b A system and its environment can also be connected in the same two different ways.

The system connections shown in Figs.4-9a and 4-10a are strongly hierarchical in character. In Fig.4-11 the same-order systems have no relation at all.

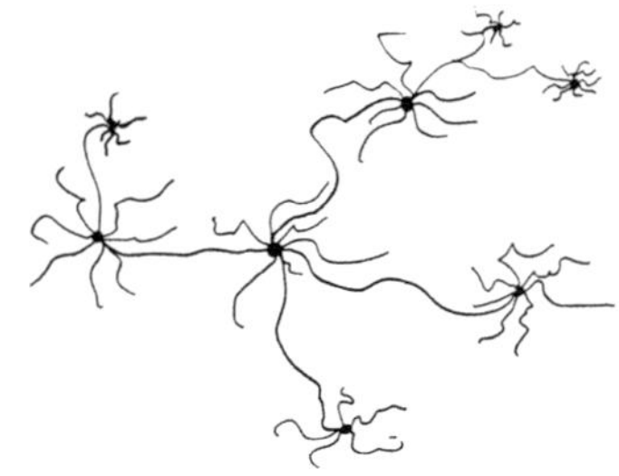

Fig.4-11 Hierarchical relation between systems (Doxiadis 1968: 115)

This hierarchical view of relations between physical urban systems was strongly disputed by the American sociologist Jane Jacobs and the American urban designer Christopher Alexander. “We are constantly being told simple-minded lies about order in cities, talked down to in effect, assured that duplication represents order. It is the easiest thing in the world to seize hold of a few forms, give them a regimented regularity, and try to palm this off in the name of order. However, simple regimented regularity and significant systems of functional order are seldom coincident in this world.” (J.Jacobs 1961: 175/176).
The two ways of connecting systems illustrated in Fig.4-9 also form the essence of Christopher Alexander’s essay *A City is not a Tree* (1966), except that he used a different method of representation: Figs.4-12a and 4-12b.

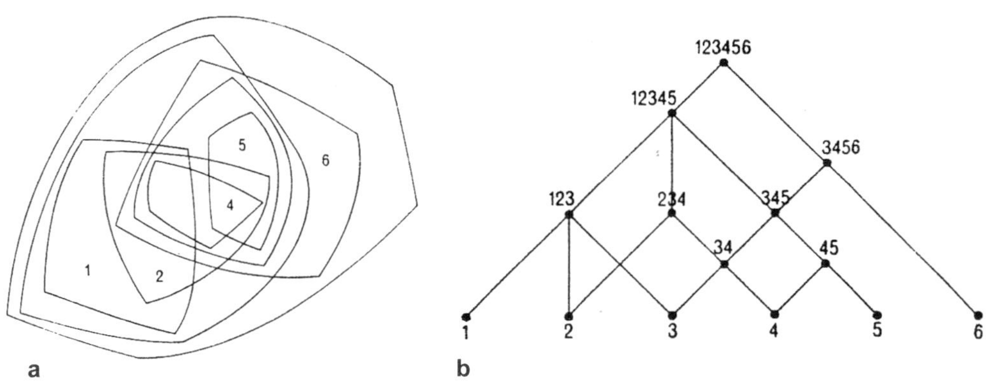

Fig.4-12a Given are six elements (1 to 6). Disregarding the complete set (1, 2, 3, 4, 5, 6), the empty set (-) and single element sets, it is possible to form 56 subsets of these elements (Alexander 1966). The same idea can be represented as a semi-lattice structure: Fig.4-12b (ibid).

They argue both in favour of system connections as represented in Figs.4-9b and 4-10b, although they do not explicitly discuss higher order systems. The scale series supported by various authors, both the functionality-based series of Doxiadis and De Boer and the scale-paradox based series of De Jong, leave no room for misunderstanding - higher order systems are always present, since they are related to the selected relevant spatial grain[36]. There is however the possibility of a considerable intended or unintended flattening of the hierarchical pyramid (see Fig.6-10). The term urban sprawl used earlier is also applicable here. In some circles in the West, however, the term ‘hierarchy’ nowadays carries an unfavourable charge.

I agree on this matter with the urban designer Henco Bekkering: “Today's proponents of urban fragmentation regard hierarchy as reprehensible. This reprehension has a moral undertone: after all, hierarchy presupposes inequality and hence power. (- - -) But formal hierarchy is not concerned with power but with meaning, legibility and comprehensibility. It is not about how people deal with one another, but about their surroundings.” (1999: 17)[37]. Van der Voort & Doevendans state, “A recognizable system and hierarchy in the organization of public space will aid the inhabitants and users in experiencing differing scale levels, and hence the relationship between part and whole.” (1984: 10).

The hierarchy may lack an urban system. Geerse (1993: 21) noted the almost complete absence of a regional system in the Santos region of Brazil, particularly due to the high cost of transportation for the population (see Fig.5-33).

Between systems of different orders, both functional and formal relations are of interest. Examples are mobility chains (Figs.4-13 to 4-16), urban cohesion (Figs. 4-17 and 4-18) and public safety (Figs.4-19 and 4-20).

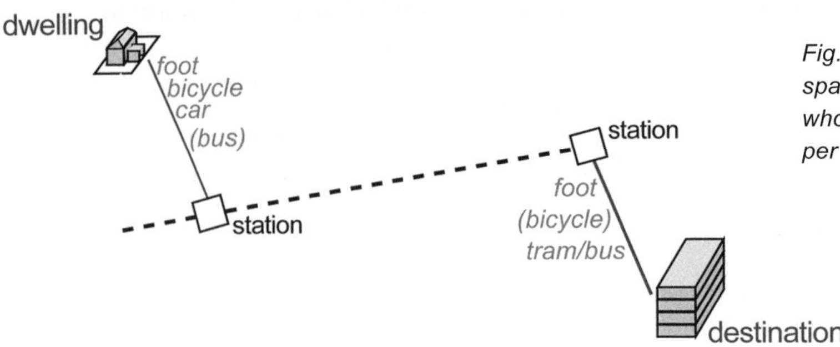

Fig.4-13 This could be the daily spatial activity pattern for someone who engages in only one activity per day away from home.

Figure 4-13 illustrates the principle of a mobility chain. The structure of such a chain is generally pre-transport/main transport/post-transport. The traveller is confronted with different physical urban systems of different orders. It is important to the traveller's time budget that the interchange points are efficiently sited and organized. If the main transport involves a collective transport mode, intensive feeder systems are desirable at each end to ensure its quality. Some examples of inadequate system nodes are illustrated in Figs.4-14 and 4-15. An example of good siting is given in Fig.4-16.

Fig.4-14 At the scale of the Amsterdam region, the major AMC hospital is directly linked to the Holendrecht metro station. This is not the case at neighbourhood level. This photo was taken at the station exit with the photographer's back towards the station. In practice, it is a lengthy walk for staff and visitors (although largely covered). (Photography by the author)

Fig. 4-15 Another example of a poorly designed transport chain, also from Amsterdam South-East, is the situation of the 'transferium' (park-and-ride with public transport connections) near Arena, the Ajax football club stadium. The transferium is sited so far from a metro station that shuttle buses are required between the car parking facility and the metro (the distance between the Bijlmer train and metro station is about 400 metres). Pedestrians are not catered for by directional signs. Not surprisingly, this park-and-ride facility is severely underused. (Photography by the author)

Fig.4-16 The right way to do it is evident in the City Hall of Amsterdam. One exit of Waterlooplein metro station is situated inside the City Hall. (Photography by the author)

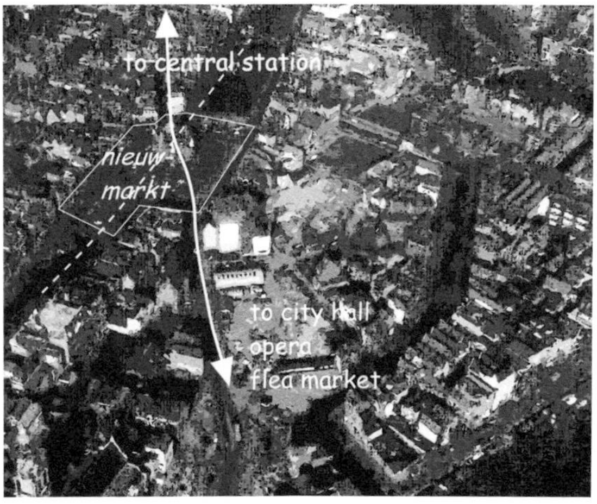

Fig. 4-17 The white line on this aerial photo of the Nieuwmarkt and its environs (in the centre of Amsterdam) marks the historic route between the present location of Central Station and the present City Hall. The route passes through the historic Waag building in the middle of the public square of the Nieuwmarkt. The Waag was originally a city gate. This route is however unrecognizable in the present spatial situation because, during refurbishment of the square in the early 1990s, no account was taken of the higher level scale.
The broken line marks the canal over which the square is constructed (as a dam). This is the direction the designers chose ten years ago for their 'long lines' in the street paving (see Figs.4-22 a and b). Designers (and officials) opted for formal coherence instead of functional coherence - or just didn't think about it ...
(Photo source: Municipality of Amsterdam)

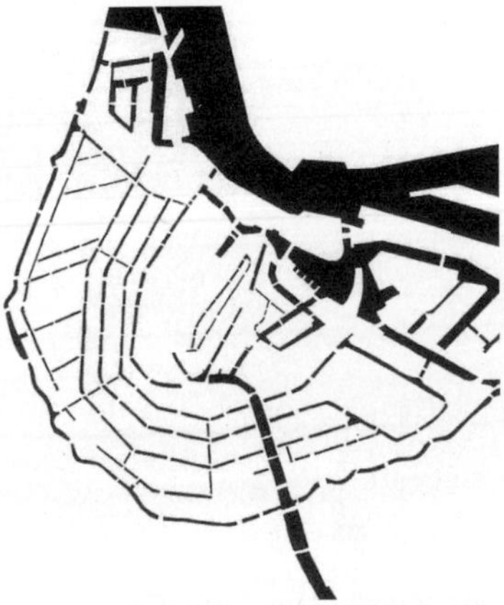

Fig.4-18 The 'Canal Girdle' of central Amsterdam is arranged like a spider's web around the original centre of the city. The clear formal structure makes it easier for residents and visitors to find their way around the inner city (Cecilia, Houtsma, Immerzeel, De Lange & Scholten 1989).

Relating levels of scale to one another means that proposals for spatial interventions at a certain level of scale have relations both with situations (existing or still to be developed) at lower levels of scale, and with those at higher levels of scale (Figs.4-19 and 4-20). Design processes should embody a combination of a top-down approach and a bottom-up approach (iterative or otherwise).

Alexander's views are interesting in this connection. He states in *A Pattern Language* that "We do not believe that these large patterns, which give so much structure to a town or a neighbourhood, can be created by centralized authority, or by laws, or by master plans" (1977: 3). Ten years later, however, he holds that bringing about an urban structure by a bottom-up approach is the 'most controversial feature' of his view of how urban areas should be designed (1987: 37). In the later book also states that "Piecemeal growth tends, in spite of all good intentions and promises, to be piecemeal in the bad sense, incoherent, scattered, fragmented. It tends to produce aggregations and assemblies ... instead of coherent wholes." (ibid.: 50).

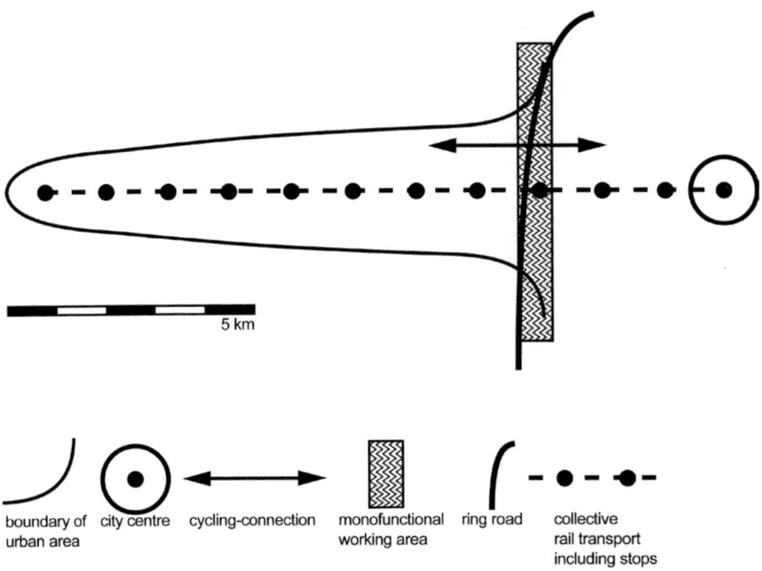

Fig.4-19 The quality of a functional spatial structure at a certain level of scale is a codeterminant of functional spatial possibilities at lower scales. Slow traffic routes with adequate public safety (which a monofunctional working area doesn't provide at night) cannot be implemented unless the higher level system meets certain conditions.

Fig.4-20 The siting of Haagse Beemden, a residential district of the city of Breda, is unfortunate. The cycling distance from the city centre is short, but people feel unsafe using the track at night because it passes through an industrial zone. The building of Haagse Beemden, it is said, promoted a considerable rise in car use in Breda.

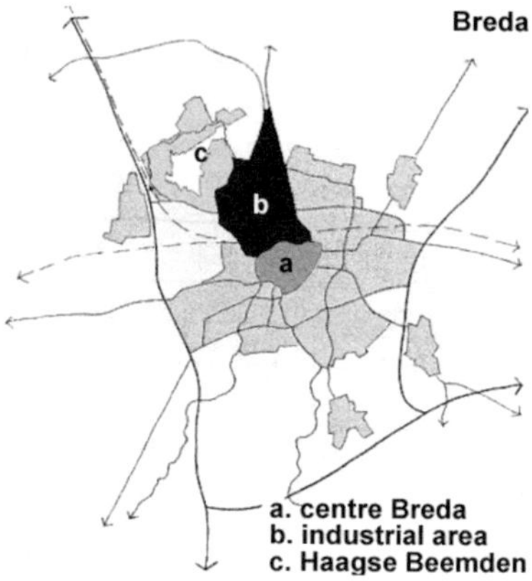

The essence of this Section may be summed up as follows. During the extension and/or renovation of an urban area, a matter of concern should be functional as well as formal relations, both within the distinguishable physical urban systems and between systems of the same or different orders. There are moreover relations with non-physical urban systems and with rural and natural systems of various orders.

4.3 Implications of working with spatial models

"There is the sound of a city beyond those windows. The sudden shriek in unison of children let out from school, the peddler behind his cart -"Hot dogs, orange drink" - the sonorous rumble of buses and automobiles, the staccato click of high-heeled pumps, the empty rattle of worn roller skates on chalked sidewalks."

(Ed McBain 1961, *Lady, lady. I did it!* : 1)

Models used as a way of communicating on existing and future physical urban systems are generally spatial in character. Models are always more or less severe reductions of systems in reality. The reduction imposes limitations which must be respected to avoid model overextension (see Section 2.3). A form of overextension that is specific to urban & regional design is due to the fact that a spatial model is a visual representation of the situation at a certain moment in the past, present or future.

Visual representation

Non-visible components are often, literally, left out of the picture. People do not experience a city only visually, however - they hear, smell and feel it. Those who cannot see nonetheless experience the city. The sensation of climate is influenced by the urban fabric. There are urban elements underground that may have above-ground effects: cables, pipes, tree root systems (Fig.4-21).

Fig.4-21 The effect of tree roots. Footpath near the Faculty of Architecture, Delft. (Photography by the author)

Societal processes remain invisible: "The disadvantage of designing by drawing is that problems which are not visually apparent tend not to come to the designers attention. Architects could not 'see' the social problems associated with new forms of housing by looking at their drawings." (Lawson 1990: 18/19).

Scale

Since the model is a scaled down representation, the visual or non-visual perception point in (future) reality will be different from the standpoint from which we view the model. This means we have to imagine the standpoint-in-reality. People sometimes forget to take this into account, an error which I call the 'parachute fallacy' - or as Bill Hillier and Alan Penn put it, "Ideal towns tend to be clear for passing balloonists, but not for the earthbound." (1991: 4) (Figs.4-22a and b, and 4-23).

Fig.4-22a and b The Nieuwmarkt in Amsterdam, seen (a) from my 4th floor apartment in a westerly direction (Zeedijk terminates at middle top). The long lines of lighter grey paving demarcate an underground waterway (see caption to Fig.4-17). In reality at ground level (b) they are experienced differently to when surveyed over a drawing-board in the design. (Photography by author)

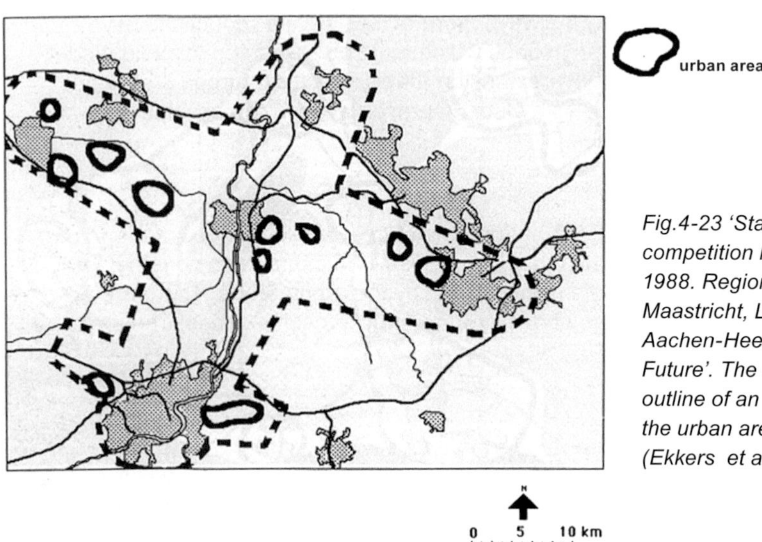

Fig.4-23 'Stad en Land op de Helling', a competition held by Eo Wijersstichting, 1988. Region covered by plan: Maastricht, Liege, Hasselt-Genk and Aachen-Heerlen. Entry: 'Flight to the Future'. The design has the general outline of an aeroplane, within which the urban areas represent the engines (Ekkers et al. 1990: 36).

The information embodied in a spatial model of reality is related to the model's spatial grain (Doxiadis 1968; Klaasen 1993). The spatial grain does not change when the scale of representation changes. The scale of representation is a matter of the required 'legibility' of the model.

A two-dimensional spatial model consists of points, lines and bounded areas (*vlakken*). It depends on the scale you are working at whether a given spatial element is represented as a point, a line or a bounded area. The use of points and lines in a two-dimensional model means that the physical dimensions of the spatial elements concerned are smaller than the spatial grain of the model, but that their functional or formal spatial sphere of influence (often representable mentally as a 'bounded area') is relevant to the structure of the system being studied or designed - e.g. the area of influence of a station, or the visibility of a tower. A graphic scale indicator on the drawing instead of scale specified as a ratio reduces the chance that misunderstandings will arise over the informative value of the model.

The lack of a temporal dimension

In a physical spatial system, the time dimension is just as important as the three spatial dimensions. Rapoport states that "the environment... can be seen as the organization of time." (1977: 12). The inability to depict the temporal dimension means that 'time' and 'process' can only be indicated indirectly using arrows to indicate the direction (Fig.4-24), using isochrones to indicate travelling time (Fig.4-25) or using a series of spatial models at different points in time (Fig.4-30 and 4-31).

Fig.4-24 In this spatial model time is represented with the help of arrows.

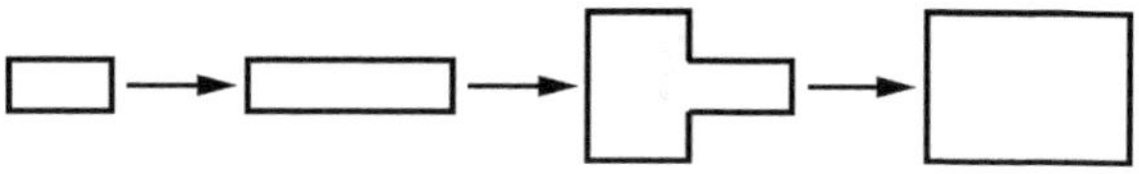

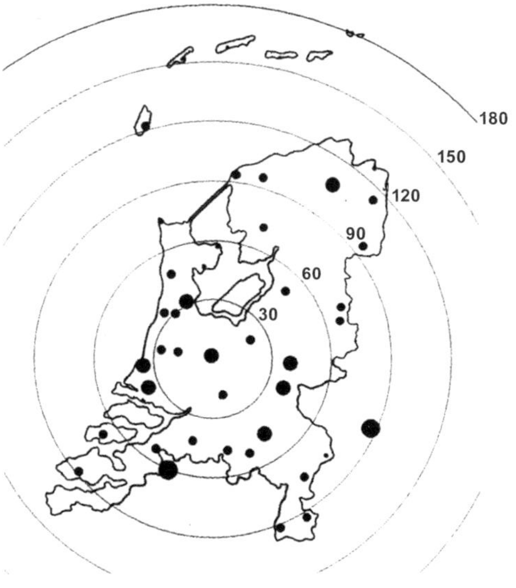

Fig.4-25 An example of a tempographic chart, measured with the Dutch city of Utrecht as origin, in 2000. The numbers indicate travel time in minutes (by car) from the origin (Reuser & Schenk 2000: 41).

Designers almost always opt to convey impressions of physical urban systems using a 'snapshot' of the situation at a given moment during the day, in summer with the sun shining and full-grown trees in leaf. This representation bypasses the fact that people's experience of a city at night, in the winter, and in a gale or heavy rain, is different from that in the summer sunshine, and neglects the differences in temporal grain appropriate to the construction of houses and, respectively, to the maturation of trees.

For example, it is only recently that, on account of the information function (public safety), people in the Netherlands have considered creating different routes for day and night use by low-speed traffic (pedestrians and cyclists) (Fig.4-26).

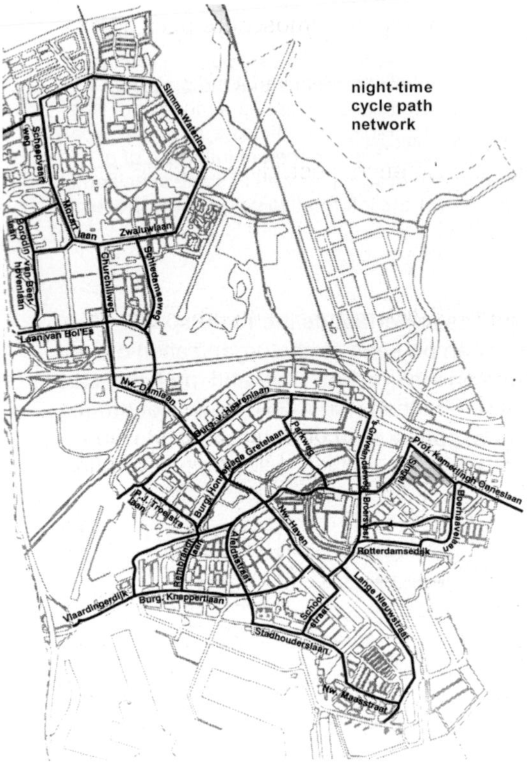

Fig.4-26 'Cycling through Schiedam at night' is the title of a pamphlet published by the Municipality of Schiedam (Neth.), which is the source of this map (Undated).

'Movement' is of course also impossible to indicate directly in a spatial model. An urban area is experienced differently according to whether it is seen from a bicycle or a moving car, for example.

The non-temporal but exclusively spatial character of models could be the reason that some proposals for spatial interventions in physical urban systems betray little if any attention to management aspects and the associated costs, and an underestimation of the dynamic of the urban situation (Fig.4-27).

Fig.4-27 (see also Fig.4-22) After completion of the refurbished Nieuwmarkt in the centre of Amsterdam, the municipal council decided to reassign part of the public space to its previous parking function. White paint was used to mark out the parking spaces, as it was for the cycle path (with the aim of drawing the attention of cyclists and motorists to this path). The part of the square not shown here is now planted with trees, despite the designers having raised successful objections to these in the initial decision phase (see Figs.4-22b).

Time, in the guise of the urban dynamic, always delivers a result that is by definition unmakeable. For example, the artificial character of a newly built housing estate that seems to have sprung from the ground without warning, gradually grows more differentiated simply 'through the passage of time'. The results of maintenance, emergency repairs and the activities of residents and visitors will eventually give the locality an atmosphere of its own.

'Building for the neighbourhood' (building to meet the needs of existing residents) in urban renewal areas and the participatory role in general accorded to the first generation residents of newly built neighbourhoods, means that the short-term carrier function and information function prevail over those of the long term. Another phenomenon, possibly related to the static character of spatial models, is that the more efficient exploitation of space is characterized (in the Netherlands, at least) by an emphasis on the multiple utilization of space, rather than multiple uses in the course of time.

The fact that an urban design is a situation model conflicts with the use of an urban design as a planning model. Planning and realization imply a duration. Unlike a design for a building, a bridge or a park, where the size of the physical system and the hence relatively short realization time make it possible to get by with a blueprint, the implementation of a design for a physical urban system, particularly when at a relatively large level of scale, is beset with uncertainties, owing to the long duration of work and the large number of actors involved (in other words, a relation exists between spatial scale/grain and temporal scale/grain) (Faludi 1973; Barnett 1982; Nio & Reijndorp 1997: 238). As Broadbent wrote, " .... there may be real dangers in presenting a model of the city in physical terms as a three-dimensional spatial model. Planning committees and the public at large, not to mention the planners themselves, become notoriously attached, or antagonistic, to the actual forms which such models present; they tend to 'freeze' development of the city in a particular state." (1988: 94).

With regard to the relation between urban & regional design and time, even though there is no direct relation with the use of spatial models, it must not be forgotten that the products of urban & regional design (implemented designs) have a long life span. This *longue durée* means that changes can and will occur in the type of use, in aesthetic evaluation etc. That is why the future value of the carrying function and the information function matters.

The essential differences between the real situation and the spatial model which designers use to work and communicate with in relation to the real situation and developments in it, are summarized below.

static spatial model	versus	**dynamic reality**
space		space and time
visible phenomena		visible and invisible phenomena
elements and spatial relations: patterns		objects, and spatial and temporal relations: patterns and processes

4.4 The carrying function and the information function of the physical urban system

"Haec autem ita fieri debent ut habeatur ratio firmitatis utilitatis venustatis." [a]

(Marcus Vitruvius Pollio About 25 BC, *De architectura*: I.3.2)

Physical urban systems make, in a conditional sense, societal activities and processes possible/impossible or probable/improbable. The significance of these systems to society may be divided into a carrying function and an information function (both with the future in mind). In the framework of the carrying function, that system consists both of elements with certain functional attributes (activity carriers which occupy a certain amount of space) and of the relationship between them (the functional-spatial structure). Moreover, there are functional-spatial relations with the environment of the system, both with systems of equal order and with systems of a higher or lower order. The functional attributes of a spatial object may differ according to the order of magnitude of the system under consideration. For example, a connection in the form of a road in a system of a certain order, may form a barrier in a system of a different order (Fig.4-28). It can even become a barrier pure and simple if no side-roads, slip roads, bridges or underpasses are provided.

Fig.4-28 Both photos show one of the routes (road combined with rail track) linking the suburb of Amstelveen with the central area of Amsterdam in one direction and national road networks in the other. In the photo left, a considerable barrier effect is apparent between two districts of Amstelveen. In the photo right, the barrier effect is greatly ameliorated by an appropriate design. (Photography by the author - see also Fig.4-7)

The information function refers to the direction-defining (*oriënterende*), identifying, cultural and aesthetic significance of built objects - independently and/or in their mutual relations (formal-spatial structure), to information from the past and about the future (Lynch 1972: 29 ff., 90 ff.). The function also refers to information that buildings and places impart about the activities to which they are dedicated, to information about safety and information about the natural

---

[a] All these should possess strength, utility, and beauty (http://www.ukans.edu/history/index/europe/ancient_rome/E/Romn/Texts/Vitruvius/home.html (04-2003))

system (e.g. the changing seasons). This information is visual, auditory, olfactory and/or tactile in nature. "Any inhabited landscape is a medium of communication. (- - -). The multiple messages of the environment affect our performance, cognition, development, and emotional and aesthetic satisfaction," Lynch states (1976: 30). With regard to the information function, the attributes of form and physical state of system elements are primary. The same is true for the relations between the elements (formal-spatial structure) and with the system environment (Fig.4-29). In order to 'read' this non-verbal information, we must understand its 'language': cultural assumptions have to be shared (Rapoport 1976: 11; 1977: 25 ff.).

The information which is imparted obviously depends on the standpoint of the information-receiver and the velocity at which that point may in some cases be moving. 'Serial vision' (Cullen 1971: 9) is velocity dependent. Differing standpoints and/or speeds of movement can give rise to conflicting wishes.

Amid the interest that has recently developed in the Netherlands in the visual designing of landscapes (incidentally, in this connection see *View from the Road* by Appleyard et al. 1964, cited in Rapoport 1977: 34) on the principle that motorways have to be provided with a pleasing decor for the benefit of their users (the mobility aesthetic), the actualization of the information function from other standpoints and/or speeds must not be left unconsidered.

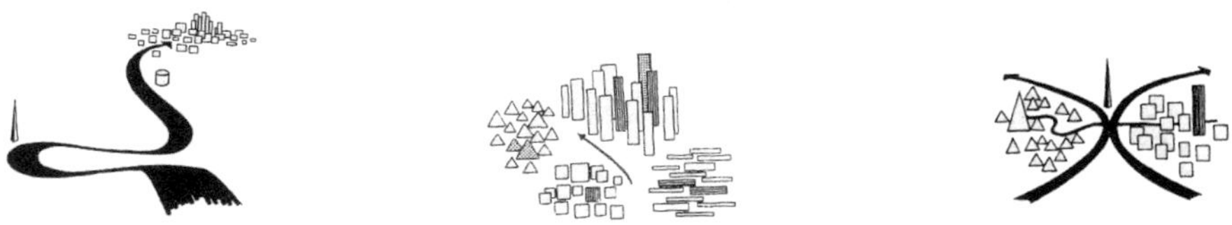

Fig.4-29 a - c Examples of formal structures (Lynch 1960: 98; 104; 108).

Societal processes have both a linear and a cyclic character (see Section 2.2 and Lynch 1972: 117). Examples of cyclic processes are the daily journey to work or school, routine shopping, retail stock deliveries, the supplies of water and gas, regular waste collection, weekly trips to football stadiums, annual holidays etc.
The daily hormonally/astronomically based human biorhythm not only imposes requirements for the availability of sufficient 'activity carriers', but also requirements for the relative siting of urban spatial objects on the grounds of their functional attributes. The time people have to spare for mobility is, after all, limited; it has been empirically set at 2 x 45 min. = 90 min. daily (studies by Vance 1977 and by Schafer & Victor 1997, see in M. Jacobs 2000: 45; 57). Particularly the cyclic daily processes, driven by the 24-hour biorhythm, impose requirements on the functional-spatial structure of the physical urban environment. Economic and cultural developments, sometimes referred to as the 24-hour economy, do nothing to diminish this effect. Other relevant factors include the culture-based weekly rhythm (Bible, Koran), although this has considerably declined in significance in the post-industrial era, and a seasonal rhythm, particularly where there is a well-marked climatic variation between seasons.

These cyclic process have a small temporal grain in relation to the time scale of a human life (see Section 2.2). Depending on the period of the cycle (a day, a week, a year), the temporal grain appropriate to this view of an urban system may range from e.g. half an hour to a week. Consider the large differences in the intensity of use of housing estates and city centres by day and by night respectively(Fig.4-30), or of urban areas in or out of the tourist season.

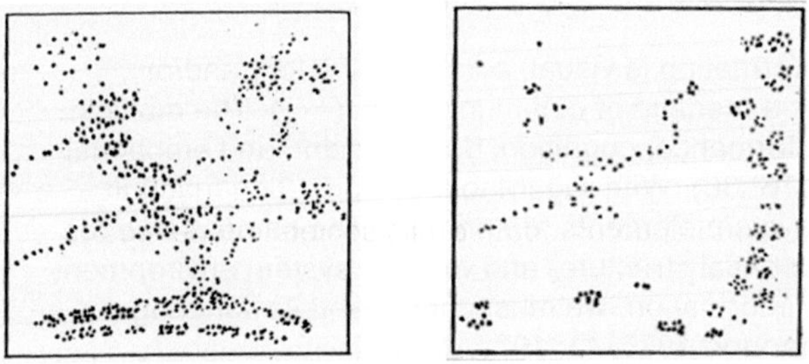

Fig.4-30 Intensity of use of the same area at differing times of day (Doxiadis 1968: 325)

Due in part to linear components in these cyclic processes, physical urban systems undergo linear changes over periods of years (Fig.4-31). These changes affect the attributes of the system elements, both the functional attributes and the formal and physical state attributes, and their spatial occupancy (in the absolute and relative sense) They may also affect their position in the system - the formal and spatial structure. These urban transformations are processes with a relatively large temporal grain[38].

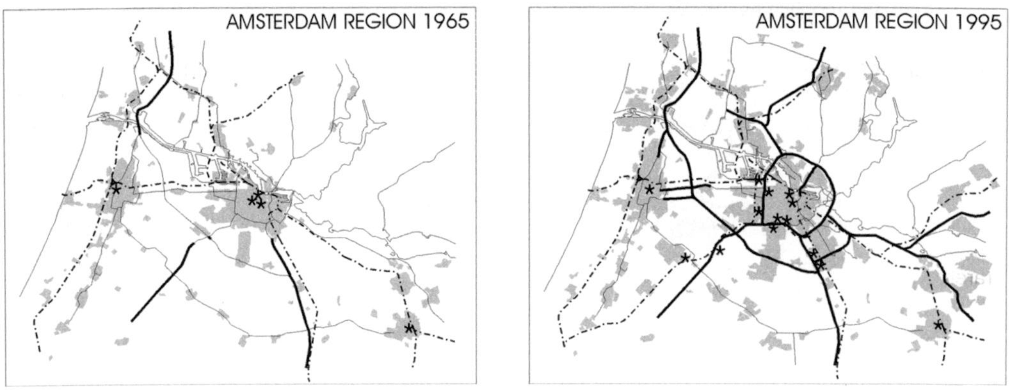

Fig.4-31 Example of a linearly changing process at a regional scale.
The maps depict two snapshots of the spatial development of the Amsterdam region. Study of these developments reveals the following interrelated development trends:
- an outward displacement taking place during recent decades of original city-centre activities to more outlying locations, mainly alongside the southern and western sections of the orbital motorway;
- an similarly outward displacement of the residential function (suburbanization, especially of the middle classes); and
- a decline in the use of bicycles and of the urban-regional public transport network.
These trends have been referred to as the 'exploding city' or the 'inside-out city' (Klaasen & Jacobs 1999: 22/23).

These linear trends influence in turn the cyclic processes. An example is the rise in car use as a consequence of increased prosperity, the resulting increase in daily action radius, the hence possible and desirable geographical dispersal of activity carriers, the resulting decline in the public transport options, and hence a rise in car use (Klaasen & van der Want 1988).

Similar processes are familiar from the natural (ecological) system. For example, the number of birds foraging in a given lake varies from hour to hour in the course of a day, and from season to season in the course of a year. If the lake gradually silts up, the number of foraging birds will decline over a period of years. The accommodation of cyclic ecological processes can also be a desirable goal in urban and regional design.

Maintenance-related physical state attributes of spatial objects may be categorized as linear (e.g. no maintenance), cyclic with a large temporal grain (e.g. periodic renovation of dwellings) and cyclic with a small temporal grain (e.g. weekly or monthly routine maintenance).

To sum up, physical urban systems are required to accommodate cyclic societal processes, and in physical urban systems linear changes (transformations) may take place as a consequence of (linear) societal and natural processes.

The terms 'use value' (*gebruikswaarde*) and 'experiential value' (*belevingswaarde*) - deontic terms - have long been used to express judgements about the adequacy with which the carrying function and the information function are being fulfilled now and will be fulfilled in the long term. Since changes in a urban physical system take place relatively slowly, the future use value and experiential/informative value are always relevant: in other words, the future value (*toekomstwaarde*) (flexibility, adaptability). 'Commodity, delight and firmness'[39] determine the spatial quality of urban areas in part or whole. "Any rigid adherence to requirements based on either the functional or the aesthetic movement may not lead to an integrated design." (Esser 1976: 137).

The designer's own judgement is clearly irrelevant to use value and experiential value. The latter case is fittingly termed 'ego design'. Ego design may be acceptable when the choice is up to the user or users. The larger the spatial and temporal scale, however, the greater is the designer's societal responsibility.

Rapoport cites a series of studies which conclude that 'planners/designers and the public represent very different value systems.' (1977: 24). He states, "The problem lies not in this, but in the fact that designers' values have not been made explicit and that the images and values of non-designers are rarely considered." (ibid.: 25).

"Visual design" (*vormgeving*), states Willem van Toorn, "is making ever greater inroads into all walks of society as a distinct discipline founded on increasingly complex theoretical grounds. In practice, however, all that 'theory' proves of little significance, and visual design manifests itself in my opinion all too often as a personal 'statement' of the designer, often dictated more by his private hang-ups and ideas and by passing fashions than by formal laws or functionality (---). But, in the organization of public space, I have no wish to be harassed by all those personal statements. If venting his 'statements' is what matters to the designer, he would have done better to become an artist." (1995).

The views people hold about urban & regional design are sometimes very naive. The jewellery designer Dini Bessems, in a newspaper interview forming part of a series on young designers, answered the (stock) question "Is there anything else you wished you could design?" as follows: "A urban district, because you have to deal with so many possibilities and constraints. Alternatively, a necklace with ten thousand sparkling gems." (*NRC-Handelsblad*, 11-10-2001).

The larger the design scale of the physical urban system under consideration (in general terms, the higher the order), the more time will be taken, and the greater capital investment will be required, both for planning of changes in this system and for their implementation. "... urban regions are conservative systems with great inertia." (Lynch 1976: 38). This entails that the future value carries more and more weight. The relative significance of the experiential value will decline with an increasing size of the physical system, because the information function is coupled to sensory perception (Fig.4-32). "Sensory quality is infrequently considered at a city or regional scale and rarely with success." (Lynch 1976: 9). This is not to say that a number 'beautifully' designed small areas necessarily add up to produce a physical regional system of high experiential value (Lynch 1958).

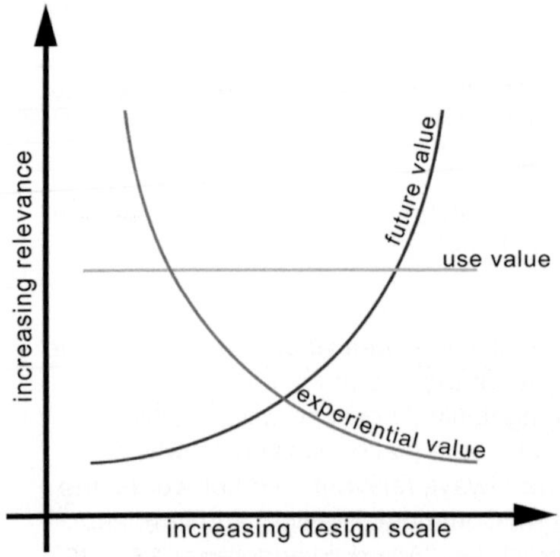

Fig.4-32 The greater the extent of a physical urban system, the less the relevance of the information function. The future value rises with extent of the system, however, because of the amount of money, time and energy that is (or will have to be) invested in it. The carrying function remains of the same relevance regardless of system size.

Criteria for use value relate to both the presence of sufficient activity-carrying elements and the spatial interrelation between the activity carriers (the functional-spatial structure). This means that the activity carriers belonging to different public policy sectors must be seen in relation to one another; for example, how do interventions in the area of public housing affect desirable or undesirable developments with regard to economic activity carriers, and vice versa? (Boer 1990: 95 ff.) Relevant from the perspective of individual users of the physical system is what potential temporospatial activity patterns are possible considering the siting of the activity carriers with regard to one another (Fig.4-33, 4-34); and, for institutions, what is their temporospatial user base (where the users may in some cases be other institutions), e.g. for the distribution and delivery of goods etc. (Fig.4-35). The functioning of institutions is dependent on activities of people (and in some cases other institutions). The situation is one of mutual interdependence: individuals can participate in a collective activity if there is a sufficient target population for the activity concerned. "...a proposed environment [should] be seen as a spatiotemporal whole." (Lynch 1972: 73). Note that I formulate 'can' participate. The organization of an urban area does not dictate how people behave but it creates (spatial) conditions for their behaviour - conditions in the sense of e.g. the space available for certain activities, and the nearness and accessibility of those activities. Within the diversity of desiderata, some will reinforce one another and others will conflict.

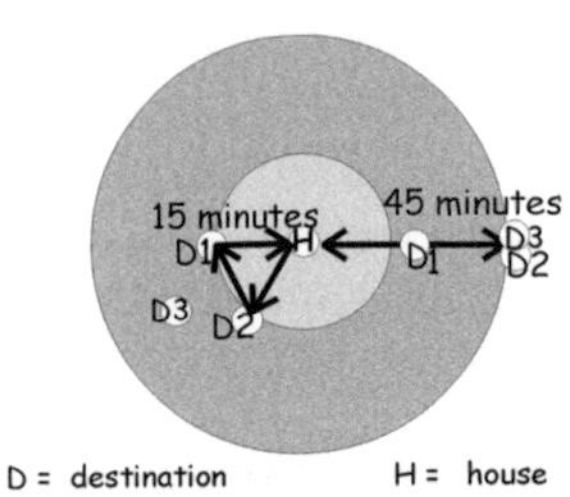

Fig.4-33 The principle of time-space activity zones. The amount of activities that can be carried out in the course of a single day increases along with the degree to which their 'carriers' are located in one another's vicinity or on a common route. With a maximum amount of available travel time of 90 minutes per day, point D3 is inaccessible if crisscross trips are called for.

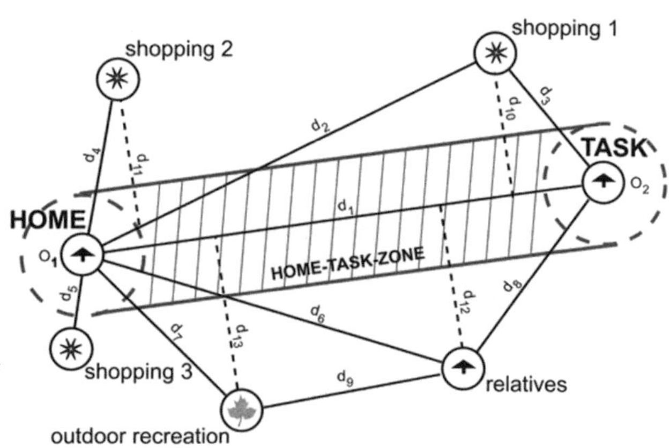

Fig.4-34 Example of a temporospatial activity pattern (after Vidacovic 1988: 122)

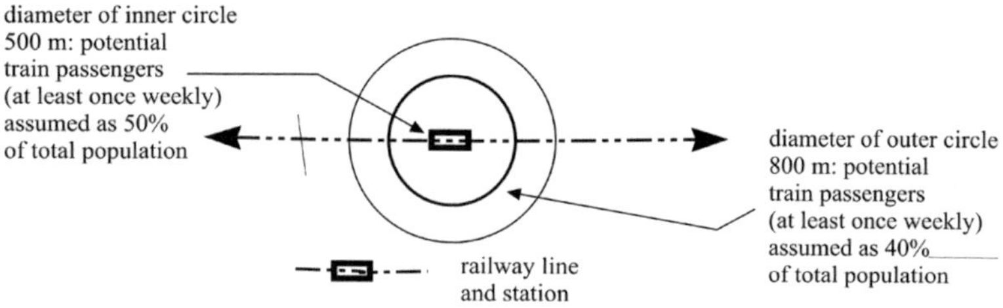

Fig.4-35 Principle of sufficient potential user base for a collective function, taking a train station as an example. The norms applied here are based on assumptions. Spatially, the number of stops a train makes cannot be extended beyond a certain limit.

The way the physical system meets the information need of users is of real importance. Experiential value is in that respect functional (Lynch 1960; Klaasen & Radema 1985: 725). A formal-spatial structure that conflicts with functional requirements results in disorientation, alienation from the environment and a sense of being 'lost' (Lynch 1960: e.g. 4; 9; 54; 56). Experiential value conversely presupposes use value. An urban system (a street, a housing estate, a city or even an metropolitan region) is after all generally experienced from a standpoint within that system (see Section 4.5.3). The term 'use value' is also applicable in connection with crime, insofar as it has a spatial component. Here too it is the information value that supports the use value (or fails to support it, depending on whose point of view one takes).

The ascribed use value and experiential value differs from person to person (and will continue to do so in the future) and is bound up with the spatial dimension of people's activities, and the associations people have with what they perceive.

Structures may lose their intended use value in the course of time due to changes of a spatial-ecological, socio-cultural and economic-technological character. Structural modifications or reconstruction can in certain cases prolong the use value. In some such cases this is accompanied by an increasing historical (information) value which eventually overshadows the use value.

Incidental needs (both per individual and in time) will not in principle be accommodated. There is a tendency in (spatial) policy to take the needs of the average user as the starting point. However, "Generalization is only possible if the diversity of (quantitatively frequently occurring) patterns is limited." (Hulsbergen 1992: 14). It is however possible to opt instead for the widest possible variety of environments, in the sense of a range of potential temporospatial activity patterns.

It is usual to take 45 minutes as the norm for home-to-work journey times (see above in this Section). However, not everyone needs a travel time budget of 90 minutes, and some people have only a much smaller travel time budget at their disposal (Drooglever Fortuijn, Hietbrink, Karsten & Rijkes 1987). The action radius of yet other population groups is increasing, and there are indications that a time budget of much more than 90 minutes is becoming acceptable (Anonymous 1998). However, assertions such as that of Jaap Modder that "The Netherlander of the 21st century lives in Almere, works in Hilversum, goes to the cinema in Amsterdam and follows a course in Haarlem" (2002) are a distortion of the real situation (see e.g. Jansen, Machielse & Vogel, undated)[40].

Within the urban community, one can identify individual and group interests which differ widely in time and place, and ideas associated with these interests about the necessary and/or desirable system elements and their attributes and relations. The built system creates the spatial conditions for what is impossible or possible, and, in the latter case, for the costs in terms of time, effort and money, and, not in the last place, under which conditions in terms of health and safety. The way the carrying and information functions are concretized is accordingly a political-administrative matter.

Good health and safety conditions, with the future in mind, seem to be the only aspect of spatial policy in which the term 'public interest' is used in a non-illusory way. Healthy, safe living conditions relate both to the sustainable preservation of processes within the natural system which are necessary and desirable to society, and to protection from undesirable processes (e.g. flooding, loud noises, explosions or traffic accidents) within that system.

To sum up the present Section, I conclude with regard to the carrying and information functions that

- the carrying function relates both to the type and quantity of spatial elements with certain functional attributes, and to their temporospatial interrelatedness (functional-spatial structure);
- the information function relates to the formal and physical state attributes of spatial elements in their mutual interrelations (formal-spatial structure);
- societal processes may be classified in the light of these functions into linear processes with a relatively large temporal grain and cyclic processes with a relatively small temporal grain;
- the information function is necessary to the carrying function and vice versa;
- the information declines in significance in physical urban systems of higher orders;
- the future carrying and information functions, and hence flexibility and adaptability, become increasingly significant in physical urban systems of higher orders.

4.5 The relevance of urban & regional design for society

"To approach a city, or even a city neighborhood as if it were a larger architectural problem, capable of being given order by converting it into a disciplined work of art, is to make the mistake of attempting to substitute art for life."

(Jane Jacobs 1961, *The Death and Life of Great American Cities* : 373)

4.5.1 Introduction

Physical urban systems are built, extended and altered, in order to fulfil (conditionally) a future-oriented carrying and information function on behalf of society. The physical urban system was identified in Section 2.4 as the object in a general sense of urban & regional design. Urban & regional designers make proposals for the framework within which urban spatial objects are realized or could be realized. A design is a proposal for a coherent package of spatial interventions in a certain urban or urbanescent area, and always relates to more than one sector.

A spatial intervention can also take the form of an explicit non-intervention.

The societal function of an urban design can also be something other than an implementation-oriented one. It could alternatively be a seductive plan made with the aim of persuading people (property developers, investors, competition juries) of something, it could function as a spur to debate, and it could function as a heuristic instrument, e.g. a volume check in relation to a schedule of design requirements. As will be argued in the next Chapter, an urban design can moreover function as a research instrument.

Determining the significance of urban & regional design to society, and hence deciding what the object of urban & regional design is, compels me to position it with regard to other disciplines that have the urban system as their object and which also address developments in physical urban systems. I do so in the light of the significance of physical urban systems to society. Traditionally these other disciplines are the empirical social-spatial sciences with a planning dimension. The growing environmental consciousness of recent years has boosted the influence in this area of sciences concerned with the natural environment.

Over 2000 years ago, Vitruvius pointed out the importance of knowledge of the natural sciences to: architects: "He should know the science of medicine, as this depends on those inclinations of the heavens which the Greeks call climates, and know about airs, and about which places are healthful and which disease ridden, and about the different applications of water, for without these studies no dwelling can possibly be healthful." (1999a: I.1.10).

Since way back there have moreover been close bonds between urban design and architecture. The positioning of urban design with regard to architecture must also be clarified.

When I refer to disciplines and their practitioners, I always speak in general terms. An individual practitioner may sometimes contribute a distinctive interpretation to his discipline.

4.5.2 Urban & regional design and spatial planning

Spatial planning

Spatial planning (*ruimtelijk planning, planologie*) has two components: a procedural one and a substantive one. The procedural component is not considered here; I refer in this connection to Section 5.1. Social-spatial sciences and sciences concerned with the natural environment which take, from a spatial-planning angle, urban systems as their object, are empirical sciences which address future reality. From a disciplinary viewpoint, the practitioners are concerned with analysing 'what is the case', and extending trends observed in these findings to 'what will probably be the case', and in normative respects to what should be desirable in a spatial-conditional sense.

A focus on what will probably be the case often induces people to ascribe spatial and societal-spatial developments with an autonomous, almost uninfluenceable character, similar to that of e.g. climatic phenomena.

From an empirical angle, knowledge and insight are supplied in quantitative and qualitative respects about the needs of individuals and groups, about functional, formal and physical-state attributes of spatial objects in relation to those needs, and about processes (both societal and ecological). The knowledge and insights obtained are both localized (*situatiegebonden*) and non-localized (*situatieonafhankelijke*). The size and the borders of research areas are also based on considerations of an empirical character.
As in other empirical sciences there is a marked tendency in the social planning-oriented sciences towards knowing more and more about an ever smaller portion of the scientific field (Doxiadis 1968: 47; Rijpma & Klaasen 1991). Expertise is developed primarily within spatial subfields, which often correspond to a certain category of activity carriers (see Fig.2-17). An exception to this trend, in the sense of non sector focussed research, is provided by empirical research into the relation between space and time, notably into the temporospatial activity patterns of different categories of households.

A pioneer in this area was the Norwegian researcher Hägerstrand during the nineteen seventies. The lead in the Netherlands was taken by Velibor Vidakovic (e.g. 1988). Other publications include: Droogleever Fortuijn, et al. 1987; Mey 1994; 1996; Dijst 1995; Mey & Ter Heide 1997). The surge in Dutch interest in this type of research parallelled the rise of gender studies.

Urban & regional design

Urban & regional design is primarily a non-empirical activity, and (potentially) a practical science (see Section 3.5). Urban plans are not based on trend forecasts but on what is possible - what can be built, in what form, and what societal activities and processes will then become possible or will be supported. " ... designers do not aim to deal with questions of what is, how and why, but rather with what might be, could be and should be. While scientists may help us to understand the present and predict the future, the designers may be seen to prescribe and to create the future. ...." Lawson states (1990: 92), referring of course to spatial-physical conditions.

An essence of urban & regional design is the act of synthesis, establishing connections, an integral approach to spatial issues. "It is the very interconnectedness of all these factors which is the essence of design problems rather than the isolated factors themselves." (ibid: 45). The synthesis referred to is one of mutually non-independently variable system variables, with formal and functional attributes and specific structural positions. The core task of urban & regional designers is to make proposals for the structuring or restructuring and the visual design of a certain urban area: proposals for packages of integrated spatial interventions (designs). Designers employ two types of strategy. They can take their primary lead on the one hand from a schedule of design requirements (*programma van eisen*), the most usual strategy in practice, and on the other from the situational possibilities (Hillier, Musgrove & O'Sullivan 1972: 29-3-7). The former strategy is often termed goal-oriented design, and the latter means-oriented design. 'Means' is understood here to include both the opportunities offered by the site (Jong & Van der Voordt 2002b: 29) and the compositional means (Jong & Van Duin 2002: 89).

Means-oriented design is of course itself also goal-oriented, the goal being the utilization of certain given facts; after all, observing and analysing without a mental framework is impossible. "All too often, however, the first step in design methods is said to be the arrangement of facts rather than a conscious decision as to which of them are considered to be relevant. Since this selection affects the results to a great degree it needs to be made explicitly" (Rapoport 1969: 140).
Among the considerations underlying this approach of designing without a schedule of design requirements, is that spatial interventions in a city set the spatial situation for a long time to come, whereas the future is uncertain in most other respects. In means-oriented designs, the probable effects are taken into account either implicitly or explicitly (Jong 1992: 83). In these effects, too, a distinction may be made between linear processes with a large temporal grain, and the spatial conditions that are created for cyclic processes with a small temporal grain.

A schedule of design requirements is based on empirical knowledge and understanding. Empirical knowledge is also utilized (sometime implicitly - see Section 5.2.1) during the design process. This may be either supplied knowledge or knowledge gathered by the designer, e.g. spatial analyses of the location or knowledge of urban systems already in existence.

A notable development in this connection is the recent (Dutch?) phenomenon of taking a 'layered' approach in spatial analyses both in spatial analyses, and in developing and presenting proposals for spatial interventions (Fig.4-36). Examples are a layer of 'water and greenery', a layer of 'infrastructure', and layer of 'settlement milieus' (*vestigingmilieus*) (in the Municipality of Amsterdam preliminary Structure Plan 2002), and a 'blue-green' layer (physical substrate), a 'network of connections' layer and an 'occupation pattern' layer (in the draft Regional Plan for Noord-Holland Zuid 2002). This approach does not differ essentially from a sector-based approach to spatial planning (policy sectors, see Section 2.4). It can hardly be otherwise than that this is associated with the use of layers in computer-aided drawing programmes. It was already stated in Section 2.4 that an urban & regional design always bears on more than one sector of the physical urban environment. Designs may well be made per sector, but without integration these do not add up to an urban design.

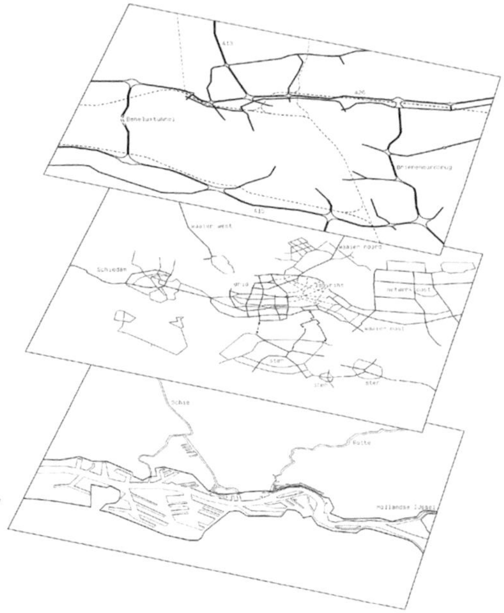

Fig.4-36 Rotterdam as a composition of three relatively independent layers. From bottom to top, they are: the course of the rivers and dykes, the system of city streets and the network of motorways and railways. (Palmboom (1987) 1990: 64).

Mutual positioning of spatial planning and urban & regional design

It is fairly generally held to be the task of urban & regional designers to integrate knowledge supplied by empirical spatial scientists into a coherent entity. The pioneers of this conception in the Netherlands were the urban & regional designer Van Eesteren (1897-1988) and the sociologist Van Lohuizen (1890-1956) (see Section 5.2.1). This division of labour between urban & regional design and those spatial sciences which have a planning dimension seems logical. Creating facilities through design without taking account of the existing needs of the community and probable future developments can hardly be termed realistic. On the other hand, sectorally localized and non-localized facts and trends should, as far as their spatial aspect is concerned, be coherently involved in the design process.

Each in its own field, the empirical spatial sciences supply knowledge and insight about needs, desiderata and probable developments. The planning-oriented social-spatial sciences focus primarily on the carrying function of the physical urban system - the functional attributes and certain physical state attributes - and in this connection on large-grain linear change processes. An exception is formed by the temporospatial research which is directed at cyclic processes with a relatively small temporal grain. Experiential research studies the information function. Those planning-oriented spatial sciences whose object is natural systems in relation to urban developments, supply insights with regard both to the carrying function and the information function into the connections between objects and processes from the natural system and the urban system respectively, with a focus on physical urban systems.

The designer's task is to explore the possibilities of synthesizing the supplied (or self-gathered) knowledge and insights, resulting in proposals for packages of integrated spatial interventions in existing urban systems or urban systems that are being developed. In principle, they thereby always establish relations with the physical urban (and natural) systems, both of equal and unequal order, that constitute the plan area. Where relevant, rural scientists will also supply knowledge, and landscape designers may play a part in the design process. Because designers bring into connection knowledge and insight from various sectors, it is also possible for them, at least in principle, not only to work towards solutions for specific problems, but also to check what new problems these solutions will entail.

The need for a new orbital road can be highly legitimate from the viewpoint of traffic capacity, but what will the road entail for the functioning of the city and the urban region as a whole? What potential-rich places for business establishments will it create, what effect will it have on the main city centre and, as a possible consequence, on living conditions in the city, etc?

The division of labour proves in practice to be only partially effective, as I will explore in Chapter 5, 'urban & regional design and science'. There is an applicability gap which can be attributed to, among other things, the unstructured character of the knowledge which becomes available (Hillier, Musgrove & O'Sullivan 1972: 29-3-2).

Furthermore, under administrative-organizational conditions such as those that prevail in the Netherlands, the development of spatial plans sometimes gives rise to a 'conflict' between interest groups about the functional designation and the layout of the available space: this conflict emerges in negotiations among official departments with their own specialist areas, between officialdom and stakeholders, and among stakeholders, in conjunction with participation opportunities for individual citizens. Obviously, a plan which arises along these lines, i.e. without a substantial contribution from urban & regional design, will show little attention to the mutual relationship between spatial objects in the different sectors, or to the effects the planned patterns and structures will have once realized[41].

In this situation, however, the synthesizing contribution of urban & regional design may nonetheless prove relevant. It emerged in some interviews in connection with a recent Dutch Masters Thesis that, "The then project leader thought he could succeed in making a plan by combining information form the various fields of policy. The "cement" needed to arrive at an added value and to concretize and visualize various aspects was however forgotten. After this planning process ground to a halt, the urban & regional designer Simon Wever was called in. He then designed three alternative regional development models. He was key to concretizing the development plan." (Teerink 2002: 101) In modern terms, one could regard the role of the designer in situations such as this as that of a mediator (Rosemann 2001: 65). Nio and Reijndorp (1997: 234) go so far as to state that the role of government policy papers in the negotiations has been supplanted by the 'spatial plan'.

The problem of the applicability gap is aggravated by the tendency, originating from the traditional bond between architecture and urban & regional design, to regard concretizing the information function, the achievement of experiential value, as the essence of urban & regional design. Relevant in this connection is that, in the Netherlands since the 1980s, the visual aspects of urban & regional design have received more and more emphasis and the connections between urban & regional design and architecture have been continually strengthened (Voort & Doevendans 1984: 4).

This development is not an international one, although it accords with views held in other countries such as Italy in Spain. In the UK, on the other hand, the same period was marked by an increased interest in social and ecological aspects in addition to visual design (Punter & Carmona 1977). The USA has seen the rise of the New Urbanism movement[42] (www.doverkohl.com/writings.html (04-2003)).

The strengthening of the connections between urban design and architecture in the Netherlands is apparent in practice from the appointment of architects (often well-known ones) for urban & regional design projects. At the Faculty of Architecture in Delft, it is evident from the strongly rising proportion of design classes in the urban planning and design (*stedebouwkunde*) course at the expense of programmatic aspects (including those relating to environmental issues), and, within the design classes, an increase of architectural design classes as against urban & regional design.

4.5.3 Urban & regional design and architecture

The view that achieving experiential value forms the essence of urban & regional design, with the experiential value often narrowed down to a visual/aesthetic and cultural value, may be encountered in the Netherlands in (among others) the Delft design professors Joost Schrijnen (1995), Pi de Bruijn (1995) and Han Meyer (in an interview with him published in Nio & Reijndorp 1997: 161 ff.). Other prominent colleagues also express this view in Nio & Reijndorp 1997.

The term 'culture' can be interpreted in many different ways, as much in the practice and science of urban & regional design as anywhere. The cultural concepts may range from preservative ones to ones based on 'trendy consumerism' (Rodermond 1997: 23).

"The goal of organizing space is to find a pattern, a coherence, a structure. The information of visual impressions and associations is ordered thereby," the Delft emeritus professor Jan Heeling stated ((1981) 2001: 16). In this outlook, the design situations and their related formal concepts play an important part in urban design (see also Westrik 2002). The physical urban system is itself considered as a cultural product: '... a design as the translation of a cultural context into an urban image' (Pasveer 1991: 6).
Urban & regional design is thus seen as a special case of architecture, albeit on a different scale, and/or concerned with public space as opposed to architecture which is concerned with buildings. "What urban & regional design is always about is the relation between the technique of making and the cultural significance of an urban element." (Meyer in Nio & Reijndorp 1997: 164). The designer Ashok Bhalotra states, "It doesn't matter if you do it as an architect or as an urban & regional designer. All the same, there is a difference between the two disciplines. The scale on which action takes place is different. The excitement is to be found at the point of meeting, where the difference vanishes. The result is then a kind of marriage of architecture and urban design ..." (Anonymous 1993: 20).

Spatial design can thus even be classed as an art form, a manifestation of the creativity of the designer as an individual. The dual meaning of the term *techné* - technique and art - is in effect here. It explains why urban & regional design is one of the categories for which the Dutch *Prix de Rome* art prize is awarded. (Fig.4-37).

Fig.4-37 The cycle/pedestrian bridges between Borneo and Sporenburg in the Eastern Docklands redevelopment zone of Amsterdam, by West8 Urban Design & Landscape Architecture, won the Footbridge Award for 2002. The bridges were nominated in the Aesthetics (medium span) category on account of their distinctive visual design and their engineering detailing. The jury had several reasons for awarding the prize to these bridges: "The visual unity of the two pedestrian bridges may be seen as an artistic element in the Amsterdam docks landscape. The robust, taut quality of the low bridge and the eccentricity of the tall bridge jointly have an imposing effect on the surroundings. The dynamic, fluid lines, and the incredible attention to detail and illumination, are a delight to the eye. The combination of colour, form and humour make these two bridges into a playful couple" (www.architectenweb.nl (04-2003)). The 'eccentricity' of the tall bridge unfortunately makes the bridge impregnable to many people, and thus worthless as a link between the extremities of two peninsulas: see the local situation sketch, left.

Designers who are primarily concerned with achieving experiential value, restrict the concept 'use value' to providing certain quantities of activity carriers (numbers of dwellings, hectares of industrial sites etc.). They treat functional-spatial organization, in relation to the carrying function, as a matter of patterns, such as distributed or clustered amenities, variations in density, etc. (see Figure 4-40). "As examples of the questions which arise in this context, should shops be situated in the centre of a residential estate or closer to its boundary in the city-centre direction? Should offices be sited along the motorway or distributed through residential areas? (---) Should a law court be sited in the city centre, as a symbol of our system of justice, or alongside a motorway to facilitate the transportation of prisoners? Should we build many small parks or one large one? What are the consequences for mobility of a given way of organizing the residential area?" (Heeling 1998: 26). This view of urban & regional design corresponds to what Punter and Carmona describe as conventional urban & regional design, concerned with external experience and notions of 'scale, density, height, massing, layout, landscape and access'. (1997: 68 ff.).

As to their positioning relative to one another, however, there are at least three non-trivial respects in which urban & regional design differs from architectural design.

Firstly, a building or other architectural structure is experienced from a standpoint outside that system (katascopically), except by its relatively few users. The architect Antonio Monestiroli, for example, formulates this idea as follows: "The house must express a culture of habitation, its forms must represent a way of living. Perhaps we can say that this is the objective of all architecture, that of expressing the life that takes place inside it." (2001: 42). By contrast, an urban system (a street, a neighbourhood, a city or a metropolitan region) is experienced primarily anascopically, from a standpoint within that system. The ability to 'use' the built environment is therefore a necessary condition to 'experiencing' it.

A street, a neighbourhood, a city or even a metropolitan region can of course be 'experienced' from a standpoint outside that system, just as a building can be experienced from outside by passers-by: e.g. from an aircraft (an aerial photo camera standpoint) or from a high point.

Secondly, if attention is indeed paid to the temporospatial aspect of the carrying function (the functional-spatial structure), there is a difference between the design and construction of a building, and the design and construction of a built-up area. A building may be treated as a semi-closed system, linked to its environment following the principle of Fig.4-10a in Section 4.2.3. A built-up area, however, is embedded in a lot of other systems of equal and higher orders; see Figs.4-9b and 4-10b. When a built-up area is designed in the same way as a building (as is often done by architects who owe their fame to designing buildings), the result is what people sometimes call an 'architect's plan' (Boer 1990: 7). Treating a design area as a semi-closed system also encourages the shifting of problems onto the neighbouring areas, e.g. by the displacement of environmentally detrimental industry (Klaasen 1993: 88).

Niek de Boer cites as Dutch examples among others the Extension Plan for South Amsterdam (1915) made by the architect H.P. Berlage, and the plans for reconstruction of The Hague following the Second World War made by the architect W.M. Dudok (Boer 1990:7). As a more recent example, one could take the restructuring and redesign of the Delft University of Technology campus by the architect Francine Houben (currently a professor of architecture at Delft University) (Klaasen 2000a: 62 ff.).

Thirdly and finally, the time factor plays a different role in architecture than in urban & regional design. An architectural design is a building design which is intended to be executed as such without change, within a relatively short time and with few if any internal and external uncertainties. The preparation of blueprints is a normal part of architectural practice. An urban design in the form of a blueprint has only a limited reality value, however. It is a framework for the creation of spatial objects, with time required for implementation and the accompanying inherent uncertainties. "If it weren't for time, all would be architecture," Stephan Gall lamented, adding, "As long as urban & regional designers continue to think in terms of urban forms, we will be stuck with making blueprints." (1996: 28).

4.5.4 Views on the object of urban & regional design

I stated earlier (Section 2.4) that in the general sense the physical urban system is the object of the discipline of urban & regional design. It is now possible to define this object more exactly. In the light of the findings of this Chapter with regard to, on the one hand, large grained linear societal processes, and on the other hand small grained cyclic societal processes, and their respectively associated views on the carrying function and information function, there are two views about the nature of the object of urban & regional design.

The view (which I hold) that the discipline of urban & regional design comprises the accommodation of (future, possibly desired) cyclic societal processes with a spatial dimension, and that experiential value presupposes use value, entails that the physical urban system cannot be seen as detached from its users and hence from the urban system as a whole.

If however achieving experiential value is considered the primary goal, and if one accordingly concentrates on the linear transformation of the urban system, then the physical urban system is seen as an autonomous system and the other components of the urban system concerned are treated as part of the environment of that physical system. An example of this kind of distinction as given in Section 2.2, where I referred to a car being regarded as a system either with our without one or more occupants.

On the grounds of these two differing descriptions of the disciplinary object of urban & regional design, we may distinguish two approaches to urban & regional design:

- pattern-oriented urban & regional design for the physical urban system as an autonomous system, and
- process-oriented urban & regional design for the physical urban system as a subsystem of the urban system.

4.6 Pattern-oriented urban & regional design and process-oriented urban & regional design

"These proposed forms seem to be static ones which do not easily grow or change, except by additions ….. or by major jumps. There is little reflection of the cyclic, process nature of a city."

(Kevin Lynch, undated statement, in *City Sense and City Design, Writings and Projects of Kevin Lynch* 1990: 60)

4.6.1 Pattern-oriented design

Pattern-oriented design is characterized by its focus on final processes with a relatively large temporal grain. This type of design addresses what is called the transformation of urban areas (Hulsbergen, Meyer & Paasman 1998; http://www.bk.tudelft.nl/onderzoek/portfolio/ Theme Urbanisme (08-2003)).

Non-urban areas are transformed into urban areas, and existing urban areas are renovated. In the latter process, the attributes of spatial elements such as form, function, intensity of use (residential density, average dwelling occupancy, number of passers-by etc.) and state of maintenance may be modified, or spatial elements may be entirely replaced.

Largely on the basis of an empirically-derived quantitative (goal-oriented, see Section 4.5.2) schedule of requirements such as numbers of dwellings, surface areas of industry sites, traffic volumes to be accommodated, square metres of park per household etc., a so-called mass-space plan is designed (cf. figure-ground design - Trancik 1986; Fig.4-38) and/or a proposal is made for the organization of the public domain. 'The composition of the urban ground plan' is the expression currently used for pattern-oriented design in the Delft University Faculty of Architecture (Fig.4-39). The possibilities offered by the design area form an important aspect. When these are allowed to play a significant role, the design may be termed means-oriented.

The composition of the urban ground plan consists of the network of public spaces, the network of bounded private spaces ('islands') and the basic units of the city-grounds and building. The difference between urban design and architecture resides in the fact that the urban designer is concerned with the organization and design of public space, and the architect with private space. (Heeling 1998); in this connection, see the concepts of 'linkage theory' and 'place theory' in Trancik 1986: 98 (Fig.4-38).

Fig.4-38 Trancik distinguishes three major approaches to urban design: "(1) Figure-ground theory: ….the starting point for an understanding of urban form is the analysis of relationships between building mass and open space. …. (2) Linkage theory: …. dynamics of circulation become the generators of urban form …. (3) Place theory: Designers increasingly become aware of the importance of historic, cultural, and scocial values in urban open space. …" (1986: 98).

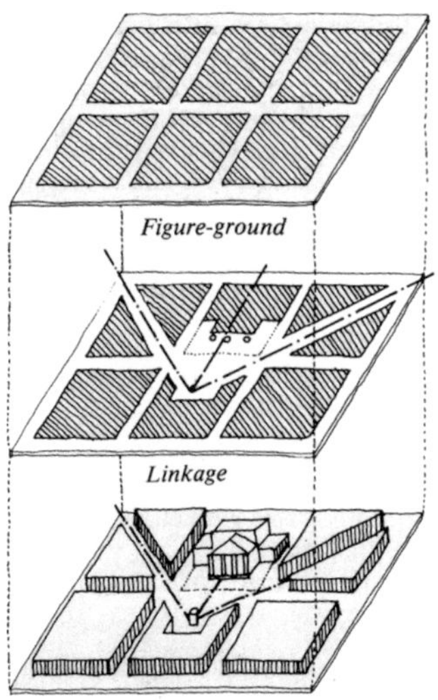

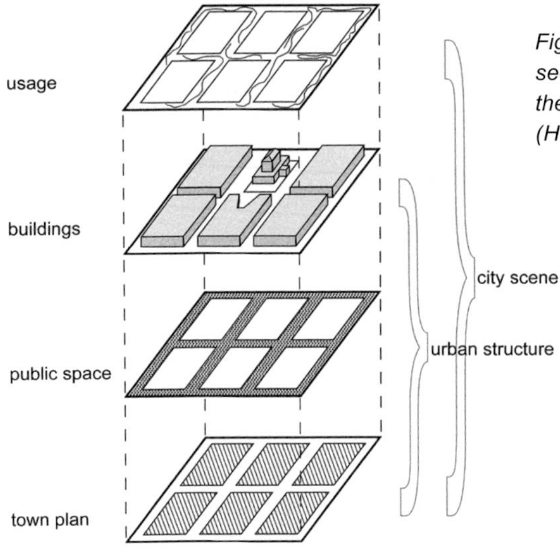

Fig.4-39 The 'core of urban & regional design' as seen in the Urban & Regional Design Section of the Delft University Faculty of Architecture (Harsema undated, ca. 2000).

The achievement of experiential value, particularly in cultural and aesthetic respects, is a central issue. Formal concepts play an important part in this (Heeling (1983) 2001: 79 ff.). As a consequence, the emphasis is on designing at lower levels of scale (see Fig.4-32). Regional design is therefore sometimes considered impossible, or is regarded as the sum of designs for parts of the region (Lynch 1976; Klaasen 1990).

The study prospectus of the Delft University has in recent years included the following statement about regional design: "Since the urban design of cities and regions is invariably restricted to very modest local interventions, much attention is paid in the course to the selection of strategic interventions."

The 'carrying function' concept does play a part in the pattern-oriented approach, but only in the limited sense of 'the carrying' of objects. As Harsema put it: "The concept 'spatial-functional organization of the city' is at first sight unmistakably clear. It is essentially a matter of the ownership, designated purpose, use and management of land, and of the execution of plans that result in alterations to these. In the jargon, the designation and actual use are termed 'functions' and the classical (CIAM) division of the organization of the city is into 'living, working, recreation and traffic'. The function of 'amenities' has subsequently been added to that list." (Undated, ca. 2000: 3). Fig.4-40 presents an example at a regional level.

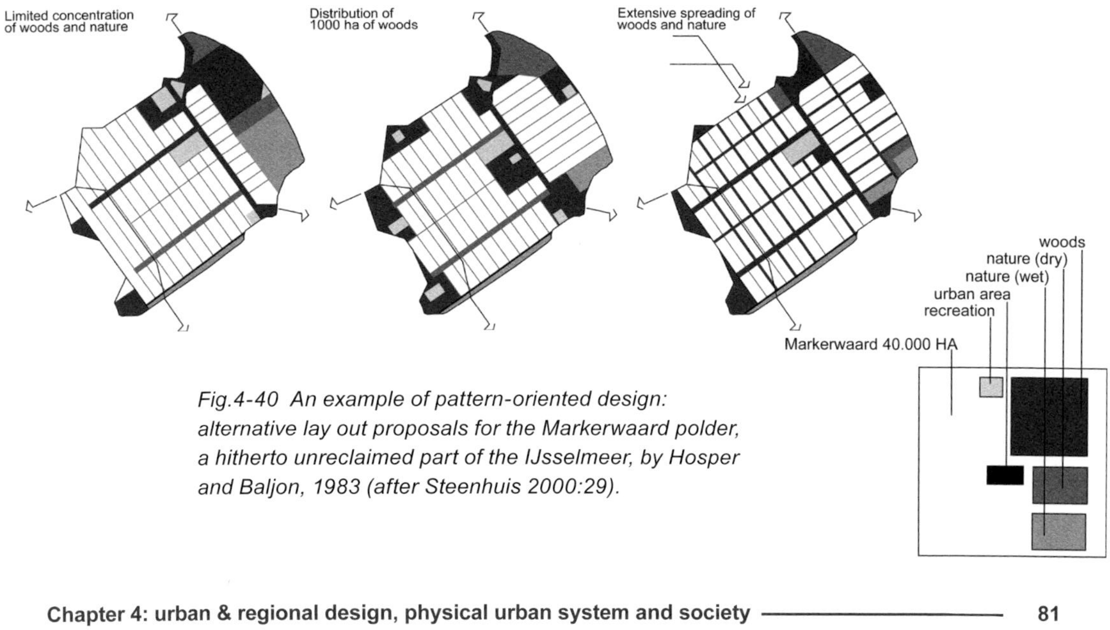

Fig.4-40 An example of pattern-oriented design: alternative lay out proposals for the Markerwaard polder, a hitherto unreclaimed part of the IJsselmeer, by Hosper and Baljon, 1983 (after Steenhuis 2000:29).

Public squares, parks and streets (avenues) are designed as 'places', public spaces where it is (presumably) pleasant to spend time (Fig. 4-41).

Fig.4-41 Master plan for the reconstruction of Dam Square, Amsterdam. Photograph of scale model viewed from south (designed by Simon Sprietsma, Municipality of Amsterdam). Source: Het Parool, *19-02-2000. The Royal Palace is on the left and the National War Monument is on the right.*

The size and boundaries of design areas are in principle arbitrary, but in practice they are determined by considerations such as the obsolescence of the original designated function (e.g. former docklands or other industrial sites, or a railway converted to underground), hydrological or similar 'natural' factors, land ownership, and units for which data are available. Distance can also be a criterion: in the Dutch official publication *Structuurschets voor de Stedelijke Gebieden* (Ministry of Housing, Spatial Planning and the Environment 1984: 6), urban regions (*stadsgewesten*) were defined by drawing circles of 8 or 12 km radius around existing regional facilities centres.

Levels of scale are defined on the basis of those originating in other systems (administrative-organizational, natural) or on the basis of distances (see Section 4.2.1).

Taking into account the stress on visual design, a design of this kind will necessarily have the character of a blueprint. Everything must be under the designer's control - even the colour of the front doors in some cases. "... All the arrangements that comprise it must be in the total, absolute and unchallenged control of the project's architects." (J.Jacobs 1961: 375). This, too, bolsters the viewpoint stated above that designing is impossible at a regional scale. It leaves little scope for modification, either in the implementation phase or in the period that follows. (Change does of course take place, but it is arbitrary and uncontrolled, essentials are after all not defined. See the caption to Fig.4-27.)

Characteristic for pattern-oriented design are

- Pattern concepts such as 'composition', 'townscape', 'carpet city', 'agglomeration', 'concentration', 'spreading', 'differentiation', 'variation', 'floor space index', 'closed building block', 'long lines of sight', 'strip', 'genius loci';
- Linear process concepts such as 'urbanization', 'suburbanization', 'agglomeration effects' (Boer 1990: 40), 'growth pole' (Zoete 1997: 33/34), 'exploding city', 'segregation', 'change of land use', 'stagnating area', 'urban renewal' etc.

4.6.2 Process-oriented design

A characteristic of process-oriented design is its concern for daily, weekly and annual cyclic processes within the urban system (and also within the natural system). Urbanized areas must be capable of accommodating a diversity of temporospatial activity patterns which take place at differing levels of scale (Fig.4-42).

“One of the gravest mistakes made in the study of human settlements is considering them as consisting of the container only … and thus depriving them of the fourth dimension, time, and of their life which is expressed in functions.” Doxiadis states (1968: 24). Similarly, Hillier and Hanson state, “However much we may prefer to discuss architecture in terms of visual styles, its most far-reaching practical effects are not at the level of appearances at all, but at the level of *space*. By giving shape and form to our material world, architecture structures the system of space in which we live and move. In that it does so, it has a direct relation … to social life, since it provides the material preconditions for the pattern of movement, encounter and avoidance which are the material realization … of social relations.” (1984: opening sentence). In Kevin Lynch’s words, “I will take the view that settlement form is the spatial arrangement of persons doing things, the resulting spatial flow of persons, goods, and information, and the physical features which modify space in some way significant to those actions, including enclosures, surfaces, channels, ambiences, and objects. Further, the description must include the cyclical … changes in those spatial distributions, the control of space, and the perception of it. The last two, of course, are raids into the domains of social institutions and of mental life.” (1981: 48).

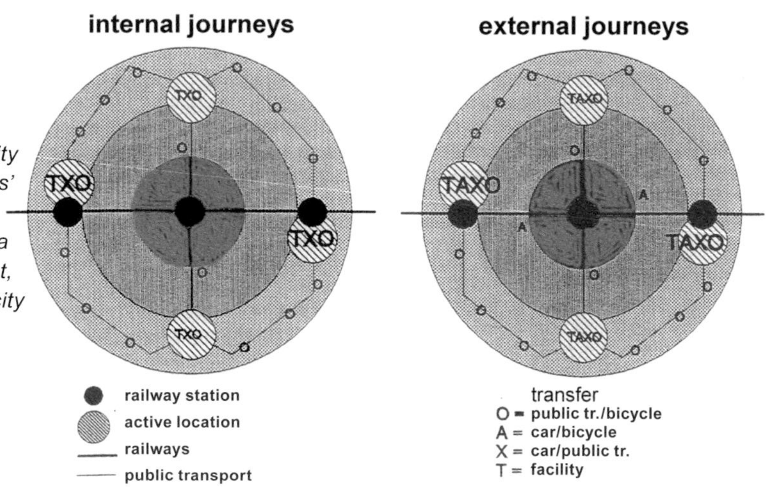

Fig.4-42 Model of a city with the emphasis on access and on mobility chains, from the report ‘Mobilopolis’ (Anonymous 1998: 28; adapted). Left, journeys within the urban area (the city as a closed system). Right, journeys to and from the city (the city as an open system).

Important components are the functional-spatial structures, supported by relevant visual design, which facilitate potentially desired processes, and the required potential user bases to enable the functioning of collective institutions. Since cyclic processes possess a linear component, this approach too entails attention to linear processes with a large temporal grain.

Functional-spatial design has no connection with ‘functionalism’. The functionalist design outlook (functional separation, light, air, traffic type separation) is a case of pattern-oriented design.

Process-oriented design addresses such questions as “what activities do people wish to participate in?”, “which places do they wish to reach?”, “can they get there?”, “can activities be combined?”, “is there a sufficient potential user base for those activities?”, “can goods be distributed?”, “do institutions have sufficiently large potential user bases to be capable of functioning?", "which target groups must be able to access a given institution?", etc. A further, far from trivial, question is "how can visual design contribute to direction-finding, identification and the creation of potential user bases?" Activity carriers from various sectors will therefore have to be positioned in a coherent relation to one another. The 'fragmented individual', who is occupied exclusively either with paid employment in a constant place or with daily routine shopping during the week and with recreation on Sundays, does not (or no longer) exists. Treating a purely categorically organized set of objectives and requirements as the basis for a design perpetuates this fragmented image of the individual. An alternative approach is that of the classification of objectives according to the method of Niek de Boer, shown schematically in Fig.4-43.

Accessibility profiles of activity carriers must moreover be matched to all relevant target groups. A prison, for example, must not only be accessible by private transport (prisoners), but also by public transport (for the benefit of staff and visitors from all over the country). Both singular and multiple journey chains must be taken into consideration. "Likewise the shrine of Ceres should be sited in a place outside the city where no one need to go except to offer sacrifice;" (Vitruvius 1999a: I.7.2).

	confrontation with (categories):		**testing against (aspects):**
	4-1 natural environment	1-4	
	4-2 spatial protection	2-4	A socio-cultural conditions
	4-3 spatial patterns	3-4	B spatial conditions
category 4 dwelling	4-4 housing	4-4	C socio-economic conditions
	4-5 amenities	5-4	D organizational conditions
	4-6 employment	6-4	
	4-7 transport	7-4	

Fig.4-43 Housing objectives matrix from: objectives matrix (Boer 1990: 96). See Fig.2-17

In the conversation with the architectural historian Ed Taverne published in Nio & Reijndorp 1997 (: 206), the term "social-scientific urban planning and design" (*sociaal-wetenschappelijke stedebouw*), although not further elaborated on, refers to process-oriented design.

The conversation mentions three approaches to urban planning and design: besides the two approaches described in the present and previous sections of this dissertation, it refers to 'administrative urban planning and design' (*bestuurlijke stedebouw*).

There are also points of correspondence with what Punter & Carmona describe as a broader, contemporary approach to urban design: "Urban design, which can be defined as a concern with the ensemble of buildings and the spaces between them; the public and private realms created; their visual, functional and symbolic qualities; and the settings for social behaviour and activities that they provide." (1997: 88).

In the process-oriented approach, functions are distinguished into different kinds: individual or collective and in the latter case further according to level of scale. A distinction is moreover made between day/night functions. Besides such traditional functional concepts as the dwelling function, the employment function etc., 'eight hours', 'sixteen hours' and '24 hours' functions are distinguished[43]. Relevant are routes, places related to them and types of node. Due to their position in a structure, certain places acquire the possibility (location value) of being able to fulfil a certain function. The functional-spatial structure is supported by the formal-spatial structure (Fig.4-44). In Lynch's words, "Forms should be manipulated so that there is a strand of continuity between the multiple images of a big city: day and night, winter and summer ...". (1960: 109).

Fig.4-44 "Paths may not be identifiable and continuous but have directional qualilty as well: one direction along a line can easily be disthinguished from the reverse. This can be done by a gradient, a regular change in some quality which is cumulative in one direction." (Lynch 1960: 54).

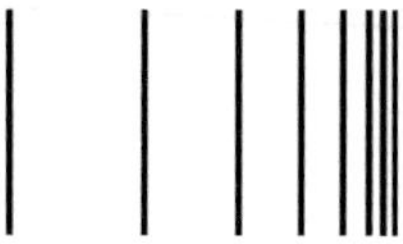

Because processes often entail multi-link journeys (mobility chains) in which differing levels of scale are involved, not only must different levels of scale be distinguished but the relation between them forms an important theme: 'hinge points' between different levels of scale ('transfer machines'). The presence of other facilities than those strictly necessary to transport enlarges the scope of potential temporospatial patterns.

Jansen, Machielse & Vogel (undated: 27) rightly point out that amenities and amenity clusters are desirable a places other than at 'transfer machines', because the latter are not the best places for everybody.

In the process-oriented approach account is taken not only of those elements of the natural system that play a part in urban systems, but also of relevant cyclic natural processes such as atmospheric currents (wind) and ecological processes.

Levels of scale are determined on the grounds of the range of influence of societal processes (see Section 4.2.1). These spatial dimensions of urban processes are not fixed, but are related to local spatial attributes and to social, cultural, economic and technological circumstances. The same is true for the boundaries and size of relevant design areas, bearing in mind that the appropriate criterion is not the present and trend-projected scope of processes, but the future desirable scope. At every scale level, there will also invariably be elements present which are relevant at one or more higher scale levels.

It is not the quantity of activity carriers that is primarily relevant, but the qualitative benefits users will obtain from certain quantities in certain densities at appropriate places (location value) in the structure. In process-oriented design, it makes a considerable difference whether institutions (hospitals, offices) enclose facilities within their own walls, or whether the facilities are directly linked to the public space and are accessible to everyone. In the latter case, institutions in urban areas contribute to the intensity of use of the public space and to the user potential user base for the autonomously situated facilities, so that persons not attached to the institution concerned can make use of them. Enclosed shopping malls and similar concentrations of facilities are in that respect anti-urban (Trancik 1986: 47).

In a process-oriented design, it suffices to indicate the functional-spatial structure and the size of the 'bounded areas' such as parking space, commercial centres etc. attached to it, plus (variations in) functional typology, height and depth values and some essential visual design indications; see Fig.6-19-7. A design of this kind is inherently more flexible than a blueprint.

Characteristic for process-oriented design are

- cyclic process terms such as 'accessibility', 'temporospatial activity pattern', 'public safety', 'hierarchy', 'transport link', 'potential user base', 'magnet facilities' (*publiekstrekkers*), 'symbiosis' (=supporting interactivity), 'network city', 'transportation nodes', 'day, evening and night functions', 'day and night routes'.
- linear process concepts as formulated under pattern-oriented design (Section 4.6.1).

Designers who have an affinity with the process-oriented design approach include (see references): Niek de Boer, Constantinos Doxiadis, Kevin Lynch, Christopher Alexander, Bill Hillier, John Musgrove, Pat O'Sullivan, Julienne Hanson, Jan Gehl, Jon Lang, the authors of Mobilopolis (Anonymous 1998), adherents of the American 'New Urbanism' movement such as Donald Chen and Robert Burchell (www.doverkohl.com/writings.html (04-2003)), and the urbanists Jane Jacobs, Gabriel Dupuy and Nikos Salingaros. The research report *Contourenschets Sociale Wijkvisie* issued by the Dutch Ministry of Housing, Planning and the Environment, in which a relation is established between urban systems and physical urban systems, also shares this outlook (Ouwehand, Fortuin, Davelaar & Kleinhans 2001).

4.6.3 Pattern-oriented design versus process-oriented design

Designers are insufficiently aware that these two types of approach, namely pattern-oriented and process-oriented, may be distinguished. Pattern-oriented and process-oriented design, share some terms with the same definitions, but each also has a terminology of its own. They also sometimes use the same terms but with different definitions. They furthermore use different types of spatial models, whether descriptive, intentional-projective or exploratory-projective[44]. The consequences are mutual incomprehension regarding the substance of the discipline, terminological confusions and poor insight into the societal significance of urban & regional design. 'When we consider the city as a problem of urban & regional design, do we mean the urban substance or the life that goes on inside it?' Jan Heeling asks (1998: 21), without offering an answer.

Essentiële verschillen tussen beide opvattingen kunnen in de volgende trefwoorden worden uitgedrukt

pattern-oriented design	versus	**process-oriented design**
pattern		process
living, working etc. (residing)		travelling / transporting
places		routes
zones		networks[45]
accessibility: distance		accessibility: journey time
distance between residential function - work function, residential function - amenity function etc.[46]		temporospatial activity pattern
(pattern-based) blueprint planning		(functional-spatial) structure planning

A revealing comparison may be made in this respect with developments in the discipline of landscape design. The increasing interest in and knowledge of ecology and ecological infrastructures has produced a similar dichotomy in landscape design: on the one hand, there is the long-existing practice of formal landscape architecture (also applicable in urban areas) which has the physical appearance of the landscape as its object (Saane 1991), and on the other there is the designing of functional ecological structures (Herngreen 1991: 16).

Terminological confusion

Incomprehension and linguistic misunderstandings are a consequence of the fact that certain terms are defined differently in the two approaches to urban & regional design, and terms thus have different meanings.

Examples of Dutch terms with differing meanings:

term	pattern-oriented design	process-oriented design
residential milieu *(woonmilieu)*	dwelling type and housing density	type of spatial activity pattern which can unfold
density (dichtheid)	dwellings per hectare	users per hectare ('houses don't buy bread')
'green' norm *(groennorm)*	area of 'green' space per dwelling	accessibility, use value and informative value of green space
zoning *(zonering)*	on basis of functions	primarily on basis of accessibility
urban region (stedelijk regio)	continuous distribution of urban elements; associated with term 'inner city'	coherent whole of cyclic urban processes; associated with term 'urban regional centre'
metropolis *(metropool)*	on basis of population density	on basis of complexity and intensity of cyclic urban processes
landmark *(landmark)*	visual point of reference	visual point of reference with a functional significance
spatial structure *(ruimtelijke structuur)*	formal structure; exists alongside functional structure	formal-spatial and/or functional-spatial structure
spatial-functional organization (ruimtelijk-functionele organisatie)	pattern	structure
mononodal/multinodal *(mono-/multinodaal)*	city or region consisting of either a continuous urban area or separate nuclei	flattened or unflattened functional hierarchical pyramid (can also occur in a formally mononodal city/ region)
lineair city *(bandstad)*	ribbon shaped	having a linear structure
organizing principle	formal concept	e.g. 24-hour biorhythm; hierarchy

A comparable confusion to this type of miscommunication is that associated with the term 'sustainability', in the sense used in the Brundtland Commission Report *Our Common Future* (1987). This term is interpreted both as a quality of spatial objects and as a quality of processes.

Examples of differences in types of model

Spatial differentiation in pattern-oriented urban & regional design relates to attributes of form and/or physical state. Examples of these are the urban models produced by the Chicago School between the World Wars: Fig.4-45 and Fig.4-46; also the image of Fig.4-6.

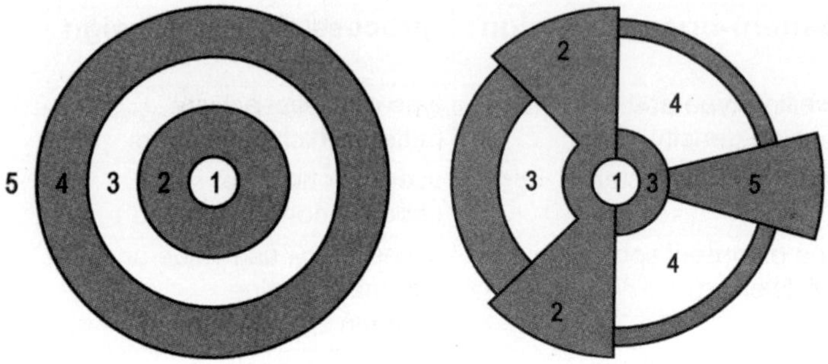

Fig.4-45 Empirically based principle-models of cities as patterns of physical state attributes; left by Burgess (1925), right by Hoyt (1939).
1 centre
2 zone in transition
3 zone of workingmen's homes
4 residential zone
5 commuters zone
(source: Eijking 2000: 22 ff.)

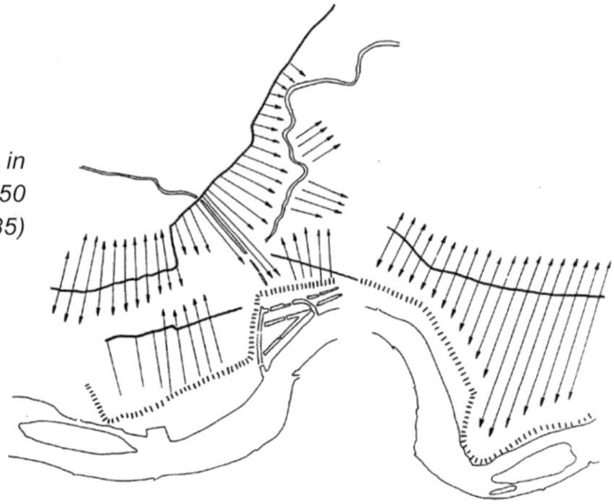

Fig.4-46 Principle plot division scheme in the Rotterdam region, circa 1850 (Wijnen 2002: 35)

Spatial models in process-oriented design are primarily concerned with the carriers of the functional-spatial structure: routes, nodes, concentrations of collective functions or collective function types, potential user bases, walking and cycling distances, bus/tram stop distances (also those between stops), journey times by tram and train: Fig.4-47, Fig.4-48, Fig.4-49 (see also Figs.6-13; 6-15.7 and 15.9 and Section 6.4.6). Auxiliary formal and physical state attributes are added to this: see Figs.6-18.8,19.7 and 19.17).

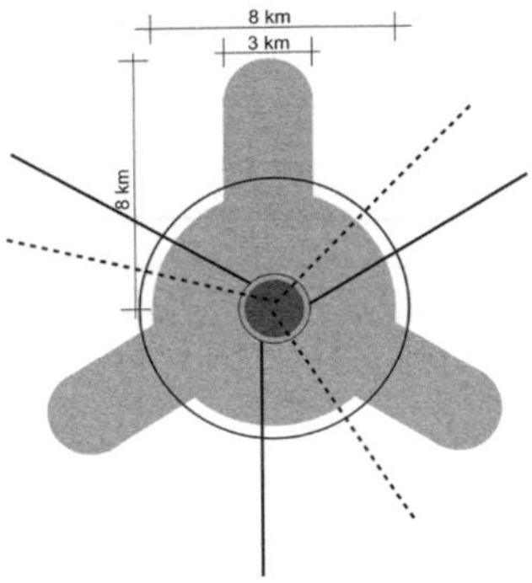

Fig.4-47 Functional-spatial theoretical model (M.Jacobs 2000: 160)

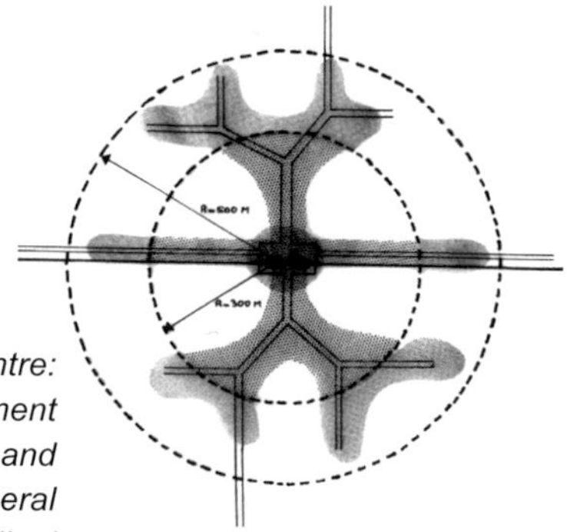

Fig. 4-48 Principle-model for the central zone of a regional centre: high concentration of facilities combined with intensive employment and dwelling opportunities around the train/regional bus station and along the (radial) main routes. Declining density in the peripheral centre areas. The mixing of collective functions with the 'dwelling' function is an outcome of the wish to create conditions for public safety.

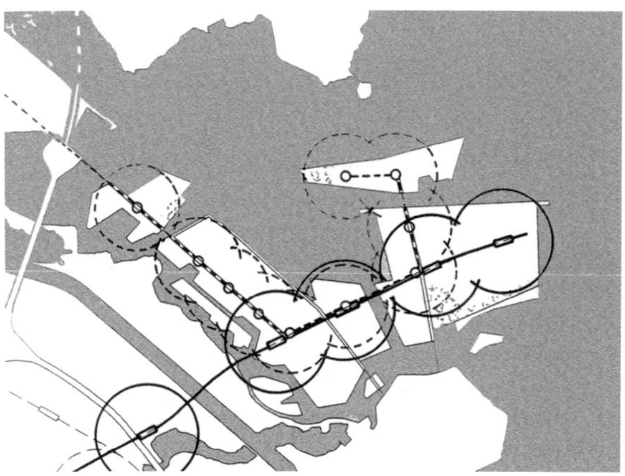

Fig.4-49 Exploratory model for the future urban extension of Amsterdam in the IJsselmeer (lake): accessibility circles of pre-transport for prospective rail link.

Examples of miscommunication

A discussion in which one interlocutor defines the term 'metropolis' on the basis of population density (Jong 1994: 34) thus enabling the western portion of the Netherlands to be labelled the 'Delta Metropolis' (Frieling, Eijking & Tisma 2000), and the other interlocutor defines 'metropolis' on the basis of the nature, complexity and intensity of cyclic urban processes and consequently concludes that 'Randstad Holland' does not exist (Boer 1996), remains a conversation between the deaf as long as this difference in the manner of definition (and thus a difference in what is considered the object of urban & regional design) is non-explicit.

Using the former definition above would moreover imply that (for example) parts of the fertile Ganges Delta in Bangladesh must be a metropolis on the grounds of population density.

The spatial organization and design policy of the Municipality of Amsterdam concentrates on keeping public space in the inner city empty (see the memorandum *Leeg, Schoon en Heel* ('Empty, Clean and Whole'), published in 1996). This is a remarkable standpoint as long as one does not realize that it represents a pattern-oriented approach, and the term 'empty' does not refer to the absence of users but to the absence of street furniture. It is to be hoped that the usage will be sufficiently taken into account; but this seems a forlorn hope when we consider the reconstruction of the Dam (see Fig.4-41).

In the light of the above, the following observation by Jane Jacobs may be cited: "This last point, that the sight of people attracts still other people, is something that city planners and city architectural designers seem to find incomprehensible. They operate on the premise that city people seek the sight of emptiness, obvious order and quiet." (1961: 37).

> " 'The square is characterless. It would be nice if it had a few benches to sit on. But it's a work of art, so it's inviolable.' A woman leans over the parapet of her little balcony. She gazes directly down onto Februariplein, the square behind her house. It's like a courtyard enclosed on four sides by brand new low blocks of flats, near Waterlooplein in Amsterdam. A few residents have put out their own benches here and there, each alongside one of the green, red or blue front doors. Actually, it is against the regulations. The municipality was afraid benches would attract loitering teenagers, so they decided to provide the new buildings with an empty square and artistic paving. From above, the 25 x 25 metre square looks just like a painting."
>
> *(source: Krita Oldenburg in* De Volkskrant, *27 August 2001)*

Urban & regional designers design possible spatial futures that cannot be predicted, Taeke de Jong states (1992: 9 ff.) In other words, what physical urban systems are possible in (in the first instance) ecological technical respects? What buildings and other structures can be built? Someone who does not realize that the pattern-oriented approach is involved here, and himself takes a process-oriented approach, will object that there is little point in designing possible spatial futures as long as the design activity does not focus on the opportunities for societal (and natural) processes offered by the designs once implemented; in other on what types of society they enable - or don't enable (Klaasen 1996). This corresponds to the difference between constructive options and utilitarian options mentioned in Section 3.2.4.

4.6.4 Pattern-oriented and/or process-oriented design

In evaluating the aspects summarized in Section 4.4 as requiring attention during concretization of the (future) carrying and information functions, the synthetizing creation of spatial potential (across more than one scale level) in order to accommodate social, economic and cultural processes with a cyclic character (in short, the use value of physical urban systems) is neglected in the pattern-oriented approach, although it may be assumed that attention is sometimes paid implicitly, in the sense of applying tacit knowledge (Section 3.4.3).

A consequence of inattention to the carrying function or use value is that when a public space such as a square is not used e.g. as a place to sit for a while, whatever the reason, the informative significance attached to it as a public square is lost: the square is not actively 'experienced' by people. In other words, if e.g. a square, a boulevard or a footpath is peripherally situated from a functional-spatial viewpoint, evokes a sense of unsafety (negative information) or is too exposed to the elements, or if there is insufficient information given about its presence (Lynch 1960), even the most splendid visual design will be a waste of effort. The recent redesign of Dam Square in the centre of Amsterdam (see Fig.4-41) is a good example. Before the new design had been implemented, I wrote in 2000 as follows: "Although the composition may be considered beautiful, the users are absent. In view of the masses of pedestrians and cyclists crossing the square, it would seem that problems of traffic safety (just think of the trams!) will be unavoidable. And where can people park all those bicycles?" (Klaasen 2000b: 63). A flood of criticism developed after completion of the square in 2001 and the predictable traffic accidents (some fatal) have alas occurred. People continue cluttering the square with parked bicycles, despite the lack of provided facilities (Fig.4-50).

a collage of articles and letters to the editor:

abstract:

A design journal: The redesign of Dam Square is a demonstration of professional skill ... with a touch of Modernity.

Composer Peter Schat: Redesign of Dam Square is major success; monumental!

Police officer: A lunatic has been at work here.
We are just waiting for the first fatality.

Editor, *NRC-Handelsblad*: It's lovely, Dam Square, but you can't walk on it .

'Letter to editor': This designer does not walk on high heels, does not cycle, has no children and is not a wheelchair user.

Editor, *Het Parool*: Proof - Dam is a disaster for cyclists.

Amsterdam Council: Decision - things cannot go on like this.

Een tijdje geleden reed ik voor het eerst over de stenen van de 'nieuwe' Dam. Ik was verbijsterd. Ik wist het meteen: deze ontwerper is geen vrouw; fietst niet; heeft geen kinderen, die in een buggy zitten; rijdt niet in een rolstoel en heeft nog nooit met krukken gelopen. Dat kan en dat je dan zo'n plein ontwerpt kan ook.

Ingezonden brief
De Volkskrant 01-06-01

Hij is mooi, de Dam, maar niet te belopen

De Dam is de afgelopen jaren omgetoverd in een plein met een onberispelijk grijs tapijt. Mooi, maar levensgevaarlijk.

(Hans Moll
NRC-Handelsblad 24-08-01)

Aangetoond: Dam ramp voor fietsers

(*Het Parool* 11-10-01)

Nu dan de Dam, ons nationale plein. De heren Schat en Montag waren enthousiast over de nieuwe vormgeving, wat begrijpelijk is. Ik heb zelf ook de neiging om de grote werken in eerste instantie mooi te vinden, want je wil geen vreugdeloze izegrim zijn. Trouwens, het was ook wel mooi.

Toch moet worden opgemerkt dat de gemeentelijke herinrichter zijn stoepvrees hier wel heel extreem heeft uitgeleefd.

(---------)

De lage, brede stoepranden die Peter Schat zag, waren er lang niet overal. Op strategische oversteekpunten was helemaal geen niveauverschil. Het gebied zag er uit als een grote voetgangerszone waar trams, auto's en fietsers dwars doorheen reden. Ik schatte dat lijn 14, die onverwacht uit de Paleisstraat opduikt, als eerste tot Amsterdamse moordenaar zou worden uitgeroepen.

Er zaten twee agenten op motorfietsen naar het gekrioel van de verkeersstromen te kijken. Het kostte maar weinig moeite om hun een mening te ontfutselen over het nieuwe plein. Anders dan bij Schat en Montag was die mening niet in de eerste plaats door esthetische overwegingen ingegeven.

„Er is hier een gek aan het werk geweest. Het is wachten op de eerste dode en dan zullen ze het over een paar maanden weer helemaal anders doen, maar ondertussen zitten wij er maar mee."

(---------)

Een goed advies. De herinrichter van de Dam ging naar Madrid om daar het Plaza Mayor te bestuderen. Dat is inderdaad een mooi plein, dat echter weinig gemeen heeft met de Dam. Het Plaza Mayor is een plein van het type 'grote huiskamer'. Hoe je een van de belangrijkste verkeersaders van de stad dwars door een plein moet leiden, kan je daar niet leren, want er is geen verkeer.

(Hans Ree in
NRC-Handelsblad
15-05-01)

Blindengeleidelijn en een oversteekstrook op Dam

AMSTERDAM - Acht maanden lag hij open voor een grondige opknapbeurt, die 14,8 miljoen euro (32,6 miljoen gulden) kostte. Het eindresultaat blijkt echter veel problemen te veroorzaken: de verkeerssituatie op de vernieuwde Dam is onoverzichtelijk voor álle weggebruikers, de keitjes voelen onder elk schoeisel aan als een spijkerbed en gehandicapten raken er het spoor bijster.

Dat kan zo niet langer, vindt nu ook het Amsterdamse college van b. en w. Op verzoek van de Stichting Gehandicapten Overleg Amsterdam (SGOA) komt er 'een beloopbare oversteekstrook' voor gehandicapten tussen Damrak en Rokin, en moet er voor blinden 'een geleidelijn' worden aangelegd. Ook wordt het zebrapad bij Madame Tussaud's doorgetrokken tot over de trambaan en zullen de rateltikkers worden verplaatst.

(Kamilla Leupen
Het Parool 23-01-02)

De vernieuwde Dam toont dat de ontwerpkeuzes volgens het ontwerpidioom dat al zo'n twintig jaar overheerst, nog steeds relevant zijn. De reorganisatie van autoverkeer en trambanen, het uitbannen van zoveel mogelijk obstakels en het met ijzeren volharding doorzetten van één materiaal levert een mentale, maar ook letterlijke vergroting van ruimte op. Net als diverse andere herontworpen pleinen laat de nieuwe Dam zien hoeveel er te winnen valt met het goed doordenken van verkeersstromen en, waar dat maar mogelijk is, het terugdringen van de belijning door lijnen weg te strepen, te bundelen en minder dominant aan te brengen. Toch zal menigeen teleurgesteld zijn dat Nederlands meest bekende plein gewoon met keitjes is bestraat die er al eeuwen lijken te liggen. De zweem van moderniteit die van het straatmeubilair moet uitgaan, maakt dat niet ongedaan. Maar de kwaliteit van de herinrichting zit hem niet in stijl en moderniteit, en ook niet in de herhaling van een beproefd recept. De herinrichting van Dam is een demonstratie van vakbekwaamheid in detaillering, materialisering en uitvoering.

(Noël van Dooren in *Blauwe Kamer*
(4) 2001: 33)

Nu de hoofdstedelijke Dam een metamorfose heeft ondergaan, is het plein zelf een monument geworden, meent **Peter Schat.** Een volgende stap moet zijn dat de rituelen die zich op het plein afspelen worden vernieuwd. Voor de kermis is geen plaats meer.

Het is al enige tijd zichtbaar dat de inmiddels een half jaar aan de gang zijnde verbouwing van het Damplein een groot succes wordt. Voor het eerst in zijn lange en grillige geschiedenis wordt het plein een eenheid, een kamer in de stad die een grote menigte kan bevatten – een nieuwe agora. Dit wordt voornamelijk bereikt door een pleinbreed tapijt van blauwgrijze en zachtgele natuursteentjes die in Portugal uit de rotsen zijn gehakt, en hier tot in alle uithoeken van het plein in waaiervormige mozaïeken zijn vastgelegd. De tramrails zijn in dit tapijt meegemetseld en de bovenleidingen worden tussen de tien schitterend omhoog priemende zilverstalen lichtmasten gespannen. Samen met de spiegelende stoeplantaarns ontmaskeren zij en passant genadeloos het protserige belichtingsgeknoei op Damrak, Rokin en Nieuwmarkt. De kleine marmeren zitbankjes komen terug maar verder is alle straatmeubilair zoveel mogelijk weggelaten.

(De componist Peter Schat in
NRC-Handelsblad 03-05-01)

Kunstprijs

Terwijl iedere (binnenstad) Amsterdammer de nieuwe inrichting en het ontwerp van de Dam in Amsterdam een ramp vindt, krijgt een medebedenker van dat ontwerp, Simon Sprietsma, een prijs toegekend van 7.000 euro uit het Amsterdamse Fonds voor de Kunsten (NRC Handelsblad, 14 maart).

Veel Amsterdammers zouden die Dam weleens goed bestraat en normaal ontworpen willen zien – zonder daarvoor prijzen uit te delen.

Ingezonden brief
NRC-Handelsblad 26-03-02

Fig.4-50 In background, the Royal Palace; in the foreground, bicycles parked in front of De Bijenkorf department store. (Photography by author 2000)

The aesthetics of Museumplein, Amsterdam (the large public square on the south side of the Rijksmuseum) were marred soon after completion of the redesign. The subtle differences in the paving of footpaths and cycle paths were unnoticeable for users of the square: Fig.4-51.

Fig. 4-51 The white lines on the ground of Museumplein, Amsterdam, are meant to make it clear to users that parts of the pavement are meant for cyclists and not for pedestrians. These lines were not part of the design...... (Photography by the author, spring 2001)

The failure of the Y-Markt (a so-called 'oriental market' intended for participation by ethnic minorities) in Amsterdam can similarly be put down to neglect of the process-oriented approach: Fig.4-52.

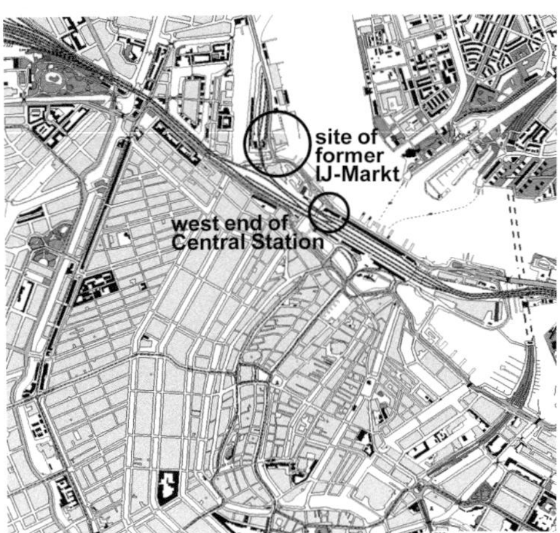

Fig.4-52 The Amsterdam Y-Markt, an 'oriental market' opened in 1993, mainly for use by traders from ethnic minorities, was supposed to become a tourist attraction with 2 million visitors per annum. It was situated in relatively isolated docklands along Westerdoksdijk, an urban arterial road, far from pedestrian routes. The forecast visitor volume was based on the market's situation at the rear of Amsterdam Central Station. The market closed down a few months after opening, never having attracted more than a few hundred visitors daily. The city alderman responsible for the market was quoted in NRC-Handelsblad (17 June 1994) as saying, "There was no time to carry out market research for a market on Westerdoksdijk." Market research was of course unnecessary to predict that the siting of the Y-Markt would prove completely inappropriate.

The assumption that regional design is impossible or must be regarded as "the sum of designs for parts of the region" (Section 4.6.1) results in fragmented regional physical systems at that scale level (see the term 'set' in Section 4.2.2). "It is noted that not only do the urban patterns created [in the Netherlands - itk] in recent decades lack sufficient coherence, but no attempt has been made to achieve such coherence." (Klaasen & Radema 1985: 721).

Criticism of this kind is not infrequently ventilated but it is characteristic of Dutch urban & regional design circles (Section 5.2.2) that it rarely prompts public debate. As stated in Section 1.1, designers are rarely held personally responsible for their products. Marginal criticisms are all one hears.

> "The buildings stand mutely alongside the square; the shops are empty and unused; you just walk across the square without stopping. Everyone was pleased at first, but the appreciation has now sunk to nothing," states Peter Drijver of Architectuur Platform Den Haag, with reference to Spuiplein in The Hague (*De Volkskrant*, 12 July 1997).

> "Either they are plans with a classical axis that stretches from somewhere to nowhere, one that isn't even a main route and is lined with countless houses like any road in a residential area." (Gall 1996: 28).

Pattern-oriented designers rarely perceive this kind of criticism as being addressed to them. In their opinion, after all, visual design is the essence of the designer's contribution to the creation of physical urban systems: the form of the built environment as an expression of culture, springing from the designer's own creativity. Functional aspects are supplied, in their view, by empirical sciences in the form of schedules of requirements or checklists; or they may be considered tacit knowledge. Process-oriented design, these designers believe, gives too little scope for creativity and sensitivity. A published interview with Ashok Bhalotra stated, 'He [Bhalotra] takes a stand with regards to the familiar distinction between future value and experiential value, and he places his emphasis on the latter. He is chiefly concerned with feeling (in the belly) and sensory experience: "I seek Quality, the Intensity of experience by all the senses. ..." (Anonymous 1993).

An obvious question is whether the rival approaches to urban & regional design are really not so incompatible that they cannot coalesce. The answer to this is affirmative: visual design is after all a *sine qua non* for process-oriented design too. It is then essential, however, that the information function presupposes the carrying function (cyclic processes). The boundaries of the areas for which the proposals are made should be determined by the territorial scope of the processes that one wishes to accommodate (in a conditional sense), in relation to the level of scale concerned. A functionally-spatially relevant bounded system can after all be considered from a pattern-oriented approach, but not vice versa (except by coincidence). Considerations of carrying functions will always necessitate the establishment of a relation with other levels of scale. This coalescence of the two approaches would make an unequivocal terminology all the more vital.

4.7 Perspectives for a scientific approach to urban & regional design

"art is I, science is we".

(Claude Bernard 1813-1878, French physiologist)

This study was motivated by the observation that despite the many problems people have with the way physical urban systems are constructed, a scientific basis for proposals for such systems - i.e. for making urban designs - is absent. The underlying assumption is that if this were indeed the case, there would be fewer problems; that the ability to draw on explicit, well-grounded, discussible knowledge both for making and for assessing proposals (*ex ante* evaluation) would reduce the part played by chance.

Chapter 3 distinguishes three types of science: the formal, empirical and practical sciences. A crucial question in practical science is 'does it work?'; a practical science develops knowledge and insight with regard to the applications of empirical and formal sciences jointly. It was established in Section 3.5 that perspectives exist, albeit with certain constraints, for developing urban & regional design as a practical science, so as to make possible a scientific basis for proposed interventions in physical urban systems.

In the development of the field of urban & regional design into a scientific discipline, the two distinct outlooks described in the present Chapter on the significance of the discipline to society will point to differently delimited objects of research. Given the fact that the substantive object of pattern-oriented design is the physical urban system itself, given the emphasis that pattern-oriented design places on cultural and aesthetic aspects of experiential value - and hence on visual design and on personal design concepts - this approach to urban design offers little perspective for a practical-scientific approach. The question 'does it work?' cannot after all be posed when elements of physical urban systems are not considered coherently with regard to the use function - coherently at a relevant level of scale, and coherently across levels of scale insofar as elements are relevant at multiple levels. After all, 'experiencing' lacks a functional significance too.

The situation is different for the process-oriented approach, in which the physical urban system is not treated separately from the urban system as a whole, and in which the use value is the primary focus of attention while the experience of the physical urban system serves to support the use. "The development of man-environment studies can be seen, in part, as an attempt to develop models which allow for specifics as a part of generalizable propositions." Rapoport (1996: 27) states in support of the above reasoning.

Pattern-oriented design could only then be considered a potential practical science when the question 'does it work?' is given a different interpretation than that above, namely, 'under what conditions can a certain type of design be executed?' This is due to the ambiguity of the word 'possible', mentioned above (Sections 3.2.4 and 4.6.3).

The next Chapter will concretize the above mentioned scientific perspectives in the framework of an outline of the relation in practice between, on the one hand, urban & regional design, and on the other, research.

5 Urban & regional design and science

5.1 Substantive science: from creative craft to practical science

"If we wish to *extend* the range of design oriented research, then other methods have to be found - or developed - which do justice to the kind [of] creative variation which is a characteristic of architectural composition."

(Jack Breen 2001, *Designerly Approaches to Architectural Research*: 54)

In the previous Chapter I made a distinction between pattern-oriented and process-oriented urban & regional design. The conclusion in the final paragraph was that a development from process-oriented design into a practical science is possible, but that the pattern-oriented approach has considerable restrictions for such a development, unless one confines oneself to the 'makeability' of designs. In this Chapter I will examine this conclusion in light of the present relationship between urban & regional design and science. My frame of reference for the concept of science has been formulated in Chapters 2 and 3, and rests upon the cornerstones of realism, objectivism and critical rationality.

It is therefore not the relativistic or structuralistic approach to reality, and its associated views on knowledge acquisition, that is used fairly often in the world of architecture and urban design. Nor can knowledge acquisition be regarded "as a restless movement, the clash between various frames of reference (----) the continuation of a conversation" (Coyne, Hawker & Wiszniewski 2001: 91). I do not regard theory as a 'view on design' (Trancik 1986; Zimmerman 2001: 56) or as a "set of activities and procedures with a specific language and a known set of protocols" (Graafland 2001: 21).

Up until the nineteen sixties the relationship between design and science was a clear one: where science played a role in design it was in a supply sense, and urban & regional design was viewed solely as a creative craft. The creative-craft view is still fairly widespread, even though the last decades have seen a shifting emphasis on the kind of empirical knowledge supplied and, certainly in the case of the Netherlands, on the relationship between knowledge input and design input (see for example Nio & Reijndorp 1997: 12 ff.) and, in relation to this, to a shift in the relationship between goal-oriented and means-oriented design. This creative-craft approach to design, characteristic of pattern-oriented design, is examined in Section 5.2. There I argue that empirical science complementing urban design is primarily wishful thinking, that in reality there is an applicability gap and that more, better or more in-depth empirical research does not produce better urban design. The creative-craft view, I argue, also does not stimulate the development of urban & regional design into a science.

In the nineteen sixties people began to distance themselves from the craft approach, particularly in the procedural sense (Lawson 1990: 2; Cross 1993: 16 ff.). "Somehow the whole process had to become more open to inspection and critical evaluation. The model of scientific method proved irresistible. Scientists made explicit not just their results but also their procedures. Their work could be replicated and criticised and their methods were above suspicion." (Lawson 1990: 18,19). Since that time designers have been wrestling with the relationship between design and research. On the one hand they seek scientific recognition for their particular field, and on the other they argue that a rational, systematic approach would be detrimental to the essential creativity when producing a design. "... architects are not used to theories that can be tested and discussed, they may be afraid that the design will be limited by the theory. " observes Krabbendam (2001: 202) for example. "Inventiveness is in inverse proportion to knowledge and experience. Knowledge and experience keep forcing us back into the old grooves of the old record of meanings..." (Hertzberger 2002: 392). Certain urban designers, however, do share the view that rationality and creativity are not at all incompatible (see Section 3.1), as is the case with knowledge and creativity, and that the creativity required for scientific research should not be underestimated. Niek de Boer states: "Methods and techniques are not tools in which all you have to do is add the ingredients to produce usable plans." (1990: 10, 11). Kevin Lynch writes: "... open and explicit methods ... goals, data and solutions must be clearly stated and rationally connected, so that they may be openly debated. Artistic mystery is no more legitimate in setting sensory policy than it is in setting economic or social policy... but intuition is not banished. It abides in the mysterious process of creation, which proposes the possibilities for public debate. It plays a crucial role in scientific discovery." (1976: 77).

In design-related science a distinction has to be made between a scientific approach to design as a process and a substantive approach to the particular type of design, in this case urban & regional design.

Following on from the distinction made in spatial planning between 'theory of planning' and 'theory in planning' (Faludi 1973), a distinction can be made between 'theory of design' and 'theory in design'.

When searching through the literature using the keyword combinations of 'architectural' or 'urban' and 'design' and 'science' or 'research', we find that in many cases design science and design research relate to the procedural side of design: to design methods and design styles, to planning and to strategies (for example Cross 1984; Vries, Cross & Grant 1993; Bakel 1995; Durling & Shackleton 2002). There has been less research published on the substantive-scientific aspects of urban design, both regarding what can be constructed under which contextual conditions and which possibilities for use are provided under what contextual conditions ('which effects, under what conditions': see Section 3.2.4).

I am not aware of any generic research carried out into the constructive possibilities - at least not in the discipline of urban & regional design itself. In view of the fact that in such research the difference between pattern-oriented and process-oriented design is not relevant, I will not discuss this type of research further in this Chapter.

With regard to the utilitarian possibilities, we can assume that apart from the supposed contrast between science and creativity, the complexity of urban systems in connection with man's considerable biological capacity to adapt plays a role (Huisman 1996). "To see complex systems of functional order, and not chaos, takes understanding." (J.Jacobs 1961: 376).

This thesis is aimed at the substantive-scientific aspects of urban & regional design. The procedural aspects of design are important to me in relation to this study in so far as

- design as method can contribute to the generation of substantive urban design knowledge, i.e. research by design (*ontwerpend onderzoeken*) in order to generate practical scientific knowledge; this is dealt with in Section 5.4;
- substantive scientific knowledge plays a role in the generation of a specific design, i.e. research-driven design (*onderzoekend ontwerpen*); this is dealt with in Section 5.5.

An alternative for 'research by design' is the term 'designerly research', which is akin to the term 'designerly enquiry' which the architect Jack Breen uses echoing the words of Bruce Archer, who introduced the term at the congress of the Design Research Society in 1980 (Breen 2001: 55). An alternative for 'research-driven design' is 'design study' (Jong & Van der Voordt 2002a).

Up until now the verb 'to design' has been viewed as the making of designs for specific sites. When 'to design' is also used in relation to research methodology it is important to make a distinction between the two. From now on if it is necessary to avoid any possible confusion, the term 'localized design' will be used.

There was also interest in the nineteen sixties for a substantive-scientific approach to urban & regional design. Names that can be mentioned in connection with this are the urban sociologist Jane Jacobs (1961) and the designers Constantinos Doxiadis (1968), Kevin Lynch (e.g. 1972) and Christopher Alexander (1977). This interest, however, subsequently declined again. But that was not the case for the need for scientific recognition. This can be seen in the fact that the congress of the European Association for Architectural Education (EAAE) in 1996 was devoted to doctoral studies in architecture and urban design. In most western countries the possibility to receive a doctorate in these fields of study as well as the actual use of these possibilities were seen to increase considerably (EAAE 1996).

At the Faculty of Architecture of the Technical University in Delft an initiative was taken in 1998 to set up a research project across the faculty aimed at substantive design related research: 'The Architectonic Intervention'. The international congress 'Research by Design' concluded this study at the end of 2000 (Ouwerkerk & Rosemann 2001; Langenhuizen, Van Ouwerkerk & Rosemann 2001). Evaluating the contributions to this international congress Richard Foqué concluded: " ... it is striking that the debate on the so-called scientific status of the design activity which started in the early 60s not only remains unsolved, but for almost forty years now is held on the same level of generality, using vague philosophical concepts, semantically based frames of reference and a total lack of understanding and vision on the true mechanisms underlying the design process on the one hand and the process of scientific research on the other. Little progress has been made since the founding fathers of modern design methodology, J.C.Jones, G.Broadbent, C.Alexander and others, established their first theories." (2001: 2).

I believe that progress has been made in 'The Architectonic Intervention' project in so far as by unlinking the proposition 'design object' and 'design context': Fig.5-1 (Frieling 2000), it seems accepted in wider circles to relate the verb 'design' no longer to just making proposals for action in specific locations. This opens the doors to theoretical models and non-localized designs, and consequently also for applied research and the development of urban & regional design as a science.

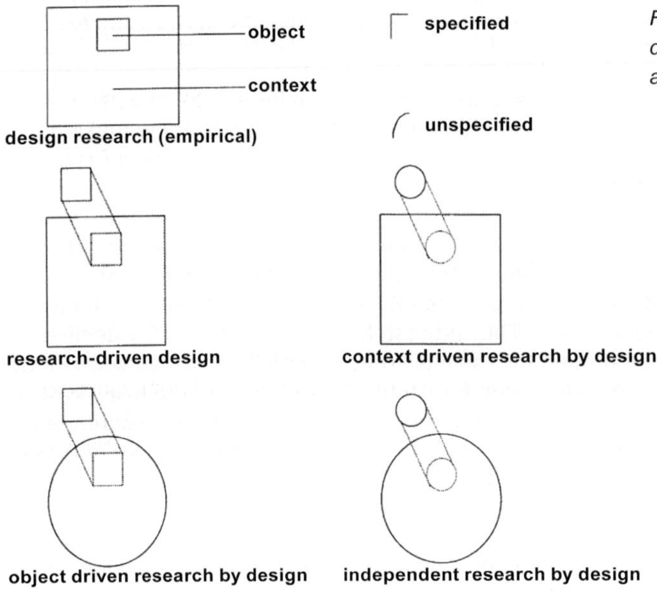

Fig.5-1 Possible relationships between design object and design context according to Frieling (2000: 12).

I understand the term 'object' to relate to the construction to be made, and 'context' to the socio-cultural, spatial-ecological, economic-technical and administrative-organizational conditions. If an object is 'specific' then it is an object that 'is the case' (or was). If it involves an object that may possibly be the case, then it will never be random in nature but always belong to the domain of urban & regional design. Essential is that the context is either spatially specific (i.e. localized, and therefore spatial-ecological and also socio-cultural, economic-technical and administrative-organizational determined) or not spatially specific while other contextual conditions (e.g. the conditions in a given country) are. Those other contextual conditions may, however, be also (partially) non-specific. In that case it involves, for example, construction possibilities and consequently associated utilitarian possibilities under various economic or cultural conditions. Since what is and is not possible changes in the course of time and given the *longue duree* of physical urban systems, the contextual future perspectives are also important.

Unlinking object and context, and regarding these alternatively as 'specific' and 'unspecific', allows us:

- to make a distinction within a substantive design-related research between urban & regional design and empirical research on the one hand, and urban & regional design as practical science on the other: respectively design research (*ontwerponderzoek*) and research by design (*ontwerpend onderzoeken* = design in the service of research);
- to clarify the difference between practical science and the application of practical science knowledge in a specific case: research-driven design (*onderzoekend ontwerpen* = research in the service of design).

The Faculty of Architecture of Delft Technical University uses the term 'design research' (empirical substantive research) as distinct from 'research-driven design' and 'research by design'. Independent use of the term 'design research' leads to confusion regarding the term as this can be and is used for all relationships between design and research, including procedural research.

There are three forms of empirical research, two of which are primarily aimed at the 'specific object':

- Ideographic research (design research), whereby a certain object in a specific context or several objects in specific contexts are described, sometimes comparatively. As the system in reality is further simplified, the descriptions of *unica* generate typologies. It is expected that the pattern-oriented approach to design, with an emphasis on the cultural and aesthetic aspects of the physical urban system, and with a creative-craft approach in relation to the substantive side, will primarily involve this type of research. This form of research is examined in Section 5.3.

- Evaluation research *ex post*, carried out after a design has been implemented aimed at gaining insight into the degree to which intended objectives have been achieved. Spatially-oriented empirical scientists carry out this kind of research. The results of this type of research can be supplied as knowledge to the designer, both directly for a localized design (Section 5.2.1), as well as in the form of a contribution from the context of application to the basis of practical-scientific theoretical models (Section 5.4.2). "... the validity and importance of [theoretical models] should be checked with existing settlements; tests and experiments to be carried out in existing settlements, the conclusions of which can be fed back in order to check the theory." (Doxiadis 1968: 285).

The third form of empirical research is primarily aimed at the 'specific context': the analysis of the design area. This type of research belongs to the domain of research-driven design: Section 5.5. Much context information is supplied by spatially-oriented empirical scientists. Designers interpret the information but also personally analyse the area's potentials. It is not so much the analysis results that deserve the predicate scientific but the analysis methods (Jong & Ravesloot 1995; Meyer 2002; Spek 2003).

Unlinking the object from its specific context creates the precondition for carrying out practical-scientific research: nomothetic research into what is possible under what conditions and with which effects (Section 5.4.) The unlinking essentially concerns research into physical urban systems independence of spatial-ecological conditions and/or socio-cultural and/or economic-technical and/or administrative-organizational aspects. This can be in the absolute sense - a certain construction is not possible (on Earth) - or in the relative sense. Because the spatial-ecological possibilities are practically endless, even if they are limited by general spatial-ecological facts (natural laws), it is wise to incorporate constraints from a socio-cultural and/or economic-technical and/or administrative-organizational point of view. In Section 5.4 the research method as developed at the Chair for Urban & Regional Design of the Delft University of Technology is related to the research approach of Lakatos described in Section 3.4.2

Non-localized design in itself is not a new phenomenon. Vitruvius described the prototype of a city: Fig.5-2.

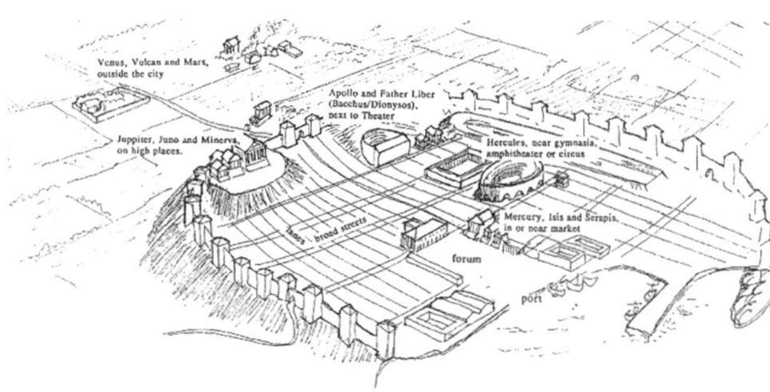

Fig.5-2 Allocations of Plots, Ports, Temples and so on: Commentary I.7.1-2 (Vitruvius (About 25 BC) 1999a: 153)

Many ideal cities have been designed since then, such as the fictitious 15th century city of Sforzinda by Filarete, the 'Ideal Cities' of Scamozzi and Cataneo in the 16th century, in the 19th century Pemberton's 'Happy Colony' and Ebenezer Howards 'Garden City'; in the 20th century Frank Lloyd Wright's 'Broad Acre City' and Le Corbusier's 'Ville Radieuse'(Fig.5-3) (Rosenau 1983). Hillier and Penn critically refer to an ideal town designed by Bofill: Fig.5-4 (1991: 3 ff.). However, these examples lack practically any scientific reasoning (see also note 9). Hillier en Penn's criticism of Bofill, which equally applies to the models in Fig.5-3, can be explained by the fact that within all three displayed models there is a confusion of scale within the model: a form of overextension of the model (see Section 2.3).

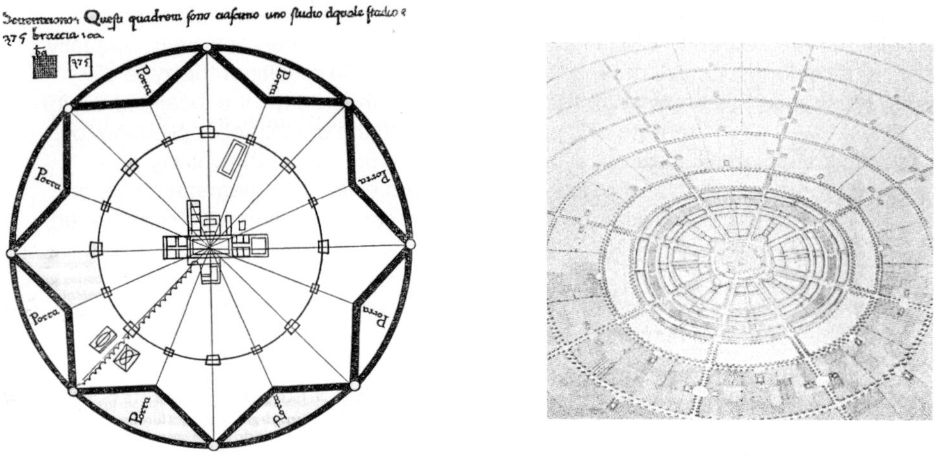

Fig.5-3 Sforzinda by Filarete from the 16th century (left) and the 19th century ideal rural city of Robert Pemberton, which was to be situated in New Zealand (right) (Rosenau 1983: 47; 160).

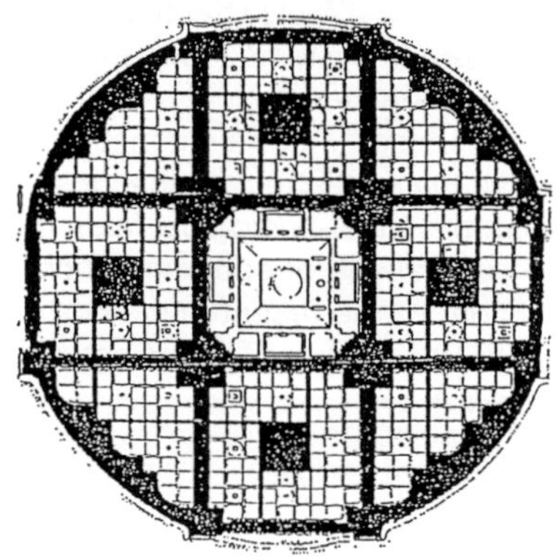

Fig.5-4 This figure "shows the plan of an ideal town designed by Ricardo Bofill. We immediately grasp the whole because a number of similar parts are brought together into similar relations - each set of buildings creates a square, groups of buildings and squares create higher order squares and so on, but it does not take much imagination to see that at ground level the rationality and repetition leads to unintelligibility." (Hillier & Penn 1991: 3 ff.).

Research-driven design makes use of this generalized design knowledge in connection with knowledge of the context. (Section 5.5). The emphasis can be on the requirements in relation to the object itself, as well as on the possibilities of the site: goal-oriented and means-oriented design, respectively (see Section 4.5.2).

In practice the breadth (*bandbreedte*) of useful research is determined by situations that occur in reality. The rationale behind this is that in urban & regional design the man-made spatial context will usually be part of the object that is to be constructed (urban renewal). This means that there is no sharp distinction between research by design and research-driven design, as I will show in Section 5.5.

The conclusion that a research-driven, localized design does not in itself provide a contribution to science leads to my examining in Section 5.6 the demarcation between science and non-science (see Section 3.4.5) regarding urban & regional design.

5.2 Urban & regional design as a creative craft

> "Whereas researchers worried over our methods, designers were fearful that these same methods might usurp their central creative skill - that a 'science of design' might suddenly seize their territory."
>
> (Kevin Lynch (1985) 1990, *Reconsidering The Image of the City*: 250)

5.2.1 The fallacy of 'the unity of town planning'

Internationally we can see that proposals for the spatial planning of cities are a matter of spatially-oriented empirical sciences and of design. The Anglo-Saxon 'survey' approach was introduced to the Netherlands in the nineteen thirties by people such as De Casseres, Van Eesteren and Van Lohuizen as complementary to urban design (Faculteit Bouwkunde TUD 1994a: 6). Van Lohuizen introduced the term 'the unity of town planning' (*de eenheid van het stedebouwkundig werk*) (1948: 3). The term 'unity' refers to the supposedly intensive collaboration between researchers and designers aimed at producing a joint result: a well-thought out and well designed plan[47]. Empirical scientists provide empirical knowledge and insight. Designers make a creative leap by integrating this knowledge into a localized design (see Section 4.5.2): Fig.5-5.

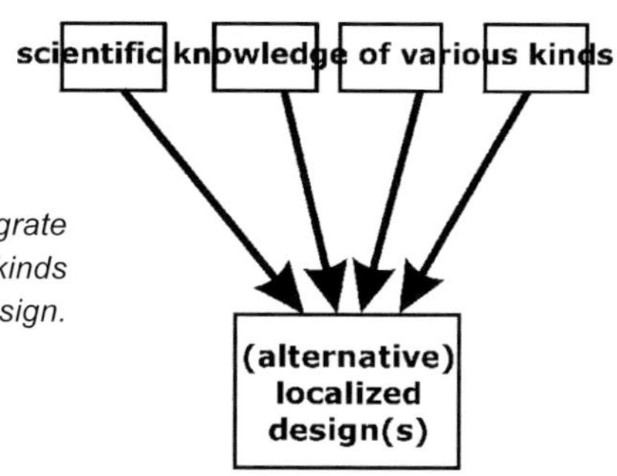

Fig.5-5 Urban & regional designers integrate knowledge of various kinds into a localized design.

Throughout the years this complementary view lost its shine as in practice there appeared to be a gap between empirical science and urban & regional design (Trombey 1984 - quoted in Hulsbergen 1992: 13; Nio & Reijndorp 1997: 239; 244). The Amsterdam professor of urban and regional planning Jaap Buit at the congress honouring the 100th birthday of Van Lohuizen in 1990 characterised the 'unity of town planning' as 'idealistic'.

In the Netherlands the harmonious view of collaboration[48] slowly shifted towards a 'legal separation': separate university chairs for urban & regional design (*stedebouwkundig ontwerpen*) and urban research, later on spatial planning (*stedebouwkundig onderzoek; planologie*). Until recently there was a professional association of urban & regional designers (in addition to that of architects) and a professional association of spatial researchers and planners. It has proved difficult to explain this distinction internationally (see 'Notes on Translation'). These two professional associations have since merged.

Hillier, Musgrove & O'Sullivan refer to an applicability gap (1972). "Regardless of the quality of research work itself, the history of attempts to link research to improvements in environmental action is largely one of confusion and failure," they state (ibid.: 29-3-2), regardless of how systematically designers work. Noting that design problems are generally badly constructed and/or poorly defined problems that need to be pre-structured in order to get a grip on them (ibid.: 29-3-3; see also Hamel 1990), they furthermore state: "Designers are left to make their own links with research by assimilating 'results' and quantification rules, and to evaluate them as they appear without any guidance on priorities or patterns of application. The designer's field thus becomes <u>more</u> complex and <u>less</u> structured." (ibid.: 29-3-5). They reason that when the number of instrumental sets (technological means) increases continually, these consequently are not recognised fully and, what is more, become masked by superfluous information, and that designers subsequently do not lose their preconceptions - on the contrary, they become more dependent upon them. "The net result is unstructured innovation, with slow and piecemeal feedback, giving the impression of arbitrary shifts in fashion." (ibid.: 29-3-8). These 'arbitrary shifts in fashion' would reinforce the fact that people quickly regard literature as being out of date, with urban design classics such as the books by J.Jacobs, Doxiadis, Lynch and Alexander being seen as irrelevant and just gathering dust on bookshelves.

The following factors contribute to making the cognitive schemes of urban designers more complex and less structured.

- The tendency in empirical research to increasingly collect ever more knowledge on an increasingly restricted part of the situation, which in turn places greater demands on the synthetisation capacity of urban designers. If a lack of information is not the crucial problem, then the spatial quality cannot be improved by simply collecting more information.

- The fact that this knowledge is not always geared towards the information need of designers (Hamel 1990: 243, referring to a series of publications on this matter; Nio & Reijndorp 1997: 244).
  - The progress of empirical science is generated by internal scientific considerations. The knowledge that is gained is therefore not always relevant for designers (Section 3.2.1; see also Hamel 1990: 244).
  - Knowledge supplied by empirical scientists is not always suitable for use by urban designers, as empirical scientists focus on 'what is the case' and therefore on 'what will (probably) be the case'. "By and large this liaison between design and social science has not been as useful in practice as was first hoped. Social science remains largely descriptive while design is necessarily prescriptive, so the psychologists and sociologists have gone on researching and the designers designing, and they are yet to re-educate each other into more genuinely collaborative roles." (Lawson 1990: 67).

When for example it is seen that the character of inner cities is changing as a result of shopping centres being set up on the outskirts of the city (or outside it) then it is not a natural development to which urban designers have to respond as e.g. Linden states (1997: 184), but a process set in motion if not by spatial then certainly by administrative decisions, which could be halted in a comparable way if this would be considered desirable.

A study of the hometowns of pupils at a certain type of secondary school in a rural part of the province of Overijssel (Neth.) (Dinteren, Krijgsman & Bout 1989) does not provide a definite answer on the accessibility of this type of school from the surrounding area. More over, only one activity was examined. Also the accessibility of the schools from the adjacent province was not considered in the study.

-The collection of social, cultural and economic-technical data and the carrying out of spatial analyses of urban systems are usually commissioned by government and other administrative bodies (local authorities, chambers of commerce, branches of industry, etc.). Administrative-organizational boundaries therefore determine what is examined and studied. The boundaries of these systems frequently cut straight across spatially distinct systems. "The organizational coherence of a region is however very rarely combined with an administrative unit, which has a negative influence on the development of the area," De Casseres long ago observed (1926: 206). For example, it may be known how many jobs are available in a certain district of town but not how many of these may be within a 500m radius of a metro stop.
- The spatial grain of information is not always geared towards the scale of the design that is to be made. Natural systems that are relevant to ecologists may differ e.g. in size and/or boundaries from those relevant to urban designers (Klaasen 1993: 92).
- Communication problems arise since empirical researchers tend to be more verbal and designers more visual in their communication (Heide & Wijnbelt 1994: 88).

There are also other communication problems between spatial planners and urban designers. An example is the use of the term 'concept'. Dutch spatial planning frequently uses the term 'planning concept'. Spatial planning concepts are action-oriented concepts whereby the government and provincial and municipal authorities are the operating bodies (Zonneveld 1991). Design concepts, even those of great communicative significance, are however of a cognitive nature. An example is the concept of the 'Green Heart', the open central region around which the Randstad more or less forms a circle. The spatial planner calls this a strong concept: it has survived in a societal and political sense for many years now. The urban designer calls this a weak concept as it requires large administrative efforts to keep this central region free from urbanisation: after all the shortest distance between points on a circle pass through the centre (Fig.4-6). See also Ter Heide & Wijnbelt (1994: 92).

Fig.5-6 The 'Green Heart' planning concept (a metaphor) (Ministerie van VROM 1996: 40).

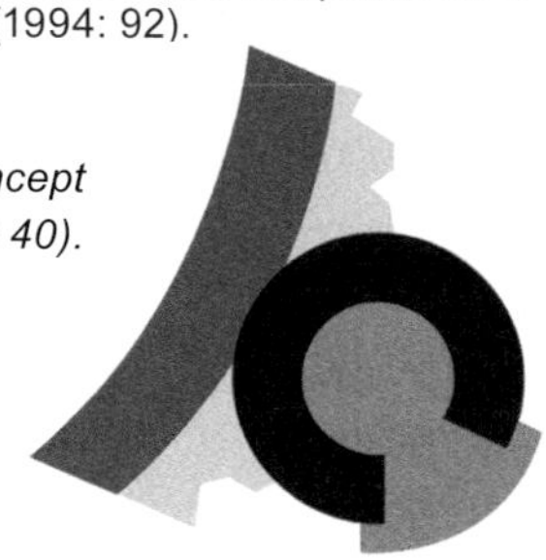

- Designers only rarely formulate synthesis-oriented research questions for spatial scientists. This applies to, for example, knowledge of (linear and cyclical) processes: processes that are to be started, processes that are to be avoided, processes that are to be halted such as, for example, the 'exploding city' (see Klaasen & Jacobs 1999) and the self-destruction of diversity (J.Jacobs 1961: 242).

At least in academic circles the complementary view in the Netherlands received a new impetus in the nineteen nineties by combining means-oriented design (see Section 4.5.2) with explicit effect analyses, sometimes in a comparative sense (Jong & Paasman 1998). Effect analyses, evaluations *ex ante*, relate to societal and physical effects in various future perspectives (Jong & Van der Voordt 2002b: 28). Effect analysis involves the estimation of probable effects, which, if they are not purely of a hypothetical nature, should be based on spatial social and physical scientific research of various kinds. Evaluations ex ante use implicit or explicit research, including evaluations ex post. Here again we see the traditional division of work. Other sciences supply knowledge to urban & regional designers.

Hulsbergen and Van der Schaaf (2002: 159 ff.) point out that evaluation ex ante can also take place with goal-oriented design.

Because in means-oriented design no goals or objectives are made explicitly in advance, means-oriented designers run the risk of circular arguments when analysing probable effects. Problem conception is, after all, a precondition in means-oriented design, too. The collection of information cannot be done at random, nor can an endless number of alternatives be designed

Research by Hamel (1990: 227) revealed that expected effects continually play a role during the design phase: in contrast to what is suggested by models of design methods, 'evaluation' is not a separate phase in a design process.

5.2.2 The creative-craft field in the light of a development into a practical science

Although the procedures of architectural and urban design have become the object of scientific research, the resulting design is regarded, apart from a few exceptions, as a unique, creative achievement. Each design site is after all unique and the creativity of the specific designer, his/her originality and the cultural value of the proposed changes are considered to be incompatible with an intrinsic scientific approach. The observation of Punter and Carmona that "Many 'designers' continue to prefer to see design as an intuitive, largely visual and artistic process ... [and that they] have little time for the view of design as a problem-solving process" (1997: XIX) cannot come as a surprise to confreres. The field of urban design, whose lavish use of terms such as 'paradigm (shift)', 'theory' and 'laboratory' instead of doctrine (shift), view and studio, suggests scientific aspirations, cannot yet outgrow its traditional craft status as long as the uniqueness of each design avoids generalisation.

The prospects of being able to develop urban design into a practical science are equally poor when on holds that design and science are two different worlds.

Examples of the pseudo scientific use of the terms 'paradigm' and 'theory':

"You are then faced with the paradigms that are implied in Dutch spatial planning. It is always the case, for example, that building is carried out against an already existing core." *(Heeling in Nio & Reijndorp 1997: 131)*

"Although here [the 20th century-itk] I believe there has been a change of paradigm at least three times, from the classic 19th century city, to an unfolded city of CIAM, to a revaluation of the urban area and the integration of functions ... as counterpoints in an expanding and mobile urban environment." *(J.Schrijnen talking at the inaugural meeting of the BNSP 6 June 1998).*

"That asymmetric profile characterizes the paradigm change." *(Cusveller 2000: 34).*

"On the basis of research ... three approaches to urban-design theory can be identified: (1) figure-ground theory; (2) linkage theory; and (3) place theory." *(Trancik 1986: 97).*

"We architects and city planners have reached the point of inventing all sorts of theories to justify the immorality of our clients." *(Oriol Bohigas,* quoted in Rodermond *1997: 25).*

According to Bunge the decisive difference between craft knowledge and regulations on the one hand and action based on technical knowledge on the other, is that the effectiveness of the action can be substantiated scientifically (Luyten & Hoefnagel 1995: 113).

It is interesting to see the term 'paradigm' in connection with this in the final report of the Commissie Midterm Review 2000 Faculty of Architecture (TUD): "Generally speaking it seems that the good results [in education-itk] are based on exemplary creative education, whereby the paradigm of the master-apprentice relationship[49] plays an important role, at the expense of the innovative contribution of the research." (2001: Prologue).

Urban design education, as is the case with architecture education at universities, takes place largely in studios where students learn the 'trade' under the supervision of design lecturers. The views of the lecturers that the students choose (or encounter) determine to a large degree the content of the education and the evaluation of the studio products (Bakel 1995).

"This recognition of individual achievement can easily give rise to the cult of the individual. In educational terms it led to the articled pupillage system of teaching design. A young architect would put himself under the care of a recognised master of the art and hope that as the result of an extended period of this service he would acquire the skills peculiar to this individual master.... The great architects of the modern movement such as le Corbusier or Frank Lloyd Wright not only designed ... but also behaved and wrote eccentrically about their work." (Lawson 1990: 18/19).

The views of the lecturer generally remain implicit as does the knowledge that the lecturer brings, and are seldom subject to public debate[50]. Both personal and social biases play a role (see Section 3.1).

The expression 'master-apprentice relationship' refers to the time when knowledge was passed on in guilds which were at the same time trade associations. Important to the transfer of this knowledge were the views of the master and historical examples. These days the master is called a professor or mentor and his examples are recorded in books and collections of plans (Risselada 1993; Bekkering, Van Ees, Bekkering & Jansen 2002). There are networks of designers who refer to one another, who have had the same teachers or a teacher/pupil relationship, who write joint articles and quote one another[51]. They tend to distance themselves from the work of their predecessors. To conclude the study the 'apprentice' submits a 'masterpiece' (graduation project; Masters Thesis). This has to be presented with conviction, without revealing any weak spots. Lecturers, in addition to their university work, are usually active or have been active in their field. The code of conduct of the Dutch organization of urban designers and planners (BNSP, September 2000) stipulates that members must respect their colleagues and cause no harm to their professional reputation and activities (art.4.b); in the event of publicly criticizing the work of a colleague that colleague must be informed (in advance if possible) (art.4.c) (www.bnsp.nl (04-2003))

"[This] principle is founded upon the idea of collegiality. The 'honour of the position' has since the guild system been an important component of the regulations for professional associations." (Comment in leading article in *NRC-Handelsblad*, 22-8-98).

".... guild regulations set down ....in minute detail how the craft must be executed. These regulations (which are both of a technical and moral nature) are transferred from master to apprentice and journeyman and forbid the individual craftsman to use his/her own technical discoveries for his/her own benefit." (Luyten & Hoefnagels 1995: 112). (See also note 49)

An educational and working climate in which it is not common for account to be given of a design; this design often as a result of the lack of explicit intentions cannot be evaluated for effectiveness; the validity of assertions can be derived merely from the status of the speaker, (Krabbendam 2001: 198)[52]; debates on professional views are avoided rather than sought;

a major part of the subject matter consists of descriptions of historical designs; due to the individual focus of graduate projects there is hardly any accumulation of knowledge; and a critical view of personal work is not encouraged, is not the most fruitful climate for a scientific development of the discipline.

It is not totally without irony that the university *'propedeuse-(kandidaats)-doctoraal'* model is now being replaced in the Netherlands by the Anglo-Saxon 'bachelor-master' model. One meaning of the term 'bachelor' is 'a junior member of a trade-guild' (Shorter Oxford English Dictionary 1988). The term 'master' of course also refers to the guild system.

Based on interviews with a large number of Dutch urban planners Nio and Reijndorp suggest that "in the last twenty-five years urban planning and design has not been a 'learning' discipline. (---). Urban planning and design no longer has 'a body of learning' that grows constantly. This is also seen in the lack of self-reflection." (1997: 245). "The one-sided emphasis on the craft is standing in the way of the development of urban planning as a discipline," writes Cusveller (1998: 11). This reiterates in other words what the American Rapoport expressed 25 years ago: "In fact the absence of evaluation, and hence a cumulative body of knowledge about buildings and cities, has been a major weakness of the design endeavour." (1977: 5). "Urban planning and design," observed Nio and Reijndorp (1997: 244) "have had a strong pragmatic impact in the Netherlands. In Dutch urban & regional design the emphasis is on realization. The generation of knowledge is practically always connected with concrete projects. (---) In actual fact knowledge development occurs within the delineation of the project." Hulsbergen suggests in connection with this that if architects, and especially urban & regional designers, dissociate themselves too much from societal problems, withdrawing themselves to the 'formal', then they will learn insufficiently from their experiences (1992: 13). I for that matter have already stated that the acquisition of practical knowledge is not the way to develop a practical-scientific discipline (Section 3.2.4).

Incidentally, in this characterisation of the discipline of urban design there are similarities with the views of Kuhn on the conducting of science and its disciplinary matrix: a closed community of teacher/ students, networks of researchers, who refer to one another, have had the same teachers, have written joint articles and quote one another. "Not 'truth' but 'power' is the decisive factor here," suggests Gerard de Vries (1984: 137). In Section 3.4.2 I rejected the scientific view of Kuhn. The lack or undesirability of scientific controversy within a group slows down scientific progress[53]. The use of the term 'paradigm' by urban & regional designers, however, does become more comprehensible.

5.3 Design research

"Then most certainly," I said, "such men would hold that the truth is nothing other than the shadows of artificial things." [a]

(Plato, *Republic*: book VII)

Under the creative-craft view of urban & regional design, research is considered either as a matter of sciences that supply knowledge to designers or as empirical design research. Since both object and site are seen as non-recurrent, it implies a primarily ideographic approach to science, similar to that taken in geography and history[54]. Ideographic research is descriptive and/or analytical in nature, sometimes in a comparative sense. Sometimes also contextual explanations are given. Only when there is a systematic approach and an explicit knowledge framework can this research be qualified as scientific (see Section 3.1). An informal collection of plans (e.g. Bekkering et al. 2002) does not meet this requirement, neither do reference images often used, relevantly or otherwise, by urban designers to clarify the intention of a design (Klaasen 2000a: 35 ff.). Examples of scientifically sound design research are Smook 1984, Boer & Lambert 1987, Broadbent 1990, Urhahn & Bobic 1994 (Fig.5-7).

Lynch on illustrative images: "Designing occurs in still another mode: 'illustrative designs' show how an area might look and work if reshaped. Because they are not complete specifications and are not directed to any single decision maker, they can be produced with relative speed." ... "Indeed, they are often carelessly done, without reference to the real limitations and functions of a place..." (1976: 51).

In Section 3.2.3 I suggested that unique wholes - spatial systems - are composed of reproducible building blocks. In the analysis of designs, the focus on similarities between designs can lead to the distinguishing of types, a categorisation based on certain object characteristics abstracted from their specific context (Fig.5-8 to 5-11). In my terminology the concept of 'type' is much the same as 'principle' or theoretical model' (see Section 2.3). Types are *a posteriori* models and theoretical models are *a priori* models (see Section 3.3). The latter are discussed in Section 5.4.

The term 'type' (*genus*) can already be seen in Vitruvius's work. He uses it to identify various kinds of classical columns (1999a: XIII). New life was breathed into the concept of type in the early nineteen century by the French architect Quatremère de Quincy, who described it as follows: "One ...applies the word *type* in architecture to certain general forms and the characteristics of the building to which they have been applied. (---) No one can ignore the many pieces of furniture, utensils, seats and clothes which have their necessary *type* in our needs and our nature." (Quoted by the English architect Geoffrey Broadbent 1990: 91 - Broadbent's italics).

Quatremère de Quincy, followed by later sympathizers such as architects Rossi and Argan, expressly does not call a 'type' a 'model', considering his view that a model is 'an object that should be repeated as it is.' (ibid.: 91).

The term 'type' in architecture and urban & regional design shows strong similarities with the term *Idealtype* introduced by the German economist and sociologist Max Weber (1864-1920). An *Idealtype* is a concept without claims to reality, but which has an empirical basis. It is formed by exaggerating or accentuating one or more attributes that are perceptible in reality.

---

[a] Translation Allan Bloom (1968) (http://www.vrc.iastate.edu/why.html (04-2003))

The type so constructed functions as a criterion for comparison. Phenomena corresponding exactly to the *Idealtype* are seldom if ever encountered. It bears no relation to a statistical average. It is an analytical tool. The *Idealtype* has a theoretical basis (Bertels & Nauta 1969: 79).

MIXED-USE AREAS WITH A THEMATIC ACCENT

Mixed and flexible working areas:
mixture of offices, business premises, catering, education etc with limited residential accomodation.

bruto f.s.i. area
0,8 - 2,7

netto f.s.i. block
1,9 - 4,0

mixed-use and dominant theme
commercial functions

residential percentage
0% or 10 - 40%

building and unit scale
freedom

MIXED-USE RESIDENTIAL AREAS WITH STACKED UNITS

Urban residential areas, high density, with primarily stacked units (duplex apartments, apartment buildings), multifunctional, primarily small scale, coupling with park.

bruto f.s.i. area
1,0 - 2,2

netto f.s.i. block
1,2 - 3,0

mixed-use and dominant theme
living and working at home

residential percentage
50 - 80%

building and unit scale
large scale max. 10%

Fig.5-7 Example from a descriptive design research project (Urhahn & Bobic 1994: 34)

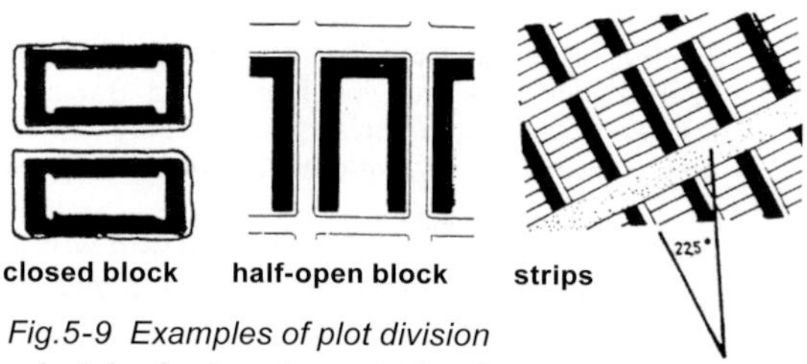

Fig.5-9 Examples of plot division principles (verkavelingsprincipes) *(Westrik 1993: 21 ff.).*

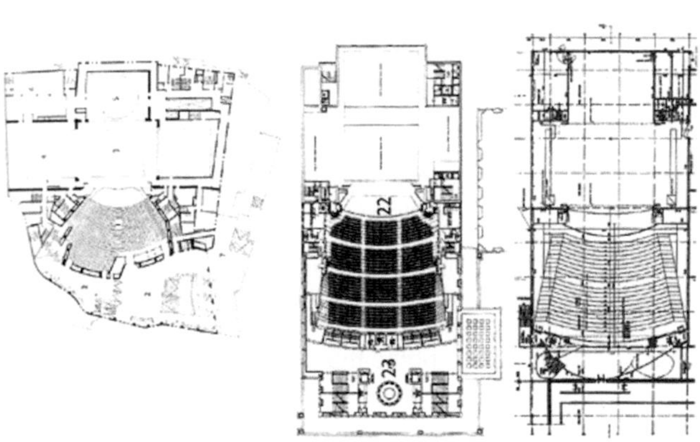

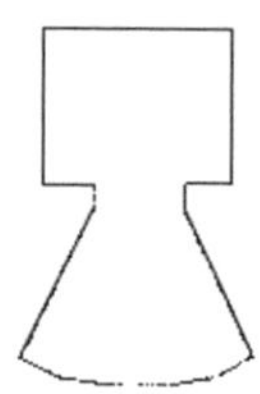

Fig.5-8 An example of typology from architecture. Three theatres of the same type: Aalto, Floor plan theatre in Essen; Rossi, floor plan theatre in Genua; OMA, floor plan Dance theatre, The Hague. The 'type', far right, comprises a framed proscenium and a shell-shaped auditorium. (Leupen 2002: 112/113).

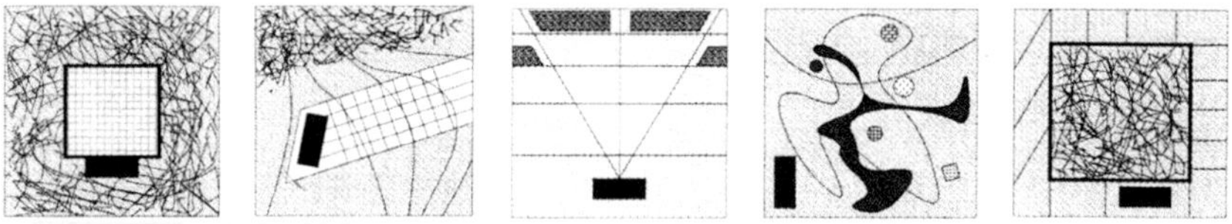

Fig.5-10 Nature images throughout the centuries. This is a cultural historical typology. From left to right: Hortus conclusus (enclosed garden); Renaissance garden; Baroque garden; Romantic garden and contemporary nature-culture. (Cate 2000: 112/113)

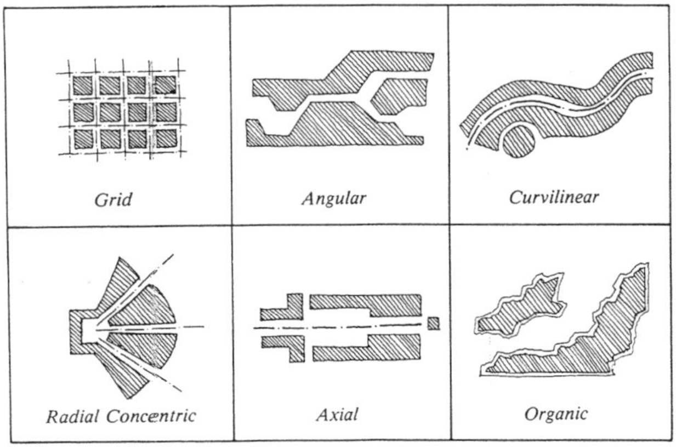

Fig.5-11 Six Typological Patterns of Solids and Void. "Most cities are built from combinations and permutations of these patterns as well as through the juxtaposition of larger and smaller patterns." (Trancik 1986: 101).

Design research, including typological research, contributes in practice primarily to the scientific body of knowledge of the history of urban & regional design. "To find urban design regarded in historic terms is not unusual, ..." (Schurch 1999: 13). Design research can only contribute to the body of knowledge of urban & regional design as a practical science when the crucial question "does it work" can be answered. The analysis should then concentrate on discovering the contextual conditions under which certain effects arise, in order to allow formulation of hypotheses that enable ex post evaluation to be carried out: now or in the future. To give an example: with regard to types of plot division (Fig.5-9), it is not enough to just collect a number of concrete examples (= a plan collection, unscientific), nor to describe, analyse, categorise and possibly explain these examples (= design research), nor to abstract them from their spatial context and carry out typological research. One must also study what effects a certain type of plot division has under which conditions (Fig.5-12). In the words of Lynch: "To some degree we can form judgements drawn from such different regions as Los Angeles, Stockholm and Paris, but these judgements are necessarily distorted by various cultural and environmental disparities. Possibly we can study certain partial aspects of city form, such as the effects of varying density or the varying composition of centres." ((1961) 1990: 61). And "...this particular concept can be analysed in terms of appropriate situation and expected performance." (1981: 283). Hillier and Hanson describe their theory on the social logic of space as "a descriptive theory of how spatial pattern can, and does, in itself carry social information and content." (1984: XI).

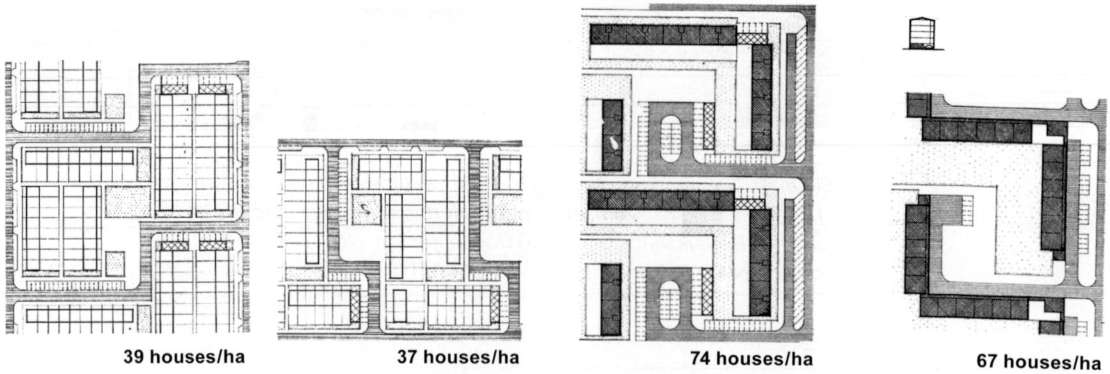

Fig.5-12 The two plot division types on the left lead to low net densities; the two types on the right lead to average net densities (Heimans 1965). Heimans observes that a lower housing density will generally lead to an increased quality of the living environment. However, a higher housing density has a beneficial effect on the accessibility of facilities. This concerns the analysis of effects in relation to cyclical societal processes with a small temporal grain.

Design research makes much use of exploratory spatial models. We could call this 'design research by drawing'. Meyer (2002) mentions as example the study of Casper van der Hoeven and Jos Louwe *Amsterdam Stedelijk Bouwwerk* (Amsterdam Urban Structure) (1985):Fig.5-13. The term 'research by design' is incorrect here, in view of the meaning of 'design',i.e. to visualise something that has not (yet) been 'the case'. The example given in Fig.5-13 involved discovering the way an Amsterdam neighbourhood had been structured.

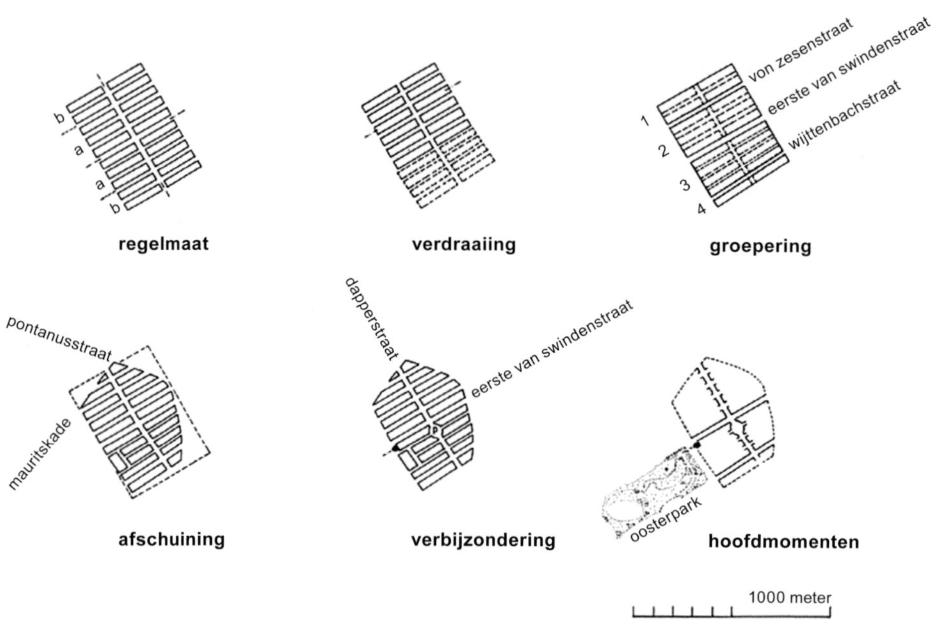

Fig.5-13 An example of design research by drawing. These six figures summarize the results of the research that Van der Hoeven and Louwe carried out into the design principles of the Amsterdam neighbourhood 'Dapperbuurt'. "In the six drawings they show what the basic principles were leading to the final spatial structure of this area." (Meyer 2002: 127).

5.4 Practical science: research by design

"Objects in cities - whether they are buildings, streets, parks, districts, landmarks, or anything else - can have radically differing effects, depending upon the circumstances and contexts in which they exist."

(Jane Jacobs 1961, *The Death and Life of Great American Cities*: 373)

5.4.1 Theoretical design

A practical science has the application of science as its object of research and is multidisciplinary in character. Relevant questions are whether it 'works', i.e. whether it can operate effectively in specific situations on the basis of knowledge generated, and what effects arise under which conditions, that is to say, what possibilities for use are created (see Section 3.2.4). It must be possible to ask these questions, which implies that a practical-scientific approach to design presumes a process-oriented approach (Section 4.7).

Instead of integrating scientific knowledge of various kinds in a particular situation in order to arrive at a (proposal for a) physical urban system, knowledge is generated by dissociating objects from any specific situation (Fig.5-14). In this way generalized knowledge is generated: a practical-scientific body of knowledge for urban & regional design, though with its limitations as summarized in Section 3.5.

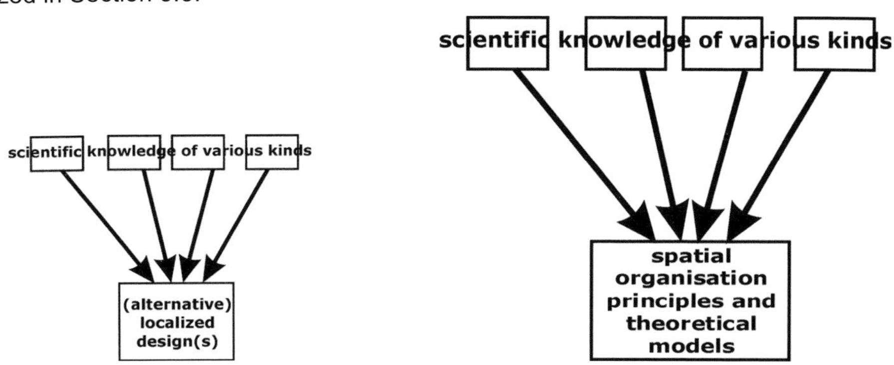

Fig.5-14 On the left the representation of a design process in which scientific knowledge is used directly in a localized design (Fig.5-1 from Section 5.2). On the right the representation of a process in which this knowledge is integrated in spatial principles and theoretical models.

By manipulating elements, element-attributes and their mutual relationships, spatial organization principles (*ruimtelijk-ordenende beginselen*) are constructed. " ... we can begin to build up theory-based descriptions of the basic elements in design. These basic elements include ranges of activities, movements, perception motivated actions, social intercourse patterns, spaces and the environmental criteria that will satisfy a classified range of possible uses, ..." (Hillier, Musgrove & O'Sullivan 1972: 29-3-13). Partly on the basis of these spatial organization principles, theoretical models for physical urban systems (*a priori* models) can then be designed. For various contextual conditions the effects that occur can be substantiated in this stage without having to attribute a value judgement. The reasoning is based on logic, mathematics and the results of empirical research, including knowledge gained from evaluations *ex post*. The latter type of knowledge should not only be used when plans (localized designs) are evaluated, in the form of checklists (Thieme, Van der Voordt & Van Wegen 1989), but must be introduced during the design process (see also Hamel 1990). Combinations of 'compositional means' (Section 4.5.2) are used to examine which objectives can be achieved: goal and means-oriented research are interwoven.

Another form of research by design could be the investigation of the possibilities, limitations and effects of building on certain types of sites, for example in areas prone to earthquakes or in Buddhist communities, for objects denoted as unspecified. I say 'could be' as I am not yet aware of any generic research into situational resources.

The manipulation of elements, element-attributes and the relationships between them, to develop theoretical models with the help of series of exploratory models, is in itself a form of design: the construction of objects that in theory 'could possibly be the case'. The term 'design' is then no longer only associated with making a specific design for a specific place. The design process is used as a method of research: research by design.

In a theoretical model, spatial organization principles - which should be regarded as building blocks - are manipulated interdependently. In organized complex systems such as physical urban systems elements, element-attributes and relationships cannot vary independently from one another, but certain variables vary simultaneously 'in subtly interconnected ways' (J.Jacobs 1961: 433).

Jane Jacobs gives an example of a neighbourhood park. "How much the park is used depends, in part, upon the park's own design. But even this partial influence of the park's design upon the park's use depends, in turn, on who is around to use the park, and when, and this in turn depends on uses of the city outside the park itself. (---) In turn, these city uses near the park and their combinations depend on still other factors, such as the mixture of age in buildings, the size of the blocks in the vicinity, and so on ..." (ibid.)

5.4.2 Spatial organization principles and theoretical models

Spatial organization principles

Spatial organization principles are the basic elements, or building blocks, for theoretical models. These principles are in part self evident, in part verified empirically and in part hypothesized (substantiated hypotheses). There are relationships between principles, and not all principles can be visualized.

Vitruvius worked with spatial organization principles. An example: "...if the directions of the streets be parallel to those of the winds, the latter will rush through them with greater violence, since from occupying the whole space of the surrounding country they will be forced up through a narrow pass. Streets or public ways ought therefore to be so set out, that when the winds blow hard their violence may be broken against the angles of the different divisions of the city, and thus dissipated." (Fig.5-15) (I.6.8; http://www.ukans.edu/history/index/europe/ancient_rome/E/Roman/Texts/Vitruvius/home.html (04-2003)).

Organization principles can be either universal in nature (applicable always and everywhere) or non-universal but non-local (a term from Radder 1996). Universal organization principles can be falsified. A distinction can, moreover, be made between functional and formal principles. The 24-hour biorhythm (visualised in Fig.4-33) is a universal, functional spatial-

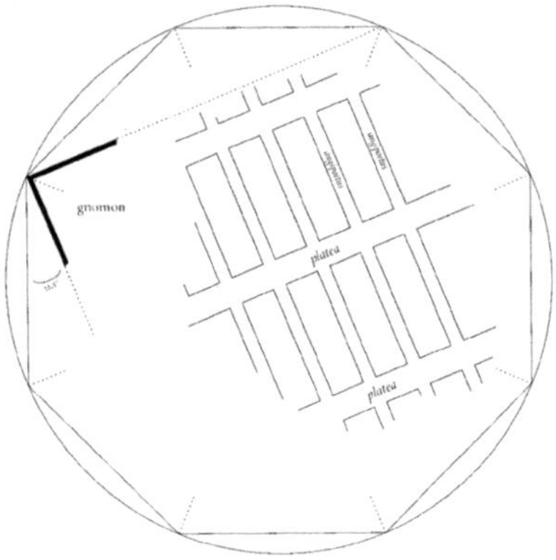

Fig.5-15 The orientation of the street plan (Vitruvius (About 25 BC) 1999b: 49): non-universal functional spatial-ecological organization principle.

ecological organization principle. Fig.5-16, from Cullen, illustrates a universal formal spatial-ecological organization principle; Fig.5-17 and Fig. 5-18 show universal organization principles developed by Salingaros and Doxiadis, respectively. The example of Fig.5-19, from Jane Jacobs (1961), is non-universal, functional, socio-cultural/economic. The patterns or environmental structures of Christopher Alexander (1977) are also spatial organization principles. Fig.5-20 shows two such principles.

Alexander uses the term 'hypothesis' in connection with his patterns (1977: XV). However, his patterns are normative, cannot be tested and sometimes rely upon circular reasoning.

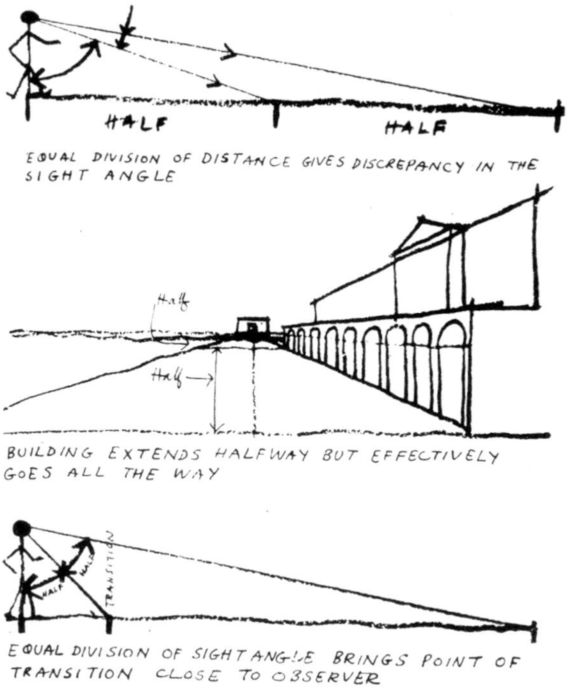

Fig.5-16 An example of human perception (Cullen 1971: 224): a universal formal spatial-ecological organization principle.

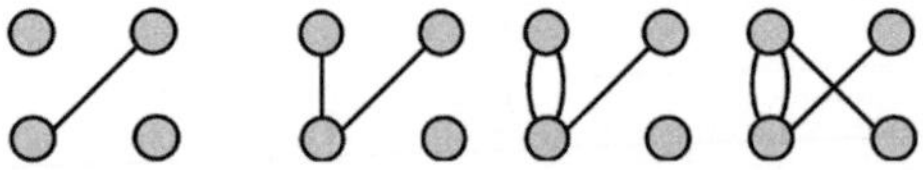

Highly simplified illustration of how random pair wise connections between N nodes link about 80 % of them at some point after N/2 steps. Here, three out of four nodes are linked together after two steps.

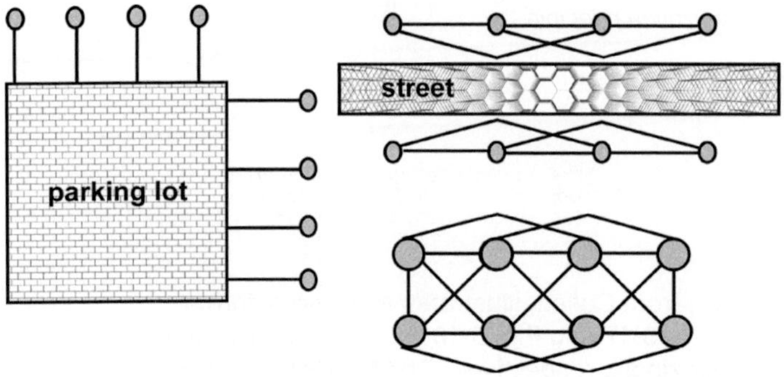

Fig.5-17 Spatial organisation principles from a mathematical viewpoint. Connections in retail areas: the worst case is when each store is connected only to the parking lot; better is a situation in which stores connect on separate sides of a street; the most successful solution connects all stores by pedestrian paths. (Salingaros 1998: 59; 64. See also www.math.utsa.edu/sphere/salingar/index.html (04-2003))

Fig.5-18 One of the many organization principles identified by Doxiadis (1968: 340; see also.: 283 ff.)

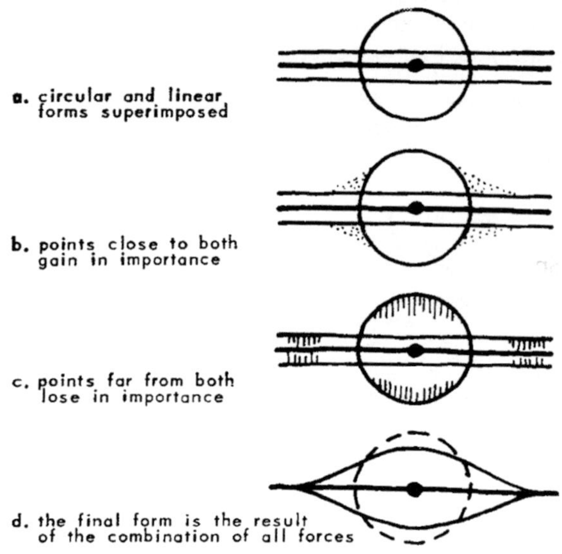

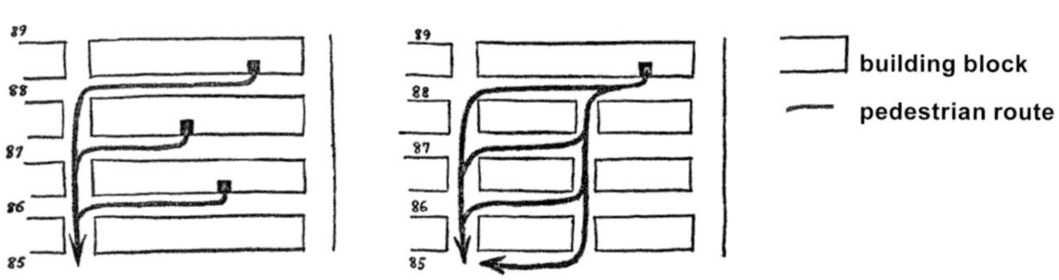

Fig.5-19 A non-universal, functional, socio-cultural/economic, spatial organization principle. The plot division in the left principle concentrates the flow of pedestrians, whereas the principle on the right spreads out this flow. Depending on the spatial, socio-cultural and economic context the effects of the two principles are valued differently. Jane Jacobs, the source of this example (1961: 179/181), argues in the context of New York for the right principle in view of the resulting reduction of the social isolation of certain streets. However, under other circumstances a concentration of pedestrian routes may be preferred, for example when considering personal safety. Having too great a spread of the flow of pedestrians can also result in insufficient location factors for certain collective functions at neighbourhood level.

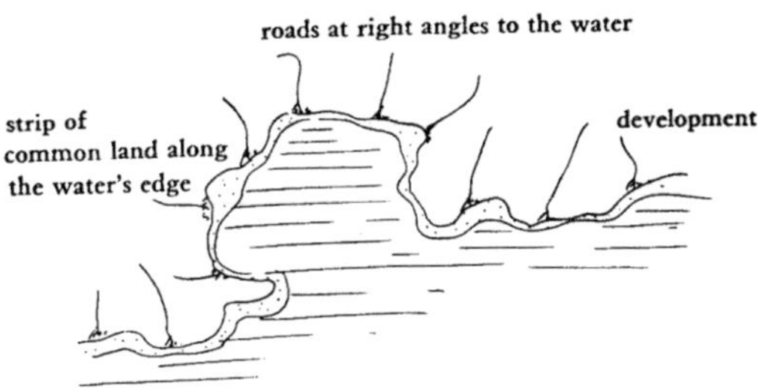

"When natural bodies occur near human settlements, treat them with great respect. Always preserve a strip of common land, immediately beside the water, and allow dense settlements to come right down to the water only at infrequent intervals along the water's edge." *(Alexander 1977: 137)*

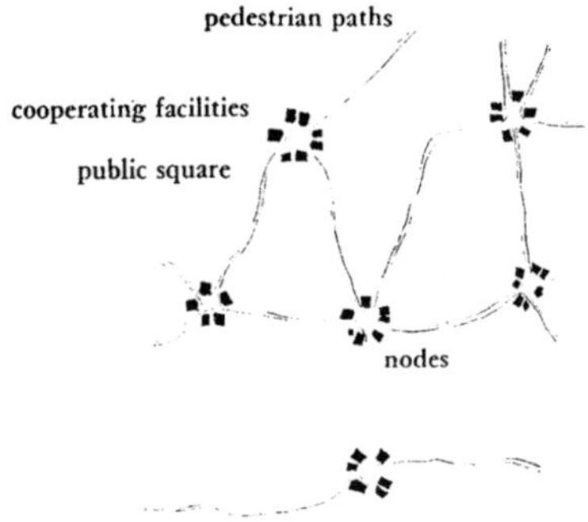

"Create nodes of activity throughout the community, spread about 300 yards apart. First identify those existing spots in the community where action seems to concentrate itself. Then modify the layout of the paths in the community to bring as many of them through these spots as possible. This makes each spot function as a 'node' in the path network. Then at the centre of each node, make a small public square, and surround it with a combination of community facilities and shops which are mutually supportive." (ibid.: 154)

Fig.5-20 Two of the 'patterns' from Alexander (1977).

Probably universal spatial-ecologic organization principles have recently been published in the Nationaal pakket Duurzame Stedebouw (National package Durable Urban Planning and Design), published by the Nationaal Duurzaam Bouwen centre in Utrecht (1999). Fig.5-21 shows an example from this. In all these examples the physical urban system is regarded as a component of the urban system as a whole, and all these examples refer to small-grained cyclic processes.

Spatial theoretical models

Theoretical models are not ready-made templates for creating localized designs. In that regard they are comparable to the 'types' from Section 5.3. However, it is not observation that leads to theoretical models, as is the case with types in empirical science, but rather (conceptual) manipulation. Theoretical models guarantee, in so far as the theoretical knowledge extends, certain explicit, substantiable qualities of a spatial-ecological, socio-cultural, economic-technical and administrative-organizational character.

An example in the realm of architecture in regard to a substantiable quality of administrative-organizational nature, is a model-based cost-quality study of schools and penitentiary institutions carried out jointly by the Dutch government department responsible for their construction and Delft University of Technology (Jonge 1986).

Niek de Boer points to the use of a spatial theoretical model in the form of a prototype made in order to control costs when making a localized design (1990: 124).

Theoretical models bridge the applicability gap discussed in Section 5.2.1. They form the 'guidances on priorities or patterns of application' which Hillier, Musgrove and O'Sullivan observed were lacking (1972: 29-3-5). As mentioned in Section 4.6.2 these are first and foremost structure models, with associated functional characterizations of bounded area, line and point elements and essential indications for visual design.

Spatial organization principles and theoretical models should be accompanied by a scale indication. Within the noted scale the models can be qualitative or quantitative in nature. Quantified theoretical models contain measurements and numbers: maximum and minimum distances, potential user bases housing densities, etc. Examples of quantitative and qualitative models are shown in Fig.5-22, 5-23 and 5-24 (see also Fig.4-42: Mobilopolis).

VERBINDEN MET BUITENGEBIED OF NIET

'Wig'
Park Sonsbeek, Arnhem

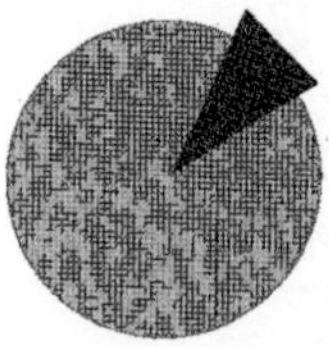

Natuur in de stad
- Hoe beter verbonden met kerngebieden, hoe robuuster het is.
- Geconcentreerd groen is makkelijk te beheren.
- Waarde als fourageer- en rustgebied voor fauna is afhankelijk van de omvang.
- Inrichting ten behoeve van natuur met recreatief medegebruik.
- Stedelijk en landelijk watersysteem kan worden verweven.

'Park'
Vondelpark, Amsterdam

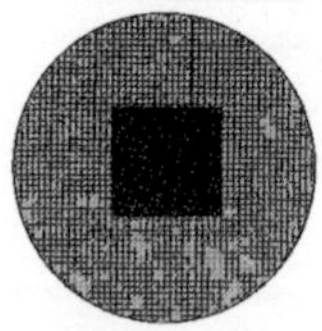

Stadsnatuur
- Hoe groter het oppervlak, hoe robuuster het is.
- Geconcentreerd groen is makkelijk te beheren.
- Waarde als fourageer- en rustgebied voor dieren is beperkt.
- Inrichting ten behoeve van recreatief gebruik.

SCHEIDEN OF VERWEVEN GROENE STEDELIJKE RUIMTE

'Uitloopgebied'

Natuur in de stad
- Recreatief uitloopgebied.
- Green belt: buffer tussen stad en ommeland.
- Zou aaneengroeien en uitbreiden van stedelijke gebieden beperken.
- Inrichting ten behoeve van recreatieve waarden met plaatselijk hoge natuurwaarden.
- Stedelijk en landelijk watersysteem kan worden gescheiden.

'Netwerk'
Plan Rose, Rotterdam

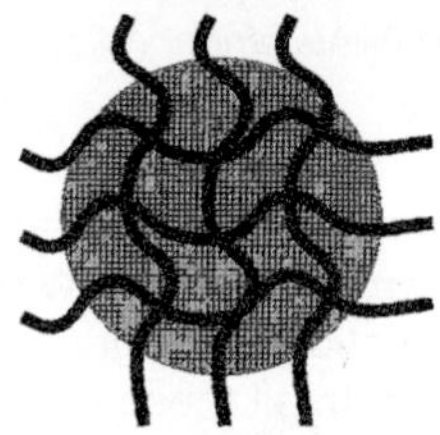

Stadsnatuur
- Combinatie van blauw-groen-recreatief netwerk.
- Waarde als migratie-route voor niet-watergebonden dieren is beperkt en sterk afhankelijk van inrichting, breedte en barrières.
- Inrichting ten behoeve van recreatieve waarden.
- Stedelijk en landelijk watersysteem kan worden verweven.

VORMGEVEN ECOLOGISCHE CORRIDORS

'Verbindingszone'
Groene corridor, Houten

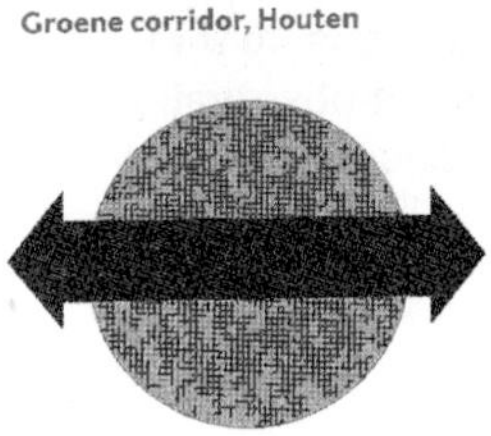

Natuur in de stad
- Als te behouden of versterken ecologische waarden een minimale breedte vereisen. De ordegrootte is afhankelijk van indicatorsoorten.
- Inrichting ten behoeve van natuurwaarden; drukte-zonering ten behoeve van recreatief medegebruik.
- Stedelijk en landelijk watersysteem is verweven.

'Stapstenen'

Stadsnatuur
- Als continue ruimte niet mogelijk
- Waarde als migratieroute afhankelijk van doelsoort en van barrières tussen de stapstenen.
- De waarde als refugium is afhankelijk van lokale omstandigheden (onderlegger).
- Inrichting afgestemd op natuurwaarden.
- De omvang kan uiteenlopen van parkenreeks tot bomenrij.

Fig.5-21 Spatial-ecological organization principles with their effects (Nieuwe Gracht, stad milieu landschap 1999)

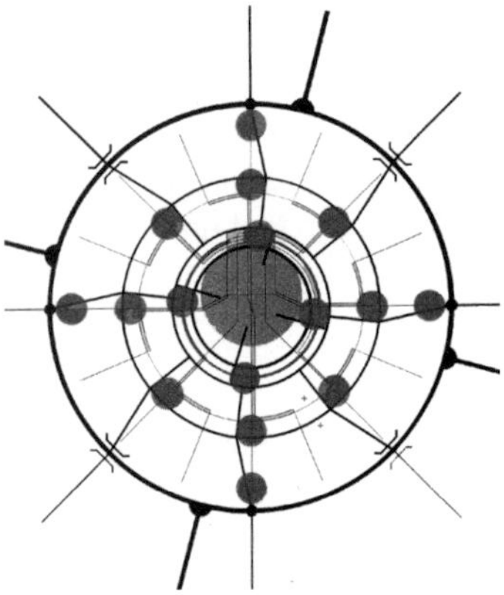

Fig.5-22 A qualitative theoretical model for a city (radius ca 4,5 km) with a centre and subcentres, tramways and roads) (Boer 1994: appendix D).

Fig. 5-23 Doxiadis' qualitative theoretical model 'Dynamopolis' (1968: 373).

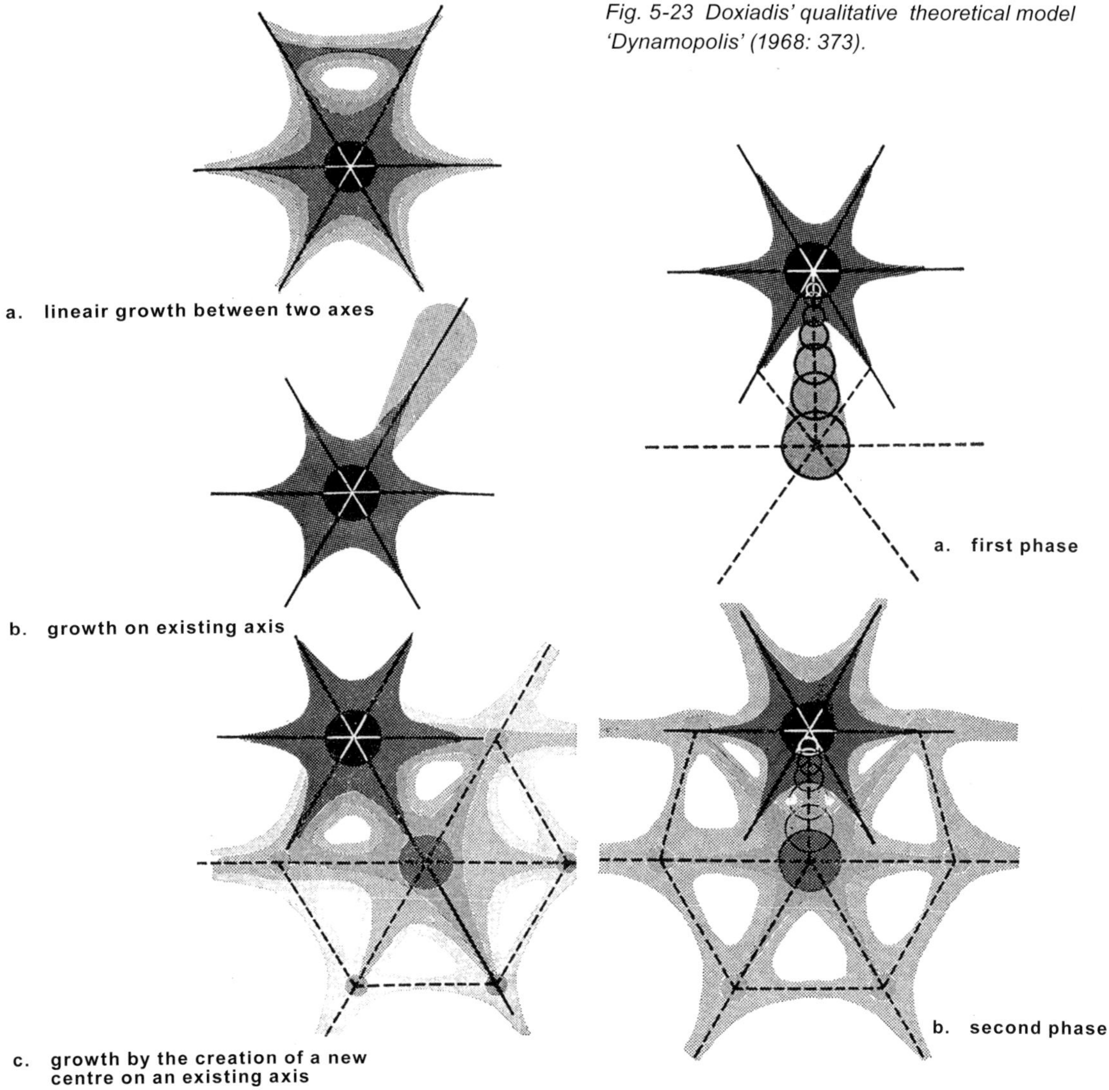

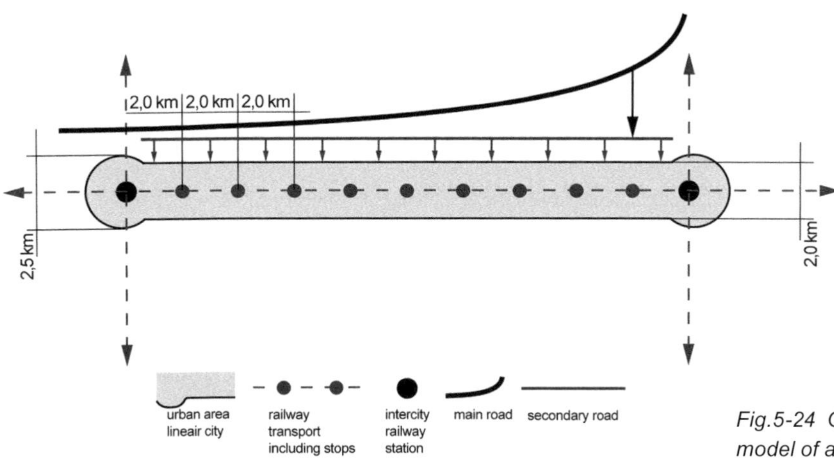

Fig.5-24 Quantitative theoretical model of a linear city.

5.4.3 Research by design: heuristics, creative abduction, plausible reasoning

One of the conclusions of the Chapter on science (Section 3.5) was that the research method employed by Imre Lakatos seemed to be a good guiding principle for the formulation of theories in urban & regional design, in view of the important role that heuristics, creative abduction and plausible reasoning, as well as the manipulation of conceptual models, have in this method. Lakatos, moreover, made use, as do urban & regional designers, of spatial models: "... conceptualisation is essential in initiating synthesis-oriented visual-spatial thinking processes." (Muller 1990: 142).

Lakatos' (and Popper's) approach has been compared before to the process of design: Hillier, Musgrove and O'Sullivan (1972: 29-3-4ff.), and following in their footsteps Muller (1990: 12ff.; 138 ff.). Gerard de Vries (1993: 4) refers to D. Lewin, who published an article on this in the first volume of Design Studies, in 1979. They all referred to localized design.

An essential concept in Lakatos' view on conducting science is the 'research programme'. A research programme comprises both an intrinsic theory (or chain of intrinsic theories), whereby a distinction is made between a 'hard core' and a 'protective belt', as well as a method of research. The method of research is also theoretical. It is neither descriptive nor prescriptive (see Section 3.4.1). Lakatos suggests: "My account implies a new criterion of demarcation between 'mature science', consisting of research programmes, and 'immature science' consisting of a mere patched up pattern of trial and error." (1978: 87). Although he alludes here to empirical science, this applies to the distinction that I made in Section 3.2.4 between practical science with the application of science as the object of research and the idea that practical science in practice would be acquired knowledge. The notion of 'trial and error' is applicable to the latter: functionalized research. "... all purely 'empirical' learning theories miss the heart of the problem." (ibid.: 38).

A report by Werkgroep Kenniswerving Bouwkunde (the 'Working Group on the Acquisition of Knowledge in Architecture') even claimed this as a major point: "Medicine and Law call for understanding. Architecture is primarily intervention. First do something, make a design, then see if it works." (Faculteit Bouwkunde TUD 1994b: 5).

For that matter the notion that intuitive design (always an implicit application of knowledge) can lay a claim to Popper's views on science regarding the development of hypotheses (context of discovery) does not take account of his views on the context of justification.

I regard the following as elements of the hard core of the research programme of the Chair of Urban & Regional design at the Delft University of Technology between 1985 and 1995:

- Viewing the built (future) reality as an open system;
- Approaching this physical urban system as an organized complex system[55];
- Viewing the physical urban system as part of the urban system as a whole;
- The fact that an element of this physical system derives its significance from its position in the system on the one hand and contributes to making the system what it is on the other;
- The distinguishing of various temporal grains in societal processes;
- The distinguishing of levels of scale within the physical urban system on the basis of societal processes that are characterised by a relatively small temporal grain;
- The consequently necessary cohesion between the system levels;
- The boundaries of design areas at various scales being defined on the bases of societal processes;

and

- Unlinking the design object from a specific design context;
- Regarding design not just in the usual sense but also as a method of research.

The essence of this research approach can be described as follows. Start with a number of basic elements of the proposed design object and manipulate them using organizational principles and other principles, in such a way that the resulting theoretical models of physical urban systems will by plausible reasoning be internally-consistent. In other words, the available formal and empirical knowledge will lead us to expect that these models will function stably when implemented.

Fig.5-25 shows an example at regional scale level.

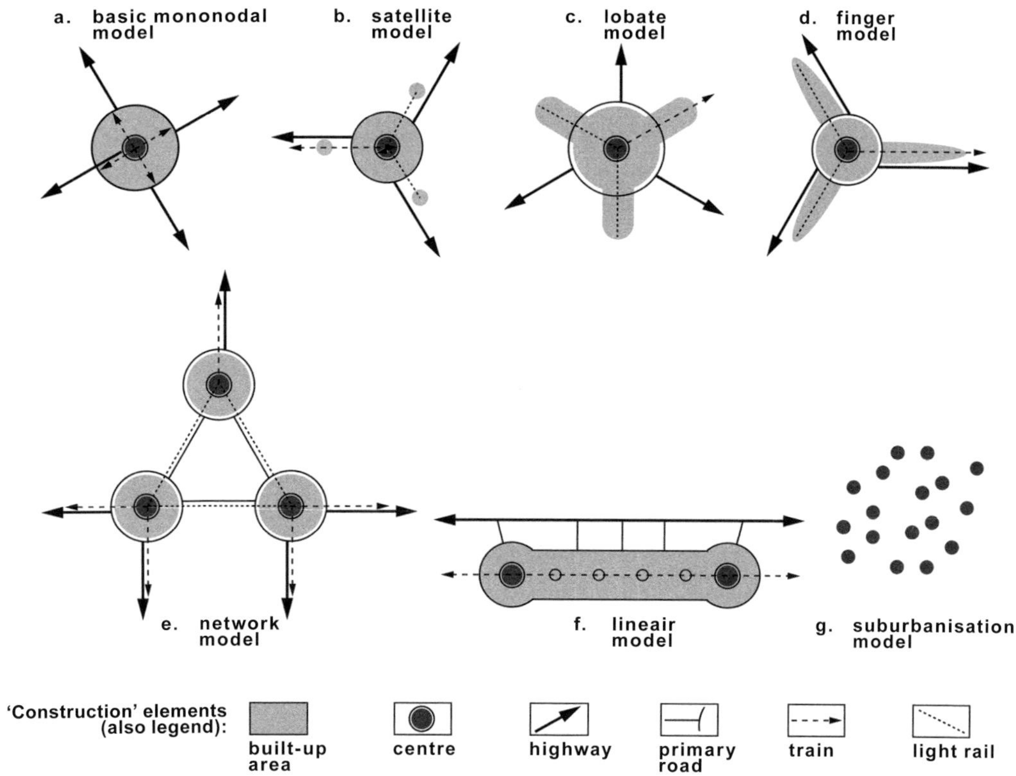

Fig.5-25 Basic elements for an urban-regional physical urban system and derived consistent basic theoretical models. The first four have one main centre and primarily a radial connection system. The difference between a finger and a lobe is that the main connection of a finger is a continuous connection and that the main connection of a lobe ends at the end of the lobe (continuous connections are located between the lobes, in the green wedges). The other two have more than one main centre[56]. The suburbanisation model is not a physical urban system (a to e: after M.Jacobs 2000: 160 ff.).

Contextual conditions and effect analyses then have to be carried out for these basic theoretical models. An example of this is illustrated in Fig.5-26.

The Lobate Model

specification:

Basic qualities: no interference from superregional transportation systems
short distance from home to natural surrounding
functional structure: radial

max radius central part depends on light-rail for short distances
max distance from center till border of urban area depends on light-rail for middle distances
max width of outer areas depends on max distance for non-motorized transport from home to green areas
minimal size of outer area depends on required exploitation of light-rail

examples: Amsterdam, Antwerp (both partly)

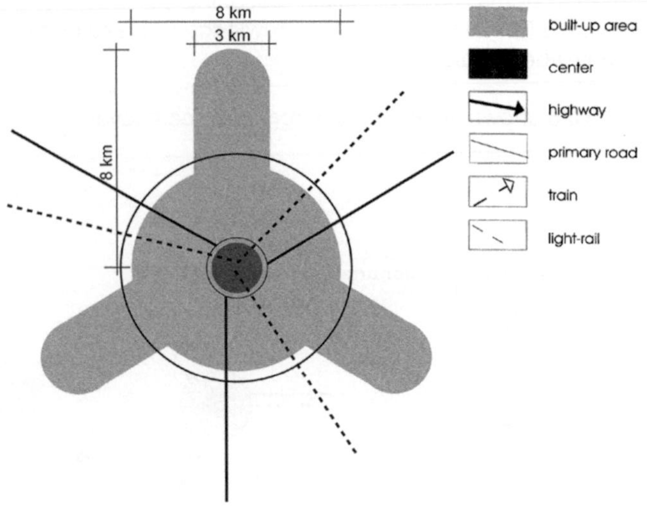

Fig.5-26 Analysis of a theoretical lobate model (M.Jacobs 2000: 160). The context (socio-cultural, spatial-ecological and economic -technological conditions) is that of West Europe.

The effect analysis can also take the form of an analysis of potentials, for example for a certain lifestyle, or such as in Fig.5-27, for the accessibility of stops/stations.

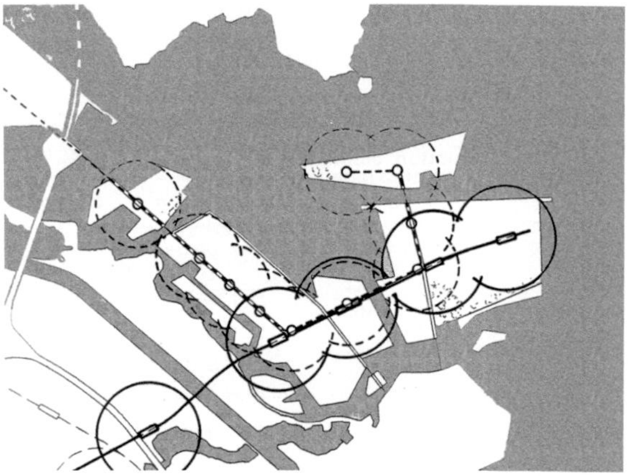

Fig.5-27 Map of the potential accessibility of planned stops on the light-rail system serving an eastward extension of Amsterdam into the IJmeer.

The fact that these basic theoretical models principles do occur in practice - often in combination - is shown in Fig.5-28.

Fig.5-28 In the Amsterdam region various theoretical models from Fig.5-25 can be identified.

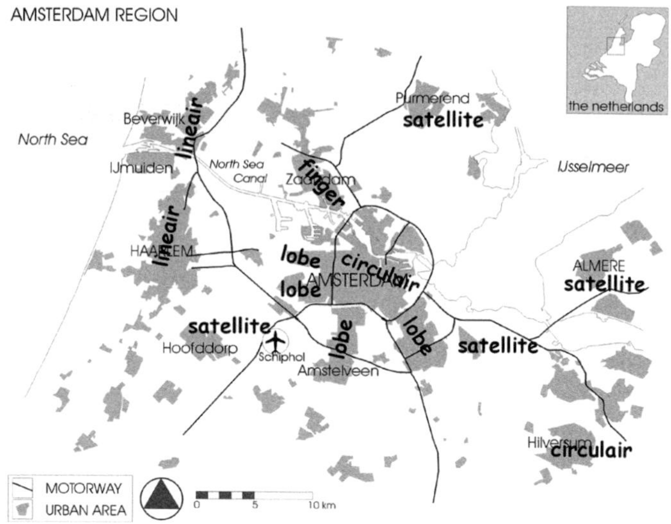

An example of an exploratory model study using the pattern-oriented approach, on the neighbourhood scale is shown in Fig.5-29. The effect analysis is restricted to residential density (making this also an example of a study into future possibilities) but the question 'does it work' cannot be answered on the basis of this analysis.

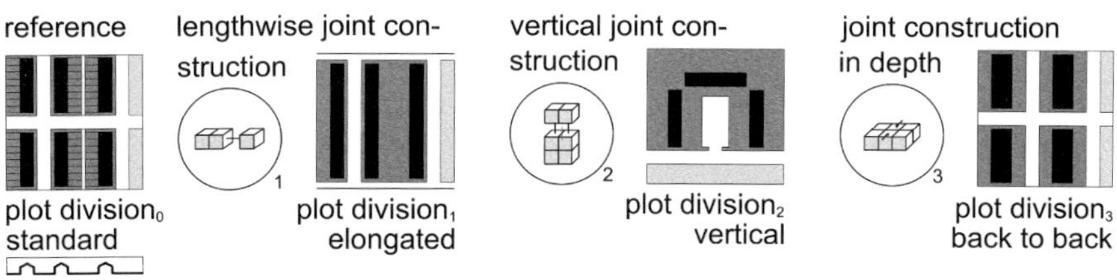

Fig.5-29 plot division transformations (Jong & Rosemann 2002: 40)

Analogies can help in deductive conjecture, for example when determining where to locate a subcentre in a lobe. Using the gravity model from physics one can, for example, reason that the more this centre shifts to the end of the lobe the greater the competitive advantage of the main centre: Fig.5-30. More over, all residents and visitors of the area of the lobe located 'behind' the subcentre will first come across the subcentre when moving towards the centre.

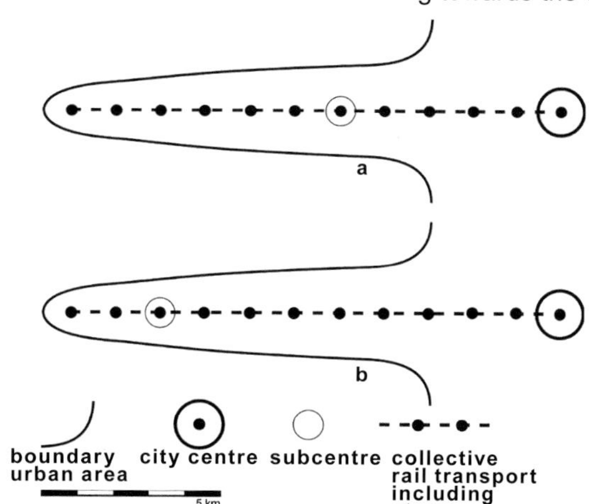

Fig.5-30 Two possible locations of a subcentre in an urban lobe. In the case of (a) the subcentre offers more competition to the main centre than in the case of (b).
No account is yet taken of travel by car: the less accessible the subcentre is locally and regionally by car, and the more expensive and limited the parking possibilities, the better the competitive position of the main centre.

On the analogy of a bicycle wheel it can be supposed that when a ring road (tangent) is constructed around a city as in Fig.5-25a with radial connections (the spokes) that are not strong enough: “things fall apart; the centre cannot hold”. This has to do with the concept of ‘location value’ (see Section 6.3).

During a process of research by design there is constant *ex ante* evaluation. A factor here which is related primarily to ‘future value’ is the degree of flexibility. On the one hand, the flexibility of the ‘construction’: i.e. openness to modification (see Lynch for a description - 1990: 384), and on the other hand, use flexibility. An example of construction flexibility is that a (functional or formal) multinodal urban system (see Fig.5-25e) is flexible in the sense that its development per unit can be (temporarily) terminated. A condition of this is, of course, that several units are not developed at the same time. The principle is inflexible in the sense that once a start has been made on the development of a unit, this development cannot be stopped without causing some degree of loss to the spatial quality. Fig.4-7 shows another example: the difficulty of modifying an area accessed by a private transport system into one opened up by a light-rail system.

To illustrate use flexibility, Fig.5-31 depicts a network of cities with both inward and outward satellite developments. The inwardly-located satellite d provides a larger degree of use flexibility than the outwardly-located satellites a, b and c. However, when efforts are made to support the potential user base of the ‘mother city’ an outward location is preferred, providing the connection between satellite and the other cities passes through the ‘mother’ city.

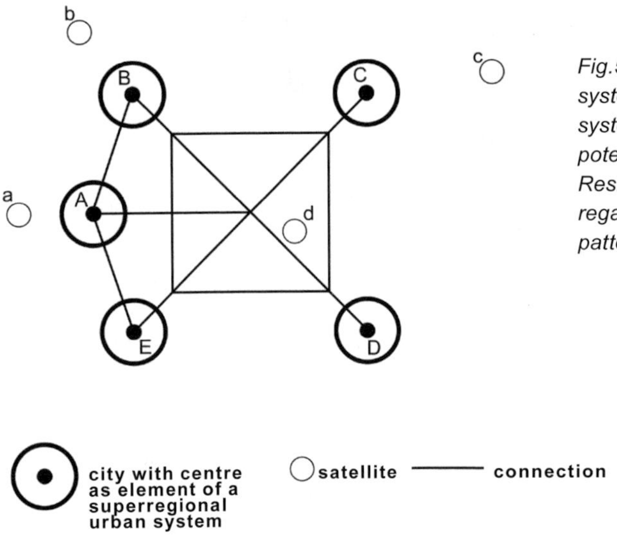

Fig.5-31 Multinodal super regional urban system combined with regional satellite systems. Satellites a, b and c reinforce the potential user bases of the ‘ mother cities’. Residents of satellite d have more options regarding their temporospatial activity patterns

If satellites are located inwards we can assume that new network units will develop. The city of Zoetermeer which developed as a satellite for The Hague provides empirical support for this assumption. (Fig.5-32).

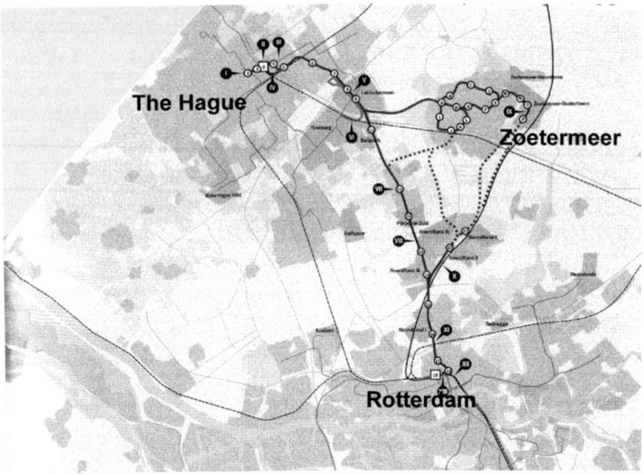

Fig. 5-32 Zoetermeer, built as a satellite of The Hague, has since developed into a city in its own right in the multinodal Zuidvleugel (South Wing) of the Randstad. This map illustrates the plan to better acces the Zuidvleugel internally with the help of the 'Randstadrail' (source of illustration: Blauwe Kamer 1999/4: 43)

Important elements in Lakatos' research approach are counterexamples or 'monsters' (his distinction between local and global counterexamples is not very relevant in the case of urban & regional design). An example of a counter argument that increases the content of a theory is the observation that in the Brazilian port of Santos the regional scale is almost completely absent (Geerse 1993): Fig.5-33. This indicates that the theoretical models of Fig.5-25 a to f contain hidden conditional assumptions, namely that the city population is evenly distributed in terms of spending power throughout the urban region, and that there are no overriding financial factors that place a constraint on movement. In Santos the regional physical urban system coincides with a local physical system where the elite, with their great spending power, are concentrated.

Fig.5-33 When the spending power within a region is not evenly distributed, the regional centre will not be located centrally (after Geerse 1993: 21).

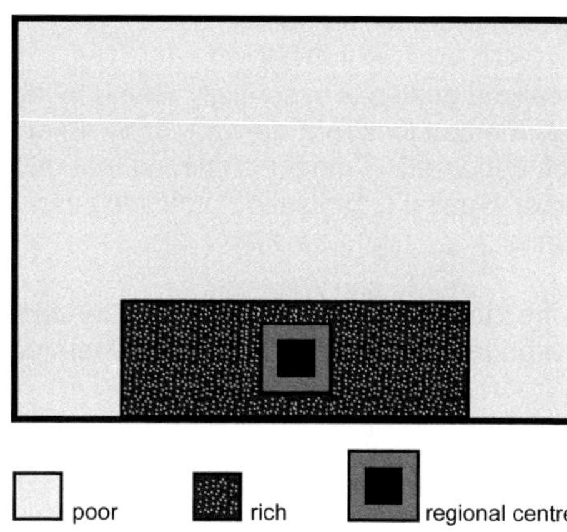

This type of research also raises questions for practitioners of sciences that supply knowledge to designers. A need arises for generalised contextual knowledge such as the vulnerability of certain physical urban systems to earthquakes, what demands are made by a lack of water or disruption through water, what requirements do certain ecological systems have? Some more examples: What impact will ICT have on spatial quality? (Drewe 2001); Is the perception of the constructed environment determined culturally, and what consequences does this have for the information function? Nikos Salingaros has shown that mathematics can contribute to providing a foundation to theoretical models (Salingaros 1998; 1999; 2001; see also www.math.utsa.edu/sphere/salingar/index.html (04-2003)): more of this kind of research is desirable.

Perception research could also offer insight concerning the information function from a neurological point of view. .

In a practical science the question is not 'true' or 'not true'. Freely rendering from Von Schomberg (1991: 59, see Section 3.4.3), urban & regional design is all about whether plausible spatial organization principles and plausible theoretical models can be derived from partially inconsistent data with abduction as the mechanism (Magnani 2001: 78). In agreement with Von Schomberg, I would suggest that any design that is based on plausible reasoning is worth carrying out. After all, urban & regional design problems are and will continue to be, ill-defined problems. (Lawson 1990: 161).

5.5 Research-driven design

"There were social reasons in Plato's time for abhorring vulgar handicraft - such work as would only be undertaken by slaves - but western culture ever since has preferred intellectual exercise to practical, a snobbery which certainly extends to the present day. It is one reason for the prestige which numerical models possess in certain circles, why it seems more respectable to devise and manipulate a mathematical model ..."

(Geoffrey Broadbent 1988, *Design in Architecture*: 92/93)

Research-driven design involves the creation of a localized design based in part on the results of scientific research.

A localized design is essentially driven by either a theoretical model with certain qualities (goal-oriented localized design), or by an analysis of the possibilities that the site offers after which a theoretical model is chosen that utilises these possibilities (means-oriented localized design). Spatial organization principles can also play a role independently of theoretical models.

For the localized design process this means that a 'design layer' is added: general design knowledge, which can be deployed when making localized designs. (Fig.5-34).

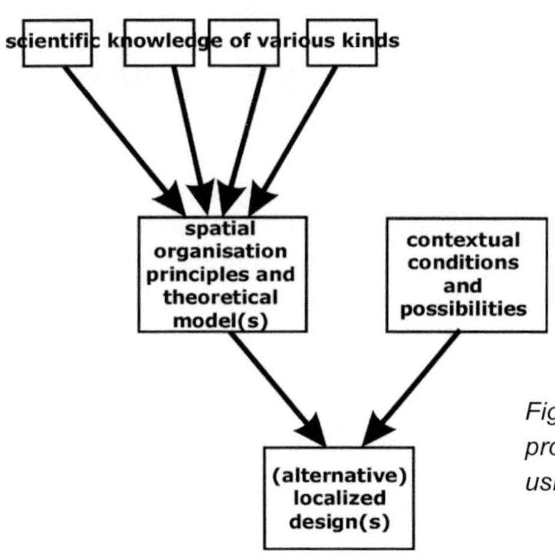

Fig.5-34 Representation of the localized design process whereby a localized design is created using the input of research by design results.

Strictly speaking each design is founded upon scientific knowledge. When designing a teapot, for example, account is taken, at least subconsciously, of the 'law of communicating vessels' (Fig.5-35). If this does not happen, then the design will fail during testing of the first prototype (and much time, energy and money will be wasted through eventually discovering the 'teapot law' for oneself).

The invention that one can position the spout of a tea container as low as one desires provided that it can be closed off by a tap, also relies upon knowledge of this law. The view that scientific knowledge would seriously hinder the conception of this solution (Jong 2002b: 449) can, according to Hulsbergen (2003: 13), be ascribed to the usually narrative and somewhat normative character of the formation of theories concerning urban & regional design.

Fig.5-35 Teapot designs where the law of communicating vessels has been ignored...

Urban & regional design also makes use of typological knowledge, such as the types of plot division (see Fig.5-9). As long as there is no insight regarding the conditions under which what effects arise, or as long as this insight is not made known explicitly, it is by no means certain that these types would also 'work' under other conditions. Even if this were the case, due to the inductive character of this way of acquiring knowledge there is always the possibility of only a sub-optimisation. "In building up a body of knowledge on human settlements we cannot regard any principle derived from existing human settlements as the sole criterion of the phenomena we are trying to interpret, describe and understand." (Doxiadis 1968: 286).

Essential to the practical-scientific approach to urban & regional design is that explicit scientific knowledge forms the foundation of localized designs. This makes a critical-rational debate over this knowledge possible. Tacit knowledge certainly also plays a role in the development of theoretical models and in research-driven localized design, but must only provide ancillary rather than essential knowledge.

Goal-oriented research input

Theoretical models are useful tools in localized design. They help to bring about a certain spatial quality. Elements of physical urban systems are considered interdependently both at a given level of scale and, as far as an element is relevant on several levels of scale, between levels of scale.

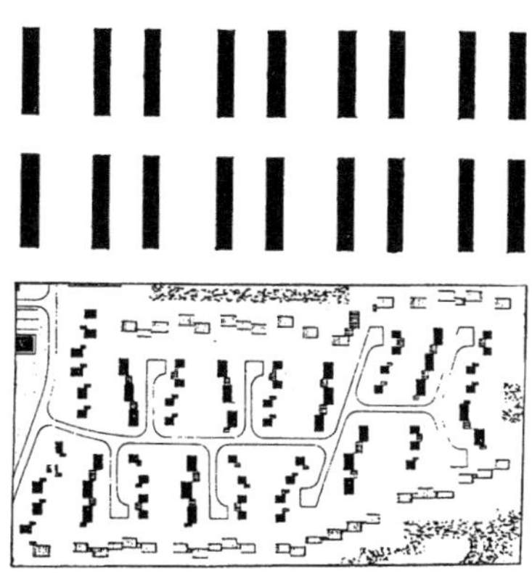

Fig.5-37 A basic plot division applied to a specific site (Westrik 1989: 76).

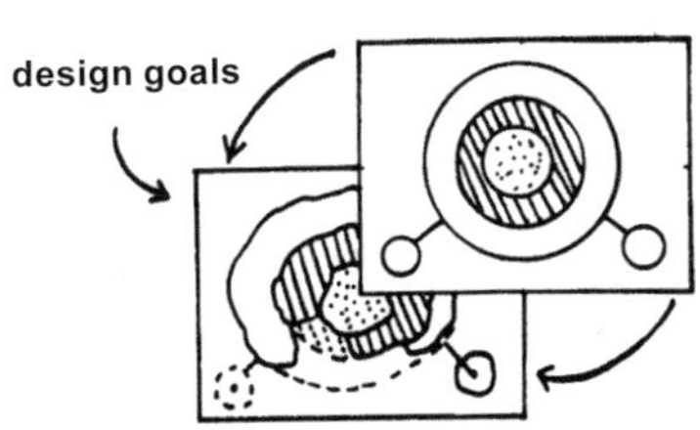

Fig.5-36 A normative theoretical model is modified 'elastically' to suit a specific site (Thüsh 1993: 62).

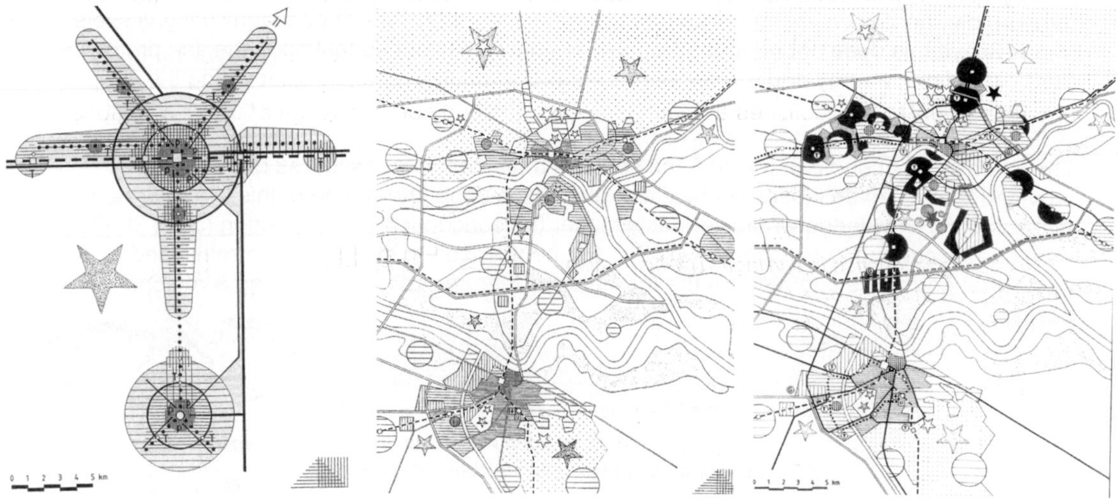

Fig.5-38 The normative theoretical model chosen for the twin cities Arnhem-Nijmegen (left) (see Fig.6-12.1-7) leads via a confrontation process with a model of the existing situation (centre) to a development model for these two cities (right) (Scholten 1992: 110; 141; legends omitted) (see also Section 6.4.1).

The task of the designer of localized designs is on the one hand to retain as much quality as possible of the chosen theoretical model - this can even be expanded with the help of specific situational potentials - and on the other to utilize the spatial individuality of the site in the design. The latter task brings about the spatial diversity that is necessary if only to make the most of the information function. Theoretical models can, metaphorically, be seen as elastically deformable: Figs.5-36, 5-37 and 5-38.

The intended effects will have to be continually checked in concrete situations, as the actual environment is not considered in the theoretical model. More over, applications of theoretical models should not only be studied in the context of their problem-solving value, but unintended consequences should also be considered. (Fig.5-39).

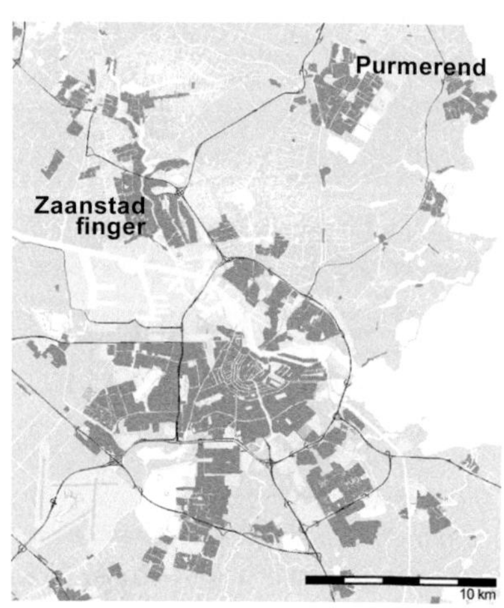

Fig.5-39 A theoretically correct direct connection between Amsterdam and its satellite Purmerend makes the ecologically valuable area between Amsterdam and Purmerend accessible, and forms a barrier in this area as well. In this case it would be better to have the connection pass through the Zaanstad finger. This also has financial advantages. However, one must check the resulting travel time.

Theoretical models can also play a role during a localized design process in the sense that a localized design process is 'taken from' the specific situation and generalized. This is the transition area between 'research by design' and 'research-driven research' mentioned in Section 5.1. A conscious simplification facilitates the studying of the (hypothesized) essence of the problem and establishes a relationship with the body of knowledge of urban & regional design: Fig.5-40; see also Fig.6-18.

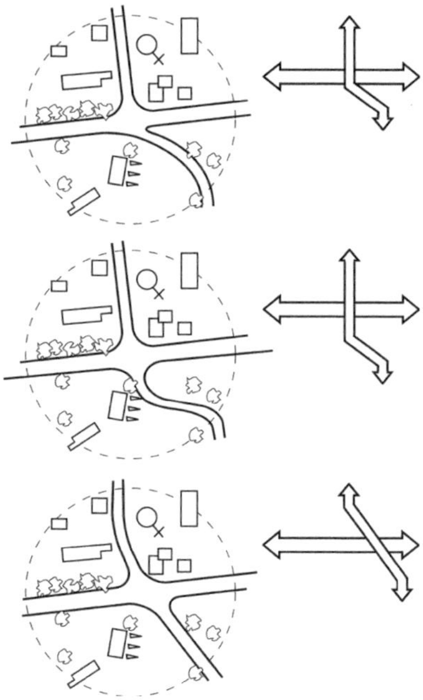

Fig.5-40 Three connection possibilities were studied for a junction in a village. The last option was considered the best.

option 1: A sharp bend in the secondary road coincides with the junction.

option 2: There are many bends in the secondary road south of the main route.

option 3: The bend is no longer sharp and does not coincide with the junction; less bends in the secondary road.

(Source: Antje Kingma, Delft University of Technology post-graduate urban & regional design project 2000)

Including existing elements in a theoretical model implies that changing their characteristics is impossible/undesirable. See for instance Section 6.18.

Creativity is needed both in using the design process as a method of research, and in applying general design knowledge to a specific situation. In research through design, creativity plays a part in the construction of organization principles and theoretical models as well as in the acquisition of insight into effects via the mechanism of heuristics or creative abduction, as Magnani called it (2001: 108; see Fig.3-3). In applying general knowledge to a specific site, creativity comes into play in adapting organization principles and theoretical models while (a) losing as little as possible of the spatial quality incorporated in the models and (b) adding as much quality as possible on the basis of the specific qualities of the site. "This first creative leap occurs not only in designing but also in the generation of hypotheses about the collection of information." (Rapoport 1969: 145). The worry of many designers, possibly in part due to their interpretation of the term 'model' as an example to be followed, that the scientific aspect of design would undermine their creative identity is therefore incorrect.

Context-oriented research input

Every localized design requires knowledge of the present state of the physical system (regardless of whether or not it is urban) and of the possibilities of transforming it, and of the relationships with other systems. This knowledge is supplied to designers and adapted by them if deemed necessary, and is also collected by the designers themselves, usually in the form of formal analyses (Fig.5-41). A situation is described by empirical research into 'what is the case', and by research into 'what can be the case'. The need for information is directed by the goals of the design in combination with relevant theoretical models. It is not possible to collect (situational) means-oriented knowledge as such, i.e. without having any goal in mind. One may think so, but then it will be a matter of following implicit directions evolving from group habits (see Section 5.2.2).

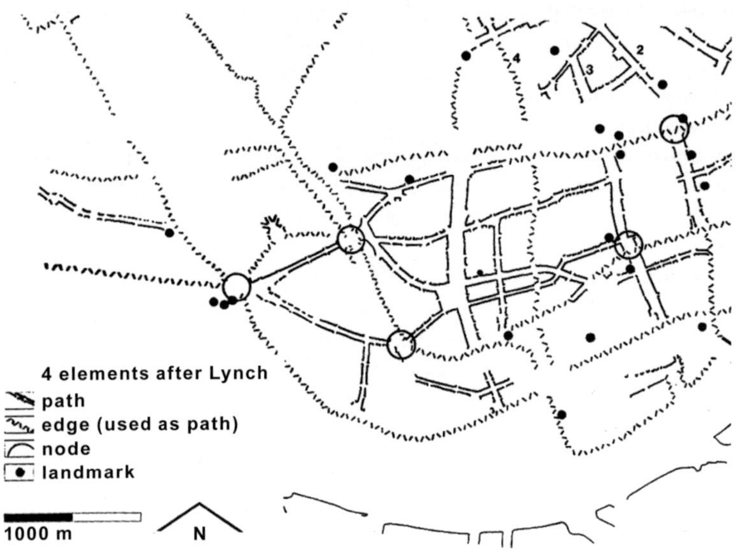

Fig.5-41 Analysis according to 'Lynch's method' (1960) of the north-western part of Rotterdam (Wijnen 2002: 38).

5.6 Design: the demarcation between science and non-science

"...we are scientists, so we will try to use arguments."

Paul Feyerabend 1991, *Dialoghi sulla conoscienza/Three Dialogues on Knowledge*)

For several years now at Delft University of Technology there has been a discussion, also involving the *Vereniging van Samenwerkende Nederlandse Universiteiten* (Association of Collaborating Dutch Universities, VNSU) and the *Discipline overlegorgaan Construerende Techniek* (Discipline Consultative Body Construction Technology, DCT), on whether a design can be regarded as scientific output. This discussion is extrascientific in the sense that it is about how university faculties are financed. It is intrascientific when it is about whether scientific results can be presented in spatial models instead of communicating them in the traditional verbal way[57]. However, the spatial sciences use spatial models as the main method of communication, a preference that is as obvious as the use of mathematic models as method of communication in mathematics and computer science.

In reality the debate is about what must be understood as 'science' and, in connection with this, what must be understood as a 'design'. If the later refers to a localized design then this, like any other application of procedural or substantive knowledge does not contribute to science, regardless of whether or not it is research-driven. Only a contribution to procedural or substantial knowledge deserves the qualification scientific. A design approach in which the emphasis lies on the differences between design situations, where each design project is seen as a unique problem, and in which a designer produces a design on the basis of personal ideas, regardless of whether or not she or he is inspired by the potentials of the situation, doesn't produce those contributions. Rather, one must search for similarities: scientists must dare to generalise. Without verifiable theoretical designs that are open to discussion, in the course of which on the basis of empirical and formal scientific knowledge insight is gained into the structuralization, lay out and visual design of physical urban systems, urban design as a field of study gets stuck in a pre-scientific phase. This is also the case if in the context of application results are not verifiable or are not assessed (Section 3.4.5), or if, in the context of application, one gets bogged down in descriptions. In neither instance is it possible to pose the question 'does it work?', and if so, under what conditions and with what effects.

Which view of science is held by the board of the Delft University of Technology has not been made explicit, although it may be deduced from the rules that are currently proposed for design - namely intersubjectivity, reliability, verifiability and practical applicability[58], that it is a realistic one. These rules are similar to those that I formulated in Section 3.4.5, these being that the process of knowledge acquisition must be rational, transferable, verifiable and open to discussion and that the conclusion must be generic, consistent and, at least in theory, testable (verification/falsification). According to these rules urban & regional designs will consequently always have to contain explicitly presented generic elements. This will restore the meaning of a localized design to what it is in essence, in relation to practical science, an instance of the applicability of generic knowledge to a specific case. Only a non-localized design can be regarded as scientific output. If one wishes to discuss whether an urban or regional design can be counted as scientific output, then a debate should be conducted on the problems in the context of justification or context of application that arise with urban & regional design more than they do with other practical sciences.

I believe that dynamism too is a characteristic of science (Section 3.4.5). To paraphrase Lakatos: a research programme should have a positive heuristic (Section 3.4.3): the programme should bear fruit. A scientific area is served by various competing research programmes which can be compared on that point. To evaluate the kind of research programme described in Sections 5.4 and 5.5, it is illustrated in the next Chapter by a number of examples.

6 Developing a practical-scientific body of knowledge for urban & regional design

6.1 Introduction

> "Those who give flight to ready and rapid practice before they have learned the theory are like sailors who go to sea in a vessel without a rudder."
>
> (Leonardo Da Vinci (1452-1519))

In this Chapter, I illustrate the application of design as a method of research (see Section 5.4) using the contributions made to the body of knowledge of urban & regional design by various individuals, including myself. This includes previously published research results. Internal publications of the Delft University of Technology have also been used, mainly the results of post-graduate projects and theses which I supervised.

The Chapter is arranged as follows. In Section 6.2 I introduce some universal spatial organization principles. The various categories are functional and formal, as well as spatial-ecologic, socio-cultural and economic in nature. Research into these principles is examined in Section 6.3.

Sections 6.4 and 6.5 give examples of, respectively, the design of theoretical models and research into theoretical models, both in relation to localized design projects. The socio-cultural, spatial-ecological, economic-technical context of the examples is western and in most cases Dutch; for example, they generally assume that the terrain is largely flat and that bicycling is a common mode of transport. These examples add weight to the arguments of Section 4.6.2 and Section 5.3.2 that designs in a process-oriented view of urban & regional design can be characterized as functional-spatial structure models, with some essential visual design indications.

6.2 Universal spatial organization principles

"Sapere aude! Habe Muth dich deines eigenen Verstandes zu bedienen."

(Immanuel Kant (1724-1804), from *Was ist Aufklärung* (1784))

6.2.1 Functional principles

24-hour biorhythm (spatial-ecological)

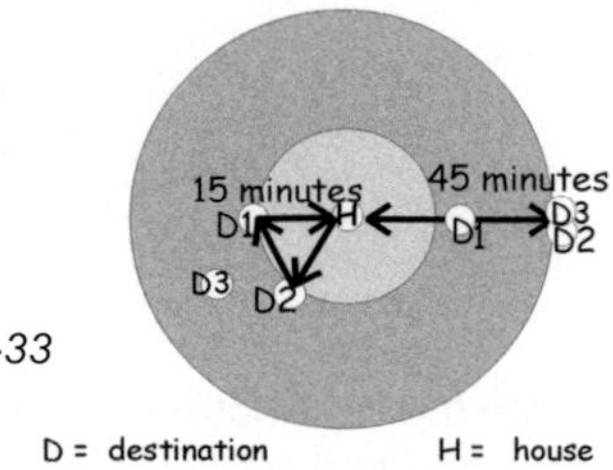

Fig.6-1 Time-space activity zones; cf Fig.4-33

The number of activities that can be carried out in the course of a single day increases along with the degree to which their 'carriers' are located in each other's vicinity or on a common route. With a maximum amount of available travel time of 90 minutes per day, point D3 is inaccessible if crisscross trips are called for (Fig.6-1).

The law of the large city (socio-cultural, economic)

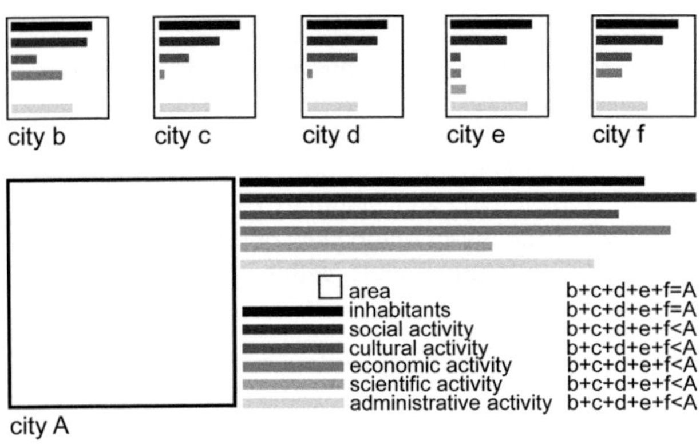

Fig.6-2 In city A with b+c+d+e+f inhabitants, considerably more happens in the socio-cultural, economic and scientific sphere than in 5 separate cities with b, c, d, e and f inhabitants respectively.

"The total level of activities in a town with 50,000 inhabitants is considerably higher than the sum of activities in five separate towns, each with 10,000 inhabitants. (----) In five cities each with a population of 250,000 far less happens in each sphere of action than in a large city with a population of 1.25 million. (---) The difference is qualitative and not just quantitative: it is not interesting whether there are more or less supermarkets or outpatients' clinics. The larger cities have institutions of a nature, size and image that are completely lacking in the group of smaller cities, or if they do exist this is an exception." (Boer 1996: 127).

Example of empirical support for this principle: VIRO-werkgroep (1992)

The rule of absolute numbers (socio-cultural and economic)

The greater the population concentration the greater the opportunity for contact and consequently the more chances there are for joint action (Boer 1996: 128). "Groups that make up a small percentage of the population can nonetheless reach absolute numbers in large cities that gives them significant scope for action. They can set up their own organizations and institutions, attract services that are specific to their needs and publicize their ideas. A climate is created where account is taken of them; (----) The rule of absolute numbers involves the most diverse minorities and elite groups, people who share an uncommon interest, hobby or commitment, who carry out an unusual job, or become companions through disposition or ethnic background. (---) Beliefs become more accepted and the city begins to attract more from these groups as inhabitants and visitors." (ibid.).

Symbiosis (economic and socio-cultural)

Symbiosis means the mutual profit that (at least) two different types of activities gain from one another (Fig.6-3). When symbiosis is present in an urban system, there is usually an attracting activity and other activities that dependent on it, such as flower stalls, street musicians, theatre cafes, ice-cream vendors, etc. Symbiotic activities are to a large degree dependent upon impulsive participation. They mainly involve pedestrians, who are the only type of traffic that can stop immediately. Cyclists may also be involved but to a lesser degree.

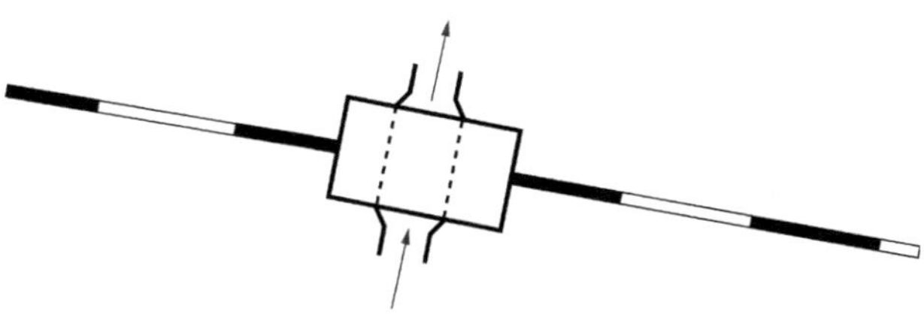

Fig.6-3 Connections at a certain scale often form a barrier at a lower level of scale. When the pedestrian/cycle routes between city neighbourhoods located on either side of a rail line converge with access to the station and its associated activities (ticket sales, kiosk, etc.), this improves public safety for all users.

Examples of empirical support: White 1988; M.Jacobs 1990 (42 ff.). See also Lynch 1990 (91 ff.). The urban planners Buit and Nozeman, who studied the consequences of relocating two hospitals in Amsterdam to the outskirts of the city, said in an interview "... fifty per cent of the shops in the vicinity of the old hospitals suffered substantial losses in profits since the move to the AMC." (Kusiak 1989: 11).

Agglomeration (economic, socio-cultural)

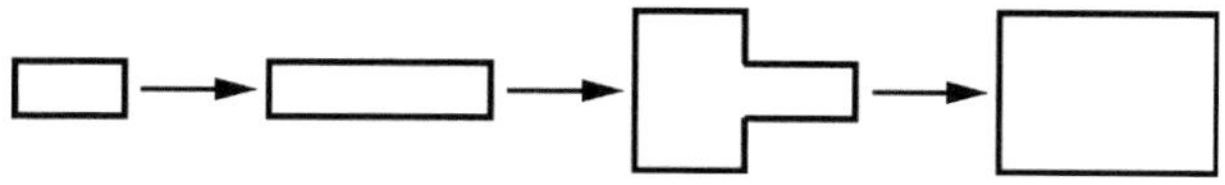

Fig.6-4 Agglomerate formation: process with a large temporal grain.

Agglomeration effects occur at all scales (Fig.6-4). “When a branch of the HEMA [a Dutch chain store - itk] opens in a small urban centre, this increases the attractiveness of the centre and its vicinity, resulting in increased employment, and more and larger shops selling a greater variety of articles. The opportunities for the retail trade may develop to such an extent that a department store such as Vroom & Dreesmann may decide to set up a branch there. The catchment area will increase in size, creating scope for specialized shops.” (Boer 1990: 40/41).

Examples of empirical support: Meulenbelt studied the effects of building The Town Hall/ Music Theatre (popularly known as the *Stopera*) in the centre of Amsterdam. “From this study we can conclude that as a result of building the Stopera the immediate area went into an upward spiral.” (1991: 43). In Oslo, after the main railway terminus was built, a variety of regional institutions developed around the new station (personal observation).

There is a close relationship between symbiosis (cyclic process with a small temporal grain) and agglomeration (linear process with a large temporal grain).

Organization principles for transport, links at the scale of city district, city and region. (economic and social)

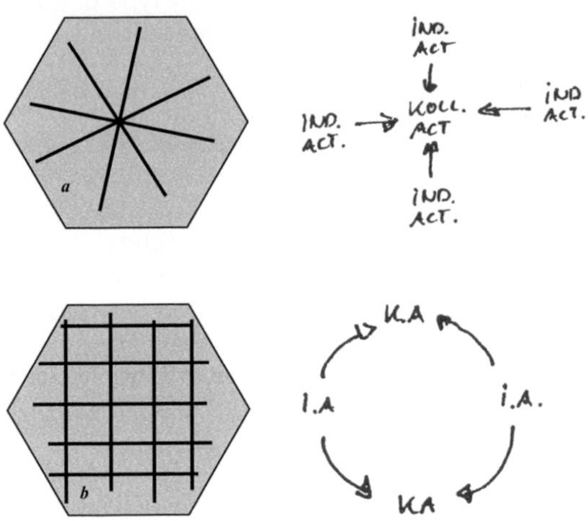

Fig.6-5 A radial and a tangential mobility structure, with the associated logically justified location of collective activities.
Koll.act (KA)= collective activities
Ind.act. (IA) = individual activities

Use of space
“A very thin man riding in a subway train during rush hours occupies 2 square feet of floor space. A fat man standing comfortably needs 5 square feet, while a man who is walking requires 8 square feet. A man in a hurry, who is running, needs 15 square feet. The same man, sitting in an automobile that is standing still, requires 200 square feet, but when he drives this automobile at a reasonable speed, he needs 600 square feet. Going at 60 miles per hour, he requires 1200 square feet.”

(Gruen 1965: 239)

The universal spatial organization principles at city level are (a) the radial mobility structure that is desirable to make collective transport possible, and (b) a tangential structure that is necessary for private car transport (Fig.6-5). Collective transport calls for the ‘bundling’ of transport movements, while cars benefit from distribution, owing to their relatively large demand for space both during driving and when parked (for example M.Jacobs 2000: 40). At a smaller scale, low-speed individual transport (walking, cycling) is once again availed by bundling and thus by a radial pattern. The bundling of transport movements creates opportunities for symbiosis (among other things public safety) along the routes and reduces the financial and spatial investment for a given link. Public transport of any reasonable quality in a tangible structure is only possible in an intensely urbanized area (for example Manhattan, New York).

An example of empirical support can be found in an article from *the New York Times* of 18-11-1997 under the headline "Getting to Jobs in Suburbs is hard for Walking Poor - Many who work but lack cars ... must spend hours on buses that run at times that aren't convenient for them."

Spatial organization principles, agglomeration effects and symbiosis processes are related to the organization principle 'hierarchy' (see Section 4.2.2) and 'location-value-on-the-basis-of-accessibility' (see Section 6.3.2). The concepts of 'junctions' and 'feeders' are related to the latter two (see Govers, Van der Ham & Van Reisen 1998). Those who say that hierarchy is outdated, or that theme-oriented, complementary centres have to be developed at an urban-regional level, argue in effect for an urban system that is dependent upon car use, or for limitationing potential spatial activity patterns. Furthermore, symbiosis potentials are only exploited to a small degree.

An example of empirical support for the relationship between the hierarchy and transport mode can be found in Gantvoort 1993.

6.2.2 Formal principles

maximum visibility of natural and artificial system elements (spatial-ecological)

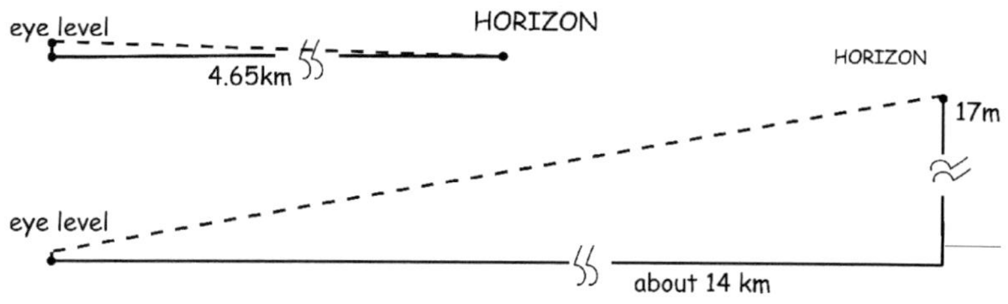

Fig.6-6 Relations between the height and the visibility of objects (after Weide, Steenbergen & Homan 2001: 34 ff.).

Due to the curvature of the earth, the relationship between the height of an object and the distance at which it is visible is not linear (Fig.6-6).

boundary length

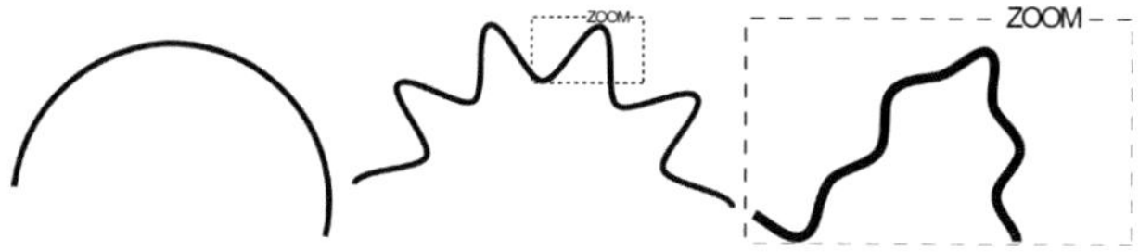

Fig.6-7 manipulating the boundary length of physical urban systems

The boundary length of the border of the urban area and the non-urban area can be increased or reduced at all levels of scale, particularly when the boundary is sharply defined (see Fig.5.15.2a). (Fig.6-7). This is thus an instance of fractal geometry (Salingaros 2001; 2003).

6.3 Researching spatial organization principles

"The value of a model is that it can be used to improve our understanding of the ways in which a system behaves in circumstances where it is not possible (for technical, economic, political or moral reasons) to construct or experiment with a real world situation."

(Colin Lee 1973, *Models in Planning*: 7)

6.3.1 Researching the location of collective functions at neighbourhood level

The fact that there is a limited amount of time available each day for travel produces spatial organization principles affecting the location of collective functions at neighbourhood level (non-universal, spatial-ecologic, socio-cultural): Fig.6-8.

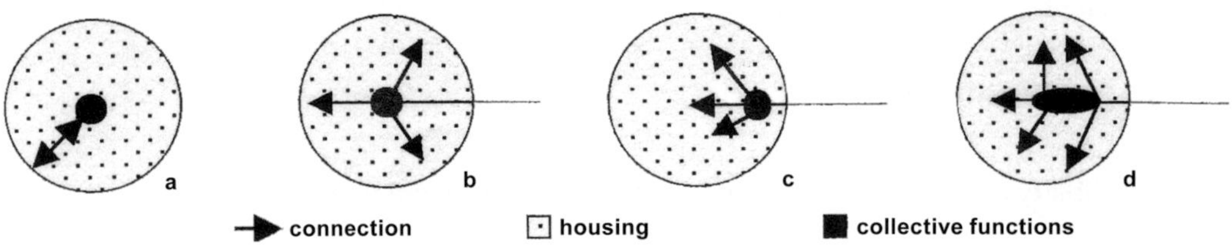

Fig.6-8 the location of collective functions at neighbourhood level under different conditions.

(a) The centre of a circle is, in a homogeneous situation, generally the most easily accessible point and thus appropriate for locating collective functions (which make an intensive use of space). The radius of the circle is a criterion for the functional spatial quality - the time and energy required for assumedly equivalent movement options (walking, cycling). The residential density and the surface area of the circle are a joint criterion for the potential quality of the collective functions.

In (b) and (c), the residential area is linked to the outside world. All residents and visitors pass through a single entry point. In (b) the point is a bus or metro station, one of the collective activities that are situated in the central zone. In (c) the entry point is for example a town-centre parking garage located on the edge of a pedestrians-only residential area. Example (d) has a combination of a bus or metro station and a parking garage. The zone between the centrally sited station and the eccentrically sited parking garage now has the highest location value for collective functions.

6.3.2 Researching location value (reproduced from Klaasen & Jacobs 1999)

Location value (universal, spatial-ecological): Each site occupies a particular position within a pattern and/or within a functional structure and derives from this a specific value in relation to other places. This value depends on the scale of the spatial system taken as a basis. Every spatial intervention brings about a change in the spatial qualities of a site and also in the relationship between the spatial qualities of this particular site compared with other sites. If the relative location value changes as the result of an intervention, spatial processes taking place at that scale may also change. Whether such spatial processes will indeed take place is determined in part by the type of intervention[59], by the extent to which it changes spatial conditions, by the internal mechanisms of relevant spatial processes and by measures or considerations of a non-spatial nature.

Research has shown that of many factors (regional) accessibility is the most significant determining the location of many regional facilities (Hughes 1991; Hessels 1992; Gordon and Richardson 1996). The term location value (A) is used to indicate the restriction to accessibility (Klaasen & Jacobs 1999: 24): Fig.6-9 and Figs.6-10.1 - 8

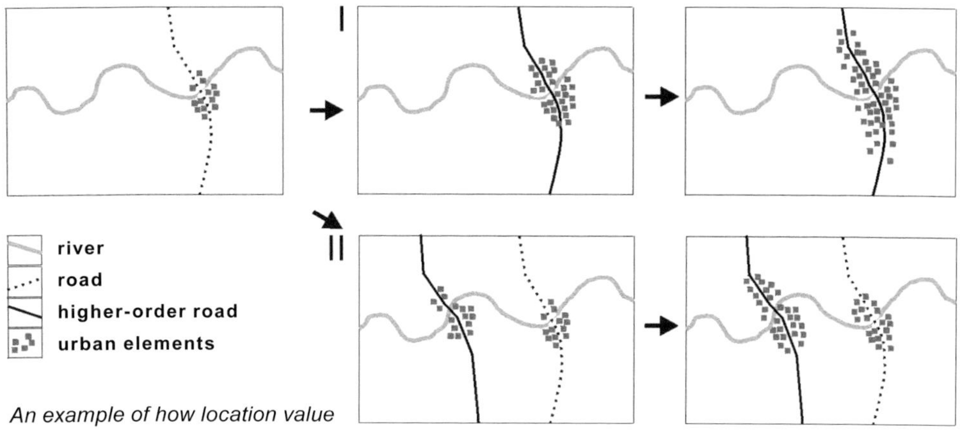

Fig.6-9 An example of how location value is influenced by spatial interventions and by ensuing effects on spatial development (Klaasen & Jacobs 1999: 25).

Fig.6-9 depicts the outcome of locating a bridge (spatial intervention) at a ford in a river (existing spatial condition). This intervention results in a higher location value at this particular site than at other places along the river, thus affecting the potential development of that area (Marchetti 1988). If the bridge and a new road were to be located elsewhere, that other location would gain a higher value and probably undergo more development than the location at the ford. The location value of the development, represented in Series I is more differentiated than that of the development represented in Series II, which is flatter (ibid.: 24).

In the above example a site with a specific topography is available. In the example below the sites concerned are generic in character.

Fig.6-10.1

Fig.6-10.2

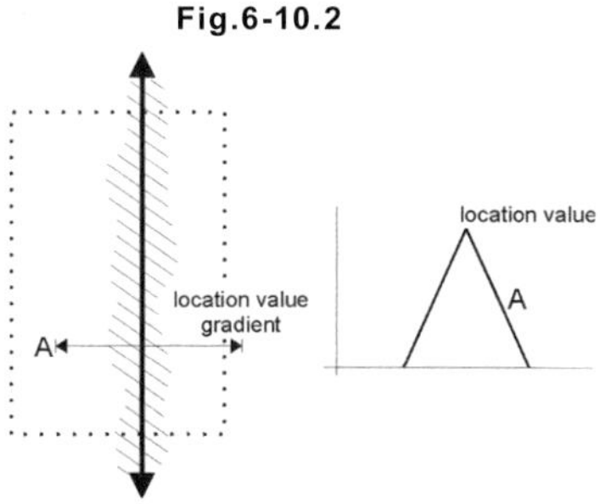

Fig.6-10.3

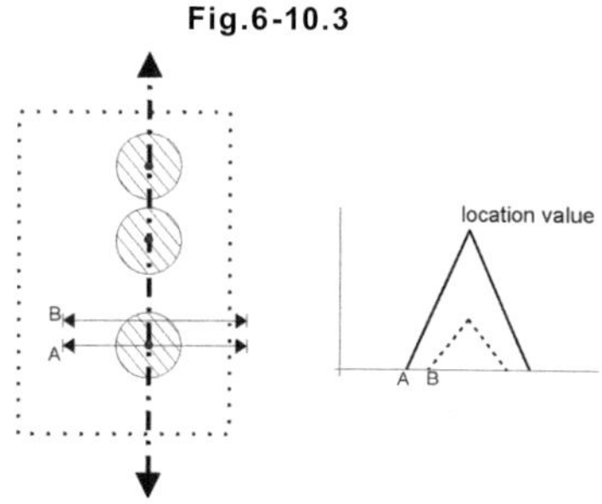

Fig.6-10.4

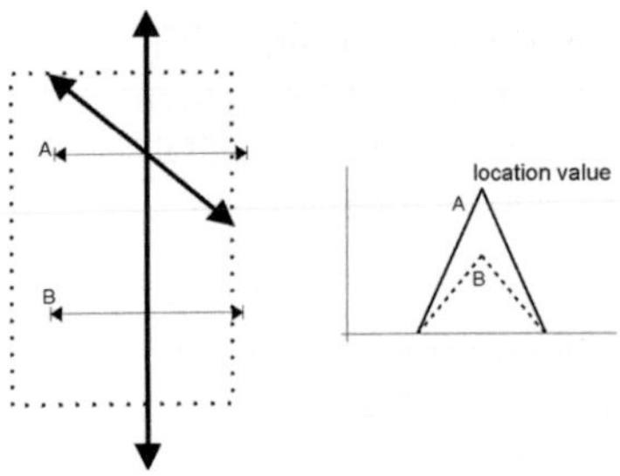

Fig.6-10.5

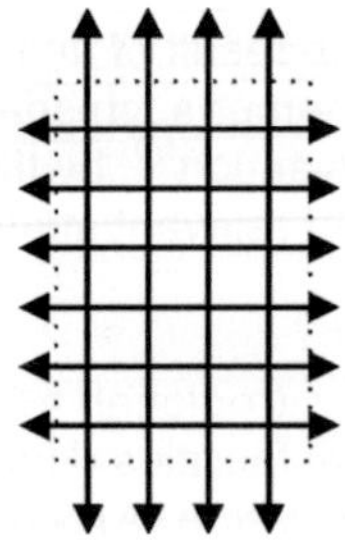

Fig.6-10.6

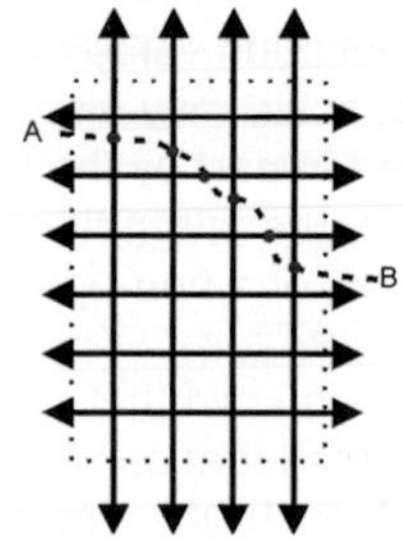

Fig.6-10 (source:Klaasen & Jacobs 1999: 25-27)

Fig.6-10.7

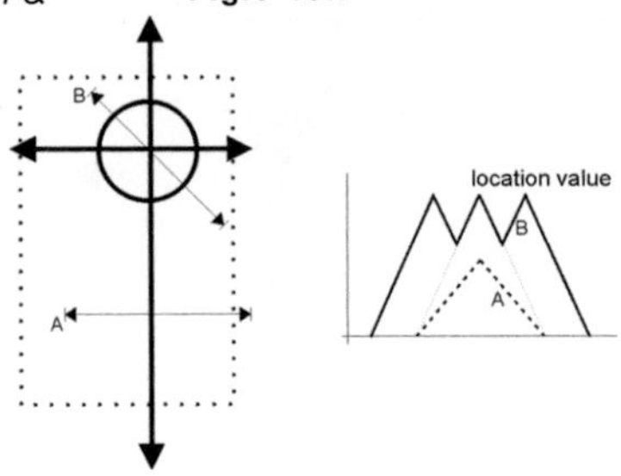

Fig.6-10.8

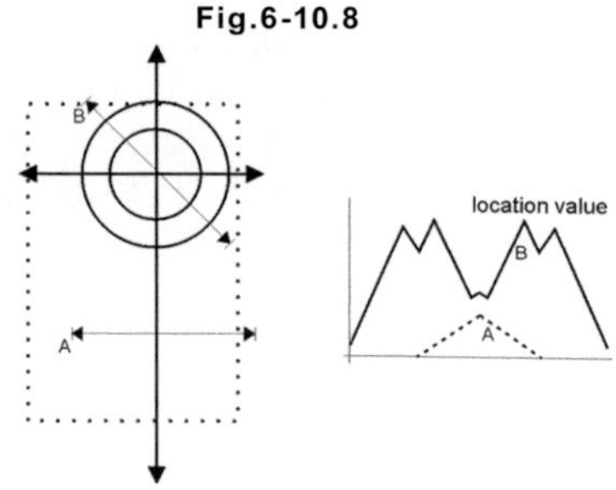

Fig.6-10.1 shows a limitless space that has not been made accessible. All the points in this space have the same accessibility. Accessibility (potential accessibility) in this example is the possibility of reaching a point x from an unspecified point y situated outside the 'limitless' space represented in the figure. The level of the location-value (A) in this space is completely flat. In fact that level is zero, since all points are equally inaccessible.

Fig.6-10.2 depicts the space shown in the previous figure but adds access by means of a path or road. This results in a marked differentiation in the location-value(A) at right angles to the road. There is no differentiation along the road itself, however. The width of the shaded zone depends on a selected criterion. For instance, it could be a ten-minute walk across difficult and varied terrain[60]. Let us suppose the path is a river. Assuming that location value is based on the availability of drinking water instead of accessibility (in accordance with the remark made in note), the resulting difference in location value would be similar.

In Fig.6-10.3 access to the area is provided by a rail link, or rather railway stations. The zone depicted in Fig.6-10.2 has been transformed into circles around these stops.

A crossroads is a unique point and is a feature of radial networks. It is the most accessible site in the area: Fig.6-10.4. The difference in the location-value(A) between this site and all others creates conditions for a hierarchical functional structure. In drawing this conclusion, we are assuming the presence of facilities for which accessibility is an important factor in determining their location.

Tangential links (networks), on the other hand, result in equality of the location-value(A). All crossings in the network shown in Fig.6-10.5 have the same location-value(A). There is considerable leveling of the location value in the area.

Thus far, we have confined the location-value(A) to the spatial system itself. Fig.6-10.6 gives an example of how the location value can be determined by the spatial aspect of systems that are largely non-spatial. Let us assume that the line A-B is an international border. The points indicated by black dots acquire a specific spatial (economic) location value as border crossings. Within the context of urban regional design, the relative location value - that is, the location value of a site compared to that of other sites - is more important than the absolute location value. The relative location value gives an indication of spatial differentiation versus leveling. Within the framework of this article, it is used as an indicator of the location value based on physical accessibility. This value can be manipulated by the introduction of infrastructure.

The situation depicted in Fig.6-10.4 changes considerably when a ring road is introduced: Fig.6-10.7. At the crossroads in the ring road, the location-value(A) is equal to that of the central intersection. It may even become equal to it or greater, depending on the quality of the ring road compared with that of the radial roads inside its perimeter. The relative location-value(A) can be reduced even more by creating additional tangential roads in the region. For example, this could be done by adding a second ring road and/or removing radial roads: Fig.6-10.8.

6.3.3 Researching accessibility of a circular basic mononodal urban system

Reflection on the access to a circular basic mononodal urban system, independent or a central part of an urban system with collective (rail) transport (see Fig.5-25) (non-universal, spatial-ecological, economic-technical) produced the following.

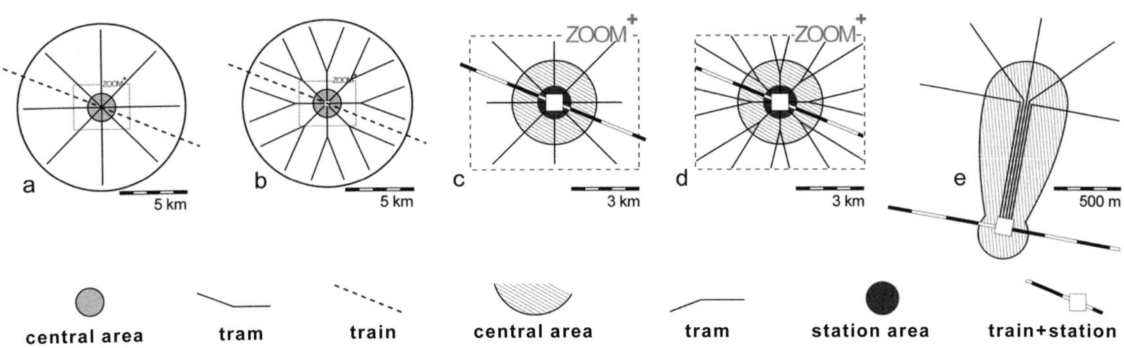

Fig.6-11 Access aspects of a mononodal urban region: collective transport.

The access pattern of a mononodal urban region with collective transport is primarily radial. The greater the radius of the area, the greater the distance that has to be travelled to and from the stops (pre-transport and post-transport) and this distance eventually exceeds the maximum acceptable distance: Fig.6-11a. Splitting the line can solve this, but at the expense of the frequency of the transport; there is a relationship between the population density, the quality of transport, the form of pre- and post-transport (walking, bicycle, volunteer bus service) and the modal split: Fig.6-11b.

In the centre of the city the rail infrastructure takes up a relatively large amount of space: Fig.6-11c. Bundling the lines not only reduces the amount of space taken up but also keeps the construction and maintenance costs to a minimum; increasing the stop frequency will help to keep down the increase of the journey time before and after the stop. The journey frequency is doubled which is of particular importance for train travellers (pre- and post-transport): Fig.6-11d. The radius of the city centre is a function of an acceptable walking distance or an acceptable metro or tram journey time before and after a train stop (including transfer and waiting times).

In the case of a station that is not located centrally, this will lead to the configuration illustrated in Fig.6-11e. The length of the route from the station to the city centre can again be related to an acceptable walking distance. The entire zone has a high location value: the circular city centre of Fig.6-11d expands asymmetrically.

6.4 Researching theoretical models

"But ideas, like butterflies, do not merely exist; they develop, they enter into relations with other ideas and they have effects."

(Paul Feyerabend 1991, *Dialoghi sulla conoscienza/Three Dialogues on Knowledge*: 163)

6.4.1 Researching development principles for a 'twin city'

The subject of the Masters Thesis of Michiel Scholten (1992) was the spatial development of the cities Arnhem and Nijmegen, for which the government ordained a coordinated project. Part of Scholten's study was the design of a number of theoretical models for the development of twin cities (Figs. 6-12.1 to 7). See also Fig.5-38.

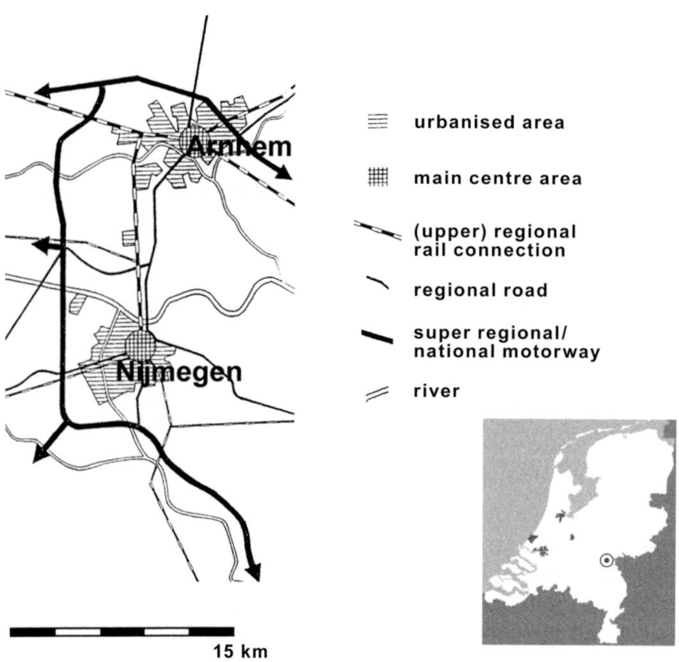

Fig. 6-12.1 The cities of Arnhem and Nijmegen (Scholten 1992: 22)

separation model (ibid.:35)

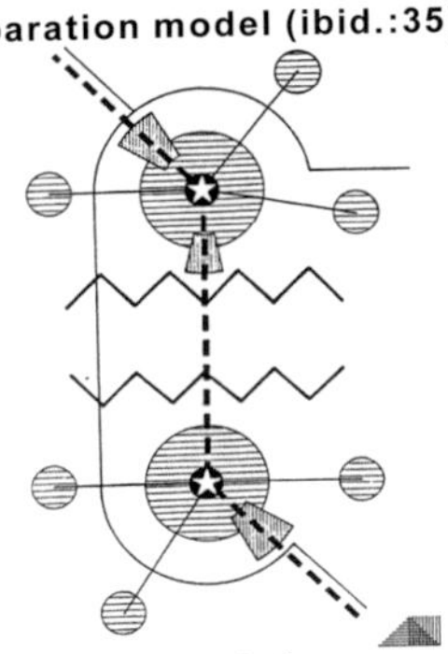

Fig. 6-12.2 This is the zero option. The two centres develop independently of one another, each according to its own structure: two mononodal systems with centres that may or may not compete with one another. There is thus no main centre. Both centres have the same quality of connection to the superregional/ national transport network. The centres are connected to one another. The area in the middle is not urbanized. The open character of this area comes under pressure, in part because no investment has to be made in an intraregional connection. Effective administrative-organizational tools are necessary in order to preserve the open character of the area. If the centres grow towards one another, however, then a weak urban structure would result due to the lack of a coherent development model.

central city model (ibid.:35)

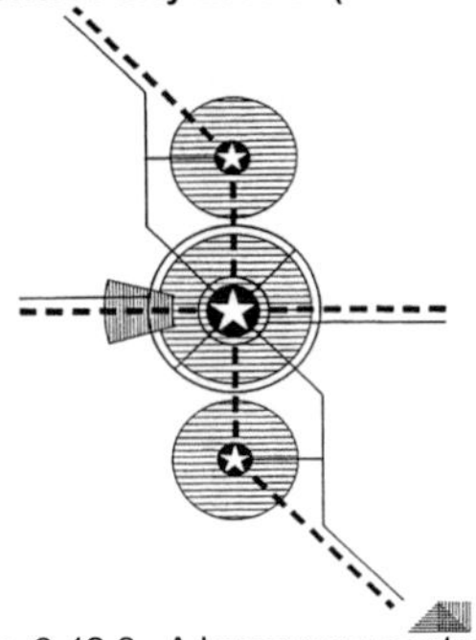

Fig. 6-12.3 A larger new centre is developed between the two centres resulting in a mononodal urban system with a main centre of a considerably higher order (given the user base) than the two existing centres. Functions from the two existing centres would have to be relocated to the new main centre, which will be the only one connected to the national/international transport network. The region would gain a coherent transport system. A larger diversity of residential milieus would result. This sort of model banks on the future. Not only does it entail a doubling of the current population and the current users of the two cities together, but its realization would also take a considerable time. It is uncertain what effects would result as a consequence, certainly with changing circumstances.

asymmetrical (ibid.: 36)

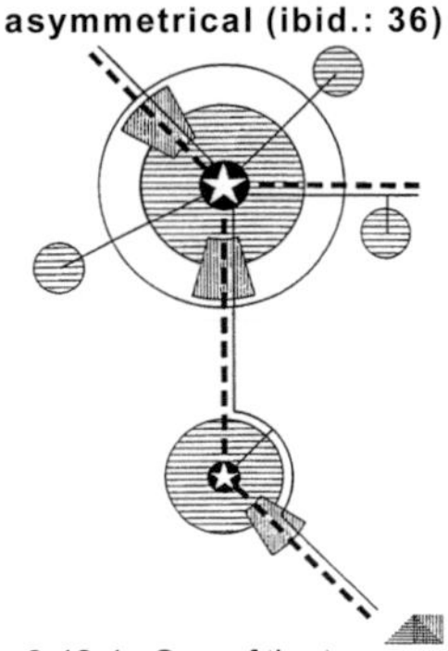

Fig.6-12.4 One of the two centres develops as main centre at the expense of the other. A mononodal urban system results but only from a functional viewpoint. Only the main centre is connected to the superregional/ national transport network. Each city has its own transport system. Connection between the two centres should be good, better than in the case of the separation model. Not only will all new developments be located in the main centre, but functions from the smaller centre will have to be relocated to the main centre (functional drainage). This could result in social problems, though a greater diversity in residential milieus would result. There will be a sunstantial pressure on the central area in this theoretical model. It displays some affinity with the satellite model (see Fig.5-25).

urbanised area	main centre	super regional rail connection	super regional road connection	business area	bordering open area

linear city (ibid.: 36)

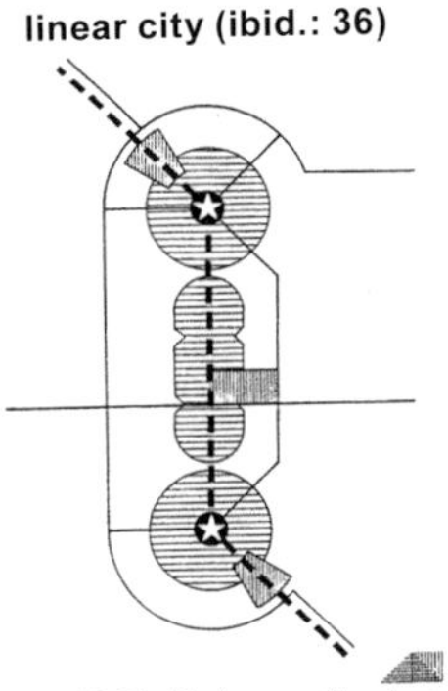

Fig. 6-12.5 Between the two cities urbanisation takes place along a central axis. The outcome is a linear city extending between two main centres. A multinodal urban system results: there is no main centre. Both centres are connected to the superregional/national transport network to the same degree. There is a cohesive regional traffic system. Depending on how the linear city develops, a larger diversity of residential milieus may develop.This theoretical model will be more stable and flexible in the future than the previous ones.

dispersed urbanization model (ibid.: 37)

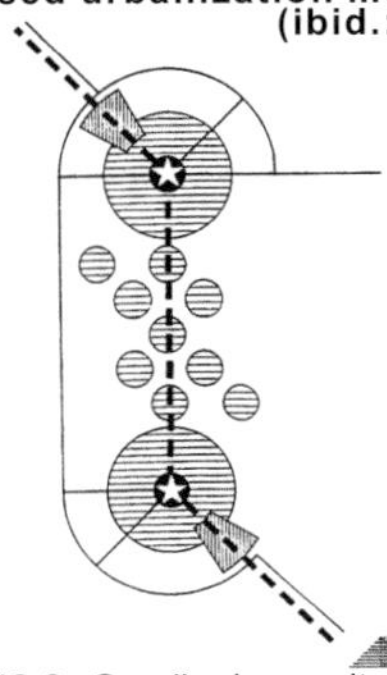

Fig. 6-12.6 Small urban units form throughout the entire central open area: de-urbanization. The urban system that results is weak: there is no main centre. The diversity of residential milieu does not increase, but a new type of milieu is created. Both centres are connected to the regional/national transport network to the same degree and have their own transport system. In the central suburbanized area a diffuse transport system develops; the potential user base is too small for effective collective transport since there are insufficient possibilities for bundling transport movements (verplaatsingsbeweging en).Without effective administrative-organizational tools, the central area will randomly suburbanize, resulting in a fragmentation of the open space.

infracity model (ibid.: 37)

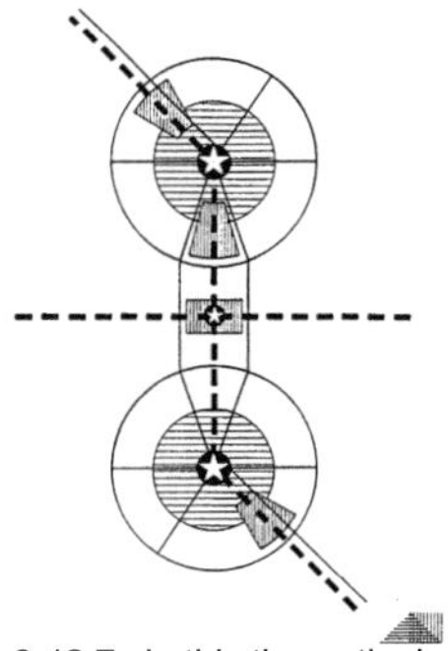

Fig. 6-12.7 In this theoretical model a junction of national, superregional and regional connections develops between the two centres. A regional transport system arises. Due to the high location value based on accessibility the junction will attract all sorts of functions, particularly economic collective functions (agglomeration effects).
The monofunctional character of the environment that develops will make it unattractive to users. Moreover, the main centres will become less lively as a result of the withdrawal of activities (symbiosis). This model will not be very stable: urbanization of the central open area will be inevitable.

6.4.2 Theoretical model for a mononodal rural region

A rural region, too, can be mononodal, or be developed as such: Fig.6-13

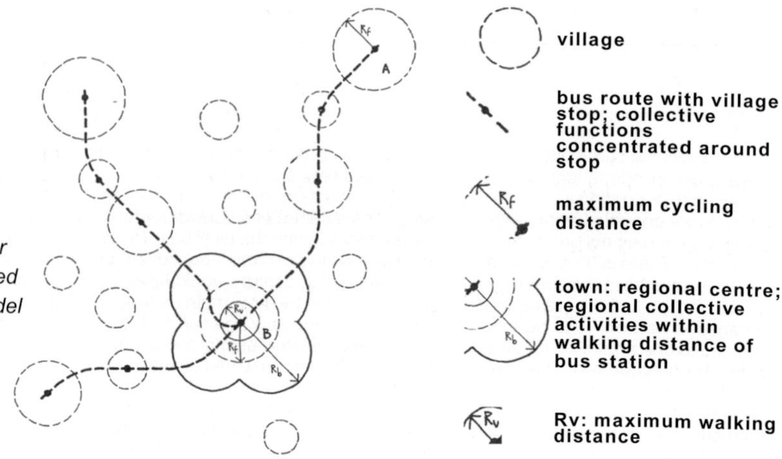

Fig.6-13 Theoretical model for a mononodal rural region based on the theoretical satellite model from Fig.5-25).

This theoretical model for a rural region accessed by collective transport - a maximum of three routes in view of the potential user base, per bus - is based on a radial urban model. In order to be able to service an as large as possible area within a certain maximum travel time, expansions of existing villages and new villages should be situated in such a way that they can support the current routes. The larger the potential user base per route the better the frequency of the bus connection and so theoretically the more users. If the number of passengers does in fact rise, the quality of the bus transport will increase even further[61].

6.4.3 Researching theoretical models on the basis of empirical discoveries

Marc Jacobs (2000) studied multinodal cities in order to develop a set of instruments for use in designing urban regions. He applied these instruments to the lobate, finger, satellite and network theoretical models (see Fig.5-25). The example given here is the lobate theoretical model (Figs.6-14.1 to 4).

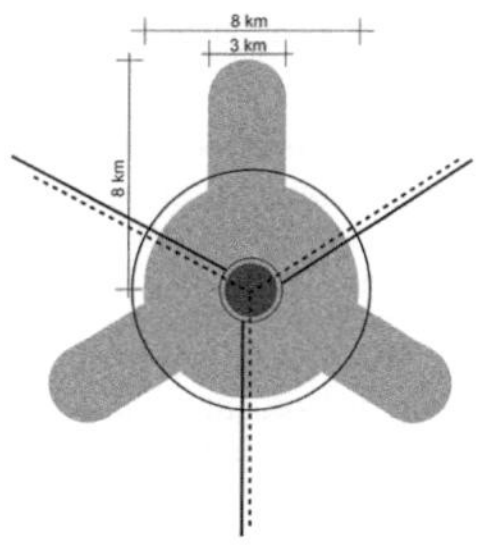

Fig.6-14.1 Theoretical lobate model (initial situation). (M.Jacobs 2000: 160)

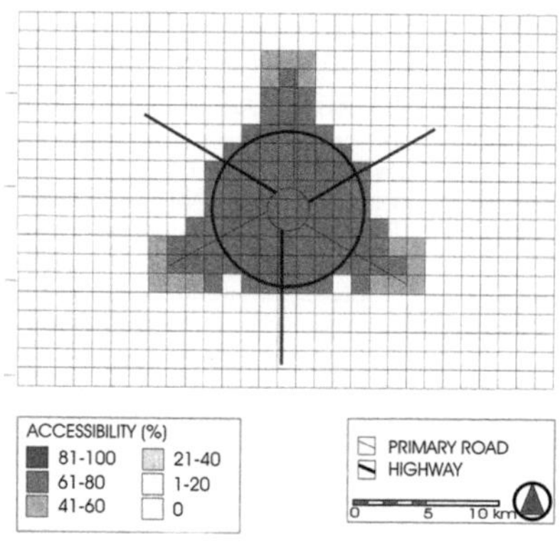

Fig.6-14.2 An accessibility analysis of this model shows it to be inconsistent with the hierarchy of centres (ibid.:164).

The lobate model is characterized by a hierarchy of centres. In a consistent model, the location-value(A) (see Section 6.3.2) must therefore be suitable for the location of urban-regional collective functions only in the main centre. An accessibility analysis of the model (Fig.6-14.2) has revealed, however, that this location value is sufficient practically everywhere for the location of this type of function. What is consistent is a theoretical lobate model in which the radius from the ring road is considerably larger than the radius from the core city. The question then is whether the ring road is still an attractive alternative route from one side of the city to the other. If the area surrounding the city is also urbanized then such a ring road would certainly pass through other urbanized parts. This could also result in objections from an ecological viewpoint, whilst the construction and maintenance costs would rise considerably. An alternative is for the ring road to be used solely for through traffic, and to build a new ring with an urban access function: Fig.6-14.3. Analysis of this new model shows that the location value (A) for the siting of urban-regional collective functions is indeed largely limited to the district centre: Fig.6-14.4.

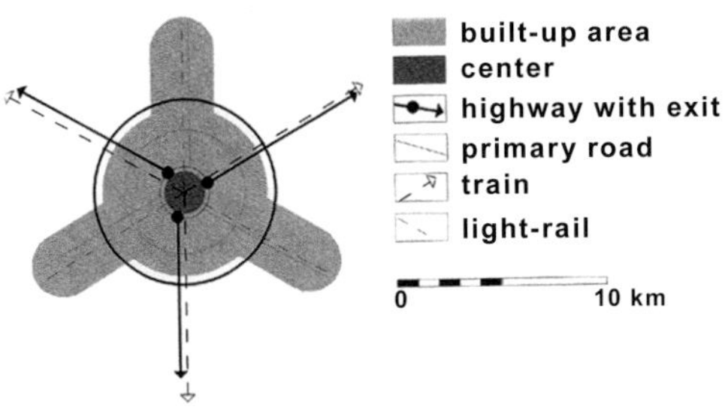

Fig.6-14.3 In this modified theoretical lobate model the ring road has far fewer exits. The access function of the road is transferred to a new primary road within the core city. (ibid.:166).

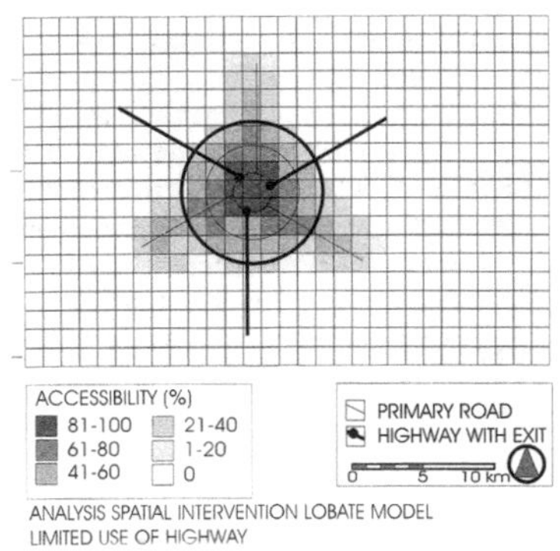

Fig.6-14.4 Analysis of the new model shows that it is now in fact consistent with the hierarchy of centre areas. (ibid.).

6.4.4 Researching the linear city

A post-graduate study project by Mia Dieters, Arno Gelderblom and Marjolein de Jong in 1991 entailed theoretical research into linear urbanisation. Their findings are embodied in the account below: Figs.6-15.1 to 11.

In a pattern-oriented approach, linear urbanization is first and foremost defined on the basis of the linear form (rule of thumb: length is at least twice the width); in a process-oriented approach it is defined on the basis of a linear main access route.

Linear urbanisation can take place at different scales:

- at street level, village level : the linear village (*lintdorp*);
- at urban and regional level: the linear city (*bandstad*).

Distinctive urban (or village) functions (primarily housing, primarily work, primarily amenities) can be located parallel to the main axis, or alternately across it. A combination is, of course, also possible: Fig.6-15.1. In both situations there is linear urbanization along a main axis. Compared with a basic circular city (see Fig.5-25a), non-urbanized areas can be reached

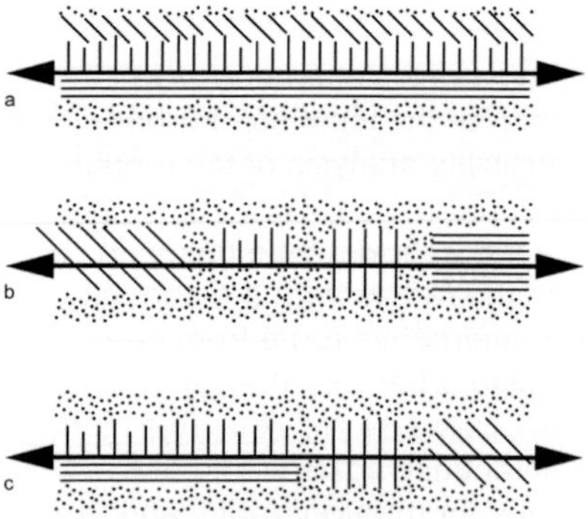

Fig. 6-15.1 Organization patterns of functions in theoretical linear urbanization models. From top to bottom;

- functions in strips along an axis → strips should be of various widths in connection with the difference in required (or affordable) surface area of functions; lengthwise there is no differentiation in informative value;
- function blocks on an axis → more flexible function development; no differentiation across the axis
- a combination of both → most flexible function development, greatest overall differentiation in informative value.

(after Dieters, Gelderblom & De Jong 1991: 6)

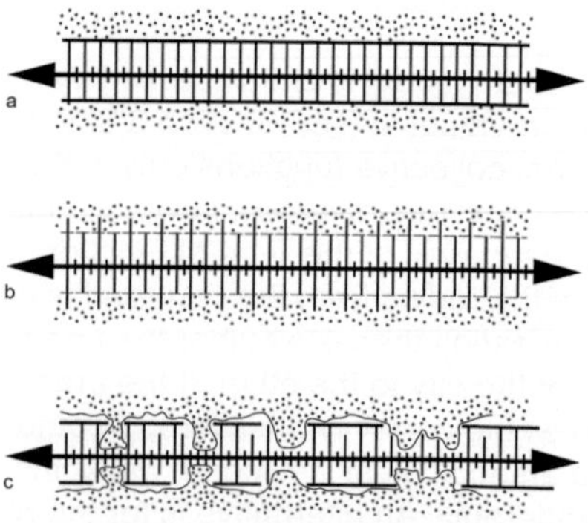

Fig. 6-15.2 Three types of transitions between urbanized and non-urbanized areas. From top to bottom:

- a distinct boundary between urbanized and non-urbanized areas → strong differentiation in informative value (experiential value);
- gradual transition between urbanized and non-urbanized areas: low building density on the edge of the urban area → a gradual difference in informative value, a larger variation in urban milieus than in the case of a sudden transition;
- a transition zone in which urbanized areas interchange with non-urbanized areas → considerable increase of the boundary length of the urban area; differentiation in potential user bases for amenities. (ibid.)

more quickly. The boundary length, moreover, is larger than that of a comparable circular city. The boundary between the urbanized and non-urbanized area can be sharp, gradual (decreasing density of urban functions[62]) or integrated: Fig.6-15.2.In a linear village, the main access route will be primarily aimed at private transport: walking, cycling, driving, with possibly the bus as supporting collective transport. A linear city is normally accessed by a motorway and in principle also by a rail connection.

Fig.6-15.3 The linear village Aguas Calientos in Peru can only be reached by rail instead of being accessed by road. (Photography courtesy Bodo Cappella)

Fig.6-15.4 The main access of Cameron Park, a small city in California, is an airstrip for light aircraft, with a lane for cars. (source: KIJK January 1994)

Interesting exceptions to road access are Aguas Calientos in Peru, which cannot be accessed by car but only by rail (Fig.6-15.3), and Cameron Park in California which is accessed by a road and an airstrip (Fig.6-15.4).

Linear cities (and their design) that are interesting from a historical point of view include: 'La Ciudad Lineal' by Soria y Mata (Spain, 1982), Tractorstoi of Miliutin (USSR, 1910), Magnitogorsk of Leonidov (USSR, 1929), Cite Industrielle Lineaire of Le Corbusier (France, 1935), Linear Industrial Town of Renaat Soetewey (Belgium, 1935), Rush City Reformed of Richard Neutra (USA, 1936) and Metrolineair City of Reginald Malcolmson (USA), 1956. These examples are taken from Dieters, Gelderblom & De Jong (1991: 11 ff.), the sources being: Angenot 1948: *De Lineaire stad, Stedebouw & Volkshuisvesting*: 128-129; Doxiadis 1963: *Architecture in Transition - linear growth* (New York): 35-36; Collins 1968: *Lineair Planning; its form & functions*, in Forum (5): 4-22; Bos, Tummers, Van Tol et al. 1984: *Ontwerp, Structuur & Vorm*, internal publication Faculty of Architecture Delft: 28 ff.

A linear system is always multinodal (see Fig.5-25).

The large space that is taken up by a central main access route for travel by car leads to a very wide barrier (when constructed horizontally) or a less wide but high barrier (when constructed vertically) - unless the car route is constructed underground (dual land use). With access by car the bundling of transport movements that characterises a linear city is not very efficient (see paragraph under Fig.6-5). If rail access as well as a central car access is possible then the car will often compete with collective transport in terms of travel time over many distances. This has a negative effect on collective transport (in turn leading to more people taking to the car and so on: a downward spiral with regard to promoting collective transport). Collective transport use can be fostered by locating the main car route outside the linear city. This also improves the environment of the urban area: Fig.6-15.5a and b. In the case of Fig.6-15.5a, the effect is that the (through) road acquires a dual function: both a connection and an access function. In the case of Fig.6-15.5b, the connection and access functions are separate.

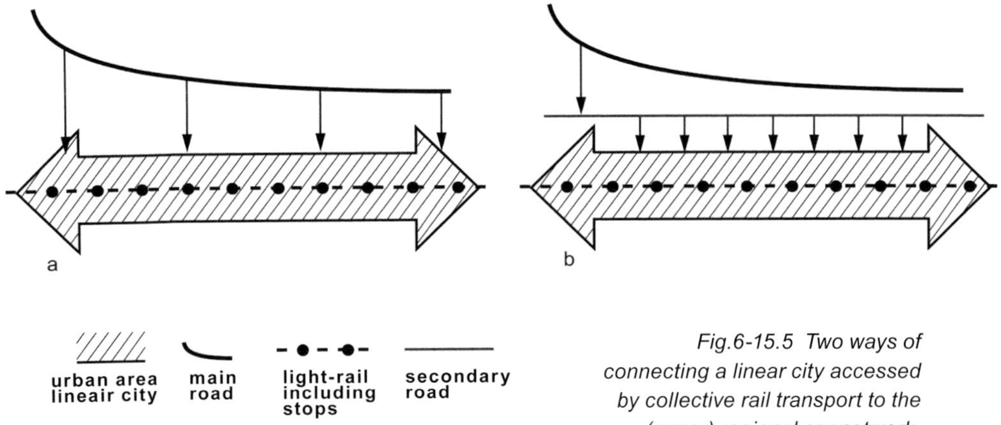

Fig.6-15.5 Two ways of connecting a linear city accessed by collective rail transport to the (super) regional car network.

A small degree of branching from the central access route (which is always the case for a collective transport connection) leads to a concentration of collective functions around intersections, due to the difference in location-value(A) (see Section 6.3). In American linear villages, the classic example is the road intersection with a petrol station at each of the four corners. In a linear city, the area around the stops is an ideal location for collective functions. Where there is a crossing of connections of similar order, the location value on the basis of accessibility will differ even further. This leads to a development such as shown in Fig.6-15.6 (symbiosis and agglomeration effects, see Section 6.2).

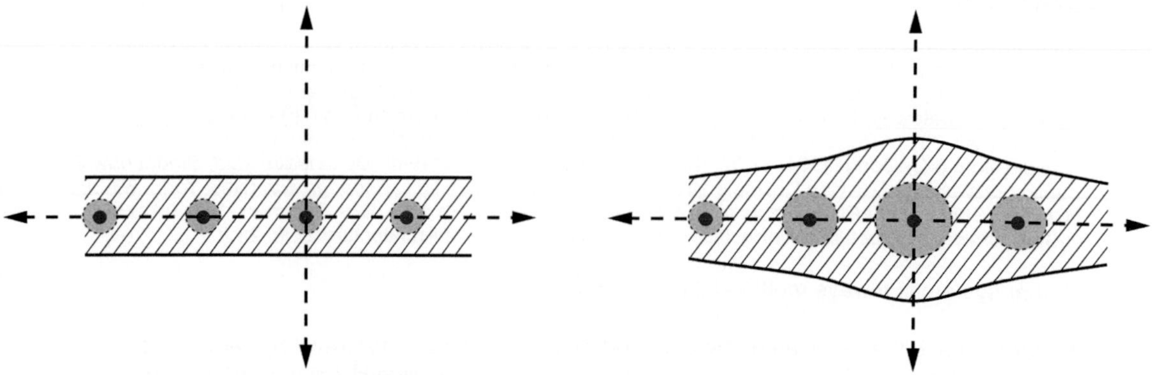

Fig.6-15.6 agglomeration effects of location value on the basis of accessibility. The situation on the left develops into the one on the right.

Due to accessibility considerations linear villages are not very efficient. This is not the case for linear cities. A more even spread of points of origin and destinations, and consequently a better spread of the demand for transport in time, means that linear cities have higher utilization of collective transport throughout the day than the mononodal satellite and lobate models.

The combination of Fig.6-15.1 (central or lowermost variant), 6-15.2 (uppermost variant), 6-15.5a and 6-15.6 produces the theoretical principle of Fig.6-15.7: a small linear city.

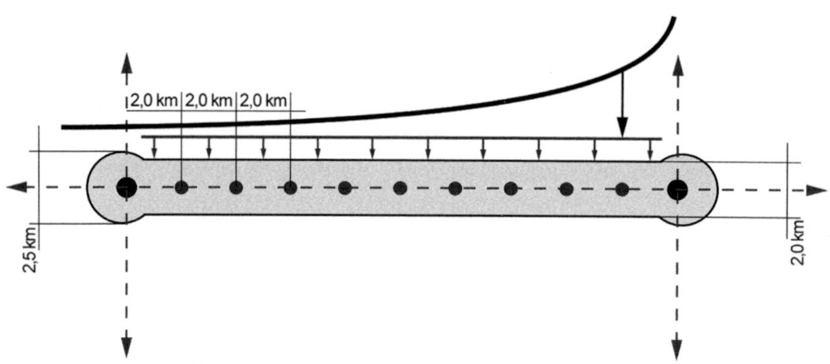

Fig.6-15.7 Theoretical model of a small linear city 'suspended' on two main centres of comparable size. The quantifications in this model are based upon administrative-societal considerations.

The width of this linear city is based upon a pre-transport distance (in the band) of a maximum of 1000 metres to a stop. Adding collective transport of a lower order according to the principle illustrated in Fig.6-15.8 allows the width to double. This leads to the theoretical model of Fig.6-15.9.

Fig.6-15.8 Adding secondary access connections, parallel to the main rail access route which cross one another at the stops, allows the width of the band to increase.

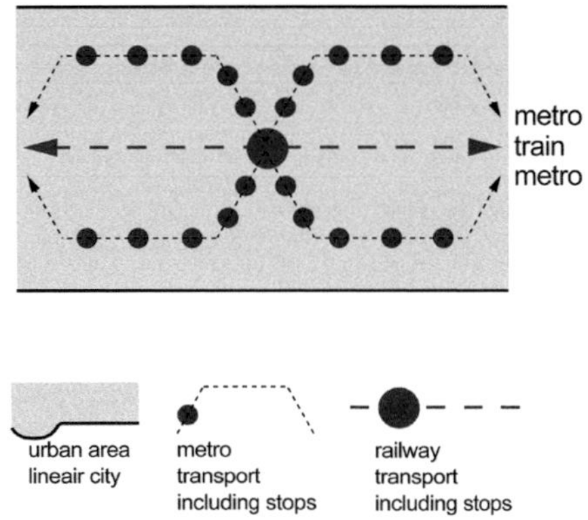

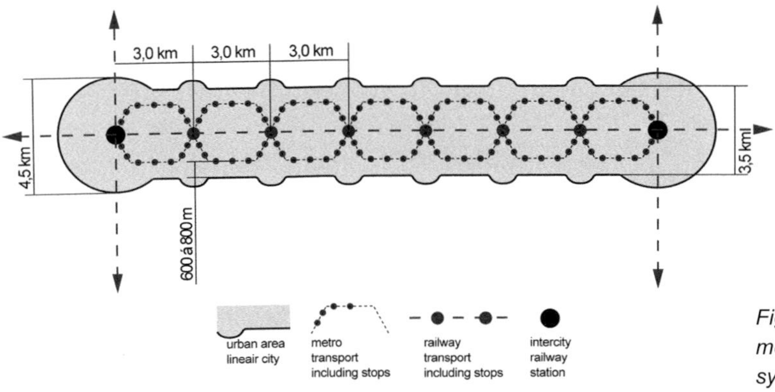

Fig.6-15.9 Variant of the theoretical model of 15.7. The user base of the system has increased considerably.

In the linear city variant of Fig. 6-15.9 conditions have been created that can lead to a greater diversity of possible urban milieus than in the narrow linear city. The location value(A) (see Section 6.3.2.) leads to positions in the system with favourable spatial conditions for regional collective functions with different accessibility profiles: Fig.6-15.10.

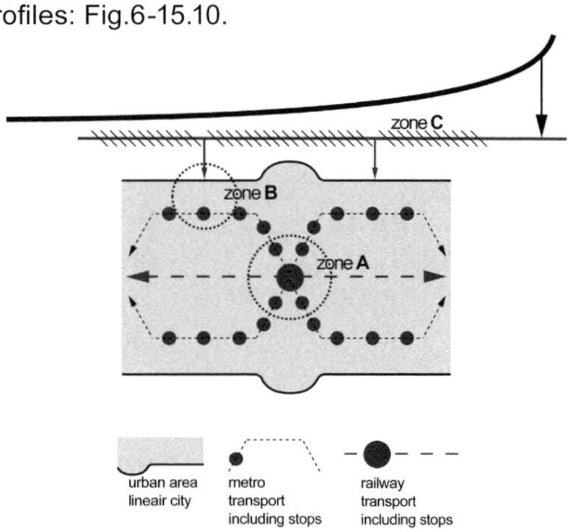

Fig.6-15.10 Around the primary station, the spatial conditions have been created for regional functions with a collective transport profile. Around the secondary stations, the spatial conditions have been created for regional functions that have a combined collective/private transport profile. In the zone along the secondary access route, a motorway, functions can be located with a private (i.e. car) transport profile.

Linear city growth takes place in practice where the natural situation encourages this (for example a river valley), or where urbanization takes place between two centres of comparable size. Fig.6-15.11 shows an exploratory model for urban developments in the province of North Holland from a provincial government paper.

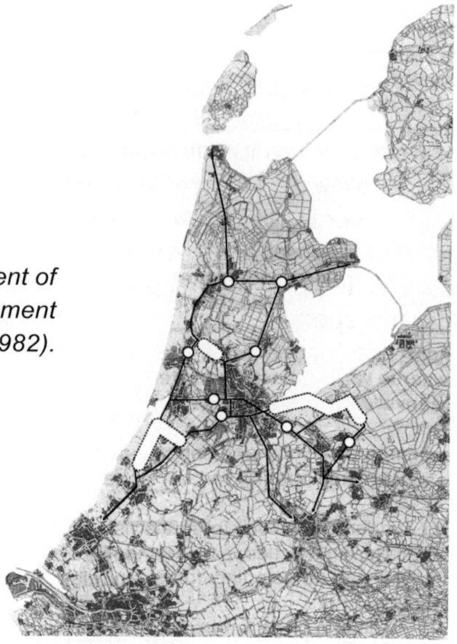

Fig.6-15.11 Exploratory model for the spatial development of North Holland on the basis of a linear urban development (Gedeputeerde Staten van Noord-Holland 1982).

6.4.5 Researching the network region

In his Masters Thesis (2001) Pepijn Verpaalen developed on the linear city principle depicted in Fig.6-15.9 to produce a theoretical model for an urban system in which information and communication technology (ICT) plays a major role. He assumed that this would mean that a substantial part of the population would feel the need for a relatively large range of temporospatial activities (Figs.6-16.1 to 11 - all from Verpaalen 2001).

In the linear city model of Fig.6-15.9 a single element can be regarded as a theoretical model. The potential user base of the main centres this element can be increased by adding lobes to this element (see Fig.5-25). This is illustrated in Fig.6-16.1.

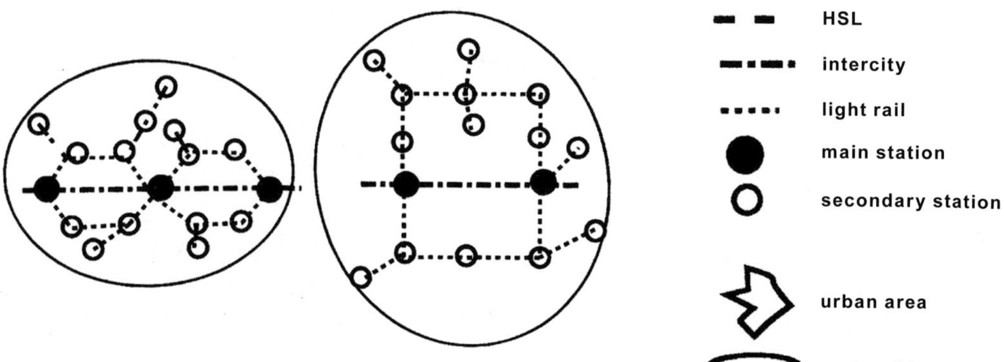

Fig.6-16.1 Linear city principle with additional lobes, the drawing on the right magnifies one element of the linear city.

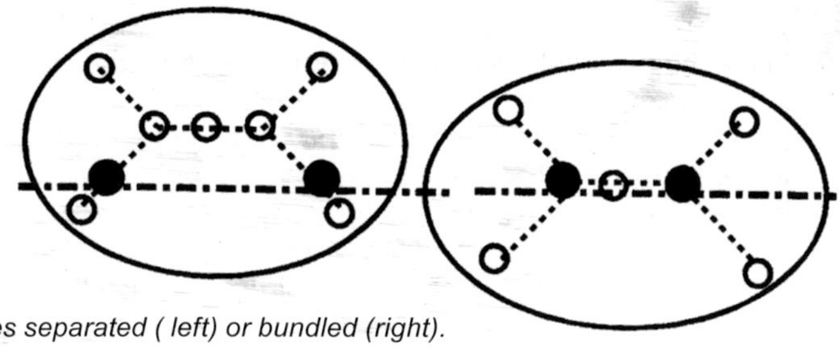

Fig.6-16.2 Parallel transport lines separated (left) or bundled (right).

Referring to the linear city element, the two horizontal, parallel transport lines may be bundled: Fig.6-16.2. Separation of these collective transport lines has a number of advantages over bundling: (1) separating local and super local transport results in a better flow and improves transport safety; (2) bundling increases the congestion in the main centres; (3) disconnecting produces a greater variety of location values, with the consequence that the collective transport system is at a competitive advantage over private transport owing to its connectivity to the superregional system.

The system is flexible, both in terms of expansion (Fig.6-16.3) and modification. In Fig.6-16.4 a high speed rail line (HSL) has been added and the existing railway has been converted into a regional light rail connection.

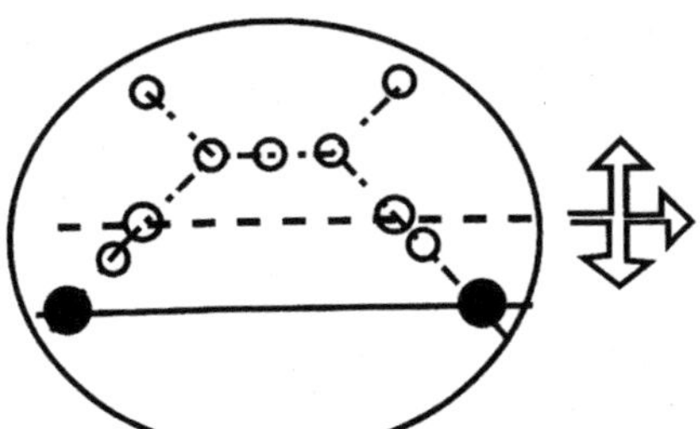

Fig.6-16.3 The theoretical model can be expanded both in height and in width.

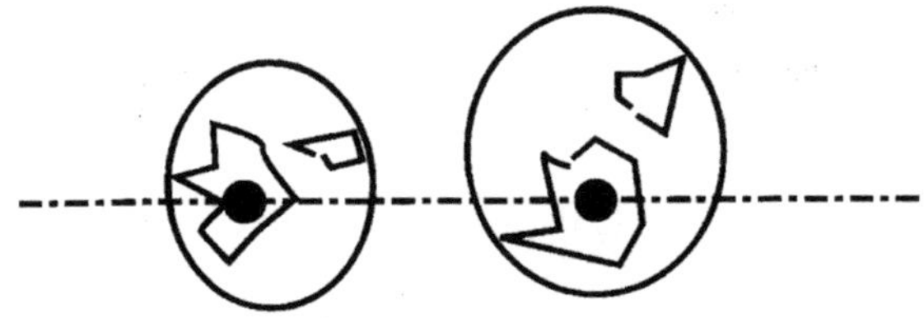

Fig.6-16.4 Initial situation

Fig.6-16.5 Introduction of high-speed line (HSL) and conversion of existing railway to a light rail connection.

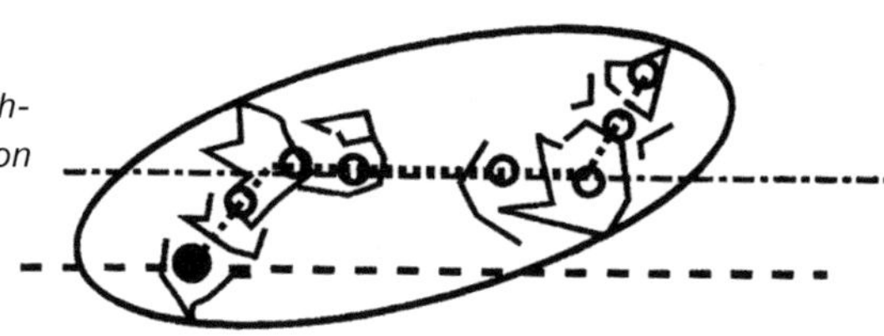

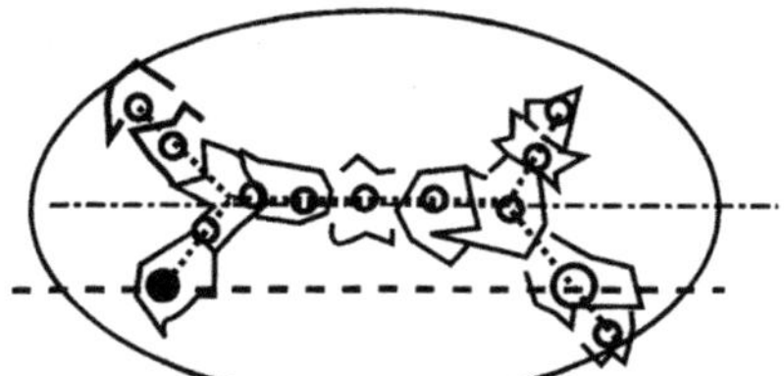

Fig.6-16.6 The system can be expanded: more lobes and possibly a new HSL station.

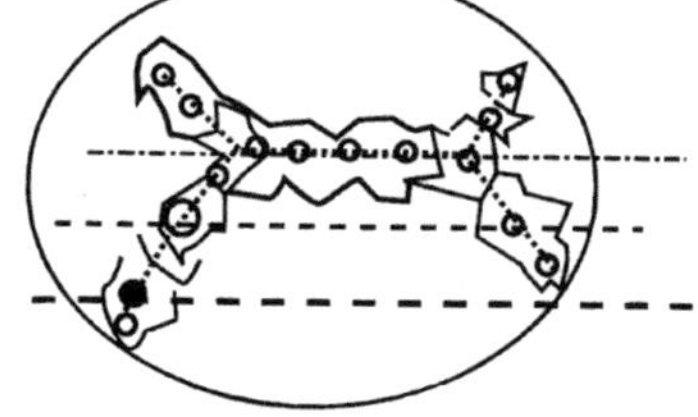

Fig.6-16.7 An even faster connection can be added.

In the models illustrated in Fig.6-16.8 to 16.10 road connections have been added in the system in such a way that (1) superlocal transport and local transport are kept separate, and (2) for superlocal transport flow and speed are the most important factors, whilst for local transport the quality and speed are such that the collective transport is a good alternative for the car. To achieve the latter in order to reach the destination by car the entire area would have to be transversed with many delay causing junctions: local roads are linked step-by-step to super regional roads: Fig.6-16.8. Compare this figure with Fig.6-16.9 where the collective transport connection is illustrated.

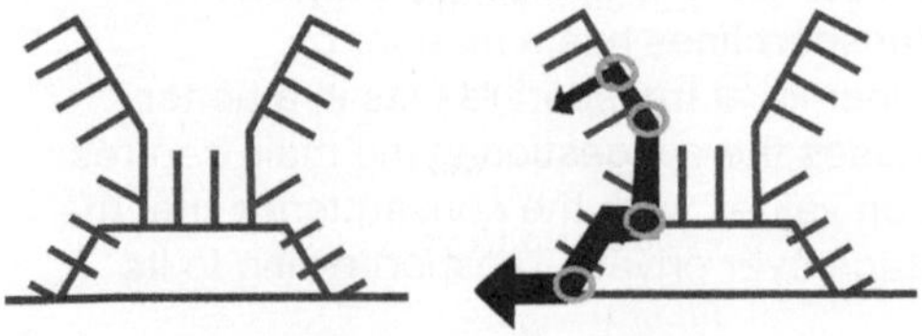

Fig.6-16.8 Car connections go through the system step-by-step: local road, district road, city road, regional road, super regional /international road.

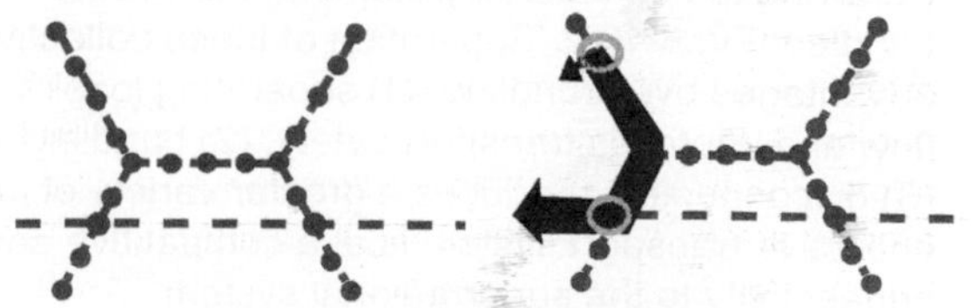

Fig.6-16.9 From local collective transport there is a direct transfer to national or international transport.

Car systems and collective transport systems can be bundled vertically. By laying the HSL above the city trunk road it is difficult to build quality-reducing intermediate stations along the HSL. On the non-urban side of the HSL good possibilities arise for connections between the car system (all levels of scale) and the collective transport system: Fig.6-16.10.

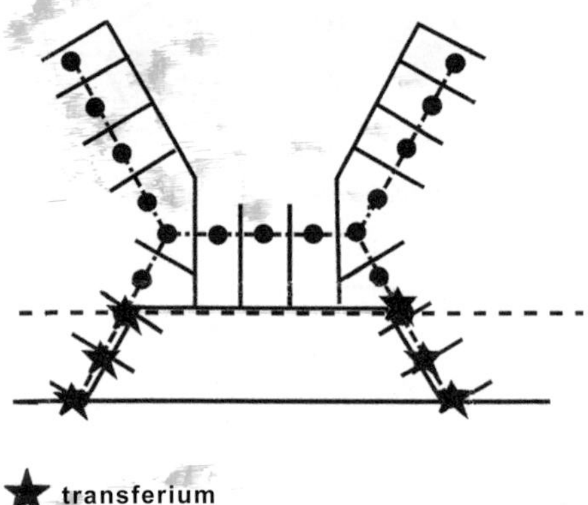

Fig.6-16.10 Location park & ride facilities.

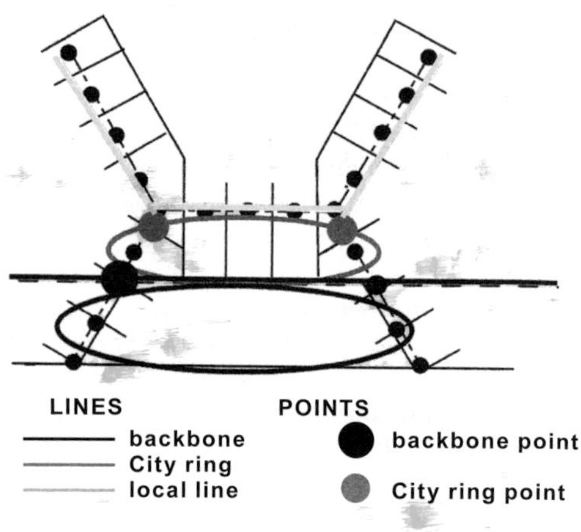

Fig.6-16.11 Introduction of ICT network.

Finally, a network of data cables has been introduced into the theoretical model. Selective 'accessibility' can be achieved with this type of network through cables with a diverse capacity. BBP stands for backbone point. Such a point can be compared with a station along an HSL. A CRP (city ring point) is also a type of station, but the accessibility is not as good as that of the BBP.

6.4.6 Theoretical model for the area around a light rail station

In a post-masters course Michiel Scholten designed a theoretical model on the basis of detailed, normative, organization principles for an area around a light rail station (metro station) (1996). A 'light rail/metro station area' is understood here to mean an area within a radius of 500 metres around the station, a distance which can be travelled by foot within 10 minutes by almost everyone. A number of elements from this study are given in Figs.5-17.1 to 10.

Collective public transport can only be operated if the demand for transport can be bundled efficiently. The effectiveness of the development of a high quality public transport system is in part dependent on the degree to which urban activities are concentrated around stations. Whatever high quality public transport network is constructed will therefore have to play a structure-giving role in further urban development. Urban activities can be organized according to their potential user base, which means that some activities have to be accessible for every resident of an urban area but that for other activities it will be sufficient if they are accessible for only some of the residents. Facilities must be accessible within acceptable journey constraints (both in terms of time and transfers) for sufficient numbers of residents in order to function. Moreover, a larger job market is necessary for specialized jobs than for non-specialised jobs. On the basis of accessibility, a hierarchy of nodes can be determined in the network of high quality public transport connections. This provides a basis for allocating urban activities to particular locations according to their potential user bases. Station areas should not be allowed to turn into motorway-style business parks, but should become high quality developments of the urban area, which mutual benefits for the station areas and the urban surroundings (symbiosis effects).

General legend

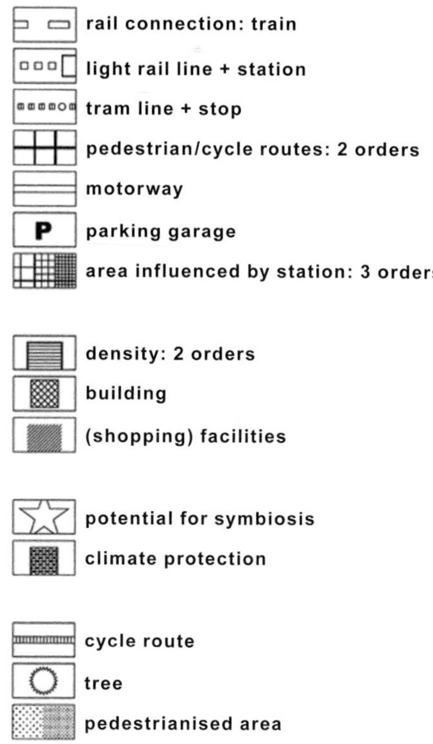

In this non-localized design three lines of approach are used:

- Accessibility: the route structure of pedestrians, cyclists, trams and cars (both local traffic and through traffic): examples of spatial organization principles ('building blocks'): Fig.6-17.1-5;
- Programme: functions and their mix, the intensity of use and the zoning - examples Fig.6-17.6;
- Protection: road safety, public safety and weather protection - examples Fig.6-17.7 and 17.8.

Accessibility

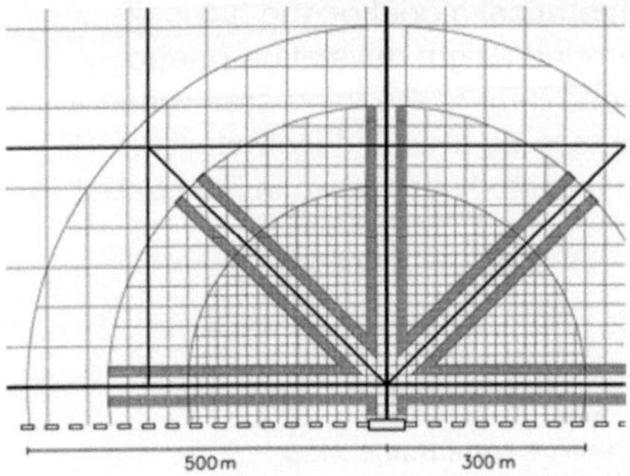

Fig.6-17.1 Cycle route structure

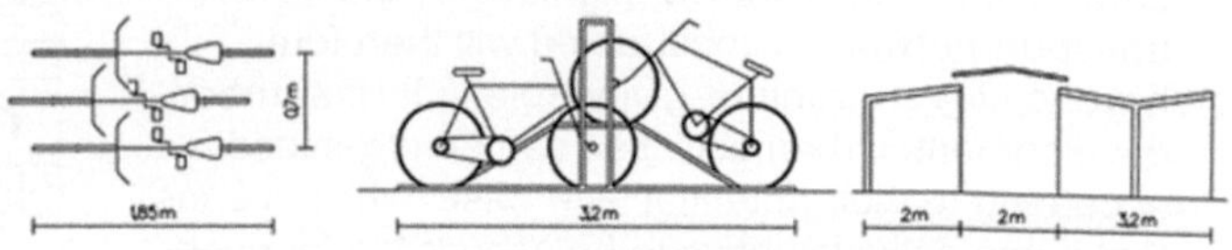

Fig.6-17.2 Cycle rack principle

For the accessibility of the metro station by bicycle, it is important that at least the main cycle routes are station-oriented and are uninterrupted. A main cycle route is characterized by being separate from car routes, by being direct and continuous and, having the highest possible priority in the layout of junctions. Cycle routes of a lower level should link up with the main routes directly and continuously. The presence of a fine-mesh cycle network in the station area will allow as many destinations as possible to be quickly accessed by bicycle. In the station area, this is important for those arriving at the station by train wishing to continue their journey by bicycle (Fig.6-17.1).

Use of a bicycle as a means of transport to the station will become more attractive if there are sufficient bicycle racks at the station where the cyclists can place the bicycle under shelter near the entrance to the station without loosing too much time. This will allow people to quickly transfer from bicycle to metro. The risk of damage to or theft of the bicycle must also be minimized.

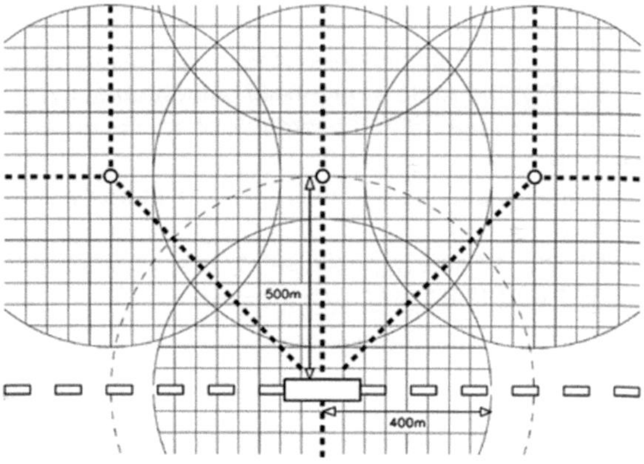

Fig.6-17.3 Tram route structure

At local level, a tram system complements the metro system better than any other. The tram system serves as pre- and post- transport feeder system and the aim therefore is to have (relatively) fast and direct connections between local concentrations of urban activities and the metro system. The route structure shown in Fig.6-17.3 is comparable to that in Fig.6-11.

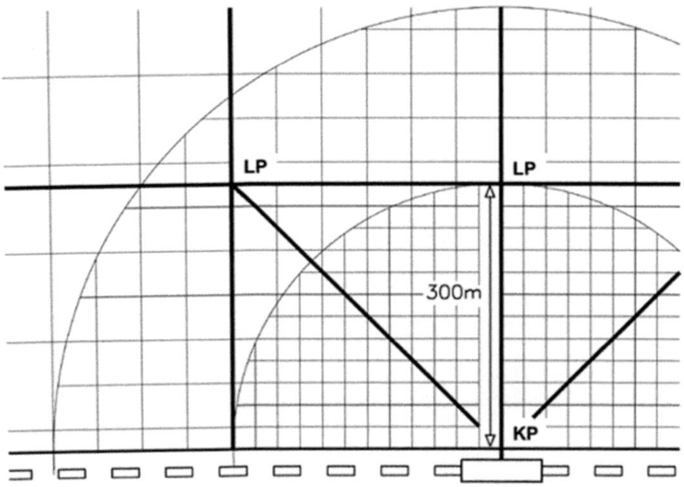

Fig.6-17.4 Siting of short stay (KP) /long stay (LP) car parking

To limit non-essential car traffic, it is important to have a policy for traffic management. Providing good accessibility to essential car traffic must not lead to an increase in non-essential traffic. The most effective measure is to apply strict parking regulations: the more accessible a station area is by alternative transport, the stricter the parking regulations must be.

A private car only needs a place outside a metro station to pick up or drop off passengers, i.e. for very short time parking only. A central parking facility (parking garage) provides parking for longer periods. Such a parking facility should be located along a direct walking route to the station - the most important destination in the station area. The walking distance to the central parking facility should be similar to the walking distance to the tram stop or longer: Fig.6-17.4.

The station is a place of exchange where metro travellers, tram and bus passengers, car drivers and cyclists can change from one mode of transport to another. The immediate vicinity of the station functions as a node of various transfer relations: Fig.6-17.5. When designing the station area it is necessary to “unravel” the node. For this it is necessary to set priorities in relation to the various forms of traffic in this area:

1 pedestrians,
2 wheelchair users,
3 cyclists,
4 collective public transport,
5 taxis,
6 cars pulling up,
7 parked cars.

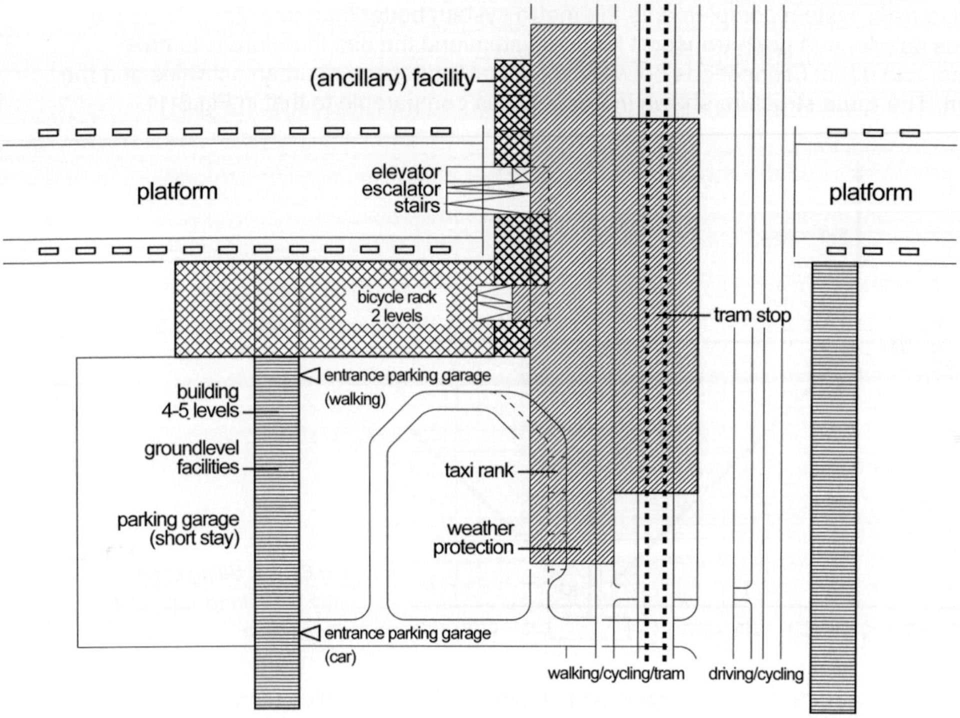

Fig.6-17.5 Transfer relationships between all available modes of transport.

Programme

In general we can say that the following functions, when located near a station, can make a major contribution to stimulating public transport:

- Public-oriented functions, such as shops, education, public buildings and healthcare. Besides generating employee traffic, these functions will also attract visitors. For some of these functions, such as hospitals, good accessibility by car is also important.
- Offices, both public and commercial. These functions tend to a large number of staff per unit surface area. The most suitable are offices with a reception function, as these attract visitors as well.

The housing function generates less public transport journeys then shops, public-oriented offices and education, but more than some other functions. Housing contributes to the public safety and the liveliness of the station area, particularly at night, in the evenings and in the weekends, when the other functions may be closed.

The more varied the functions are, the more attractive the station area. When locating functions in the station area one must also aim towards a mixture of functions that produces a spread in the demand for public transport through the day and not only to a relative increase in the use of public transport during the rush hour.

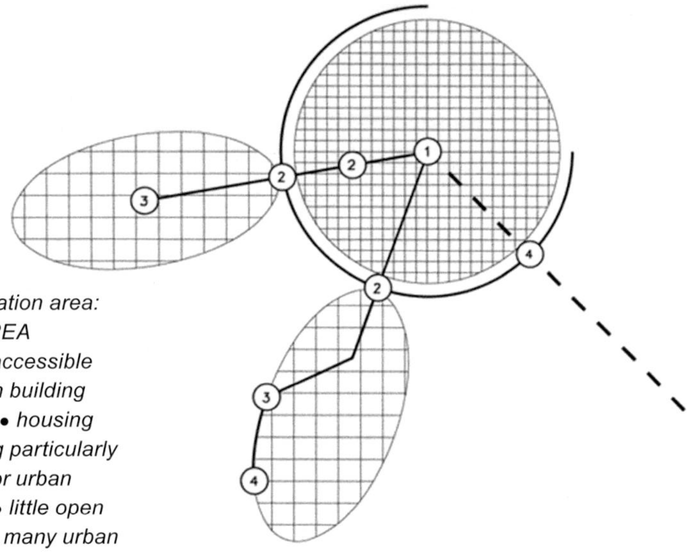

Fig.6-17.6 Intensity of functions in station area:
1 CENTRAL URBAN STATION AREA
central in the urban system o easily accessible by high quality public transport • high building density • strong mixture of functions • housing not dominant but important • housing particularly in form of apartments • preference for urban residence among small households • little open space • little greenery • many jobs • many urban facilities • gross fsi : 3.5
2 URBAN STATION AREA
near the centre of the urban system • best location is relatively central in relation to more peripheral districts • easily accessible by at least metro and tram • high building density • strong mixture of functions • relatively large proportion of housing • small households are most heavily represented • urban forms of housing • little open space • little greenery • gross fsi : 2.5
3 SEMI-URBAN STATION AREA
at some distance from the centre of the urban system • easily accessible by metro and tram • moderately low, building density • function mixture but housing is dominant • differentiation of small and larger households • differentiation of forms of housing • potential for subcentre or district centre • more open space • more greenery • gross fsi : 2.0
4 PERIPHERAL STATION AREA
in transition phase from urban to rural system • easily accessible by metro and tram • peripheral choice location lies at crossing of metro and train line and has better accessibility then other locations in the area • relatively low building density • practically monofunctional area • all housing in form of housing estates • more open space • more greenery • gross fsi : 1.0

The station area should be designated for functions that lead to a high intensity of users and a high density of buildings at a walking distance from the station. The functions with the highest intensities are best located in the area for pedestrians around the station - within a radius of 300 to 400 metres of the station (along direct main routes for pedestrians). Lower, but not absolutely low, intensities are possible in zones that are located further from the station and further from the main routes for pedestrians. The zoning of functions in the station area can be further differentiated by locating public-oriented functions along the direct main routes for (slow-moving) traffic from the station. On the one hand this increases the accessibility of the public-oriented functions for (occasional) visitors, and on the other hand it promotes increases an attractive urban atmosphere by the presence of large numbers of the public. When locating functions, account will also have to be taken of the characteristics of the travellers generated by a particular function. A hospital, for example, attracts a large number of visitors with impaired walking, and should thus be located as close as possible to the station (see Fig.4-14).

Protection

To obtain a high utilisation rate of the metro, also in the early and late hours, public safety in the waiting and transfer areas of the station is important. In addition to the general measures in relation to public safety, there are specific measures for the waiting and transfer areas at the station (Fig.6-17.7).

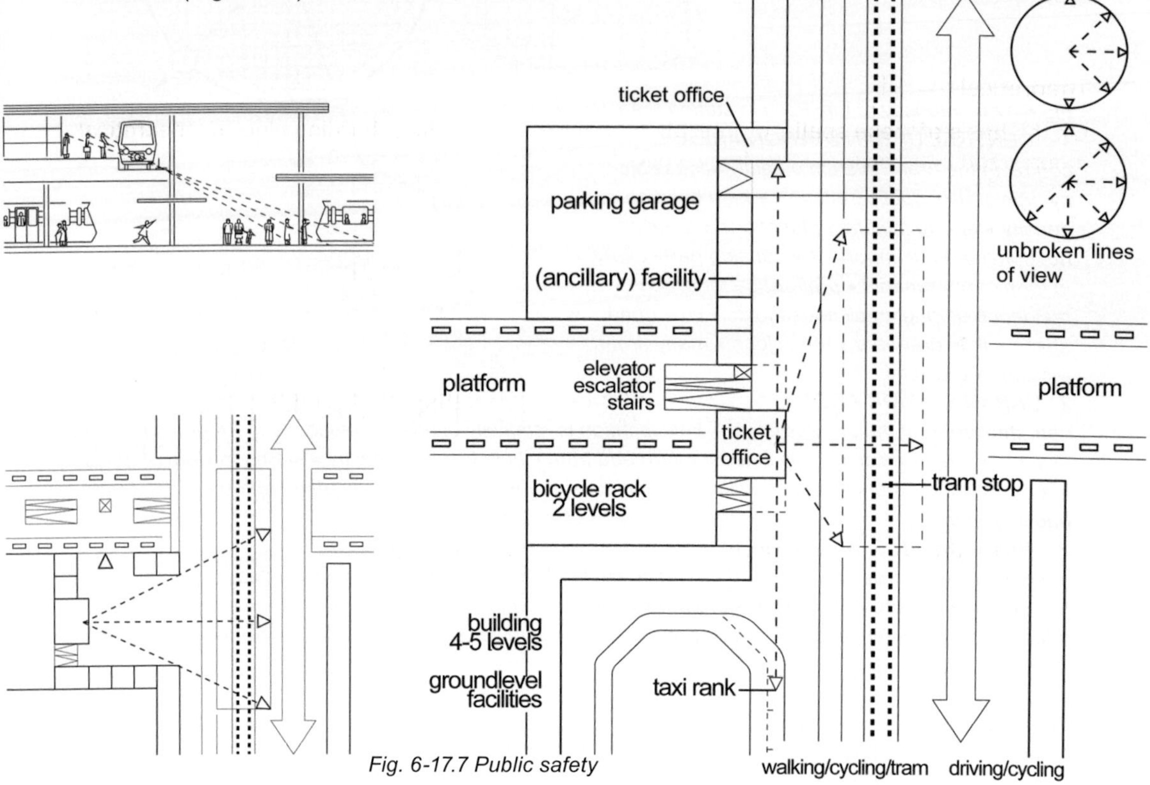

Fig. 6-17.7 Public safety

Measures:

- Locating public-oriented functions at or around the waiting and transfer areas at the station.
- Locating (ancillary) functions at the waiting and transfer areas at the station, with opening hours corresponding to those of the station.
- Locating the waiting and transfer areas along and in view of (continuous) main traffic routes. Avoid placing the waiting and transfer areas in a secluded location.
- Locating all the waiting and transfer facilities of the metro, tram, bus, bicycle, taxi and car in view of the other waiting and transfer facilities. At a taxi rank there will usually be drivers present.
- Unbroken lines of view between the various waiting and transfer facilities at or near the station: Avoid placing opaque bus shelters or advertising boards in the lines of sight.
- Avoid (long) windowless building fronts near the station, e.g. a bicycle shed. Integrate the bicycle shed with other (public-oriented) facilities.
- Good escape routes for potential victims. For example, avoid locating waiting facilities between two busy car lanes.
- Direct, immediately recognisable and publicly safe walking routes between the main entrance of the station and the tram stop, bicycle shed, taxi rank and car parking facilities.

Protection against sun and rain or snow is visualized in Fig. 6-17.8

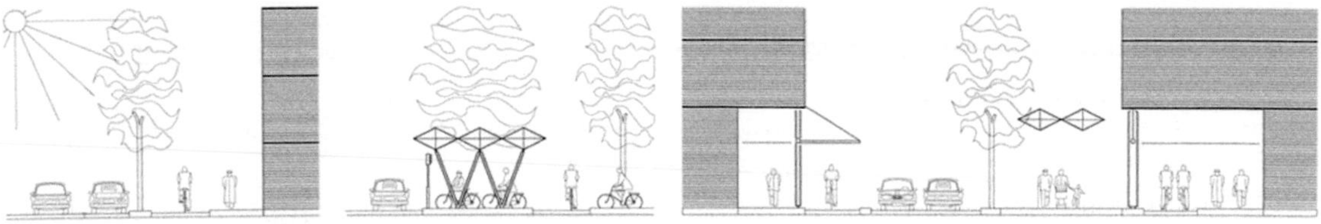

Fig. 6-17.8 Weather protection.

Theoretical models

On the basis of these spatial organization principles (theoretical 'building block's') theoretical models can be constructed on two levels of scale: fig.6-17.9 and 17.10.

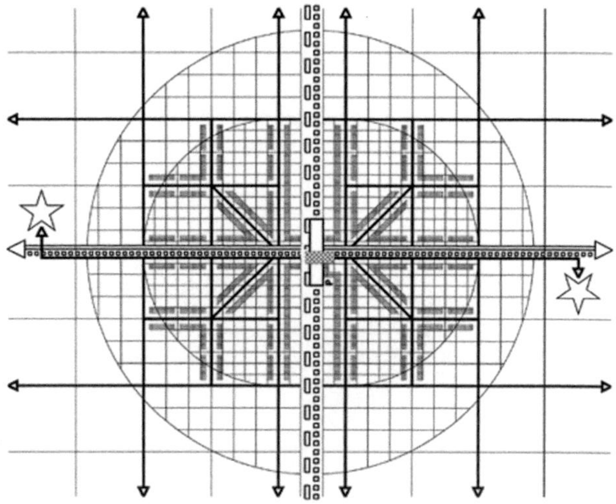

Fig.6-17.9 Theoretical model for the area around a metro station on the basis of spatial organization principles (theoretical building blocks).

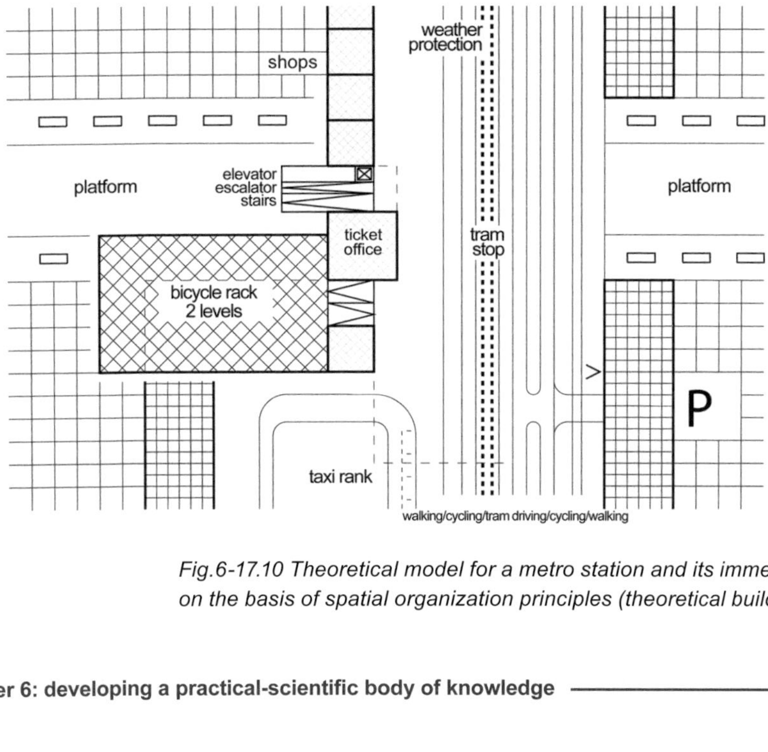

Fig.6-17.10 Theoretical model for a metro station and its immediate surroundings on the basis of spatial organization principles (theoretical building blocks).

6.5 Researching theoretical models in relation to localized design projects

"…. I have used quite a number of Greek examples; this is not intended to mean that similar cases from other countries were not of universal value. But rather that I wanted to be completely sure that I was not misinterpreting the causes of the phenomena because of any lack of knowledge of the details in each situation."

(Constantinos Doxiadis 1968, *Ekistics*: 18)

6.5.1 A design for the Amsterdam inner city

The description below is based on the results of a post-graduate project by Cecilia, Houtsma, Immerzeel, De Lange and Scholten (1989) (Figs.6-18.1 to 10).

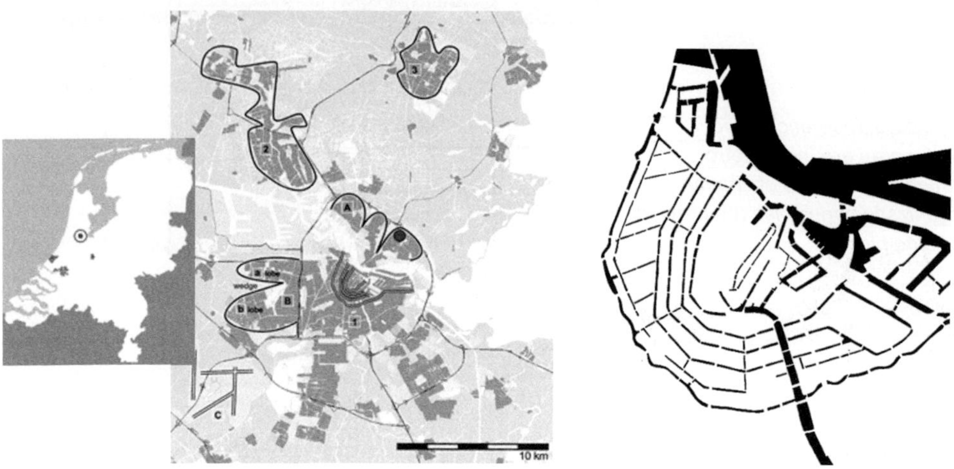

Fig.6-18.1 Amsterdam and its inner city

In the design for the inner city of Amsterdam, it must be borne in mind that functional-spatially this area is the main centre of the Amsterdam region, which is a combination of the lobate, finger and satellite models (see Fig.5-25). The development plan for this region, shown in Fig.6-18.9, came about after a development vision was formulated for both the region and the main centre area, and a development plan was made for the entire region (not shown here). Fig.6-18.2 is a representation of the working method. Only the grey coloured elements in this diagram are presented here: Figs.6-18.3 to 11.

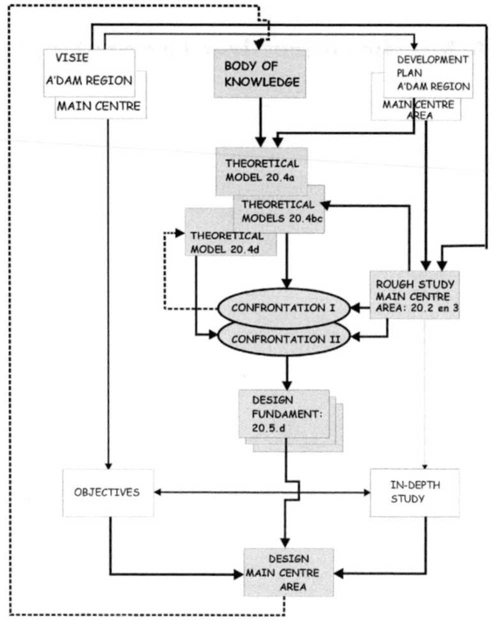

Fig.6-18.2 Working method. In the diagram, rectangle represent products and ovals represent actions. The dotted lines indicate feedback. Only the grey coloured elements in this diagram are presented here.

Functional and formal structure analyses were made of the existing situation (Fig.6-18.3 and 6-18.4).

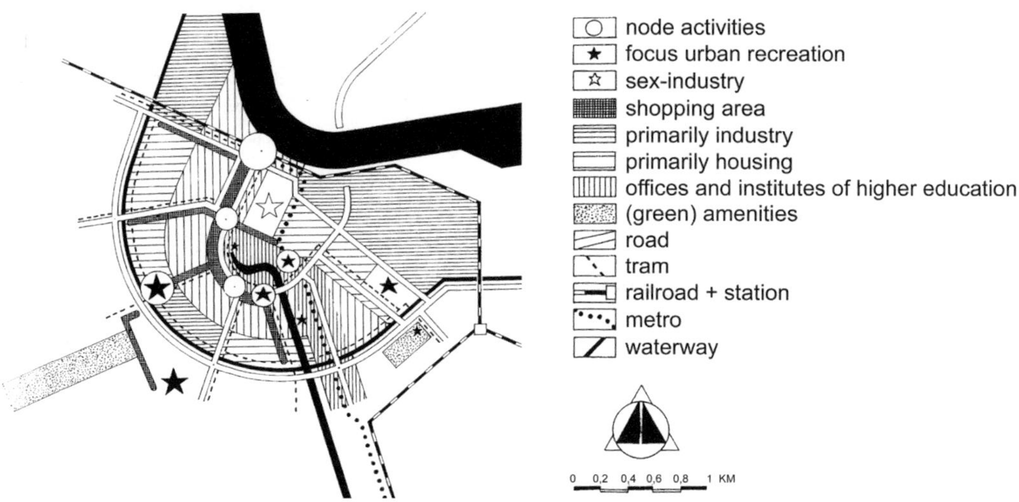

Fig.6-18.3 Functional structure analysis of the inner city of Amsterdam (Cecilia et al. 1989: 77).

Important elements of the functional structure are:
- the transecting of the city by a waterway (*het IJ*);
- the location of the regional main station on the *IJ*;
- the linear centre zone between this station via Dam to Muntplein;
- the radial routes to and from this centre zone;

- a partial inner ring road for car traffic;
- magnet functions in the centre with connencting routes: main station, Dam, Leidseplein, city hall/music theatre.

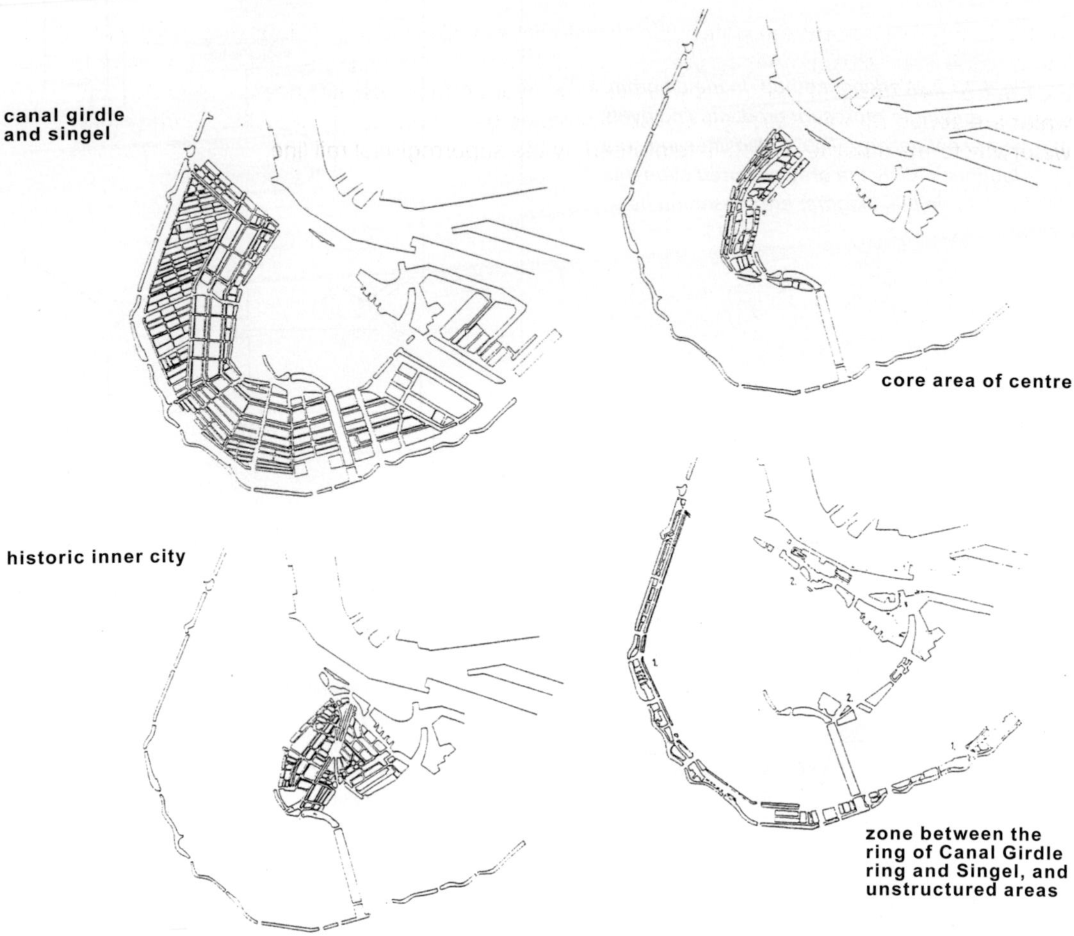

Fig.6-18.4 Formal structure analysis of the inner city of Amsterdam. Five distinctive zones are identified (ibid.: 82).

There are certain relationships between the formal structure, in which the canal girdle is particularly important for identification and orientation, and the functional structure:
- the magnet functions lie in the centre core area (with the exception of Leidseplein) - the historic inner city is less suitable for this;
- functional routes are located along the radials;
- the unstructured area in the western part of the inner city was not considered to be a part of the centre area until recently.

A theoretical model for an urban-regional centre of a scale appropriate to a mononodal region of 1,5 million inhabitants is illustrated in Fig.6-18.5a. In Fig.6-18.5b, elements of the existing system that are considered unchangeable are introduced in this theoretical model. The main station is in reality not located in the middle of the centre. Since the focus of the centre activities does not coincide with this station, a zone is created between these two magnet functions. Some of the internal urban-regional connections run through this zone to the station. The bundling of these lines results in a high frequency collective transport service.

Added in Fig.6-18.5c are the waterway intersecting the city (*het IJ*), and the superregional rail line and the main station on the bank of this waterway. This means that tangential access to the centre area (the inner ring road) has to pass over or under *het IJ*. Located on and in the water are zones with a relatively high location value based on various considerations. The waterway forms a barrier which is reinforced by the superregional rail line.

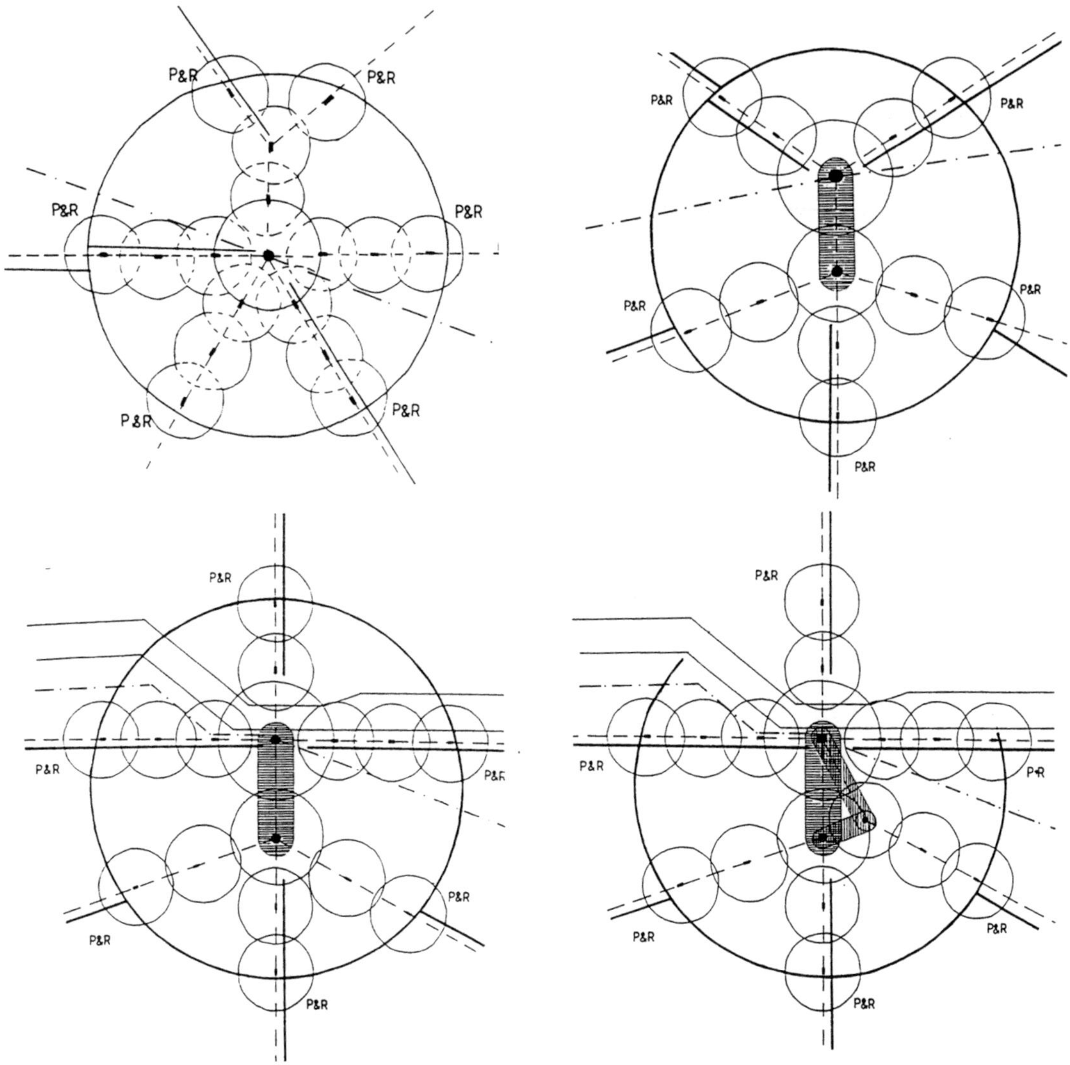

Fig.6-18.5 Four theoretical principles for an urban-regional centre area. The principles are successively geared more closely to the existing situation in Amsterdam (ibid.: 84). The circles indicate areas in walking distance of a station.

Fig.6-18.5d was obtained by confronting 6-18.5c with the existing situation. The siting of the the city hall/music theatre attractor outside the main centre zone leads to the addition of two secondary centre zones which form a triangular circuit together with the main centre zone.

The confrontation of the theoretical model with the actual situation is illustrated in four steps in Fig.6-18.6a to d. When confronting models it is important that their structures are comparable. The confrontation allows differences to be observed. These differences may lead either to a modification of the theoretical model (as illustrated above) or to the observation that they are a positive addition in the case of Amsterdam, but have no implications on the scale of the inner city. They may also lead though to the identification of problems for which a solution or partial solution can possibly be found.

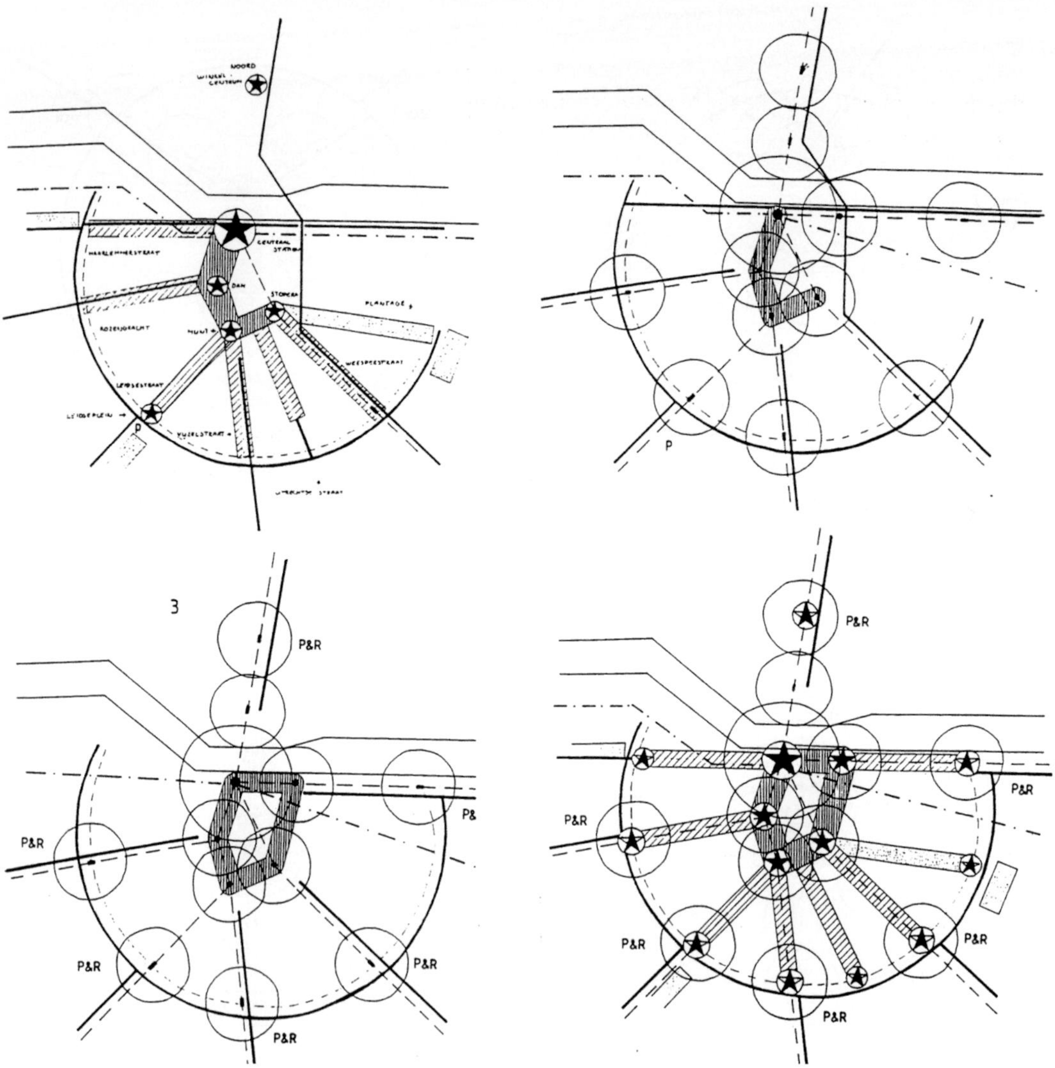

Fig.6-18.6 Four stages in the process of producing a general development model for the inner city (ibid.: 86).

Steps in the confrontation were the introduction of the existing radial rail lines and their stops, and the introduction of city dependences (subcentres which require a good connection with the main centre area). The triangular circuit from 18.5d has been modified according to the actual situation in Amsterdam to avoid an undesired transection of the historic inner city (see Fig.6-18.4) and has become pentagonal. The unstructured zone on the eastern side of the inner city is suitable for centre-type developments. A 'centre-zone' around the historic inner city is thus created. The whole centre remains compact. The distances are walkable, and criss-cross relationships can develop through the historic inner city. The radials connect to this centre pentagon.

The final result of the confrontation is Fig.6-18.6d, a functional-spatial design basis.

Examples of positive aspects:
- the monumental quality of the inner city;
- the dominant pattern of tangential and radial canals;
- an easily accessible inner ring road for car traffic;
- the existence of places in the city with 24-hour activity;
- places with 24-hour activity are connected to one another.

Examples of problems are illustrated in Fig.6-18.7.

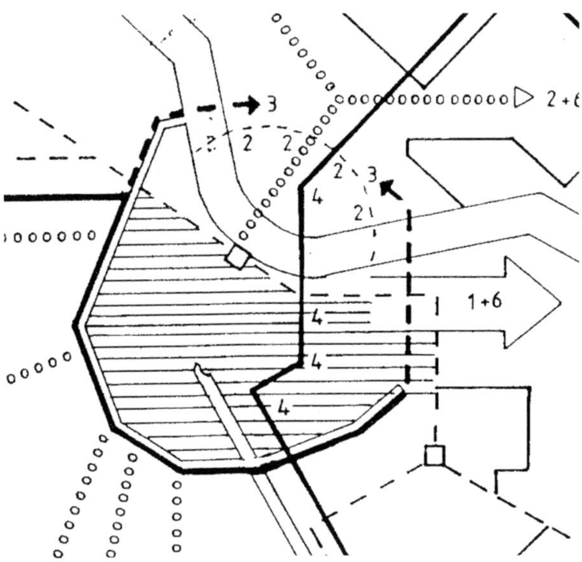

Fig.6-18.7 A few of problems revealed by the confrontation (ibid.: 91 ff.).

1. *The through road for cars on the north side of the main station forms a barrier for the development of this side of the station. This road functions more as a connecting road than an accessing radial.*
2. *Amsterdam-North (across* het IJ*) is disconnected from the urban-regional centre: there is a lack of high-quality collective transport and cycle/pedestrian connections, and hence poor access to urban-regional functions from the north.*
3. *The inner ring road for car traffic does not extend to Amsterdam-North.*
4. *The motorway from Amsterdam-North transects the main centre area.*
6. *A radial connection is lacking.*

Fig.6-18.8 depicts a research question that was formulated as a result of the confrontation. In view of the fact that the inner ring road is fairly narrow, is it possible to split it into two concentric rings with one-way traffic?

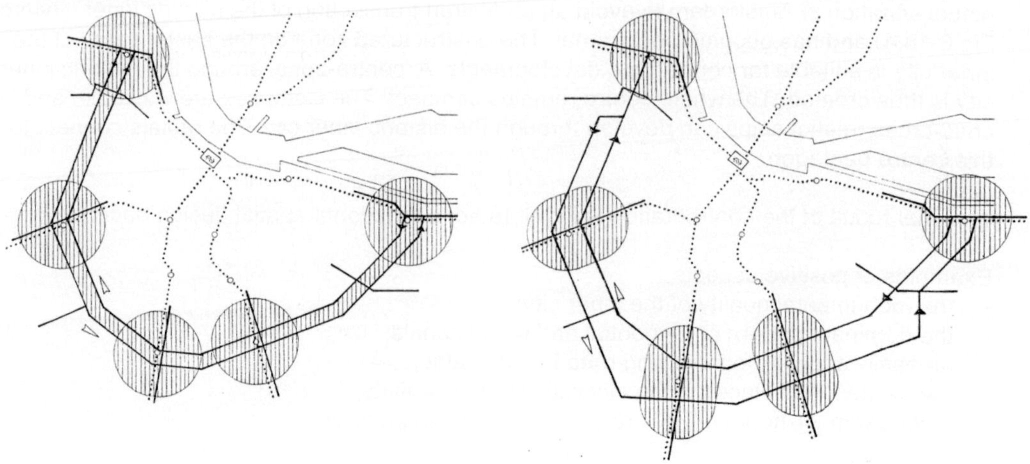

Fig.6-18.8 Considering that the inner ring road for is fairly narrow, is it possible to split the inner ring? Note the changed form of the areas that have potential for the development of city dependences (ibid.: 97).

Important conclusions to be drawn from the confrontation are:

- The main station is largely surrounded by water. This water could be partly used for centre-related functions (e.g. new buildings on foundations or floating in the water).
- There is an unstructured zone between the inner ring road for car traffic and the road for collective transport traffic. Special functions could be located in this zone at the junctions with the radials.
- The structure element 'Singel' may become clearer (information function) if the now unstructured zone along it becomes involved.
- The urban-regional centre can be expanded in the eastern unstructured part of the inner city. Moreover, an expansion there would strengthen the position of the main station.
- The land around the main station is used too extensively.
- The historic inner city offers possibilities for transverse relationships between the various parts of the centre zone circuit.
- The water on both sides of the main station provides starting points for the development of special urban milieus.
- The radials have to be strengthened - some by the construction of a light rail connection, others by the provision of new tram connections.
- All (new) light rail stations generate potential for urban-regional functions, but not every area around such a station is suitable for this (monumental character, barriers present, etc.). Furthermore, the various locations will have to be weighed up against one another, e.g.as part of a phased development plan.

On the basis of the objectives based on the vision for the Amsterdam region (see Fig.6-18.2) and on further, specific, research into the current situation, the basic development model of Fig.6-18.6d. leads to a functional-spatial design for the inner city.
This design is shown in Fig.6-18.9.

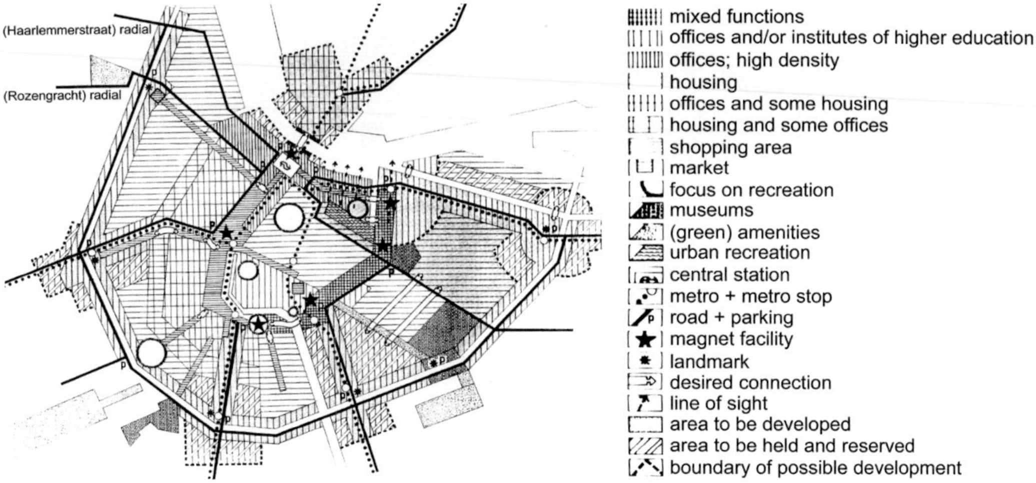

Fig.6-18.9 Functional-spatial design for the inner city of Amsterdam (ibid.:115).

A few essentials of this design are

- the super regional rail line along the waterway that cuts through Amsterdam has been laid underground, providing space for an extension of the urban-regional centre close to the main station;
- the water on the north side of the main station provides another extension of this centre;
- radial light rail lines have been added;
- Amsterdam-North is connected to the current city centre area by a light rail line;
- the southern point of Amsterdam-North is involved in the centre development;
- parking facilities are located at the peripheral end of the radial rail connections;
- in the inner city, the radial connections are clearly marked at the beginning and end;
- the shopping route in the main centre zone is extended into the main station;
- on the north side of the station the shopping route is extended eastwards.[63]

This study concludes by zooming in on all radial routes. Two examples are shown here: the Rozengracht radial connection in the direction of Amsterdam-West, the connection with the Slotermeer-Geuzeveld lobe and the Osdorp-Slotervaart lobe (see Section 6.5.2 below), and the Haarlemmerstraat radial, the continuation of which forms a barrier between the Slotermeer-Geuzenveld lobe and the wedge to the north (idem) (Figs.6-18.10 and 18.11).

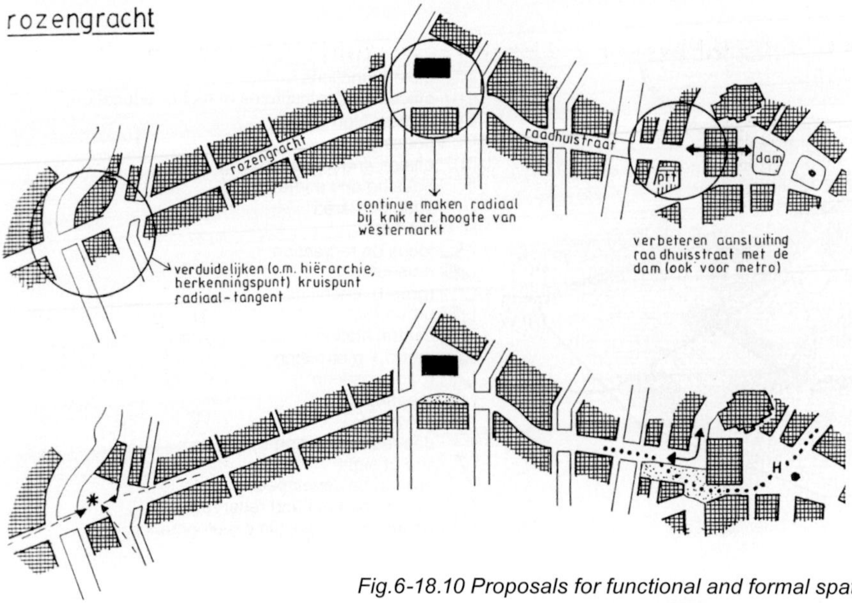

Fig.6-18.10 Proposals for functional and formal spatial interventions in the western (Rozengracht) radial from Fig.6-18.8, arising from the design for the inner city (ibid.: 119).

Fig.6-18.11 Proposals for functional and formal spatial interventions in the north-western (Haarlemmerstraat) radial from Fig.6-18.9, arising from the design for the inner city (ibid.: 118).

6.5.2 Researching the lobate model based on actual situations in Amsterdam

The Amsterdam region is partially developed according to the lobate model (Fig.6-19.1). A study of the development possibilities of this region requires a further study of this theoretical lobate model: Fig.6-19.2 to 19.17.

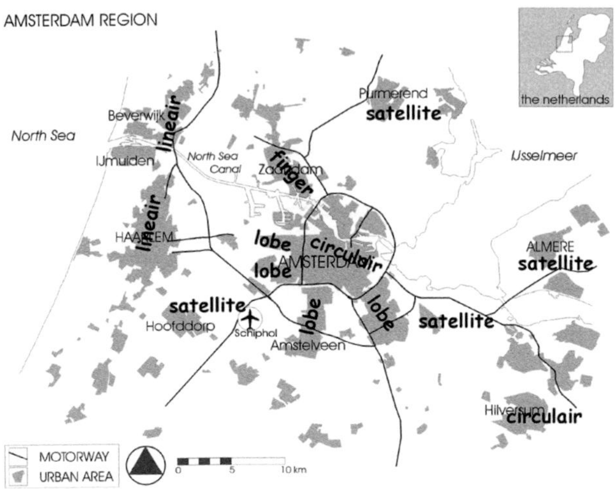

Fig.6-19.1 The Amsterdam Region

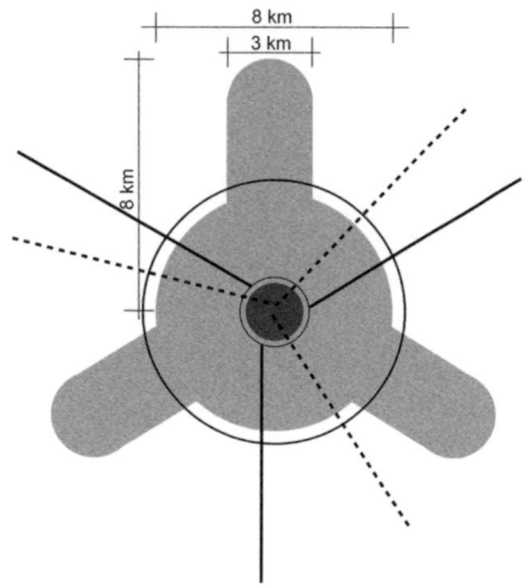

Fig.6-19.2 A lobate theoretical model (Jacobs 2000: 160); see Fig.5-25

The lobate model (Fig.6-19.2) is one of the theoretical models depicted in Fig.5-25. The lobate principle can be elaborated further, embroidering upon the situation found in the western part of Amsterdam (Fig.6-19.3). One of the qualities of the lobate model is the considerable length of the edge of the built-up urban area (see Section 6.2). An effect of this long boundary is that more people can live and work in and along the fringe of the urbanized area. People living and working in the lobes can get out of town fairly quickly by foot and/or by bicycle to spend their leisure time in a natural setting, provided of course that the lobe is not too wide and that there are no barriers along the lobe that cannot be crossed. The inhabitants of the central part of the city can also reach the countryside by bicycle, as long as the radius of this area does not exceed a certain length. Preferably it will be an attractive green bicycle route that continues in the wedge. The most easily accessible parts of the open space, lie either in the point of the wedge or at the edges; therefore, these areas should be developed for intensive use (Fig.6-19.4).

On the other hand, the width of the lobe depends on the desired quality of the collective transport that provides access to the lobe, in relation to the maximum acceptable walking distance to and from the transport stops (Fig.6-19.5).

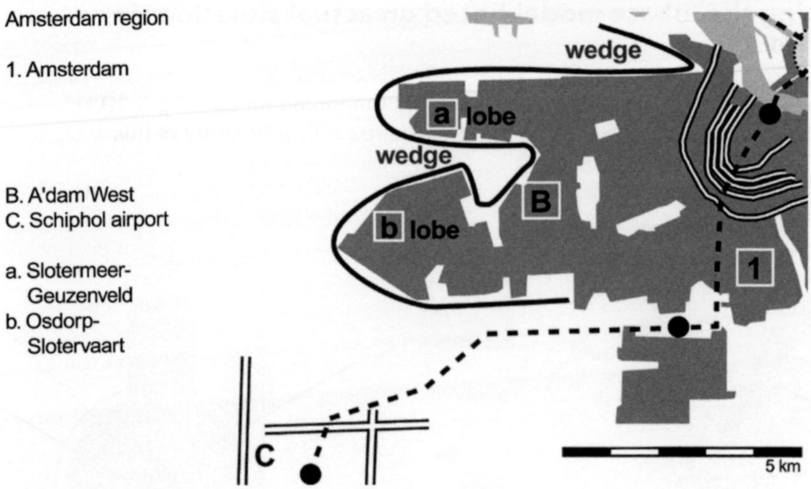

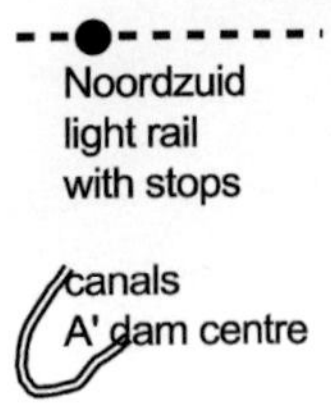

Fig.6-19.3 The lobes and wedges of Amsterdam West.

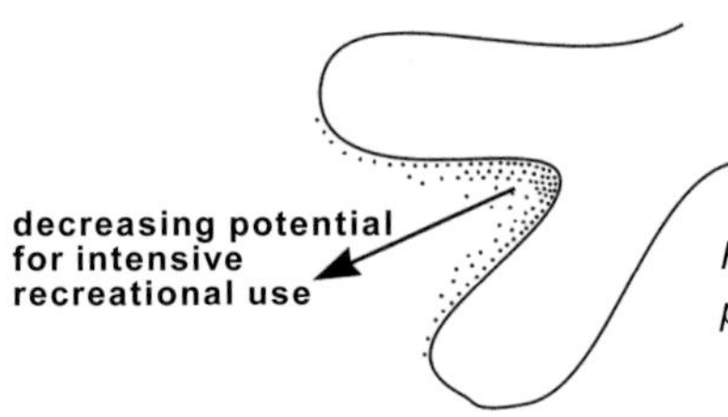

Fig.6-19.4 The recreational potential of a wedge.

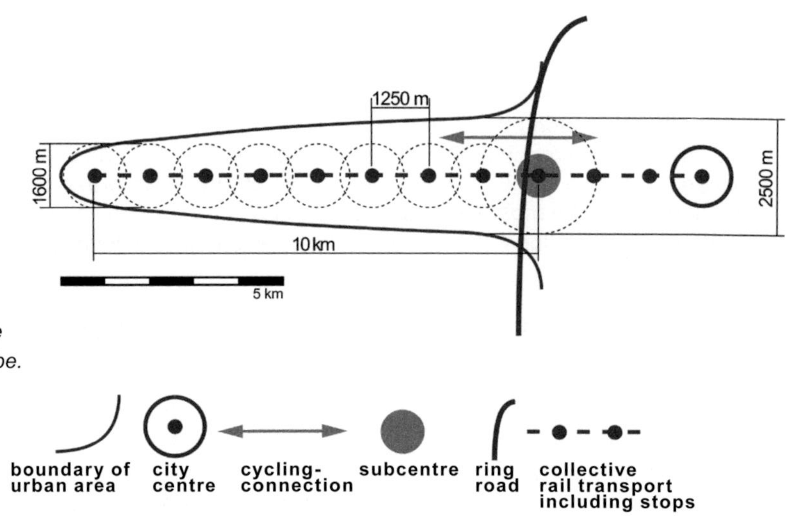

Fig.6-19.5 A quantitative theoretical model of a lobe.

The quality of collective transport also depends on the number of passengers using that service - in other words, on the 'user density' of the area, and on the modal split. The speed of the mode of transport, in connection with the distance between the stops, subsequently determines the length of the lobe in relation to travelling time. Of course one has to take into account the length of the route that has to be traversed in the central part of the city.

In a post-graduate project, students analysed the Slotermeer-Geuzenveld lobe in Amsterdam and proposed a reconstruction (Damen, Jacobs & Van der Want 1988). They confronted this northern of the two western lobes with (among other things) the spatial organization principles depicted in Fig.6-19.4 and Fig.6-19.5. They observed the following.

- The wedge on the south side is largely inaccessible to the public. The use of the sports parks here is restricted to club members. The 'arm pit' of this wedge contains an artificial lake (*Sloterplas*) which does not allow for any intensive recreational development.
- The wedge on the north of the lobe is narrow, and large areas are also not easily accessible or are built-up or cultivated (sports fields, allotment gardens, offices). Barriers, in the form of a motorway, a canal and a railway line, also make the wedge difficult to access.
- The travelling time by tram from the end of the lobe to city centre is too long: well over 35 minutes including transport to and from the stop. The frequency is low, as is the reliability and the comfort of the service.

In the specific situation of this lobe, the zone of transition between the lobe and the central part of Amsterdam accommodates a circular rail line and a ring road with slip roads. When we add these elements to the lobate model, a circular area around a station/parking garage (radius = walking distance) will have great potential for high quality urban activities, including a park & ride facility because of its excellent accessibility. It is a potential 'city dependence' (De Boer 1994: 24). A subsequent observation was therefore:

- The potential for high quality urban activities at the transition from the lobe to the central city area is not taken advantage of.

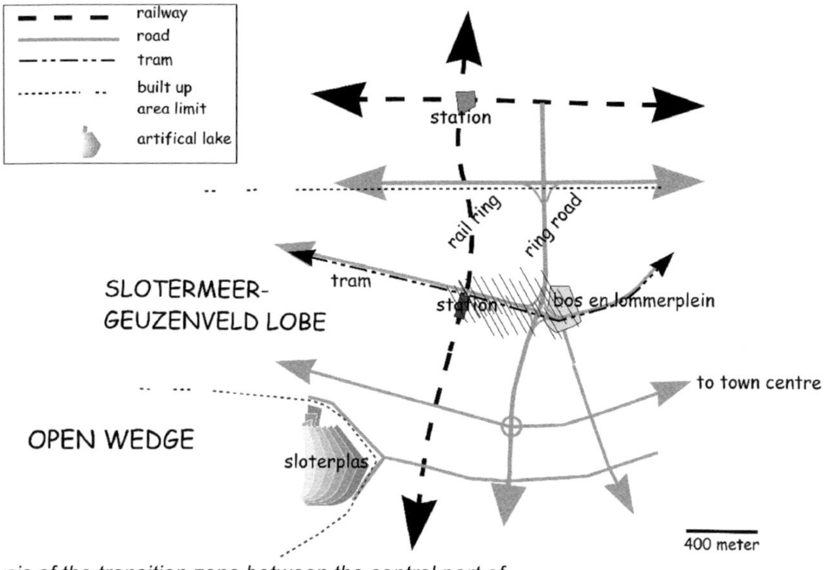

Fig.6-19.6 Analysis of the transition zone between the central part of Amsterdam and the Geuzenveld-Slotervaart lobe. The shaded zone is a potential subcentre area (after Damen, Jacobs & Van der Want 1988).

Zooming in on the transition zone between the lobe and the central district (Fig.6-19.6) revealed that the slip roads of the motorway ring and the railway station did in fact provide access to the lobe, but that there was no high-quality radial rail connection with the centre of the city, nor a suitably recognizable radial city road in the direction of the centre. On the city-centre side of the motorway ring, there is a square (*Bos en Lommerplein*) which in view of its location has much promise, but in fact is a rather disappointing city junction. The fact that one has to head in a southerly direction on the square in order to get to the centre of the city is not made clear by the visual design of the square. The square is not an inviting place to stay. It cannot be seen from the station (and vice versa). Between the station and the square, the strip with the greatest potential, is a large, windy, visually unattractive space.

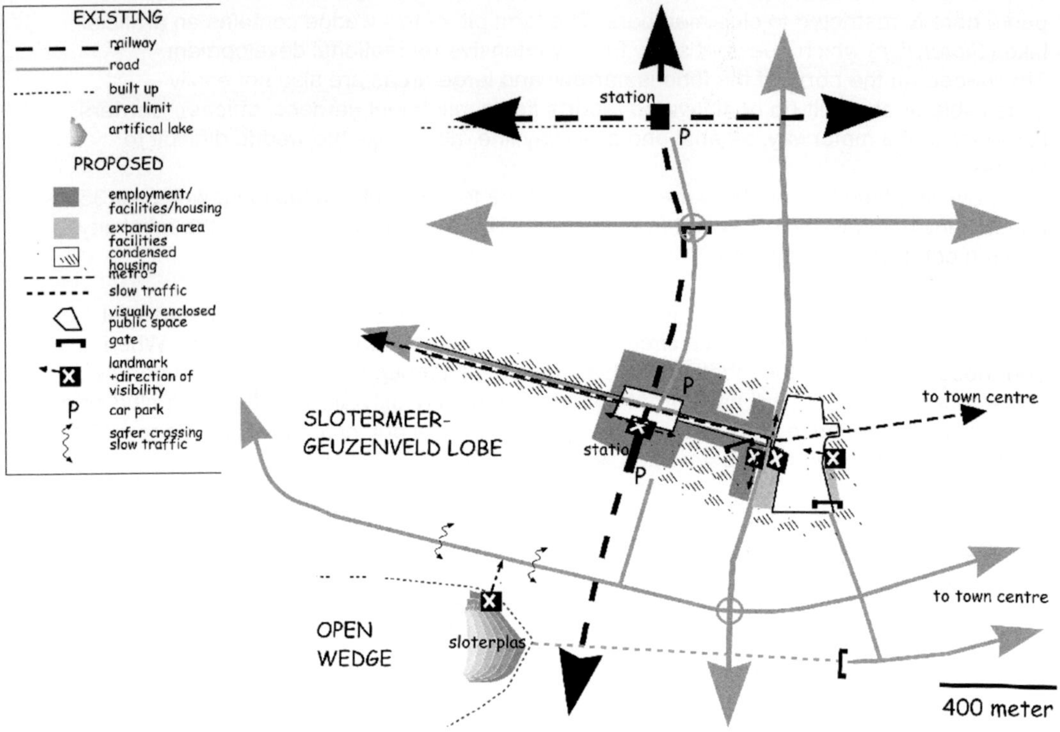

Fig.6-19.7 Improvement proposals for the transition zone between the lobe Geuzenveld-Slotervaart and the central part of Amsterdam (based on Damen, Jacobs & Van der Want 1988).

Their proposals for restructuring lead to this lobate design geared towards this specific situation, illustrated in Fig.6-19.7. Improvements include that the lobe and city dependence as well as the *Bos en Lommer* square are no longer accessed from the motorway ring, that the car connection with the centre of the city is made clearer and that the facilities for slow traffic (pedestrians and cyclists) are improved.

In the actual situation in Amsterdam the zone of transition between the lobe and the central part of the city accommodates a orbital rail line with a station, and a motorway ring with slip roads. When we add these elements to the lobate model, because of its excellent accessibility from within a circular area (radius = walking distance) the station will prove of great potential for high-value urban activities, including a park & ride facility.

In Amsterdam West there is not one lobe but two (Fig.6-19.3). This raises the question of the minimum desired distance between two lobes. The wider the lobe, the greater the potential for diverse forms of more and less intensive recreation, which of course depend on the nature of the area. A possible criterion is also the visibility of the urban area for people located at a certain point in the wedge. Using the spatial organization principle of Fig.6-6 it is possible to calculate the visibility of buildings. A rule of thumb tends to be used which states that half way along the lobe the width of a wedge has to be at least one-and-a-half times that of a lobe.

In a situation like that found in Amsterdam West, the bases of the lobes touch each other (Fig.6-19.3). This produces a variant on the lobe. This leads to yet another possible development of the theoretical lobate model which is directly applicable to the situation in Amsterdam West, depicted in Fig.6-19.8.

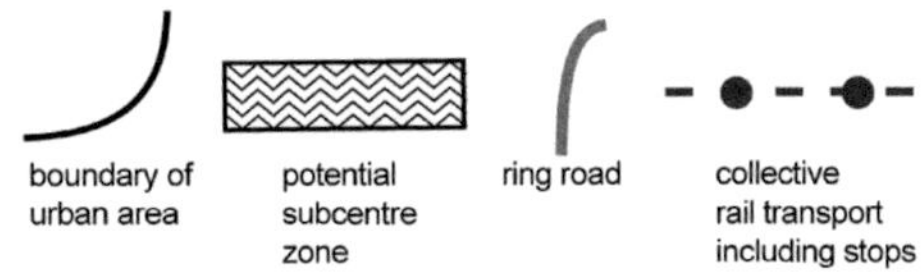

Legend to Fig.6-19.8-11 and 15

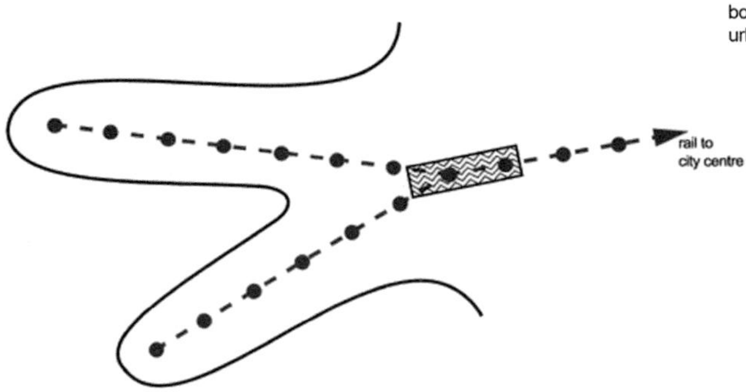

Fig.6-19.8 One of the possible developments of the lobe principle: a double lobe of which the bases overlap.

In this variant, the 'critical mass' necessary to support the subcentre has potentially been doubled without reducing the degree of accessibility from the lobes. On the light rail line to the city centre, moreover, the frequency would be in principle doubled, while the length of the pre- and post-transport routes would increase only slightly if at all. The costs of putting in this transport infrastructure would obviously be considerably reduced. The elongated dark grey zone is the strip where a railway stop could be located, together with a subcentre for the two lobes.

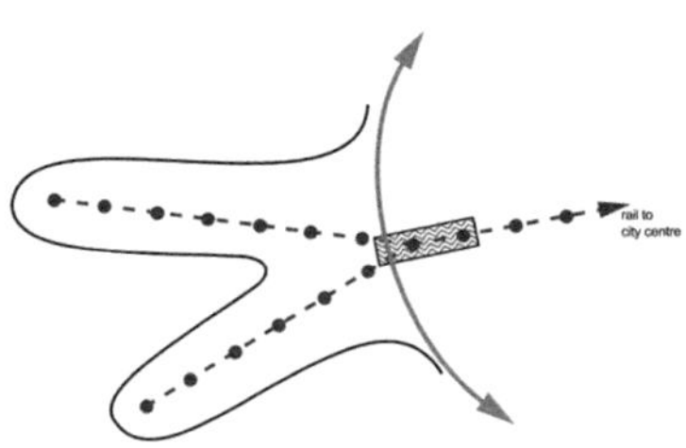

Fig.6-19.9 Ring road without junctions

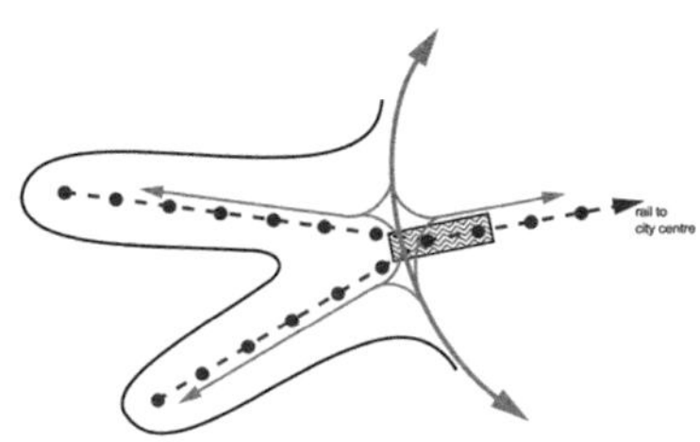

Fig.6-19.10 Ring road with slip roads on both sides

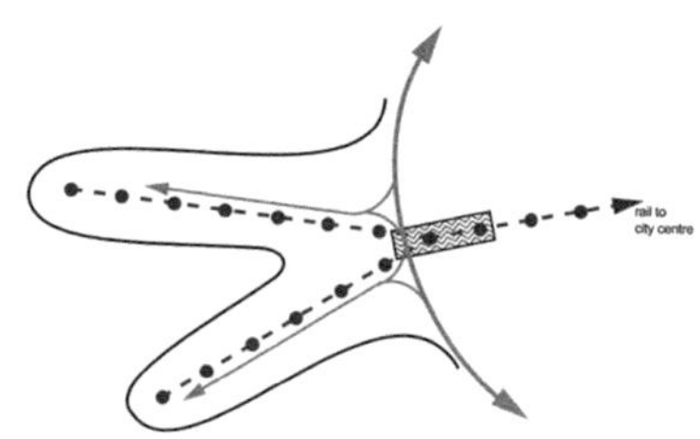

Fig.6-19.11 Ring road with slip roads on the lobe side only.

Adding a ring road (Fig.6-19.9) creates many new possibilities. The crossing of the road and the light rail line would probably be the best place to locate the subcentre, if we give the ring road slip roads. We could provide slip roads both in the direction of the city centre and the lobe (Fig.6-19.10). We could alternatively make the access to the city centre by car difficult by only providing access to the lobe (Fig.6-19.11). Reaching the city centre would make it necessary to park the car and travel by light rail or by taxi, or to make a detour through the lobe. This, however, might result in businesses and some regional facilities leaving the city centre for locations in the lobe, which we might not actually want.

A proposal for a restructuring of Amsterdam West, based on the organization principles of Figs.6-19.9 to 11, is shown in Fig.19.12. Here the station serves both western lobes, and there is no direct access to the lobes from the ring road. It is, however, possible to transfer from private transport to collective transport at the station. The potential user base for the station is larger here than in the development proposals shown in Fig.19.7. The black circle indicates the potential size of the subcentre area based on a walking distance of 500 m.

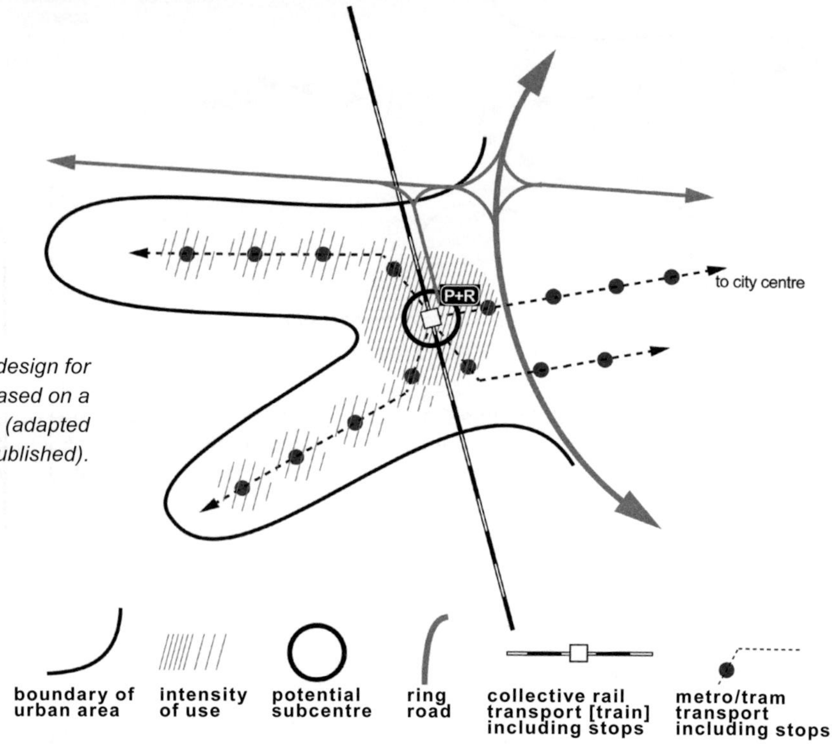

Fig.6-19-12 A design for Amsterdam West based on a 'double lobe" principle (adapted from Chr. van Ees, unpublished).

The question of where to locate high-quality urban activities is currently on the political agenda of the Amsterdam North city district (Figs.6-19.13 and 19.14).

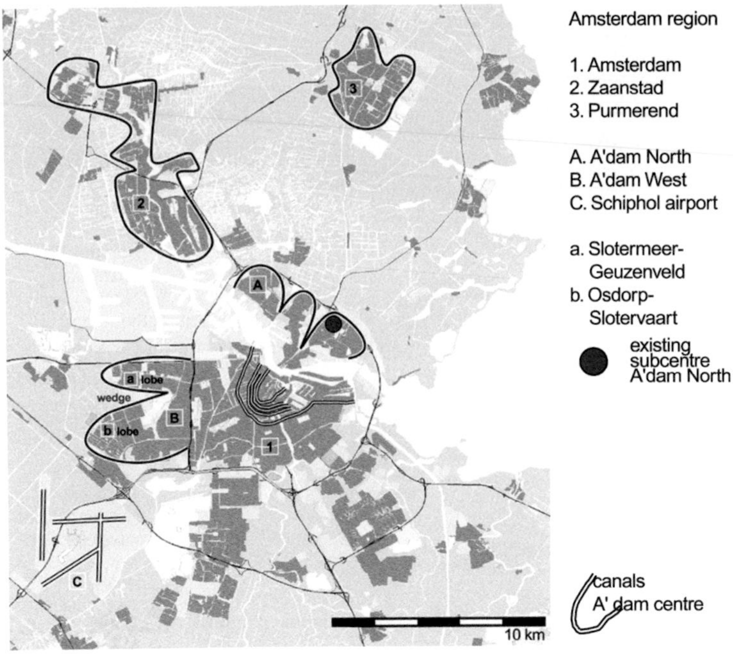

Fig.6-19.13 The Amsterdam Region with an emphasis on the northern part..

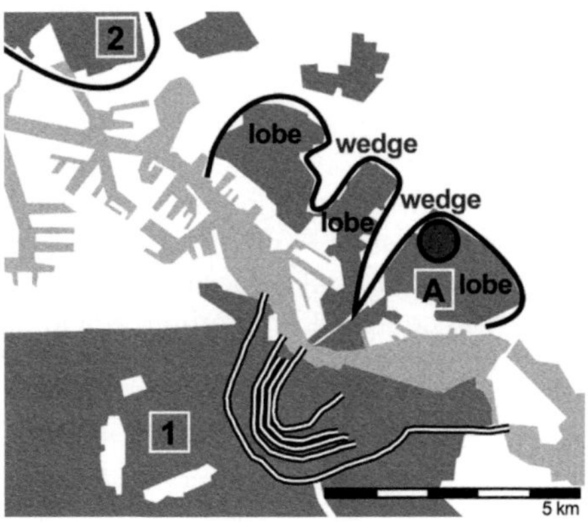

Fig.6-19.14 Amsterdam North viewed as lobate model.

Amsterdam North, which at present still lacks urban rail transport, theoretically has the potential to develop as part of the central city area (without lobate expansion), but can also be viewed as having the characteristics of a lobate model: a double - or even triple - lobe (Fig.6-19.14). The wide water barrier, which separates this part of Amsterdam from the rest of the city, forms a serious obstacle to developing Amsterdam North as part of the central area of Amsterdam. The qualities that are specific to a compact circular urban principle (such as a range of possible spatial activity patterns for slow traffic) cannot be realized due to the water barrier, whilst this barrier cannot really be narrowed to any significant degree.

The current subcentre of Amsterdam North is located not far from the ring road, near one of its junctions and has plenty of parking space. Now that a light rail link is being constructed traversing the Amsterdam Region from north to south (the *Noord-Zuid* line), plans have been developed for an expansion of this subcentre to include national as well as regional facilities.

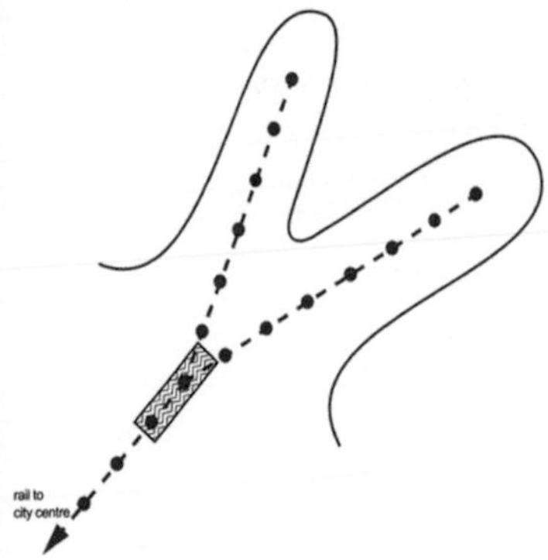

Fig.6-19.15 The double lobe of Fig.19.4 'interpreted' for Amsterdam North.

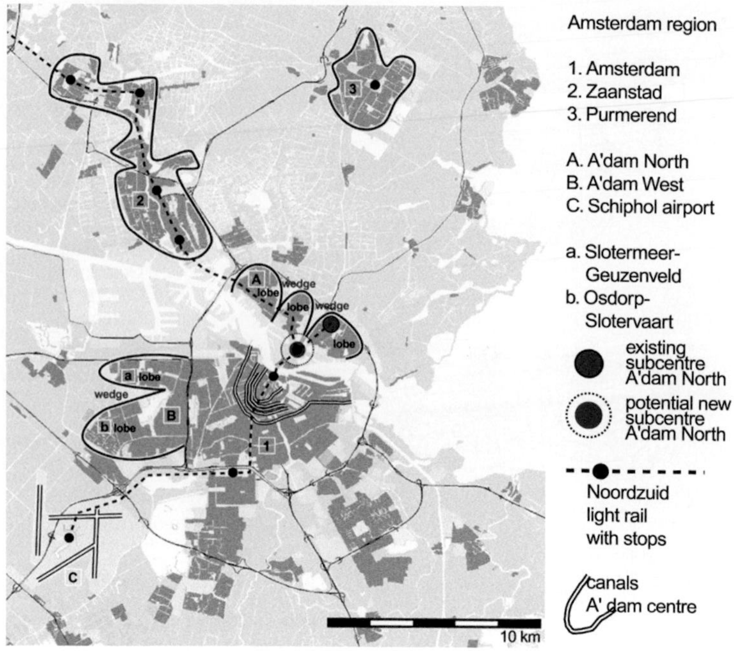

Fig.6-19.16 The planned north to south light rail line, without extension to Purmerend, but with a branch line to Zaanstad.

When we confront these proposals with the lobate development shown in Fig.5-30 and Fig.6-19.15 we see that this subcentre would end up in an unfavourable position at the end of a radial rail link (Fig.6-19.16). If the Noord-Zuid line were to be extended further northwards to the satellite city of Purmerend then this location would no longer be a problem. Due to the greater potential traffic value, however, a more obvious option, would be to invest in a rail line which branches off in the northern IJ shore zone in a north-westerly direction towards Zaandam (drawn in Fig.6-19.16). The area before or at the point of the fork would be an ideal location for high-quality facilities. Apart from the advantages already mentioned, the distance to the main centre of Amsterdam would be short - one metro stop. The main centre would also visible, across the IJ, in the form of the Amsterdam Centraal Station. The reverse would also apply, providing the new subcentre were given a vertical landmark (Fig.6-19.17). The fact that the area borders the water, which the north bank enjoying good sun penetration, and that this area is easily and quickly reached from the ring road by car, increases its location value still further.

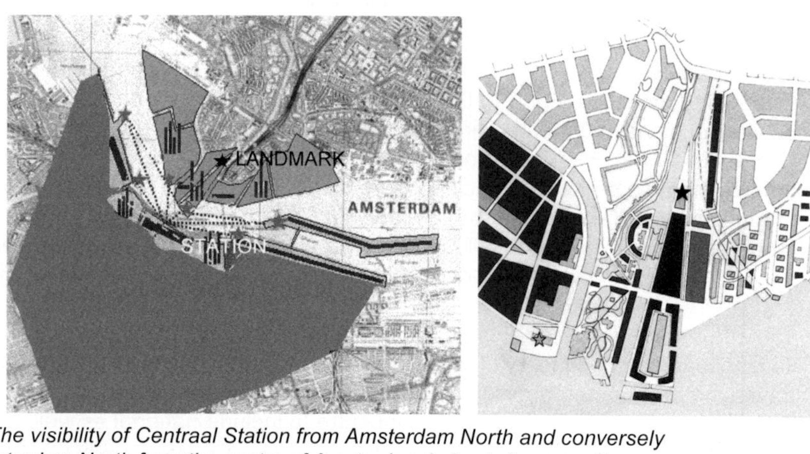

Fig.6-19.17 Left: The visibility of Centraal Station from Amsterdam North and conversely the visibility of Amsterdam North from the centre of Amsterdam helps to increase the cohesion of the two areas. Right: development of the southern part of Amsterdam North with the location of the landmark (Rambhajan & Zijp 2002: appendix 'IJ-sprong': 19).

7 Findings and implications for research and education

7.1 Findings

"Those junior scholars who are attracted to currently unfashionable parts of any discipline soon learn the price of wandering from the straight and narrow path, and only the obstinate and the odd ducks among them persist in doing so, rather then let their own intellectual inquiries be distorted and frustrated."

(Stephen Toulmin 2001, *Return to reason*: 140)

In Chapter 1, I described my research as an intellectual quest into whether a substantive-scientific approach to the discipline of urban & regional design was valid and recommendable. This quest was guided by four questions:

1. What position could urban & regional design potentially take in relation to the sciences as a whole?
2. How far is this position connected with opinions on the significance of urban & regional design for society, and on the consequent definition of the object of urban & regional design?
3. Does the actualization or non-actualization of this potential position of urban & regional design within the field of sciences, or the manner of such actualization, depend on the view held about the definition of the object of urban & regional design?
4. What avenue or avenues may be followed, starting from the view that usefulness (including future usefulness) to society is a central aspect of urban & regional design, in order to build up a scientific body of knowledge?

These four questions were answered in the subsequent Chapters. In Chapter 3 (Science), I considered the field of sciences from the standpoint of my views on reality, on the nature of science and on the relationship between them. I concluded that within that field urban & regional design must be positioned among the practical sciences, that is to say within the sciences that have the application of science as their object of research.

Applied research aims to acquire knowledge of what effects actions will have, under which conditions; and for this knowledge to be generic, i.e. independent of its application to a specific case. In the case of urban & regional design this means:

- What theoretical physical urban system models can be constructed, and under what socio-cultural, spatial-ecological, economic-technical and administrative-organizational conditions?

And

- What effects do these theoretical physical urban system models have in the sense of spatial conditions for (cyclic) processes in urban societies, and under what socio-cultural, spatial-ecological, economic-technical and administrative-organizational conditions?

The unique character of a localized design is no reason to suggest that design cannot be scientific. In the case of urban or regional design, unique spatial compositions can be seen as constructions of reproducible 'building blocks'. The unique character of each design arises once the generic knowledge has actually been applied in a specific situation.

I did however conclude that the position of urban & regional design within the practical sciences is a special one. Due to the nature of the discipline the scientific justification of hypotheses is problematic and the emphasis in a scientific approach is on the context of discovery, supported by findings in the context of application. My examination of the field of sciences also revealed that the research method that was developed by Imre Lakatos, due to its affinity to design, provides points of departure for applied research in the area of urban & regional design.

As a result of the conclusions of Chapter 5 (Urban & regional design and science) the answer given in Chapter 3 (Science) to the first question has to be modified somewhat. Urban & regional design is not only (potentially) a practical science, but also an empirical science. Designs whether implemented or on paper, can be examined and can thus contribute to the body of knowledge of urban & regional design history. In the case of implemented designs, provided they are analysed for conditions/effects relationships, the findings can contribute to the development of a practical-scientific body of knowledge of urban & regional design.

In order to answer the second question - regarding the role played by the definition of the object of urban & regional design - it was necessary to examine the significance of urban & regional design for society, and to establish whether the assumed difference in views in this respect does exist and does indeed lead to a difference in defining of the object of the discipline. My findings in this regard are outlined in Chapter 4 (Urban & regional design, physical urban systems and society). I concluded that, considered from a systems approach to (urban) reality, two views can be distinguished with respect to the object of urban & regional design. In one view, the present and/or future usefulness of the physical urban system is the central issue and the experiential value supports the use value in a functional sense. The physical urban system is seen as a subsystem of the urban system. I call this view - which I myself take - 'process-oriented design'. The term 'process' refers here to cyclic processes in society with a small temporal grain. In the other view, the physical urban system is regarded as a autonomous system and the other components of the urban system are regarded as belonging to the environment of this physical urban system. In this view, which I call 'pattern-oriented design', the experiential value of the composition of that physical urban system is central, and designers focus on long-term changes in this composition (transformations of the physical urban system).

In terms of practical science, a relevant question in both the above approaches concerns the conditions under which theoretical models can be implemented. If we interpret the relationship between conditions and effects in the sense of the conditions under which various utilitarian options are generated, then the potential position of urban & regional design in the field of sciences does indeed depend on how the object of urban & regional design is defined. In the process-oriented approach, the essential question of the practical sciences, 'does it work?', is directly applicable: can such spatial conditions be created that a certain type of urban society is accommodated, and are they flexible enough that future societies might also be accommodated?

The pattern-oriented approach is potentially a historical science. Interesting and useful though historical data are, if they are not accompanied by analysis of conditions and effects, then they do not offer a rational, substantial basis for designs which are, by definition, aimed at the future. It is difficult to answer the question 'does it work' in this approach, because the physical urban system is designed without a direct relationship being established, in a conditional sense, with daily and weekly societal processes. The question may be relevant but cannot be answered: it is not the aim of this approach to urban & regional design. Moreover, the pattern-oriented approach usually places an emphasis on visually perceptible design, with much attention to the cultural aspect, in both a historical and an artistic-creative sense. Together these considerations hamper a practical-science approach except in the sense of whether a designed physical urban system can actually be constructed.

The third question - whether, and if so in what form, urban & regional design manifests itself scientifically - is the theme of Chapter 5 (Urban & regional design and science). As far as I have been able to ascertain no applied research has been done by urban & regional designers in relation to constructive options. In the process-oriented design approach, some research has been done into the contextual conditions under which various utilitarian options are possible. Examples of this kind of applied research were presented in Section 5.4. Research which takes the pattern-oriented design approach manifests itself almost exclusively as descriptive historical research, which is ideographic and typological in nature. As I mentioned above, the question of whether this design approach is potentially a practical science is not easy to answer. Fig.5-29 suggests that it is in fact a practical science. By altering one variable the effects on the housing density can be examined - although these effects are not explicitly named. However, as long as such non-localized building blocks cannot be incorporated into a physical urban system, with the rest of the urban system being treated as the system environment, the complex organized character of the urban system (see Section 2.4) still prevents us answering the question of 'does it work?'. “Cities ... do not exhibit *one* problem in organized complexity, which if understood explains it all. They can be analysed into many such problems or segments which, as in the case of the life sciences, are related with one another. The variables are many, but they are not helter-skelter; they are 'interrelated into an organic whole' “ (J.Jacobs 1961: 433). Jane Jacobs suggests that many societal problems that are connected with the configuration of physical urban systems can be attributed to a lack of attention for this complex organized character. Lynch also points to the impossibility of determining the effects of single variables (1972: 229).

From the examples given, particularly in Chapter 4 (Urban & regional design, physical urban systems and society), we see that not only cyclic societal processes receive little attention in the pattern-oriented design approach, but also people and their needs seem generally to receive little attention. “The experience of space is defined by its interaction with people, yet in the late twentieth century people tend to conceive of space as an empty volume,” writes Salingaros (1999: 29). Jon Lang says: “It has been suggested that if the profession would recognize the habits, needs and desires of building users as primary determinants of form, it will need to know more about the relationship between the designed environment and human behaviour than it does at present. Moreover, if the profession is to use this information creatively, it must be organized in such a way which lends itself to that use. The design process is presently largely mimetic; typological solutions are adjusted to new situations ...“ (1987: 247).

The fourth and last question - what avenue or avenues may be followed, starting from the view that the use value is a central aspect of urban & regional design, in order to build up a scientific body of knowledge - is also answered in Chapter 5 (Urban & regional design and science). In general, urban & regional designers tend to follow the path of empiricism and/or of norms and values. "Testing and evaluation are the only way of deciding whether a design is a success and of building up a body of knowledge." (Rapoport 1969: 146). The research approach of a practical science is however one which is not directed at applying scientific knowledge to the design of a specific site, but to developing an application-oriented scientific body of knowledge. This is achieved by introducing an extra, non-localized, design phase, in which design is used as a method of research. The application of knowledge is distinguished from applied knowledge. System elements, element-attributes and relationships can be varied and analysed in relation to one another: knowledge-based design to generate knowledge. Fig.7-1 represents a combination of the ideas illustrated in Fig.5-14 and Fig.5-33.

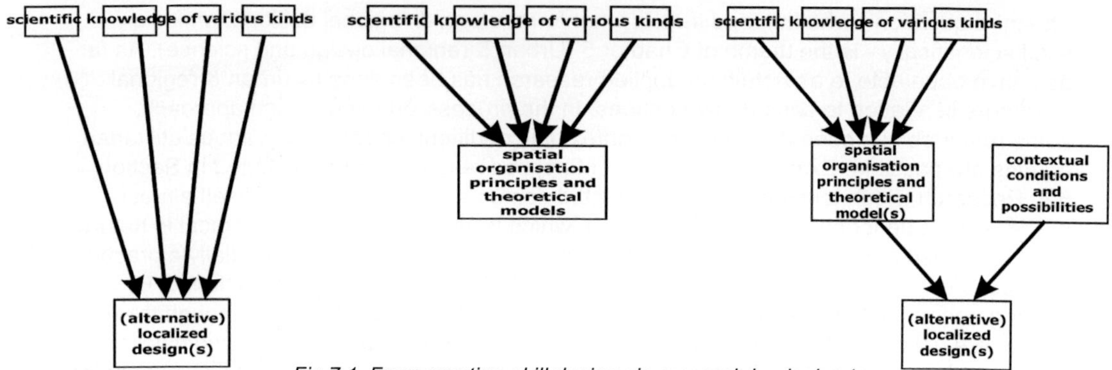

Fig.7-1 From creative-skill design via research by design to research-driven design.

The purpose of my study, to substantiate the possibility of a substantive-scientific approach to the discipline of urban & regional design, and to give this approach concrete content, has been achieved. The examples from Chapter 6 (Developing a practical-scientific body of knowledge for urban & regional design) underline this statement.

The question raised in the first Chapter about the usefulness of a practical scientific approach still remains unanswered. In the terms of Lakatos, the question is whether this research programme has a positive heuristic, i.e. is it fruitful in the sense of its significance for the practice of building physical urban systems. In view of the practical examples, I answer this question positively from a scientific point of view. This is not to say that this is the only fruitful research programme in the practical-scientific discipline of urban & regional design. I characterized the method I have followed in my research in Chapter 1 as an 'intellectual quest' and I also referred to it as the type of research known as an 'interpretative-theoretical study'. This type of research, in which the researcher is guided by an idea formulated at an early stage, unmistakeably shows the characteristics of a design process. Just as a design process - either localized or non-localized - can never result in a uniquely possible building, or a uniquely possible development of an area, my research cannot yield a uniquely possible answer.

The question of the usefulness of any particular research programme in urban & regional design, has another aspect: the administrative-organizational conditions. In a democratic context, it is not scientific specialists /professional urban & regional designers who decide what happens, but the elected administrators whom they provide with information and insight. Providing more and better information however does not mean that better decisions will be taken. Various mechanisms in the administrative-organizational system influence spatial policy decisions on improper grounds. More and better information is no more than a contribution to better decision making.

Examples of mechanisms in the Netherlands that improperly influence spatial decisions: the method of calculating the amount of funding a municipal council receives from central government; the level of the conveyance tax when buying a house, which also has to be paid when people go to live near their work; the fact that the spatial planning of the government does not play a role in the hospital planning of central government (Kusiak 1989)[64].

The initial motive behind my research was that I believed that better decisions regarding our physical urban systems, are necessary, and therefore we need more and, above all, better-substantiated information. During my 'quest' I have become even more convinced of this. Jane Jacobs, had she been writing now, would have been able to include many contemporary Dutch examples in her book *The Death and Life of Great American Cities.* To mention but a few instances:

- "To build city districts that are custom made for easy crime is idiotic. Yet it is what we do." (1961: 31). How about Amsterdam-Bijlmermeer, the Amsterdam Lelylaan station and surrounding area?
- "It is uncanny to see a city neighborhood ... walled off ...". " ....the middle and upper income housing occupying many acres of city .... 'new concepts of city living', ..." (ibid.: 48). In the Netherlands the 'controlled neighbourhoods', called 'gated communities' after the American example, are on the rise.
- " ... the tendency for outstandingly successful diversity in cities to destroy itself; the tendency for massive single elements in cities to cast a deadening influence; ..." (ibid.: 242). Urban redevelopment projects tend to push up rents which are then no longer affordable for small-scale activities such as artists' studios. Huge building complexes known in the Netherlands as 'solids' are currently in vogue.
- "It is so easy to fall into the trap of contemplating a city's uses one at a time, by categories. Indeed, just this - analysis of cities, use by use - has become a customary planning tactic.(---) The overall pictures such methods yield are about as useful as the picture assembled by the blind men who felt the elephant and pooled their findings." (ibid.: 143; 144). This could apply to typical Dutch contemporary urban expansion schemes, e.g. the VINEX developments.

7.2 Implications for scientific education and research

"In today's atmosphere of team research, relatively structured and rigid post-graduate education, and centralized funding, it may become necessary to provide institutional mechanisms which discourage too much consensus and uniformity among scientists."

(Noretta Koertge 1978, *Towards a New Theory of Scientific Inquiry*: 266)

Universities, including universities of technology, serve two masters these days with regard to research and education: 'Science' and 'the Market'. Both aim to meet the needs of society. Although Science and the Market both benefit from research carried out on the basis of a scientific attitude characterised by a mentality of rational problem-solving, the interests of Science and the Market do sometimes clash (Huisman 1996: 208 ff.). Lecturers are expected to obtain income for their university through market-initiated projects and the education system is forced to focus on generating a speedy and cheap supply of graduates to meet the needs of the Market. The ambition of students are primarily oriented towards a professional career. It is nonetheless a societal necessity to maintain a scientific attitude in university research and education. In interest of their cross-fertilization, scientific research and education must thrive in close contact with one another. Chapter 6 (Developing a practical-scientific body of knowledge for urban & regional design) underlines this importance.

For the discipline and scientific area of 'urban & regional design' it is not so much a question of maintaining a scientific attitude as of developing such an attitude. It is characteristic of the discipline of 'urban & regional design', as stated, that it has a guild-like character which expresses itself in professional conformity, an almost complete lack of scientific debate and the persistence of a master-apprentice relationship in the disciplinary education (see Section 5.2.2).

Based on my findings, a scientific attitude towards carrying out research and providing education implies:

- general scientific standards are learned and upheld;
- insight into the various views concerning the nature of science, particularly in relation to urban & regional design;
- knowledge and insights that are developed are related to already existing knowledge and insights;
- one's own professional and scientific views are viewed critically, related to those of others and are made the subject of public debate;
- rational argumentation lies at the basis of evaluating research and education products, also when they involve design.
- the language used, including images, is coherent and clear.

"... disciplines which encourage, thrive on, or revel in, incestuous private languages should always arouse suspicion. Coherence and clarity are not simply aesthetic attributes: they are the most reliable and consistent indicators of the integrity and intelligibility of a discipline," stated Janet Daley at a symposium on design methods in architecture some 30 years ago (1969: 75). Huisman campaigned against 'plastic language' (1996: 147).[65] "In science," she suggests, "we must therefore ... focus on the shortcomings in the use of terms. Inventing terms, overusing terms resulting in their losing their significance and applying terms to cover a wide range of meanings are often seen in science, but can be remedied." (ibid.).

Research

A practical scientific body of knowledge for urban & regional design hardly exists. Any knowledge and insight that has been acquired over the last 40 years is widely dispersed, difficult to access and insufficiently coherent.

Using design as a method of research, this body of knowledge must be further developed and made coherent. The research approach developed by Lakatos, including the search for counterexamples, can be a stimulus due to its similarities with design methods. It is also worthwhile to carry out research into heuristic strategies that are specifically significant in urban & regional design (see Radder 1997: 45 ff.).

With respect to functionality, the socio-cultural aspects of urban design must certainly be incorporated in research by design, in addition to the spatial-ecological aspects (including of course sustainability) and the economic-technical aspects. Urban areas are after all designed and built to be used. Research into cyclic processes with a small temporal grain, and particularly into linear changes within this, is necessary in light of constant and changing activity patterns in space and time, which are partly the result of developments in information and communication technology (Drewe 1996; 2000)[66]; not only human temporospatial activity patterns, but also those in areas of production and trade (distribution and contribution systems). Not only empirical knowledge is important, but also the acquisition of insight into what can be made, both in terms of construction and utilitarian options. Vulnerable social groups should be given specific attention (Hulsbergen 1992). The problem of mobility, to mention but one example, has more aspects to it than increased car ownership and congested roads.

With respect to formal-spatial organization principles, designers require practical knowledge of the manner in which people perceive and interpret information from their environment visually and otherwise, both objectively and subjectively. Perceptual psychology can act in this case as a supplier of 'building blocks' for general knowledge on urban design (see Dorst: to be published). It may be interesting to consider recent neurological views in this respect. Lynch suggested decades ago that perception is an important research subject because the perception of users can vary considerably from that of professional designers ((1960) 1992: 157). Ter Heide and Wijnbelt observed, "We remain convinced that too little use ... is made of this type of research [perception research - itk] ...... This has various causes. Designers do not give much credence to the results of perception research, perhaps because they feel threatened by it." (1994: 87).

Both with regard to the perception issues and to possibly desired activities and temporospatial activity patterns, account should be taken of the increasing diversity of cultural backgrounds of users of physical urban systems: see for example Rapoport (1976; 1977) and Esser (1976). Concepts such as 'street', 'front and back', 'private' and 'comfort' have different implications in different cultures. (Rapoport 1977: 28).

Literature research alone will produce series of principles, which may or not be of a universal functional-spatial nature, at various scales. Based on the outcomes, existing theoretical models should be further developed and new ones should be designed. Important in this respect is the transformation of verbal and mathematical models into spatial models in order to make them suitable for use in spatial design.

Last but certainly not least, supporting empirical knowledge should be sought; existing knowledge, including knowledge available in the so-called 'grey circuit' (unrecorded scientific material), as well as newly acquired knowledge. Designers should be encouraged to formulate researchable questions, possibly as an addition to research conducted by empirical scientists, and possibly even as a preliminary to new research projects.

The usefulness of research into adaptability was already touched upon by Lynch in 1958: "... it appears that adaptability to future change unspecified is a significant goal in city planning, and that there are some physical means of attaining it." ((1958) 1990: 379 ff.). In the existing field of tension between 'blueprint' design and structure-oriented design (Section 4.3), knowledge of adaptability in relation to structure, form, function and variation may act as a catalyst.

Lynch mentions the following as means to achieve adaptability: (1) excess capacity, (2) generous communication facilities, (3) a separation of elements likely to change from those unlikely to change and (4) leaving space for growth. (1972: 108/09).

Education

If I were to present here a blueprint for an educational programme comsistent with the views with which I started my research and the resulting findings, then I would be guilty of the authoritative way of thinking that I opposed so explicitly in Section 5.2.2. However, my research did imply a number of structural principles for this education, affecting both content and form.

Research carried out by Hamel into the way architects think (1990) revealed that when designing, his subjects made much more use of their prior knowledge and data supplied with the project than of information from other sources. Hamel called the designer's knowledge that was activated for a particular project the 'problem conception', and he observed that this problem conception is mainly a product of the architect's education and professional experience. "Training and education carry much weight," Hamel concludes on the basis of empirical research. "Subjects that do not play a substantial role in training and education have a smaller chance of being part of the problem conception of the educated designers than subjects that do play a substantial role. If the education of architects omits any attention to the behavioural science dimensions of design projects, we can expect this to be evident in the problem conception of the graduates." (1990: 242). This means that education plays a major role in determining the details of what Hillier, Musgrove and O'Sullivan describe as the cognitive schemes with which designers interpret the world (1972: 29-3-3).

Based on this observation, I argue that an urban & regional designer should possess procedural and substantive-scientific knowledge (a theoretical framework) as well as integrating insight and visualizing skills with regard to physical urban systems at various scales. Urban and regional designers should also have insight into the influence on these systems of specific spatial-ecological, socio-cultural, economic-technological and administrative-organizational conditions and into the influence of these conditions on physical urban systems, as well as knowledge and skills in the application of this insight into specific situations (localized design).

If a university education wishes to set itself apart from a purely vocational training then the cultivation of a specific scientific attitude as described above is necessary. The emphasis should not be on the acquisition of an encyclopaedic knowledge and skills in reproducing this knowledge, but rather on identifying connections and on learning to develop knowledge[67], as well as on the ability to substantiate the theoretical framework within which a design has to be positioned or research by design has to take place. This has consequences for the organization of university courses.

In university courses for urban & regional designers, as for architects, it is usual to find a project approach in the form of studio classes (Graaff & Cowdroy 1997). A characteristic feature of this form of education is the master-apprentice relationship, which as I argued in Section 5.2.2. does little for the development of the discipline urban & regional into a science. Recently a member of the Delft Faculty of architecture, Prof. van Duin, concluded that "a research culture is urgently needed as a driving force inside the profession," thereby calling into question the training of students in studio classes: "Is the design studio still the appropriate place to educate design students?" (2001: 12.). This is a provocative question which has however so far failed to instigate a debate on the topic.

Problem-based learning (PBL), a method of education that is becoming increasingly popular among practical science courses, does not seem, at least at the moment, to be a step in the right direction for educating urban & regional designers, as the introduction of this method at the Faculty of Architecture in Delft has shown. The essence of PBL is that students are faced with a specific problem which forces them to acquire knowledge, insight and skills without direct instruction and in a way that motivates them. A necessary condition for this form of teaching is that there are one or more theoretical frameworks in the form of an (accessible) procedural and substantive scientific body of knowledge. Such frameworks exist in medical science where this didactic form has been developed and is already well established. Theoretical frameworks aid in making disciplinary views less sensitive to trends[68].

In my research, I have shown that a coherent theoretical framework can also be developed for urban & regional design. My personal educational experience with problem-based education within my proposed theoretical framework (in so called 'discipline projects', see Graaff & Kolmos: to be published), leads me to observe that this method of education can indeed be fruitful, and moreover can be instrumental in strenghtening the theoretical framework. Broadly, speaking, however scientific theoretical frameworks still have to be developed, i.e. made accessible for urban & regional design. Without these frameworks, problem-based learning results in a form of project education ('task projects'; ibid.) in which the personal views of the lecturers involved in setting up the projects determine the curriculum and internal balances of power between lecturers play an important part. This tends to preserve the traditional master-apprentice relationship and thus further bolsters the guild-like character of the discipline.

Steps in the direction of developing urban & regional design education as a truly scientific university discipline can be made by instilling concrete aspects of the scientific attitude as described above into the training, and by demanding of students an application of this knowledge and their acquired insights in their studio work.

This of course places demands on the 'masters'. It is not a matter of telling them what views to teach on the essence of the discipline, on the appearance of designs, or on what consecutive steps have to be taken in a design process. It is rather that the educators must be prepared to substantiate their views, including how they implement them in their method of working, scientifically, that is to say that their arguments must be based upon a conscious and specific, explicit thinking process, in which logical and coherent connections are made. They must be ready to enter into a debate regarding these views. In studios - here I am adopting a suggestion of Janis who introduced the concept of 'groupthink' - raising substantive criticism in an open debate should therefore be a group norm (1972: 178).

As in all practical and/or empirical university courses the acquisition of skills in research should be a *conditio sine qua non* for all students of urban & regional design. In this respect students should have freedom of choice regarding both their specific research projects and the theoretical framework under which they wish to operate - insofar as it has been developed and is coherent and accessible.

Many students have ambitions oriented towards a professional career at this time of 'higher education for all'. A specific space should accordingly be created within the master courses on urban & regional design for those students who have shown an explicit interest in pursuing the discipline as a science. It is after all these students in particular who will help expand the body of knowledge of urban & regional design. Without them, Chapter 6 (Developing a practical-scientific body of knowledge for urban & regional design) would have been considerably shorter. Universities are subject to the same maxim as stated by Jane Jacobs for cities: "It takes large quantities of the 'average' to produce the 'unaverage'." (1961: 443).

Samenvatting

Knowledge-based Design: Developing Urban & Regional Design into a Science

Ina T.Klaasen

Een stedebouwkundig ontwerp bepaalt na uitgevoerd te zijn voor lange tijd hoe mensen hun leven op een gezonde en veilige manier in (tijd)-ruimtelijk opzicht kunnen organiseren. Hetzelfde geldt voor het functioneren van sociale, culturele en economische instellingen en organisaties. Gezien het feit dat zowel mensen als instellingen bij dit functioneren de nodige problemen ondervinden – variërend van verdwalen in nieuwbouwwijken tot de moeizame bereikbaarheid van werkplekken - is het opmerkelijk dat in een wereld als de onze waarin wetenschap en toepassingen van wetenschap zo'n grote rol spelen, het (her)structureren en (her)inrichten van stedelijk gebied niet of nauwelijks gebaseerd is op inhoudelijk-wetenschappelijke kennis op het gebied van stedebouwkundig ontwerpen. Van expliciete, onderbouwde en bekritiseerbare kennis is slechts sprake in toeleverende zin, vooral van de kant van de sociaal-ruimtelijke wetenschappen, niet bij het ontwerpen zelf.
Binnen de vakwereld is voor het ontwikkelen van een wetenschappelijk fundament voor stedebouwkundig ontwerpen, zeker de laatste decennia, ook nauwelijks aandacht. De wijdverbreide opvatting dat ieder ontwerp uniek en gebaseerd is op het creatieve vermogen van de ontwerper, laat weinig ruimte voor een inhoudelijk-wetenschappelijke benadering, terwijl ook de grote complexiteit van stedelijk gebieden een rol zal spelen.
Aan mijn onderzoek liggen de veronderstellingen ten grondslag dat stedebouwkundig ontwerpen wel als een maatschappelijk zinvolle wetenschap te ontwikkelen is, dat daarbij een rol speelt welke opvatting aangehangen wordt over de maatschappelijke betekenis van het vakgebied 'stedebouwkunde' en derhalve van stedebouwkundige ontwerpen, en het uit deze betekenis af te leiden object van het vakgebied. Deze veronderstellingen baseer ik op de kennis en inzichten die in de afgelopen vijftien jaar eerst bij de leerstoel 'stedelijk en regionaal ontwerpen', en vervolgens bij die van 'ruimtelijke planning' verkregen zijn.
Het onderzoek is daarmee te karakteriseren als een interpretatief-theoretische studie, een term van de methodoloog A.D.de Groot ((1961) 1968: 325 e.v.). Kenmerken van zo'n studie zijn dat binnen een bepaalde verzameling van gegevens (tentatieve) verbanden worden aangebracht, dat het onmogelijk moet zijn het probleem direct door een toetsingsonderzoek op te lossen, en dat de interpretatie niet de enige mogelijke is. Dit maakt het onderzoek tot een 'intellectuele zoektocht'.

Een eerste te beantwoorden vraag is hoe stedebouwkundig ontwerpen in het veld der wetenschappen gesitueerd zou moeten worden, zo van een inhoudelijk-wetenschappelijke benadering sprake zou zijn. Het 'stand'punt van waaruit ik mijn zoektocht aanvang is dat de werkelijkheid te kennen is onafhankelijk van het kennende subject. Aangezien de ken-capaciteit van de menselijke soort genetische en cultureel bepaalde beperkingen heeft, kunnen we de werkelijkheid echter slechts bij benadering kennen (correspondentietheorie van de waarheid). Mensen nemen selectief waar volgens algemene ordeningsprincipes van vereenvoudigen, categoriseren en generaliseren. Ze leggen verbanden en vormen zich zo een bepaalde voorstelling van de wijze waarop de werkelijkheid 'samen-gesteld' is, was of

zal kunnen worden. De werkelijkheid, waaronder de stedelijke werkelijkheid, is derhalve op te vatten als een (open) systeem, dan wel een stelsel van (open) systemen van gelijke en ongelijke orde. Elementen van een systeem ontlenen hun betekenis (plaatswaarde) aan de positie die zij in dat systeem innemen. Processen in een systeem kunnen lineair of cyclisch zijn. Of veranderingen in ruimtelijke of temporele zin waargenomen worden hangt af van de ruimtelijke of temporele korrel van de waarneming (Jong 1992: 16). Binnen stedelijke systemen zijn fysieke stedelijke systemen te onderscheiden met als elementen gebouwen, straten, parken, rioleringsbuizen, stations, maar ook stelsels van gebouwen, van straten e.d. die bepaalde vormkenmerken, gesteldheidskenmerken en functionele kenmerken bezitten. Deze onderling en met elementen uit het natuurlijke systeem samenhangende ruimtelijke objecten worden ge(re)construeerd om voor de stedelijke samenleving een draagfunctie en een informatiefunctie te vervullen. De visuele verschijningsvorm op een bepaald moment wordt de compositie van het stedelijk gebied of stedelijk landschap genoemd.
Wetenschappelijke kennis berust op rationele overwegingen. Taal, waar onder beeldtaal, heeft een ordenende functie bij het denkproces en is een middel om wetenschappelijke denkbeelden over te dragen. Wetenschap beperkt het 'toeval' in de zin van 'willekeurig gebeuren'.
Wetenschap veronderstelt generalisering. Men moet daartoe systemen vereenvoudigen, en zich richten op overeenkomsten in plaats van verschillen.
Communiceren en reflecteren over deze systemen doen we met behulp van modellen: bewuste vereenvoudigingen van de (vroegere, huidige, toekomstige) werkelijkheid. Relevant bij stedebouwkundig ontwerpen zijn pragmatische (analoge) modellen, met name ruimtelijke, en in functioneel opzicht vooral descriptieve, intentioneel-projectieve en exploratief–projectieve. Het begrip 'model' vat ik dus anders dan met name in de architectuur gebruikelijk is, niet op als 'voorbeeld ter navolging'.
Een stedebouwkundig ontwerp is een model dat een voorstel bevat voor een samenhangend pakket ruimtelijke ingrepen in een al dan niet reeds bestaand fysiek stedelijk systeem, en heeft altijd betrekking op meer dan één beleidssector.

In het veld der wetenschappen is een driedeling mogelijk: (1) formele wetenschappen zonder empirische inhoud, (2) empirische wetenschappen die gericht zijn op wat 'het geval (geweest) is' en wat derhalve 'waarschijnlijk het geval zal zijn' en (3) praktische, handelingsgerichte, wetenschappen die de toepassing van wetenschap tot object van wetenschappelijk onderzoek hebben (Peursen 1986: 61) (schema A). Bevindingen van praktische wetenschappen worden vervolgens toegepast in concrete gevallen (schema B). Praktische wetenschap is niet in de praktijk verkregen kennis (Drenth 1995: 157; Gunsteren 2001): de praktijk genereert slechts vragen.

empirische wetenschap	*epistèmè*: (intersubjectieve) kennis	wat *waarschijnlijk* het geval zal zijn	voortgang gegenereerd door wetenschaps-interne overwegingen	kenmerkend: explicatieve en predictieve modellen
praktische wetenschap	*technè*: (intersubjectieve) kennis	wat het geval zal *kunnen* zijn	voortgang gegenereerd door wetenschaps-externe overwegingen	kenmerkend: descriptieve, intentioneel- en exploratief-projectieve modellen

Schema A

praktische wetenschap	*technè* = (intersubjectieve) kennis	wat in algemene zin het geval zal kunnen zijn (onder welke condities met welke effecten)
toepassing van kennis	*phronèsis* = beslissing in redelijkheid	wat concretiseerbaar is in een specifieke situatie, gegeven condities en verwachte effecten (voorspellingen, zo mogelijk empirisch onderbouwd)

Schema B

Centraal bij praktische wetenschappen staat de vraag 'werkt het': onder welke condities zijn welke effecten van het handelen te verwachten. Hierbij gaat het zowel om inzicht in de constructiemogelijkheden als in de gebruiksmogelijkheden. Gegeven de buitenwetenschappelijk probleemstelling is een monodisciplinaire aanpak onwaarschijnlijk. Op grond van het bovenstaande kan geconstateerd worden dat stedebouwkundig ontwerpen, als alle technische wetenschappen maar ook bijvoorbeeld de medische wetenschap, als wetenschap gesitueerd zou moet worden bij de praktische wetenschappen.

Dezelfde wetenschappelijke regels en normen gelden in empirische en praktische wetenschappen. In de opvatting over die regels zijn twee hoofdstromen te onderscheiden, objectivisten en subjectivisten/relativisten, met als belangrijke exponenten respectievelijk Karl Popper en Thomas Kuhn. Kuhn's opvatting dat het bedrijven van wetenschap overwegend een niet-rationele, consensus-gerichte aangelegenheid is moge in beschrijvende zin juist zijn, vanuit een realistische opvatting over wetenschappelijk kennis – bij een praktische wetenschap de enige mogelijke – is deze niet houdbaar als nastrevenswaardig. Hoe 'natuurlijk' het inductief verifiëren van hypotheses/theorieën ook moge zijn, wij hoeven deze natuurlijke neiging niet te volgen, net zomin als de neiging om 'zekerheid' te prefereren boven 'twijfel'. Ook Popper's opvattingen zijn in hun strikte zin niet houdbaar. Vanuit objectivistische hoek is met name kritiek geleverd op het feit dat hij de 'ontdekkingscontext' wetenschappelijke irrelevant achtte: ook hypotheses en theorieën kunnen rationeel onderbouwd worden. Popper's leerling, de objectivist Imre Lakatos had – mede onder invloed van Kuhn – met name ook kritiek op de 'tegennatuurlijkheid' van de exclusieve gerichtheid op falsificatie in tegenstelling tot op verificatie/corroboratie. Dit bracht hem tot het ontwikkelen van een onderzoeksaanpak die door zijn nadruk op heuristiek, abductie en plausibel redeneren interessante overeenkomsten vertoont met (stedebouwkundige) ontwerpprocessen. Deze aanpak biedt perspectieven voor de ontwikkeling van een praktisch-wetenschapsgebied stedebouwkundig ontwerpen. Bij praktische wetenschappen komt echter de 'rechtvaard igingscontext' in een ander licht te staan dan bij empirische. Om ethische en financiële redenen en vanwege de factor tijd, kunnen praktisch-wetenschappelijke hypotheses niet altijd experimenteel, onder beheersbare, herhaalbare condities getest worden. In die gevallen moet men op basis van een reeks van toepassingen waarschijnlijke conclusies trekken aangaande noodzakelijke condities en optredende effecten. Omdat de term 'rechtvaardiging scontext' in die gevallen aanzienlijk aan betekenis inboet, is het dan beter om te spreken van 'toepassingscontext'.
De hier opgesomde toetsingsbelemmeringen doen zich wanneer het gaat om de (re)constructie en (her)inrichting van stedelijke gebieden cumulatief voor. Het verkrijgen van informatie uit de 'toepassingscontext' wordt bovendien gehinderd doordat de condities waaronder in de praktijk voorstellen geïmplementeerd worden relatief weinig overeenkomsten vertonen en deze condities niet gemanipuleerd kunnen worden. Op grond hiervan ligt het

accent bij het praktisch-wetenschappelijk benaderen van stedebouwkundig ontwerpen op de 'ontdekkingscontext': wat wordt verondersteld mogelijk te zijn, en welke effecten zullen waarschijnlijk onder welke condities optreden. Empirische en formele wetenschappelijke kennis, mede gevoed door de 'toepassingscontext', dienen hierbij te zorgen voor de benodigde inperkingen.

De vraag is vervolgens aan de orde of bij het al dan niet ontwikkelen van dit vakgebied 'stedebouwkundig ontwerpen' tot een wetenschapsgebied, het object van het vakgebied zoals dat voortvloeit uit de opvattingen over de betekenis van stedebouwkundig ontwerpen voor de samenleving, een rol speelt. Opvattingen over de betekenis van stedebouwkundig ontwerpen voor de samenleving, duid ik door dit vakgebied te positioneren ten opzichte van de vakgebieden 'ruimtelijke planning' en 'architectuur'. Invalshoeken hierbij zijn (1) het beschouwen van de (toekomstige) stedelijke werkelijkheid als systeem, (2) de aan het werken met ruimtelijke modellen inherente beperkingen waarvan de belangrijkste is dat factor 'tijd' en derhalve processen slechts indirect kunnen worden weergeven (schema C), en (3) een uitwerking van de begrippen 'draagfunctie' en 'informatiefunctie', in gesubjectiveerde vorm de begrippen 'gebruiks'- en 'belevingswaarde.' Wat dit laatste begrippenpaar betreft beargumenteer ik onder meer dat het kunnen gebruiken van een fysiek urbaan systeem, anders dan bij een bouwwerk, een noodzakelijke voorwaarde is voor het kunnen beleven ervan.

statisch ruimtelijk model	VERSUS	dynamische werkelijkheid
ruimte		ruimte en tijd
zichtbare verschijnselen		zichtbare en onzichtbare verschijnselen
objecten en hun ruimtelijke relaties: patronen		objecten en hun ruimtelijke en temporele relaties: patronen en processen

Schema C

Deze positiebepaling maakt helder dat de algemene omschrijving van het fysieke urbane systeem als het object van stedebouwkundig ontwerpen, op twee manieren te interpreteren is en in de praktijk ook geïnterpreteerd wordt. Enerzijds wordt het fysieke urbane systeem als een zelfstandig systeem gezien, met de overige componenten van het stedelijke systeem als systeemomgeving, anderzijds wordt dat fysieke systeem gezien als onlosmakelijk onderdeel van het stedelijke systeem als geheel.
In de eerstgenoemde benadering wordt gefocust op het de compositie van het fysieke systeem en op lineaire veranderingsprocessen hierin (gekenmerkt door een grote temporele korrel). Ik noem dit de patroongerichte benadering. Dit type stedebouwkundig ontwerpen richt zich op wat de transformatie van stedelijke gebieden genoemd wordt. Onder invloed van het vakgebied 'architectuur' staat, meestal op basis van een in functioneel opzicht kwantitatief programma van eisen, het creëren van door persoonlijke vormconcepten gestuurde belevingswaarde centraal. Mede gezien deze nadruk op de vormgeving hebben patroongerichte ontwerpen het karakter van blauwdrukken, hetgeen ze weinig flexibel maakt.
In de tweede genoemde benadering, die ik procesgericht noem, richt men zich in de eerste plaats op wat het tijdsaspect betreft kleinkorrelige cyclische stedelijk-maatschappelijke processen met een ruimtelijke dimensie. Ook deze hebben overigens een grootkorrelige

lineaire component. Bij deze ontwerpopvatting ligt de nadruk op de gebruikswaarde, met de belevingswaarde als onmisbare, functionele, ondersteuning hiervan. Belangrijke componenten zijn de door relevante vormgeving ondersteunde functioneel-ruimtelijke structuren die mogelijk gewenste processen faciliteren, en draagvlakken voor het kunnen functioneren van collectieve instellingen. Bij procesgericht ontwerpen kan volstaan worden met het aangeven van de functioneel-ruimtelijke structuur en een aantal essentiële vormgevingsaanwijzingen.

Van het feit dat deze twee typen benaderingen onderscheiden kunnen worden, zijn stedebouwkundig ontwerpers zich onvoldoende bewust. Patroongericht en procesgericht ontwerpen hebben naast gedeelde begrippen met overeenkomstige definities, zowel ieder een eigen terminologie als bij een zelfde begrip verschillende definities. Ze maken bovendien gebruik verschillende typen ruimtelijke modellen. Vakinhoudelijk onbegrip, spraakverwarringen, en onvoldoende inzicht in de maatschappelijke betekenis van stedebouwkunde zijn het gevolg.
Essentiële verschillen tussen beide opvattingen kunnen in de volgende trefwoorden worden uitgedrukt:

patroongericht ontwerpen	VERSUS	procesgericht ontwerpen
patroon		proces
wonen, werken etc: verblijven		verplaatsen
plekken		routes
zones		netwerken
bereikbaarheid: afstand		bereikbaarheid: verplaatsingstijd
afstand woonfunctie-werkfunctie; woon-functie-voorzieningenfunctie; werk-werkfunctie, etc		tijdruimtelijke activiteitenpatronen
(patroonmatige) blauwdrukplanning		(functioneel-ruimtelijke) structuurplanning

Schema D

Geconcludeerd wordt dat samenhangend met deze opvattingen de perspectieven voor een praktisch-wetenschappelijke benadering van stedebouwkundig ontwerpen verschillend zijn. Patroongericht ontwerpen biedt weinig perspectieven voor een praktisch-wetenschappelijke benadering. De vraag 'werkt het' in de zin van gebruiksmogelijkheden, kan immers niet gesteld worden wanneer elementen van fysieke urbane systemen niet in samenhang met elkaar beschouwd worden. Ook 'beleving' heeft dan geen functionele betekenis. Bovendien ligt de nadruk op culturele en esthetische aspecten en op persoonlijke vormconcepten.
Dat ligt anders voor de procesgerichte benadering waarin het fysieke urbane systeem niet los gezien wordt van het urbane systeem als geheel, en waarin de gebruikswaarde het primaire aandachtspunt is en de beleving van het fysieke urbane systeem het gebruik moet ondersteunen.

Deze perspectieven concretiseer ik in het kader van een schets van de relatie tussen stedebouwkundig ontwerpen en onderzoek in de praktijk.
In het algemeen is er bij het doen van voorstellen voor de ruimtelijke ontwikkeling van steden een taakverdeling waarbij op ruimtelijke planning gerichte empirische wetenschappers kennis en inzicht aanleveren, die door ontwerpers in een 'creatieve sprong' geïntegreerd wordt in een ontwerp voor een specifieke situatie (Fig.E). In Nederland wordt hiervoor wel het begrip gehanteerd van 'de eenheid van het stedebouwkundig werk' (Lohuizen 1948: 3). Ook bij het zogenoemde middelengericht ontwerpen, waarbij met name de mogelijkheden van de situatie richtinggevend zijn en het ontwerpresultaat *ex ante* geëvalueerd wordt, gaat deze arbeidsdeling op. In de praktijk blijkt er echter tussen empirische wetenschappen en stedebouwkundig ontwerpen een kloof te bestaan. Voor deze 'toepassingskloof' zijn een aantal redenen te geven. Een belangrijke is dat er steeds meer kennis van allerlei aard beschikbaar is gekomen, ontwerpers het overzicht hierop kwijt raken, te meer daar overbodige informatie hierbij versluierend werkt (Hillier, Musgrove & O'Sullivan 1972). Ontwerpers komen als gevolg daarvan niet los van vooraf reeds ingenomen standpunten - ze worden er in tegendeel afhankelijker van (op.cit.).
De in de jaren zestig van de vorige eeuw opkomende belangstelling voor het wetenschappelijk benaderen van stedebouwkundig ontwerpen, richtte zich niet alleen op de procedurele kant van ontwerpen, maar gedurende enige tijd ook op de inhoudelijke kant (o.m. J.Jacobs 1961; Doxiadis 1968; Alexander 1977). Tegen het wetenschappelijk benaderen van stedebouwkundig ontwerpen rees echter, en rijst nog steeds, veel verzet: een rationele, systematische aanpak zou de bij het maken van een ontwerp onmisbare creativiteit nadelig beïnvloeden. Ook de gildeachtige wijze waarop de wereld van stedebouwkundig ontwerpers, in navolging van die van architecten, georganiseerd is, stimuleert het ontwikkelen van een wetenschappelijke aanpak niet. Een opleidings- en werkklimaat dat gekenmerkt wordt door een meester-gezelrelatie, waarin verantwoording afleggen over het tot stand gebrachte product niet gebruikelijk is, geldigheid van beweringen aan de status van de spreker ontleend wordt en een debat over vakinhoudelijke opvattingen eerder ontweken dan gezocht wordt, is niet het meest vruchtbare voor een wetenschappelijke ontwikkeling van dat vakgebied. Voor zover in deze context (realistisch) wetenschappelijk onderzoek bedreven wordt is dit vrijwel zonder uitzondering empirisch beschrijvend onderzoek van (cultuur)historische aard: ontwerponderzoek.

Voor praktisch-wetenschappelijk onderzoek is het noodzakelijk de gedachte los te laten dat ieder ontwerp uniek is, met andere woorden het is noodzakelijk het object van ontwerpen los te koppelen van de specifieke ontwerpcontext. Dit opent de deur voor het ontwerpen van principemodellen met ruimtelijk-ordenende beginselen als bouwstenen: ontwerpen die in ruimtelijk-ecologisch en/of sociaal-cultureel en/of economisch-technologisch opzicht situatieonafhankelijk zijn - dit in onderscheid van situatieve ontwerpen. De activiteit 'ontwerpen' staat dan in dienst van onderzoek en is een methode van onderzoek geworden: ontwerpend onderzoeken (Fig.F).

In een situatief ontwerp wordt dan niet door iedere ontwerper kennis steeds opnieuw rechtstreeks geïntegreerd toegepast, maar via een 'extra' ontwerpfase, waarin geïntegreerde algemene wetenschappelijke stedebouwkundige kennis ontwikkeld wordt (Fig.G). Essentieel in deze praktisch-wetenschappelijk benadering van stedebouwkundig ontwerpen is dat sprake is van expliciete wetenschappelijke kennis omdat dit een kritisch-rationeel debat over deze kennis mogelijk maakt.
Principemodellen overbruggen de eerder genoemde toepassingskloof. Zowel bij het ontwikkelen van deze kennis als bij het toepassen daarvan in specifieke situaties, is creativiteit onmisbaar.

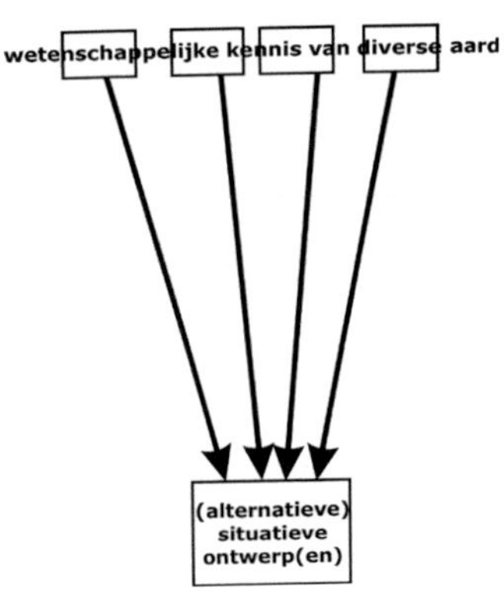

Fig.E Weergave van een ontwerpproces waarin toegeleverde wetenschappelijke kennis direct wordt toegepast in een situatief ontwerp

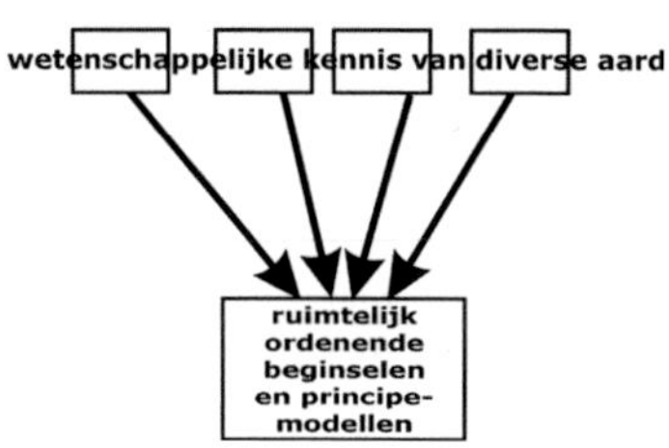

Fig.F Weergave van een ontwerpproces waarin toegeleverde kennis geïntegreerd wordt in ordenende beginselen en principemodellen.

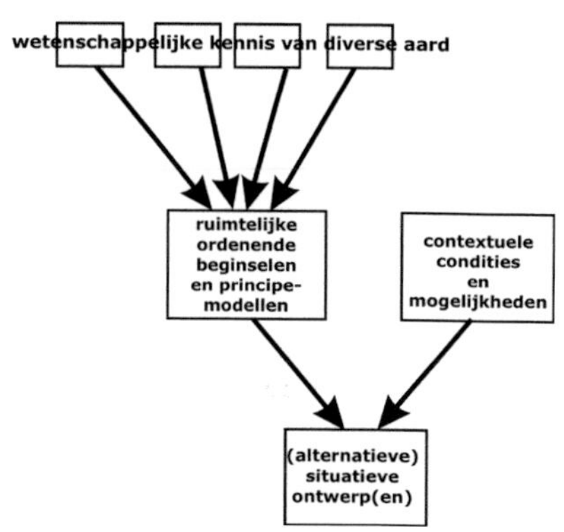

Fig.G Weergave van een ontwerpproces waarbij een situatief ontwerp tot stand komt met behulp van de input van resultaten van ontwerpend onderzoeken

Wordt de onderzoeksaanpak van Lakatos gerelateerd aan de aanpak zoals ontwikkeld bij de leerstoel stedelijk en regionaal ontwerpen, dan kan als harde kern van het praktische-wetenschappelijke stedebouwkundigeontwerponderzoek beschouwd worden:

- Het als open systeem opvatten van de gebouwde en aangelegde (toekomstige) werkelijkheid;
- Het benaderen van dit fysieke stedelijke systeem als een georganiseerd complex systeem;
- Het fysieke stedelijke systeem zien als onderdeel van het stedelijke systeem als geheel;
- Het feit dat een element van dit fysieke stedelijke systeem enerzijds zijn betekenis ontleent aan zijn positie in het systeem en anderzijds eraan bijdraagt het systeem te maken tot wat het is;
- Het onderscheiden van verschillende temporele korrels bij maatschappelijke processen;
- Het onderscheiden van schaalniveaus binnen het fysieke urbane systeem op basis van maatschappelijke processen die gekenmerkt worden door een relatief kleine temporele korrel;
- De noodzakelijkerwijs daaruit voortvloeiende samenhang tussen deze systeemniveaus;
- De eveneens daarmee samenhangende begrenzing van ontwerpgebieden op verschillende schaalniveaus;

en

- Het loskoppelen van het design object van een specifieke design context;
- Ontwerpen (ook) zien als een methode van onderzoek.

De essentie van de onderzoeksaanpak kan als volgt beschreven worden. Start met een aantal basis-elementen van het indicatieve object en manipuleer deze zodanig, mede op basis van ordenende beginselen, dat gebaseerd op plausibel redeneren intern consistente principemodellen op hoofdlijnen van fysieke ruimtelijke systemen resulteren. Dat wil zeggen constructies die op grond van ons beschikbare formele en empirische kennis geacht kunnen worden bij uitvoering stabiel te functioneren. Analyseer deze basisprincipes op welke effecten onder welke condities te verwachten zijn mede op basis van empirisch onderzoek. Ook tijdens het proces van ontwerpend onderzoeken is voortdurend sprake van *ex ante* evaluatie. Om het in principe onbegrensde aantal mogelijkheden te beperken wordt de 'bandbreedte' van

zinvol onderzoek bepaald door in werkelijkheid voorkomende situaties. Tegenvoorbeelden (Lakatos' 'monsters') spelen een belangrijke rol: ze vergroten de theoretische inhoud van principemodellen. Het gaat er bij stedebouwkundig ontwerpen om of uit deels inconsistente gegevens met heuristiek en creatieve abductie als mechanismen (Schomburg 1991: 59; Magnani 2001: 78) plausibele ruimtelijk ordenende beginselen en plausibel theoretische modellen kunnen worden afgeleid.
Principemodellen zijn geen kant-en-klare ontwerpvoorbeelden voor specifieke ontwerpsituaties, het zijn hulpmiddelen. De taak van de situatieve ontwerper is enerzijds zoveel mogelijk hoedanigheden van het gekozen principemodel te bewaren - mogelijk deze zelfs uit te breiden met behulp van specifieke situationele potenties - en anderzijds de ruimtelijke eigenheid van de situatie in het ontwerp te benutten. Dit laatste om de ruimtelijke diversiteit tot stand te brengen die alleen al vereist is om de informatiefunctie tot zijn recht te laten komen. Principemodellen kunnen, metaforisch beschouwd, gezien worden als gemaakt van elastiek.

Steeds zullen de met een principe model beoogde effecten in concrete situaties gecheckt moeten worden omdat in dat principemodel de concrete omgeving niet is meegenomen. Ook op eventuele onbedoelde gevolgen moet een ontwerper bedacht zijn.
Tijdens een situatief ontwerpproces kunnen principemodellen ook een rol spelen in de zin dat een situatief ontwerpprobleem 'uit' de specifieke situatie 'gelicht' wordt en veralgemeniseerd wordt. Dit is het overgangsgebied tussen ontwerpend onderzoeken en onderzoekend ontwerpen. Een bewuste vereenvoudiging vergemakkelijkt het bestuderen van de (veronderstelde) essenties van het probleem en legt een relatie met generieke stedebouwkundige kennis.

Al enige tijd is bij de TU Delft een discussie aan de gang of een (stedebouwkundig) ontwerp als een wetenschappelijk product gezien kan worden. Deze discussie lijkt te gaan over de vraag of een ontwerp, een ruimtelijk model dus, een acceptabel wetenschappelijk communicatiemiddel is. De werkelijke discussie gaat, of zou moeten gaan, over de vraag of stedebouwkundig ontwerpen behalve een vakgebied ook een (praktisch-)wetenschapsgebied is - gezien de beperkte mogelijkheden tot rechtvaardiging van hypotheses een serieus te nemen vraag. De hier beschreven, bij de leerstoel 'stedelijk en regionaal ontwerpen' van de faculteit bouwkunde van de TU Delft ontwikkelde onderzoeksaanpak, tezamen met de in dit boek opgenomen voorbeelden van concrete onderzoeksprojecten, maakt dat deze vraag bevestigend beantwoord kan worden. Dit wordt ondersteunt door voorbeelden van (aanzetten tot) praktisch-wetenschappelijke kennis, in de vorm van ordenende beginselen en principemodellen, uit met name de jaren zestig en zeventig van de vorige eeuw.

De in dit boek gepresenteerde onderzoeksprojecten van zowel wetenschappelijke staf als bij de leerstoelen betrokken studenten, tonen ook aan dat het onderzoeksprogramma vruchtbaar is, dat er in termen van Lakatos sprake is van een 'positieve heuristiek'. Niet kan geconcludeerd worden dat dit onderzoeksprogramma het enige mogelijke is. Een interpretatief-theoretische studie levert geen onderzoeksresultaat dat andere resultaten uitsluit. Dit maakt dit type empirisch onderzoek verwant aan ontwerpen: ook een ontwerpproces levert nooit het enige mogelijke ontwerp op.

Meer en betere kennis met betrekking tot stedebouwkundig ontwerpen, hoe zinvol ook in het licht van de problemen die er zijn met de ruimtelijke structuur, inrichting en vormgeving, en derhalve met het functioneren van mensen en instellingen, betekent echter als zodanig voor de toekomst nog geen verbetering van de situatie. In een democratische context zijn het niet de deskundigen die bepalen wat er gebeurt, maar gekozen bestuurders, die door deskundigen voorzien worden van kennis en inzichten. Meer en betere kennis wil nog niet zeggen dat ook betere besluiten genomen zullen worden.

Mijn bevindingen leiden tot aanbevelingen voor universitair onderzoek en onderwijs. De belangrijkste zijn dat als een wetenschappelijke benadering van stedebouwkundig ontwerpen wenselijk geacht wordt, een cultuurverandering nodig is. De gilde-achtige cultuur die de stedebouwkundige ontwerpopleidingen kenmerkt, moet dan getransformeerd worden in een cultuur waarin algemene wetenschappelijke spelregels gehanteerd en aangeleerd worden en inzicht aanwezig is in verschillende opvattingen over wat wetenschap is, in het bijzonder met betrekking tot stedebouwkundig ontwerpen. Eigen vak- en wetenschapsinhoudelijke opvattingen dienen kritisch beschouwd worden, gerelateerd worden aan die van anderen, en onderwerp zijn van publiek debat.
In inhoudelijk opzicht zullen naast de ruimtelijk-ecologische en de economisch-technologische, de sociaal-culturele aspecten van stedebouwkundig ontwerpen nadrukkelijk aandacht moeten krijgen, waarbij deze aandacht zowel lineaire als cyclische processen moet gelden - en veranderingen daarin. Ordenende beginselen en principemodellen moeten verder ontwikkeld worden, mede met behulp van kennis uit andere wetenschapsgebieden. Deze kennis moet 'vertaald' worden in voor ontwerpend onderzoeken bruikbare vormen.
Onderwijs en onderzoek moeten gezien hun wederzijds bevruchtende werking - onder andere blijkend uit de voorbeelden in dit boek - nauw met elkaar verbonden zijn. Aandacht zou in het bijzonder uit moeten gaan naar die studenten die van een wetenschapgerichte ambitie blijk geven. Met name deze studenten zullen immers bijdragen aan het ontwikkelen van gegeneraliseerde stedebouwkundige ontwerp-kennis.

Summary

Knowledge-based Design: Developing Urban & Regional Design into a Science

Ina T.Klaasen

An implemented design of an urban area imposes long-term conditions on societal processes, such as the opportunities people have to organize their lives in temporospatial respects in a healthy and safe living environment, and the way social, cultural and economic institutions and organisations can function. In view of the fact that both people and institutions experience recurrent problems - ranging from getting lost in new housing estates to the awkward accessibility of workplaces - it is striking that in a world as ours laden as it is with scientific knowledge and its applications, the design/redesign of urban areas is based on scarcely any substantive-scientific knowledge in the area of urban & regional design. Designers are supplied with knowledge, particularly from social-spatial sciences, which is explicit, well-founded and open to critique, but design itself is not considered to be scientific.
As to the professional field, there has been very little concern to develop a scientific foundation for urban & regional design, particularly during the last few decades. The widely held notion that each design is unique and based on individual creativity has hitherto left little room for thinking about urban & regional design as a science, whilst the immense complexity of urban areas plays a role as well.

The assumptions underlying my research are that urban & regional design can be developed into a societally relevant science, that this depends on the view held regarding the significance of urban & regional design to society, and what is considered to be the object of the discipline derived from this view. I base these assumptions on the knowledge and insights I have acquired during the last fifteen years; the first ten years within the Chair of Urban & Regional Design, and after that within the Chair of Spatial Planning, both of the Faculty of Architecture of the Delft University of Technology.

The research can therefore be characterised as an interpretative-theoretical study, a term from the methodologist A.D.de Groot ((1961) 1968: 325ff.). The characteristics of such a study are that within a particular collection of data (tentative) connections are made, that it must be impossible to solve the problem directly by experimental tests, and that the interpretation is not the only one possible. This makes the research an 'intellectual quest'.

The first question that needs to be answered is where urban & regional design fits into the field of sciences, if a substantive-scientific approach is indeed possible. The standpoint from which I start my quest is that the real world exists independently of us as knowing subjects. As the cognitive power of human beings is limited by 'nature' and 'nurture', the real world is only knowable by approximation (the correspondence theory of truth). People are selective in their perception in accordance with general organization principles of simplification, categorisation and generalisation. They make connections, so forming a picture of how reality 'fits together', or can be fitted together. Reality, including urban reality, can therefore be approached as an (open) system, or a system of (open) systems of equal and unequal order. Elements of a system derive their significance (location value) from the position they hold in that system. Processes in a system can be either linear or cyclic. Whether changes are perceived in a spatial or temporal sense depends on the spatial or temporal grain of the perception (Jong 1992: 16). Within urban systems we can distinguish physical urban systems, made up of spatial elements such as buildings, streets, parks, sewers, stations, or made up of configurations of spatial elements like buildings, streets etc. which have certain characteristics in terms of form, physical state and function. These urban spatial objects, in mutually coherent combinations and in coherent combinations with natural spatial objects, have been and are constructed or reconstructed in order to fulfil a carrying function and an information function, on behalf of the urban society. The visual manifestation at a particular moment is called the composition of the urban area or urban landscape.

Scientific knowledge is based upon rational considerations. Language, which includes visual language, has an organizational function in the thought process and is a means for conveying scientific ideas. Science limits 'chance' in the sense of 'random events'.

Science presupposes generalization. For this purpose we must simplify systems and focus on similarities rather than differences.

In order to communicate about and/or reflect on these systems we have to use models: conscious simplifications of (past, present and future) reality. Relevant to urban & regional design are pragmatic (analogue) models, particularly spatial ones, and from a functional viewpoint particularly descriptive, intentional-projective and exploratory-projective models. I therefore do not regard a model as an 'example to follow' as some (if not most) architects do. An urban or regional design is a proposal for a coherent package of spatial interventions in a certain urban or urbanescent area, and always affects more than one sector.

Sciences may be divided into: (1) formal sciences without empirical content, (2) empirical sciences which concentrate on 'that which is (or was) the case' and therefore 'that which will probably be the case' and (3) practical, action-oriented sciences that have the application of science as their object of scientific research (Peursen 1986: 61) (Fig.A). The findings of practical sciences are then applied in concrete cases (Fig.B). Practical science is not knowledge that is acquired in practice (Drenth 1995: 157; Gunsteren 2001): practice only generates questions.

empirical science	*epistèmè*: (intersubjective) knowledge	what will *probably* be the case	progress generated by intrascientific considerations	characteristic: explicative and predictive models
practical science	*technè*: (intersubjective) knowledge	what *can* be the case	progress generated by extrascientific considerations	characteristic: descriptive, intentional and exploratory-projective models

Fig.A

practical science	*technè* = (intersubjective) knowledge	what generally could be the case (under which conditions, and with what effects)
application of knowledge	*phronèsis* = reasoned decision	what is concretizable in a specific situation, given the applicable conditions and expected effects (predictions, empirically grounded as far as possible)

Fig.B

The ultimate question for the practical sciences is 'does it work? i.e. which effects are to be expected and under what conditions. This involves both insight into constructive options and utilitarian options. Given the extrascientific problem statement a monodisciplinary approach is unlikely to be fruitful.

On the basis of the above we can conclude that urban & regional design as a science would have to be categorised among the practical sciences.

The same scientific rules and standards apply in empirical and practical sciences. In the views regarding these rules two main approaches can be distinguished: an objectivistic one and a subjectivistic/relativistic one, the primary exponents of which are, respectively, Karl Popper and Thomas Kuhn. Kuhn's conclusion that science should be conducted in a primarily non-rational, consensus-driven manner may be correct in a descriptive sense, but from a realistic view of scientific knowledge - the only one possible for practical sciences - this is not tenable as a goal. However 'natural' the inductive verification of hypotheses/theories may be, we do not necessarily have to follow this tendency, no more than we do the tendency to prefer 'certainty' over 'doubt'. Popper's views in their strictest sense are not tenable either. From an objectivistic point of view criticism has primarily been levelled at the fact that he regards the context of discovery as scientifically irrelevant: also hypotheses and theories can have a rational foundation. Popper's student, the objectivist Imre Lakatos - to some extent influenced by Kuhn - also criticised in particular the 'unnaturalness' of the exclusive focus on falsification instead of on verification/corroboration. This led him to develop a research approach, which due to his emphasis on heuristics, abduction and plausible reasoning, shows interesting similarities with (urban & regional) design processes. This approach offers perspectives for the development of urban & regional design into a practical-scientific discipline. In practical sciences the context of justification is however viewed in a different light from in empirical sciences. Ethical and financial considerations as well as the time factor may make it impossible to test a practical science hypothesis experimentally, under controlled, repeatable conditions. In these cases one will have to draw plausible conclusions on the basis of a series of applications, regarding the necessary conditions and effects that arise. Because the term 'context of justification' has much less significance in these cases, the term 'context of application' is preferable.

In urban & regional design the above-mentioned testing limitations apply in a cumulative manner. Acquiring information from the context of application moreover is hindered because the conditions under which proposals are implemented in practice show relatively few similarities and these conditions cannot be manipulated. Based on this, the emphasis in the practical-scientific approach to urban & regional design lies on the context of discovery: what is assumed to be possible, and what are the probable effects, under which conditions.

Empirical and formal scientific knowledge, in part derived from the context of application, should provide the necessary constraints.

The next question is whether, in the development or non-development of 'urban and regional design' into a substantive-scientific discipline, what one regards as the object of that discipline - arising from what one considers to be the significance of urban & regional design to society - plays a part. To answer that question I position urban & regional design in relation to the disciplines of 'spatial planning' and 'architecture'. Lines of approach are (1) the systems approach to (future) urban reality, (2) the limitations inherent to working with spatial models of which the most important is the time factor and consequently that processes can only be shown indirectly (Fig.C), and (3) an examination in further detail of the concept of the 'carrying function' and the 'information function' (subjectively use value and experiential value). With regard to the latter two terms I argue, for example, that to be able to experience a physical urban system, unlike a building, the ability to use that system is a necessary condition.

static spatial model	VERSUS	dynamic reality
space		space and time
visible phenomena		visible and invisible phenomena
objects and their spatial relations: patterns		objects and their spatial and temporal relations: patterns and processes

Fig.C

This positioning makes it clear that the general description of the physical urban system as the object of urban & regional design can be interpreted in two ways and in practice is indeed interpreted in two ways. The physical urban system can be seen on the one hand as an autonomous system, with the other components of the urban system as the system environment, and on the other hand as an inextricable component of the urban system as a whole.

The first approach mentioned focuses on the composition of the physical system and on the linear processes in this system (characterized by a large temporal grain). I call this the pattern-oriented approach. This type of urban & regional design focuses on the so-called 'transformation' of urban areas. Influenced by the discipline 'architecture', and usually based on a quantitative programme of functional requirements, the creation of an experiential value guided by personal form concepts is seen as the main task for urban & regional designers. In part due to this emphasis on the design, pattern-oriented designs have the character of blueprints, which makes them fairly inflexible.

In the second approach mentioned, which I call process-oriented, the focus is primarily on small-grained cyclic urban-societal processes with a spatial dimension. These processes do of course also have a large grain linear component. This design view emphasises the use value, with the experiential value as an essential, functional support of this value. Important components are the functional-spatial structures, which are supported by relevant visual design that facilitates any desired processes, and the potential user bases needed for the functioning of collective institutions. For process-oriented design it is sufficient to indicate the functional-spatial structure and a number of essential indications with regard to visual design.

Urban & regional designers are insufficiently aware of distinction between these two types of approach. In addition to having shared concepts with similar definitions, pattern-oriented and process-oriented designs each have their own terminology as well as different definitions for the same concept. They also make use of different types of spatial models. This results in a lack of understanding in the field, confusion in the language used and insufficient insight into the societal significance of urban & regional design.
The essential differences between the two approaches can be expressed in the following key words:

pattern-oriented design	VERSUS	process-oriented design
pattern		process
living, working etc. (residing)		travelling / transporting
places		routes
zones		networks
accessibility: distance		accessibility: journey time
distance between residential function - work function, residential function - amenity function etc.		temporospatial activity pattern
(pattern-based) blueprint planning		(functional-spatial) structure planning

Fig.D

We can conclude that the perspectives for a practical-scientific approach of urban & regional design differ according to which standpoint is adopted. Pattern-oriented design offers little perspective for a practical-scientific approach. We cannot ask 'does it work?' with regard to possible uses, unless the elements of physical urban systems are seen in mutual relation. 'Perception' therefore also has no functional significance. What is more, the emphasis lies on cultural and aesthetic aspects as well as personal form concepts. This is different for the process-oriented approach in which the physical urban system cannot be regarded as We can conclude that the perspectives for a practical-scientific approach of urban & regional design differ according to which standpoint is adopted. Pattern-oriented design offers little perspective for a practical-scientific approach. We cannot ask 'does it work?' with regard to possible uses, unless the elements of physical urban systems are seen in mutual relation. 'Perception' therefore also has no functional significance. What is more, the emphasis lies on cultural and aesthetic aspects as well as personal form concepts. This is different for the process-oriented approach in which the physical urban system cannot be regarded as separate from the urban system as a whole, and in which the use value is the primary point of interest and the perception of the physical urban system supports the use.

I concretize these perspectives by outlining the relationship between urban & regional design and research in practice. In general, when making proposals for the spatial development of cities, there is a division of tasks whereby empirical scientists supply knowledge and insight into spatial planning, which is integrated by designers in a 'creative leap' into a design for a specific situation (Fig.E). In the Netherlands the term 'the unity of town planning' is applied (Lohuizen 1948: 3). This division of tasks also applies to means-oriented design, whereby the possibilities of the situation provide direction and the design result is evaluated *ex ante*. In practice, however, there seems to be a gap between empirical science and urban & regional design. There are a number of reasons for this 'applicability gap'. An important one is that increasingly more knowledge of a varied nature has become available, and designers as a consequence no longer have a comprehensive grasp of this knowledge, the more so as much of the information is irrelevant (Hillier, Musgrove & O'Sullivan 1972). Designers are consequently unable to let go of their preconceptions; on the contrary, they become more dependent upon them (ibid.).

In the nineteen sixties the rising interest in the scientific approach to urban & regional design focused not only on the procedural side of design but also for a while on the substantive side (e.g. J. Jacobs 1961; Doxiadis 1968; Alexander 1977). However, there was and still is much resistance against the scientific approach to urban & regional design: a rational, systematic approach is thought to adversely affect the essential creativity needed when making designs. Also the guild-like manner in which the community of urban & regional designers is organized, similarly to that of architects, does not stimulate the development of a scientific approach. An education and working climate that is characterized by a master-apprentice relationship, in which often no account is given of the resulting product, where the validity of claims are derived from the status of the speaker, and where debates regarding views held in the field are avoided rather than sought, is not the most conducive for a scientific development of that discipline. For so far as (realistic) scientific research is carried out in this context, it is almost without exception empirical descriptive research of a (cultural) historical nature: design research.

For practical-scientific research one must not think in terms of each design being unique; in other words it is necessary to dissociate the object of design from the specific design context. This opens the doors for the design of theoretical models with spatial organization principles as 'building blocks': designs that in spatial-ecological and/or socio-cultural and/or economic-technical terms are independent of the situation. The activity of design acts to serve research and has become a research method: research by design (Fig.F).

In research by design knowledge is not integrated directly and individually into each localized design, but general, integrated scientific urban & regional design knowledge is developed in an additional design phase (Fig.G). Explicit scientific knowledge is essential in this practical-scientific approach to urban & regional design as this makes a critical-rational debate regarding this knowledge possible. Theoretical models bridge the previously mentioned applicability gap. Creativity is crucial in both the development of this knowledge and its application in specific situations.

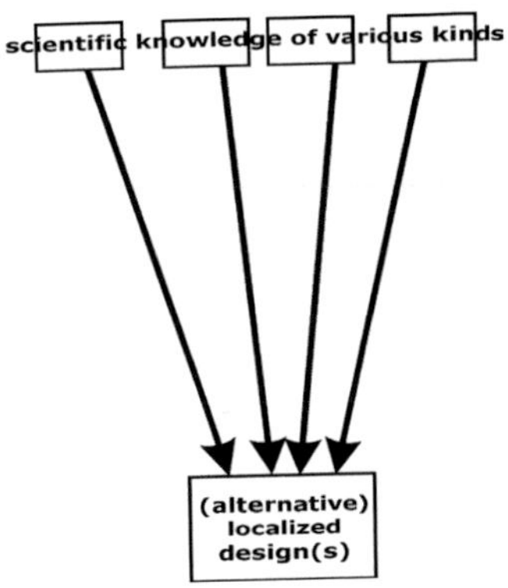

Fig.E The representation of a design process in which supplied scientific knowledge is used directly in a localized design.

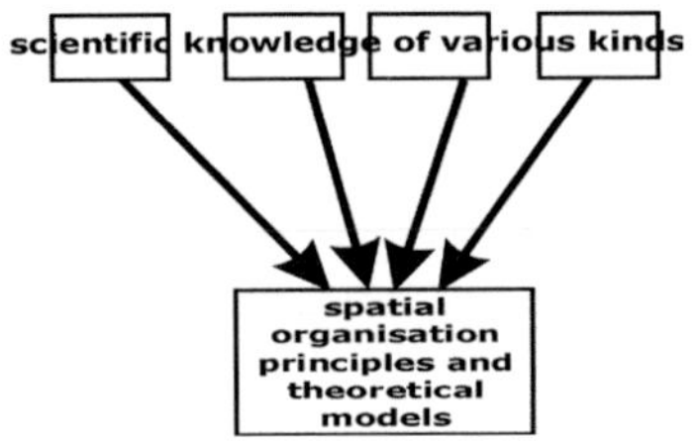

Fig.F The representation of a design process in which supplied knowledge is integrated in spatial principles and theoretical models (research by design).

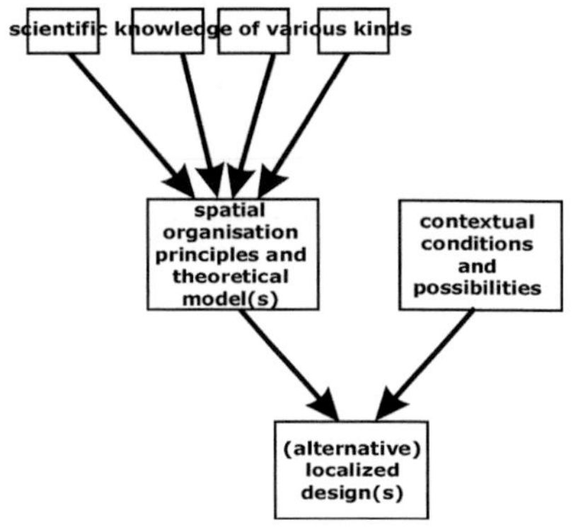

Fig.G The representation of the design process whereby a localized design is created using the input of research by design results.

If the research approach of Lakatos is related to the approach developed at the Chair of Urban & Regional Design, then I regard the following as elements of the hard core of the practical-scientific research programme:

- Viewing the built (future) reality as an open system;
- Approaching this physical urban system as an organized complex system;
- Viewing the physical urban system as part of the urban system as a whole;
- The fact that an element of this physical system derives its significance from its position in the system on the one hand and contributes to making the system what it is on the other;
- The distinguishing of various temporal grains in societal processes;
- The distinguishing of levels of scale within the physical urban system on the basis of societal processes that are characterised by a relatively small temporal grain;
- The consequently necessary cohesion between the system levels;
- The boundaries of design areas at various scales being defined on the bases of societal processes;

and

- Unlinking the design object from a specific design context;
- Regarding design not just in the usual sense but also as a method of research.

The essence of the research approach can be described as follows.
Start with a number of basic elements from the object under study and manipulate them, in part on the basis of organizational principles, in such a way that the resulting theoretical models of physical urban systems are logically plausible and internally-consistent: constructions which, in the light of our available formal and empirical knowledge, are likely to function stably when implemented. Contextual conditions and effects analyses then have to be carried out for these basic theoretical models, in part based on empirical research. During the process of research by design there is also a continual *ex ante* evaluation. In order to limit the theoretically infinite number of possibilities, the breadth of useful research is determined by situations that occur in reality. Counter examples (Lakatos's 'monsters') play an important part: they increase the theoretical content of theoretical models. Urban & regional design entails the question of whether plausible spatial planning principles and plausible theoretical

models can be derived from partially inconsistent information with heuristic and creative abduction as mechanisms (Schomburg 1991: 59; Magnani 2001: 78).

Theoretical models are not ready-made templates for creating localized designs, but ‘tools’. The task of the designer of a localized design is on the one hand to retain as much quality as possible of the chosen theoretical model - this can even be expanded with the help of specific situational potentials - and on the other to utilize the spatial individuality of the site in the design. The purpose of the latter is to bring about the spatial diversity that is necessary even if it is only to make the most of the information function. Theoretical models can be seen metaphorically as being made of elastic.

The intended effects will have to be continually checked in concrete situations as the actual environment is not considered in the theoretical model. A designer should also consider any unintended consequences.

Theoretical models can also play a role during a localized design process in the sense that a localized design problem is ‘taken from’ the specific situation and generalised. This is the transition area between ‘research by design’ and ‘research driven research’. A conscious simplification facilitates the studying of the (hypothesized) essence of the problem and establishes a relationship with generic urban & regional design knowledge.

For several years now a debate has been going on at the Delft University of Technology whether a design can be regarded as scientific output. This debate seems to deal with the question of whether a design, a spatial model, is an acceptable means of communication. The debate in fact deals, or should deal, with the question of whether urban & regional design is indeed a (practical) scientific discipline. As there are limited possibilities for proving hypotheses this question ought to be taken seriously. The research approach described here together with the examples in this book of concrete research projects, allows this question to be answered affirmatively. This is supported by examples of practical scientific knowledge, dating mainly from the nineteen sixties and seventies, in the form of organizational principles and theoretical models (or initiatives in that direction).

The research projects by academic staff and students described in this book also show that the research is bearing fruit, that in the terms of Lakatos there is a ‘positive heuristic’. It cannot be concluded however, that this research programme is the only possible one. An interpretive-theoretical model study does not produce research results that exclude any other result. This makes this type of empirical research similar to design, in that it is a process that always has more than one possible outcome.

More and better knowledge regarding urban & regional design, however useful in light of the spatial problems and consequently with regard to the functioning of people and institutions, does not in itself improve the (future) spatial situation. In a democratic context it is not the experts who determine what happens, but the elected administrators whom these experts supply with knowledge and insights. More and better knowledge does not necessarily mean that better decisions will be made.
My findings lead to recommendations for university research and education. The most important of these is that a change in culture is necessary if urban & regional design is to be scientifically approached. The guild-like culture that characterises urban & regional design education should therefore be transformed into a culture in which general scientific rules are applied and taught, in which lecturers possess knowledge about the various views regarding science, in particular in relation to urban & regional design, and in which critical debates are encouraged.

From a substantive viewpoint, not only spatial-ecological and economic-technological aspects but socio-cultural aspects of urban & regional design should receive attention. This attention should concern linear as well as cyclic processes including changes in these processes. Organizational principles and theoretical models should be further developed. Knowledge from other fields of science should be 'translated' into forms that are suitable for research by design.

In view of the cross fertilisation between education and research - as shown in this book - the two have to be considered in close connection. Special attention should be given to those students who show interest in a scientific approach to the discipline. It is after all these students in particular who will help feed the body of knowledge of urban & regional design.

Notes

Chapter 1

1 The term 'urban & regional design' is used throughout this book as a translation of the Dutch term *stedebouwkundig ontwerpen*. See "notes on the translation from Dutch into English" for observations regarding this translation.

Chapter 2

2 The height of a tower in the 'here and now' can be measured with only a limited measure of accuracy. Equating this measurement to measuring the height of that same tower on the contract drawing, as the architect Lawson (1990: 4) does, amounts to a denial of the independent existence of reality.

3 The term 'formal', which in an urban design context is treated as the adjectival form of 'form', refers here to an uninterpreted mathematical system.

4 Isolated 'as an approximation', because in principle the system is always affected by the observer and/or researcher.

5 This means that a representation of reality in the form of a photograph or a graphic record of seismic waves is not a model in its own right since it concerns only objectively filtered registrations. Obviously, representations of this kind can be used as the basis for a model (e.g. the interpretation of an aerial photo: a topographical map is an example of a spatial model based (partly) on aerial photos.)

6 These are terms used in the so called 'Global Ecological Model' (GEM) (Ministerie van Volkshuisvesting en Ruimtelijke Ordening 1977).

7 The term 'culture' can be understood in either a broad or a narrow sense. When the term is used as here without further qualification, it has the narrow meaning; in combination with 'social' (e.g. 'socio-cultural') it carries the broad meaning.

8 The socio-cultural dimension often remains implicit. In the respect of the information function, it is for example the interpretation we give to the shapes of buildings and public spaces such as schools, churches, sports fields and residential care homes. 'Interpretation in architecture is based on psychological mechanisms and cultural patterns.' (Lawson 1990: 148).

9 "Public life can be divided into sectors, within which various administrative layers of government can take regulatory action to promote activities and developments, among other means by creating suitable spatial and financial conditions." (Boer 1990: 13). Examples of sectors are traffic, public housing, health care and open air recreation.

10 A design process can also be for the purpose of research (see Chapters 5 and 6).

Chapter 3

11 In his inaugural address, Prof. J. de Mul (Erasmus University, Rotterdam) distinguished three forms of 'chance': contingency (the non-necessary), accident (the secondary, non-essential) and fortuitousness. Non-necessary chance means that there are also alternative possibilities (there is no question of logical compulsion). Accidental (in the single case) is opposed to the universal (in all cases). For neither contingency nor accident is there any question of randomness, as there is in chance determined by fate (Huisman 1996: 138).

12 'Objective' in Popper's words: "the *objectivity* of scientific statements lies in the fact that they can be *inter-subjectively* tested (Popper (1959) 1968: 44).'Intersubjective' is not meant here in a Kuhnian sense, but in the sense of epistemic reliability: "the capacity of scientists to get it (approximately) right about the things they study." (Boyd (1985) 1991: 350).

13 Cf. Popper's categorization of three 'worlds', with 'World 3' being that of the 'objective contents of thought' or knowledge 'without a knowing subject'. The most important inmates of this world are 'critical arguments'. Popper's 'World 1' and 'World 2' are respectively those of 'physical objects or of physical states' and of 'states of consciousness ... or ... behavioural dispositions to act' (Popper 1972: 106ff).

14 '*Scientific* realism': according to Boyd, Gasper and Trout (1997: Glossary), "the view that the subject matter of scientific research and scientific theories exists independently of our knowledge of it, and that the goal of science is the description and explanation of both the observable and the unobservable aspects of an independently existing world."
'*Metaphysical* realism: "In the widest sense, the view that (a) there are real objects (usually the view is concerned with spatiotemporal objects), (b) they exist independently of our experience of our knowledge of them, and (c) they have properties and enter into relations independently of the concepts with which we understand them, or the language with which we describe them. (---) Metaphysical realism, in all of its three parts, is shared by commonsense, the sciences, and most philosophers." (Audi 1995, lemma 'metaphysical realism'). According to Van Peursen (1994: 84) metaphysics as a key to reality must not be sought in the supernatural, but in human consciousness; metaphysics is thus not only culturally but also individually determined. "To be real in the scientific sense means to be an element of the system; hence this concept cannot be meaningfully applied to the system itself.' (Carnap (1956), 1991: 86); "No system can validate itself." (Toulmin 2001: 80).
'*Naive* realism' = commonsense, Aristotelian commonsense (Feyerabend 1978). "Today we can add as a defence of commonsense: commonsense-perception, -thought, and –action are results of evolution and therefore liable to be better, closer to nature than bright ideas of intellectuals." (ibid.: 169).
'*Critical* realism' (Huisman 1996): "There is a reality which is external to us and which we can come to know, and a realistic view of our cognitive capacities helps us understand *how* we can come to know it."
'*Instrumental* realism' focuses on the importance of natural-scientific technology as a means of making discoveries and developing knowledge (Ihde 1991).
'*Referential* realisme': refers to 'elements of a human-independent reality' (Radder 1996: 77, 108; see also Larry Laudan in Boyd, Gasper & Trout 1991: 225 ff).
'*Constructive* empiricism': the accumulation of scientific knowledge relates exclusively to phenomena (Bas van Fraassen, Princeton University (USA), in Science supplement of *De Volkskrant* 24-12-99).

15 Foqué(2001), Bax, Doevendans and Trum (2001), Besteliu and Doevendans (2001), however, see urban design as an example of a pragmatic conception of science such as developed by Peirce et al. Their view is based on a direct relation between theory and (localized) practice. Practical science (see Section 3.2.4) does not imply a pragmatic conception of science, unless all practical science must be regarded as pragmatic.

16 A grey (transitional) zone exists between pure empirical research and practical research: long-term, application oriented research is sometimes referred to as 'fundamental strategic research'.

17 This multidisciplinary scientific character should not be confusedwith a multidisciplinary approach of a specific (societal) problem.

18 The Dutch words *kunst* (art) and *kunde* (1. skill 2. used as a suffix to denote various branches of technology, e.g. *bedrijfskunde*, business science) are etymologically cognate.

19 The Dutch word *kunst* (art) can also mean 'artifice' and is often used as a prefix in the latter sense, e.g. *kunstwerk* (1. a work of art, 2. a civil engineering structure such as a bridge or tunnel) or *kunstgebit* (false teeth).

20 Inter alia, art as mimesis (Plato), as an expression of the artist's feelings, as *l'art pour l'art*, as free beauty (Kant, Mondriaan), art in the form of concepts (Burg 1999).

21 The study of e.g. medicine is, however, a practical science that has traditionally been studied at conventional universities. In recent years, the conventional universities in the Netherlands have been increasingly offering (professionally oriented) courses in practical sciences.

22 Instead of projective, the term prospective is sometimes used. The use of these terms in the spatial sciences is not unambiguous (e.g. Vught & Van Doorn 1976; Kleefmann 1984).

23 *Methodos*, originally in Greek the pursuit of any goal without a particular reference to obligatory procedures. From there: the pursuit of knowledge as a special case (Toulmin 2001: 84). Methodology is understood as meaning both 'the procedures and techniques governing inquiry' and 'the study of such procedures and techniques.' (Boyd, Gasper & Trout 1997: Glossary).

24 The 'context of discovery' is currently also sometimes termed the 'context of invention', particularly in connection with practical sciences. A three-way distinction is also made: 'context of invention','context of pursuit' and 'context of justification'. The 'context of pursuit' relates in this case to the phase in which an idea is worked out as a hypothesis (Jong & Schipper 1987: 148). In the present research report the term 'discovery' will be used.

25 A practical example of an *ad hoc* hypothesis of the kind 'forbidden' by Popper is that of the 'transferred semen trace' theory submitted as evidence in the Putten murder case, and later rejected as a judicial error (2002). (http://www.leidenuniv.nl/mare/2002/06/101.html;04-2003).

26 The difference between 'verification' and 'corroboration' is that corroboration could also support an alternative theory or hypothesis.

27 Kuhn apparently conflates two meanings of the word 'discipline': the Latin *disciplina*, according to Lipsius (late 16th century), refers to 'the rules governing the professional conduct of soldiers.' (Toulmin 2001: 35).

28 Lakatos developed his methodology in the domain of mathematics. In an article in the *Journal for the Philosophy of Science* (1963-64), the basis for his posthumously published book *Proofs and Refutations* (1976), he set out five rules for research:
"Rule 1. If you have a conjecture, set out to prove it and to refute it. Inspect the proof carefully to prepare a list of non-trivial lemmas (proof-analysis); find counterexamples both to the conjecture (global counterexamples) and to the suspect lemmas (local counterexamples).
Rule 2. If you have a global counterexample, discard your conjecture, add to your proof-analysis a suitable lemma that will be refuted by the counterexample, and replace the discarded conjecture by an improved one that incorporates that lemma as a condition. Do not allow a refutation to be dismissed as a monster. Try to make all 'hidden lemmas' explicit.
Rule 3. If you have a local counterexample, check to see whether it is not also a global counterexample. If it is, you can easily apply rule 2." (Lakatos 1976: 50).
"Rule 4. If you have a counterexample which is local but not global, try to improve your proof-analysis by replacing the refuted lemma by an unfalsified one." (Ibid.: 58).
"Rule 5. If you have counterexamples of any type, try to find, by inductive guessing, a deeper theorem to which they are counterexamples no longer.' (Ibid.: 76).

29 Popper gives the same example in Appendix XI of his 1968 edition of *The Logic of Scientific Discovery* (p. 442). Unlike Gooding, Popper cites an original source.

30 "The outstanding historical example is Lysenko. T.D. Lysenko was a biologist in the Soviet Union to whom Stalin granted the power to enforce his theories upon fellow biologists (-). From approximately 1927 to 1964, Lysenko ruled his discipline using the draconian methods of a totalitarian state. Biological science was virtually destroyed, and replaced by data fabrication in the service of propaganda –great agricultural progress was claimed: meanwhile the peasants starved. Disobedient scientists who criticized or resisted were removed from their posts – some were imprisoned and killed."
(http:/www.hedweb.com/bgcharlton/cargocult.html – 04-2003)

31 Incidentally, Patrick Abercrombie, a professor of Town and Country Planning at the University of Liverpool in the early years of the 20th century, described the Garden City as a laboratory for social and town planning experiments. (Preface to Casseres 1926: XIV). In his book *What Time is This place?,* Lynch proposes testing design hypotheses by establishing ''centres to conceive and evaluate possible new environments along with the new institutions and ways of living they imply." (1972: 228).

Chapter 4

32 The Netherlands Architecture Institute distinguished four approaches within urban planning and design in 1990 (Nio & Reijndorp 1997: 15): urban planning and design as

- an aspect of city marketing,
- a script in a theatrical spectacle,
- a morphological instrument for ensuring the continuity of urban form,
- a synthesis of architecture and urban planning.

The interview with Taverne in the same book distinguishes:
'visual designing', administrative and social-scientific urban planning and design (ibid: 206).
Henk van Blerk (1997) noted four different angles in urban design in the Netherlands in the 1990s: caring-critical, idealistic-innovative, altruistic-moralistic and hedonistic-realistic.

33 The design must of course indicate both the proposed interventions and the existing situation. In practice, this distinction is not always made clear.

34 The scale series used by De Jong agrees reasonably well with one based on types of transportation and the associated acceptable journey time: walking system ca 300 m (neighbourhood), walking/cycling system 1 km (estate or village), bus/tram system 3 km (city borough or small town), high-grade urban railway system/car system 10 km (city), regional railway/car system 30 km (urban region), intercity railway system 100 km (national region).

35 Jacobs develops a number of spatial interventions on the basis of his research which create conditions for either a nodal or multinodal urban system development (M. Jacobs 2000). I return to this example of 'research through design' in Chapter 6.4.3.

36 Spatial grain and scale level are also relevant in historical settlement patterns. The Romans settled along main routes, in the Netherlands on the banks of major rivers; the native farmers settled along the tributaries. Until recently, people concluded from research, which had been confined to a high level of scale, that the local population had retreated from the river area in Roman times (verbal information, with reference to archeological finds made in connection with research on a lower level of scale for the 'Betuwe Route', a new railway route crossing the Netherlands from west to east at the position of the so called 'great rivers').

37 This moral undertone is also evident in Lynch's rejection of hierarchy. Lynch (1981) argues for this rejection on the basis that all parts of a city are equally important. The fact that American cities are primarily structured around accommodating car journeys (see Section 6.2) plays a part in this outlook.

38 'Large' in relation to a human lifespan, but small of course in comparison to many processes that take place in the natural system.

39 Compare the translation of the terms employed by Vitruvius in the opening quotation of this Section. This translation used here corresponds to that of the architect Broadbent (1990: 37).

40 Assertions of this kind are a product of the human tendency to regard oneself as the measure of things. Architectural engineering students, for example, invariably overestimate average cycling and walking speeds. Similarly, Dutch gender studies of the 1980s tended to treat 'women' and 'mothers with small children' as virtually interchangeable concepts.

41 A personal experience in this connection is the 1979 decision process for a new satellite town for Amsterdam in the vicinity of Schiphol Airport (known as the 'NORON' location). Neither of the two design variants attracted a majority in the provincial government. A vote on various aspects of the two variants, with the outcome that only those components which occurred in both variants would be accepted, was averted only at the last moment.

42 The American 'New Urbanism' movement that arose in the 1980s addresses itself principally to lower levels of scale, e.g. on such urban processes as pedestrian access to facilities. The thinking behind is movement is much broader in scope, however, and returns in certain respects to Ebenezer Howard's concept of the Garden City from the early 1900s. The New Urbanism movement's main criticism is of the urban sprawl so typical of the USA (Leclercq 1999; Smit 2002).

Conventional Sprawl	Authentic Neighborhoods
- sprawl	- neighborhoods
- experimental, since 1945	- field tested, for 5000 years
- segregation of uses into pods	- mix of uses in streets and blocks
- car is a prerequisite to survival	- car is an option
- measurable in car trips	- measurable in walking distances
- consumes wildlife habitats and farmland	- conserves wildlife habitats and farmland
- horizontal zoning	- vertical zoning
- confusing, ambiguous form	- legible public spaces
- financed and constructed all at once	- financed and constructed incrementally
- has "developers"	- has "founders"
- forgettable and disposable	- memorable and lasting

(http://www.doverkohl.com/writings_images/authentic.html)

43 In thinly populated areas, there may even be 20-minute functions, e.g. mobile shops (*De Volkskrant*, 27 November 1993)

44 In other words, there is no neutral 'language of observation'. This is reminiscent of Kuhn's 'incommensurability' (see Section 3.4.2).

45 The term 'networks' is associated with the term 'space of flows', coined by Castells (1996). (Incidentally, Lynch referred to the 'flow system' as long ago as 1958: 361.) Introduction of the 'flow' concept does not however entail admission of the 'time' concept to pattern-oriented thinking.

46 It is hard to avoid seeing a relation here to the traditional division of labour between men and women (Klaasen 1985).

Chapter 5

47 'Policy' is sometimes included as a third component of the Unity of Town Planning, for example by the Van Eesteren-Fluck & Van Lohuizen foundation (EFL foundation). *De eenheid van het stedebouwkundig werk* (The Unity of Town Planning) was the title of his inaugural address as Professor of Town Planning(Delft University of Technology, then still *Technische Hogeschool Delft* (Delft Technical College). The subject of this address (contained as appendix in Valk 1990) was the collaboration between researchers and designers.

48 Arnold van der Valk however in his biography of Van Lohuizen did question this suggested smooth transition between research and design in which knowledge and intuition were combined (1990: 92). "What the designers accepted from the surveyors were the quantitative results: how many inhabitants, how many school children, how many cars, how many shops, etc." he says quoting one of Van Lohuizen's colleagues from before the Second World War (ibid.: 83).

49 In guilds a distinction was made between masters, journeymen and apprentices (*meesters, gezellen* and *leerlingen*). Masters can be compared to professors, journeymen to lecturers, and apprentices to students. For further information visit: http://www.twingroves.district96.k12.il.us/Renaissance/guildhall/guilds/guildinfo.html#anchor1484127 (05-2003)

50 In 1993 the description of the Delft Chair of Urban & Regional design (*stedebouwkundig ontwerpen stad/regio*) read: "The Chair ... focuses primarily on the design of functional-spatial structures of the city and the region." (*Vakgroep Stedebouwkunde* (departement of Urban Planning & Design) 1993: 8).In 2002 (another professor had been appointed): "Because the urban planning design of a city and region will always be limited to very minor local interventions, the education system spends a great deal of attention on the selection of strategic interventions." This change has never been publicly debated.

51 A quote: "Janet Daley castigated Alexander and his colleagues... for inventing 'private languages'. People who use ordinary words in special ways are obviously unsure of their ground. (---) We have some fairly complex things to say, (---), but it should be possible to say them all by means of good, honest, simple words, used with the meanings by with most people understand them.She is right of course, but perhaps she underestimates the power of 'in-groups' in the architectural scene, and

of the desperate need that many environmental designers have to be recognized as 'respectable' by science. And it is easy to acquire a tolerant imitation of respectability by expressing simple thoughts in complex jargon." (Broadbent 1969: 18).

52 The example that Krabbendam discusses is the statement of Le Corbusier 'the curved line paralyses everything'. It is difficult to deny that Le Corbusier's preference for straight lines has influenced many followers...

53 For me a personal sobering experience in this respect was the refusal by my co-editors on the editorial board of *Stedebouw & Volkshuisvesting* to publish a submitted article on spatial hierarchy with as reason given that 'spatial hierarchy' is an outmoded concept. It did, however, thanks to my protest eventually get published: Gantvoort 1993.

54 This ideographic approach can incidentally be found in other sciences as well. Medical science has, for example, the so-called narrative approach, where the background and story of the patient are particularly important. (*De Volkskrant*, 11-01-03).

55 In relation to this point the views of Jane Jacobs on Howard's 'Garden City' are interesting. "His aim was the creation of self-sufficient small towns, really very nice towns if you were docile and had no plans of your own and did not mind spending your life among others with no plans of their own." (1961: 17). "... Howard attacked the problem of town planning much as if he were a nineteenth-century physical scientist analysing a two-variable problem of simplicity. The two major variables in the Garden City concept of planning were the quantity of housing (or population) and the number of jobs. These two were conceived of as simply and directly related to each other, in the form of relatively closed systems. (---)And on this simple base of two-variable relationships was created a theory of self-contained towns as a means of redistributing the population of cities and (hopefully) achieving regional planning." (ibid.: 435).

56 In addition to the functional multi-nodality referred to here, there can also be, though not necessarily simultaneously, formal multi-nodality. The new town Almere in the IJsselmeer polder of South Flevoland is an example of a formal multinodal, but a functionally mononodal urban region.

57 At Delft University of Technology the public debate on a PhD thesis is purely verbal in nature, unless the desire to use visual aid to support the arguments used is stated well in advance.

58 From a memorandum of the *Voorbereidingsgroep* (preparation group) BTA advice output criteria for design, to the Deans of a number of faculties including the faculty of Architecture, dated 09-01-2003.

Chapter 6

59 For example, the first motorway exit in a particular area has a greater effect on the relative location value than the second. A tenth motorway exit will no longer make any difference.

60 An interesting article in this context appeared in the Dutch newspaper *De Volkskrant* on 16 May 1994. On the subject of some market research carried out in Vietnam, it stated that in the absence of any other criteria, social classes are determined by the walking distance between the dwelling and the main road: "The poverty line is a distance of more than half an hour."

61 This model was made as part of a regional development plan for the West-Friesland region in de nineteen eighties

62 Intensive recreation is an urban function; extensive recreation a function of non-urban areas.

63 At present work is being carried out in Amsterdam on points d and i. This also applies to other essentials of this study that have not been mentioned here. Point e, which has a clear relationship with point d, is not (yet) policy.

Chapter 7

64 Walen and Nozeman researched the consequences of moving a hospital from the centre of a city to the outskirts. They found that this stimulated car use and increased the total number of kilometres traveled by car. For the less mobile section of the population it resulted in reduced accessibility (1985).

65 An example of plastic language: management, process and evaluation can be used in random order, e.g. management of the evaluation process etc.

66 One of these ICT developments is the mobile phone. Research into the effects of this on the desired design of physical urban systems promises to be an interesting project.

67 The philosopher L.Floridi, when working at Oxford University, suggested in an interview that defining knowledge as the collection of information is a typical phenomenon of the book age. He wrote *The Extension of the Mind, an introduction to information and communication technology for philosophers* (*De Volkskrant*, science Section 4-5-96).

68 At the Faculty of Architecture in Delft, the introduction of Problem Based Learning (PBL) in the 1990s led to the type of project Graaff and Kolmos called ‘task projects’. These projects entail a high degree of planning and direction on the part of the teacher. “Both the problem and the subject-oriented methods are chosen in advance, so that for the student the primary concern is to complete the project according to the guidelines provided.” Graaff and Cowdroy regard the implementation of PBL in this faculty as a failure (1997). A new educational programme has been introduced in 2002 in which the concept of PBL no longer has a place. At this faculty incidentally, in collaboration with other Delft faculties and faculties of other universities, PBL -avant-la-lettre existed from the nineteen sixties to 1984 in the form of multidisciplinary projects for advanced students (*Interuniversitaire Studiegroepen Stedebouwkunde/Planologie*), which were based on problems that occurred in practice and were raised by social organizations.

References

Alexander, Christopher. 1964. Notes on the Synthesis of Form. Cambridge (Mass., USA): Harvard University Press

Alexander, Christopher. 1966. "A city is not a tree.". *Design* (Februari issue)

Alexander, Christopher; Sara Ishikawa & Murray Silverstein. 1977. A Pattern Language. New York (N.Y.): Oxford University Press

Alexander, Christopher; Hajo Neis; Artemis Anninou & Ingrid King. 1987. A New Theory of Urban Design. New York (N.Y.): Oxford University Press

Angyal, A. (1941) 1969. "A Logic of Systems." Excerpt from Foundations for a Science of Personality; Harvard University Press . Reprinted in 1969 in: Systems Thinking, edited by F.E.Emery; pp.17-29. Harmondsworth, Middlesex (UK): Penguin Books.

Anonymous. 1993. "Interview met Ashok Bhalotra." *Blauwe Kamer/Profiel* (1): 20.

Anonymous. 1998. Mobilopolis; de actieve fietsstad. Nota in opdracht van Projectbureau Integrale Verkeers-en Vervoersstudies. Nijmegen/Deventer (Neth.): Vakgroep Planologie (K.U.Nijmegen), Haskoning & Goudappel Coffeng

Apostel, Leo. 1961. "Towards the formal study of models in the non-formal sciences." In: The concept and the role of the model in mathematics and natural and social sciences, edited by H.Freudenthal; pp.1-37. Dordrecht (Neth.): D.Reidel Publishing Company

Aristotle. 1958. The Pocket Aristotle, translated by W.D. Ross, edited by Justin. D. Kaplan. New York (N.Y.): Simon & Schuster

Audi, Robert (ed.). 1995. The Cambridge Dictionary of Philosophy. Cambridge (UK): Cambridge University Press

Bailer-Jones, Daniela M.. 1999. "Tracing the Development of Models in the Philosophy of Science." In: Model-based Reasoning in Scientific Discovery, edited by Lorenzo Magnani, Nancy Nersessian & Paul Thagard; pp.23-40. New York (N.Y.): Kluwer Academic/Plenum Publishers

Bakel, Anton P.M. van. 1995. Styles of architectural designing: empirical research on working styles and personal dispositions. PhD Thesis. Faculty of Architecture TU Eindhoven (Neth.)

Barnett, Jonathan. 1982. An Introduction to Urban Design. New York (N.Y.): Harper & Row

Bax, Thijs; Kees Doevendans & Henk Trum. 2001. "Research Design and Education: Von Humboldt revisited." In: Research by Design, International Conference Faculty of Architecture Delft University of Technology in co operation with the EAAE/AEEA, November 1-3 2000, Proceedings B, edited by Anja Langenhuizen, Marieke van Ouwerkerk & Jürgen Rosemann; pp.31-35. Delft (Neth.): Delft University Press

Bekkering, H.C. 1999. Voetlicht op het stedebouwkundig ontwerpen in het *fin de s*(c)*iecle*. Inaugural address. Delft (Neth.): Delft University Press

Bekkering, H.C.; C.H.E. van Ees; D. Bekkering & M. Jansen. 2002. 9 Projecten voor blok stad. Internal publication Faculty of Architecture TU Delft .

Bertels, Kees & Doede Nauta. 1969. Inleiding tot het modelbegrip. Bussum (Neth.): W.de Haan

Besteliu, Ion & Kees Doevendans. 2001. "Generating Knowledge Through Design." In: Research by Design, International Conference Faculty of Architecture Delft University of Technology in co operation with the EAAE/AEEA, November 1-3 2000, Proceedings B, edited by Anja Langenhuizen, Marieke van Ouwerkerk & Jürgen Rosemann; pp.43-48. Delft (Neth.): Delft University Press

Blerck, Henk van. 1997. "Het stedebouwkundig beroep - ambachtsmens, deskundige, artiest en/of antichrist." In: De Stedebouwkundige als regisseur; essays bij de Cor van Eesterenmanifestatie 1997; pp.5-14. Amsterdam: Bond van Nederlandse Stedebouwkundige en Planologen

Boer, N.A. de. 1978. "Provinciegrenzen en regionaal beleid." *Economische en Statistische Berichten* (1): 32-37

Boer, Niek de. 1989. "Metropolitaine Zorgen – perifeer gelegen city-elementen. "*Stedebouw en Volkshuisvesting* (5): 58-65.

Boer, N. A de. 1990. Stedebouwkundige Planvorming. Internal publication Faculty of Architecture, TU Delft

Boer, N. A de. 1994. Strategische plekken in Amsterdam. Amsterdam: Architectura & Natura

Boer, Niek A. de. 1996. De Randstad bestaat niet. Rotterdam: NAI uitgevers

Boer, Niek de & Donald Lambert. 1987. Woonwijken: Nederlandse Stedebouw 1945-1985. Rotterdam: Uitgeverij 010

Boyd, Richard; Philip Gasper, & J. D. Trout (editors). 1991. The Philosophy of Science. Cambridge (MA, USA): MIT- Press

Boyd, Richard. (1985) 1991. "Observations, Explanatory Power, and Simplicity: toward a Non-Humean account." In: Observation, Experiment, and Hypothesis in Modern Physical Science, edited by P.Achinstein and O.Hannaway. Cambridge (Mass., USA): MIT Press. Reprinted 1991 in The Philosophy of Science, edited by Richard Boyd, Philip Gasper & J.D. Trout; pp.349-377. Cambridge (Mass., USA): MIT Press

Breen, Jack. 2001. " Designerly Approaches to Architectural Research." In: Research by Design; International Conference Faculty of Architecture Delft University of Technology in co operation with the EAAE/AEEA, November 1-3 2000, Proceedings B, edited by Anja Langenhuizen, Marieke van Ouwerkerk & Jürgen Rosemann; pp.54-61. Delft (Neth.): Delft University Press

Broadbent, Geoffrey. 1969. " Design method in architecture." In: Design methods in Architecture, edited by G.Broadbent & A.Ward; pp.15-21. London: Lund Humphries

Broadbent, Geoffrey. 1988. Design in Architecture. London: David Fulton Publishers

Broadbent, Geoffrey. 1990. Emerging Concepts in Urban Space Design. London (UK): Van Nostrand Reinhold

Bruijn, P. B. 1995. Bouwstenen. Inaugural address. Delft (Neth.): Publicatiebureau Bouwkunde

Burg, Simone van der. 1999. Denken Doorzien. Hilversum (Neth.): Stichting Educatieve Omroep Teleac

Carnap, Rudolf. (1956) 1991. " 'Empiricism, Semantics, and Ontology." In: Meaning and Necessity, enlarged edition. Chicago: University of Chicago Press. Reprinted 1991 in: The Philosophy of Science, edited by Richard Boyd, Philip Gasper & J.D.Trout; pp. 85-79. Cambridge (Mass., USA): MIT Press

Casseres, J. M. de. 1926. Stedebouw. Amsterdam (Neth.): S.L. van Looy.

Castells, Manuel. 1996. Rise of Network Society. Oxford (UK): Blackwell Publishers.

Cate, Marije ten. 2000. "Landgoed, a culture of decongestion." In: Buiten Plaats- City Escape, edited by E.v.d.Kooij; pp.112-123. Delft (Neth.): Delft University Press

Cecilia, Cathy; Irene Houtsma; Frank Immerzeel; Ineke de Lange & Michiel Scholten. 1989. Kloppend Kloppend Hart - voor Den Haag en Amsterdam. Internal publication Faculty of Architecture TU Delft

Chorley, Richard J. & Peter Haggett. 1969. "Models, Paradigms and the New Geography." In: Physical and Information Models in Geography, edited by Richard J.Chorley & Peter Haggett; pp.19-41. London: Methuen & Co

Cohen, H. Floris. 1997. "Wil de echte Galilei opstaan." In: Newtons God & Mendels Bastaarden, edited by Bert Theunissen, Casper Hakvoort et al.; pp. 17-38. Amsterdam: Meulenhof/Kritak

Commissie Midterm Review 2000 Faculteit Bouwkunde TU Delft. 2001. Eindrapport. Delft (Neth.): Faculty of Architecture TU Delft

Coyne, Richard; Adrian Hawker & Dorian Wiszniewski. 2001. "Educational Practice and Interpretation." In: Research by Design, International Conference Faculty of Architecture Delft University of Technology in co operation with the EAAE/AEEA, November 1-3 2000, Proceedings B, edited by Anja Langenhuizen, Marieke van Ouwerkerk & Jürgen Rosemann; pp.88-93. Delft (Neth.): Delft University Press

Cross, Nigel (editor). 1984. Developments in Design Methodology. Chichester (UK): John Wiley & Sons

Cross, N. 1993. "A history of design methodology." In: Design Methodology and Relationships with Science, edited by M.J.de Vries, N.Cross & D.P.Grant; Nato ASI Series D: Behavioural and Social Sciences Vol.71; pp.15-27. Dordrecht (Neth.) Kluwer Academic Publishers

Cullen, Gordon. 1971. The Concise Townscape. London (UK): Architectural Press

Cusveller, Sjoerd. 1998. "Groeten uit Zoetermeer." *Blauwe Kamer* (1): 9-11

Cusveller, Sjoerd. 2000. " Helder concept met ondoorzichtige slingers." *Blauwe Kamer* (2): 34.

Daley, Janet. 1969. "A philosophical critique of behaviourism in architectural design." In: Design Methods in Archtecture, edited by G.Broadbent & A.Ward; pp.71-75. London: Lund Humphries

Damen, Leo; Marc Jacobs & Jaap van der Want. 1988. Structurering en vormgeving op stedelijk niveau. Graduate Study. Internal publication Faculty of Architecture TU Delft

Diderot, Denis. (1749) 1951. "Lettre sur les Aveugles a l' usage de ceux qui voient." In: Diderot Œuvres; pp. 841-902. Paris (Fr.): Librairie Gallimard

Dieters, Mia; Arno Gelderblom & Marjolein de Jong. 1991. Haarlem als Bandstad. Graduate Study. Internal publication Faculty of Architecture TU Delft

Dijst, M. J. 1995. Het elliptische leven - Actieruimte als integrale maat voor bereik en mobiliteit. PhD Thesis. Faculty of Architecture TU Delft

Dinteren, J.H.J; A.R.Krijgsman & H.Bout. 1989. "Bereikbaarheid van onderwijsvoorzieningen. "*Stedebouw & Volkshuisvesting* (2): 11-17

Dorst, Machiel van. De (Over)Levende Stad. PhD research project. Faculty of Architecture TU Delft. To be published

Doxiadis, Constantinos A. 1968. Ekistics - An Introduction to the Science of Human Settlements. London: Hutchinson & Co

Draaisma, Douwe. 1995. De Metaforenmachine, een geschiedenis van het geheugen. Groningen (Neth.): Historische Uitgeverij

Drenth, P. J. D. 1995. "Psychology as a science: Truthfull or Useful." *U&H (Tijdschrift voor wetenschappelijk onderwijs)* (5/6): 147-168

Drewe, Paul. Undated (about 1975). Sozialtechnik. Unpublished manuscript.

Drewe, Paul. 1996. The Network City. Key note Address NUTAU '96; International Seminar on Architecture and Urban Design Technology: Sao Paulo (Brazil) October 11 - November 2.

Drewe, Paul. 2000. " ICT and urban form, Urban planning and design - off the beaten track." In: Design studio 'The Network City'. Delft (Neth.): Faculty of Architecture TU Delft

Drewe, Paul. 2001. "Physical and Virtual Space. How to Deal with Their Interaction?" *Journal of Design Research* (1): http://jdr.tudelft.nl.

Droogleever Fortuijn, J.S.; S. Hietbrink; L. Karsten & M. Rijkes. 1987. Van hot naar her, het combineren van taken in de ruimte en tijd door tweeverdieners, alleenstaande ouders en alleenwonenden in Haarlem, Enkhuizen en Stede Broec. Haarlem: Provinciale Planologische Dienst

Duijvestein, Ilse. 1997. Mitla. Masters thesis. Faculty of Architecture TU Delft

Duin, Leen van. 2001. "Architectural Strategies and Design Methods Questions." In: Research by Design, International Conference Faculty of Architecture Delft University of Technology in co operation with the EAAE/AEEA, November 1-3 2000, Proceedings B, edited by Anja Langenhuizen, Marieke van Ouwerkerk & Jürgen Rosemann; pp. 9-13. Delft (Neth.): Delft University Press

Dunk, H.W von der. 1994. "Geschiedenis en Wetenschap." In: Overtuigend Bewijs, edited by P.B.Cliteur, H.D.Papma & R.T.P/Wiche; pp.38-64. Amsterdam/Meppel (Neth.): Boom

Dupuy, Gabriel. 1993. "A revised history of network urbanism/Een herziene geschiedenis van netwerkstedenbouw." *Oase* (53): Nijmegen (Neth.): SUN Publishers

Durling, David & John Shackleton. 2002. Common Ground. Proceedings of the 2002 International Design Research Society Conference in London (UK). Book and CD-ROM. Staffordshire University Press

EAAE (European Association for Architectural Education) and Delft University of Technology, Faculty of Architecture. 1996. Doctorates in design and architecture, EAAE/AEEA-conference, February 8-10 1996, Proceedings. Vol 2. Results and Reflections. Delft (Neth.): Publicatiebureau Bouwkunde

Eijking, Bart. 2000. "Tijd als ordenend principe." In: Deltametropool – Tijd als instrument van ordening, edited by D.Frieling, B.Eijking & A.Tisma; pp.22-36. Delft (Neth.): Delft University Press

Ekkers, Paul et al. 1990. Regionaal ontwerp en beleid - plananalyse 'Stad en Land op de Helling'. Den Haag: Eo-Wijersstichting

Ende, Tonja van der. 2000. Denken doorzien II. Hilversum (Neth.): St. Educatieve Omroep Teleac

Esser, Aristide H. 1976. "Design for Man-Environment Relations." In: The Mutual Interaction of People and their Built Environment, edited by Amos Rapoport; pp.127-144. Den Haag: Mouton Publishers

Faculteit Bouwkunde TU Delft. 1994. Onderzoeksprogramma Stedebouwkunde 1994-1998. Internal publication Faculty of Architecture TU Delft .

Faculteit Bouwkunde TU Delft. 1994. Uitgangspunten voor verbetering van het kennisonderwijs, Nota Werkgroep Kennisverwerving Bouwkunde. Internal publication Faculty of Architecture TU Delft .

Faludi, Andreas. 1973. Planning Theory. Oxford (UK): Pergamon Press Ltd.

Feyerabend, Paul K. 1978. "In Defence of Aristotle." In: Progress and Rationality in Science, edited by G. Radnitzky & G. Andersson; conference, Kronberg, July1975, selected papers; pp.143-180. Dordrecht: D. Reidel Publishing Compagny

Feyerabend, Paul K. 1991. Dialoghi sulla conoscienza/Three dialogues on Knowledge. Oxford (UK) Cambridge (Mass., USA): Basil Blackwell Ltd/Inc

Finch, Vernon C.; Glenn T.Trewartha; Arthur H.Robinson & Edwin H.Hammond. 1957. Elements of Geography. New York (N.Y.): McGraw-Hill Book Compagny

Foqué, Richard. 2001. "On the True Meaning of Research by Design." In: Research and Design, International Conference Faculty of Architecture University of Technology in co operation with the EAAE/ AEEA, november 1-3 2000, Proceedings B, edited by Anja Langenhuizen, Marieke van Ouwerkerk & Jürgen Rosemann; pp.1-8. Delft (Neth.): Delft University Press

Frey, G. 1961. "Symbolische und Ikonische Modelle." In: The concept and the role of the model in mathematics and natural and social sciences, edited by H.Freudenthal; pp.89-97. Dordrecht (Neth.): D. Reidel Publishing Company

Frieling, D. H. 2000. "De noodzaak van gemeenplaatsen." In: de Architectonische Interventie Halverwege, edited by G.Wigmans; pp.8-13. Delft (Neth.): Delft University Press

Frieling, D; B.Eijking & A.Tisma (editors). 2000. Deltametropool – Tijd als instrument van ordening. Delft (Neth.): Delft University Press

Frijlink, Frank & Leon Leferink. 1991. Waar het leven goed is - een stedebouwkundig ontwikkelingsplan voor West-Brabant. Masters thesis. Faculty of Architecture TU Delft

Gall, Stephan. 1996. "De tussenschaal als stedebouwkundig werkterrein." *Blauwe Kamer/Profiel* (3): 26-29.

Gantvoort, J. Th. 1993. "Functionele hiërarchie opnieuw ter discussie." *Stedebouw en Volkshuisvesting* (4): 12-18

Gasparkski, W.W. 1993. "Design, science and philosophy: the praxiologival perspective." In: Design Methodology and Relationships with Science, edited by M.J.de Vries, N.Cross & D.P.Grant; Nato ASI Series D: Behavioural and Social Sciences Vol.71; pp.165-187. Dordrecht (Neth.): Kluwer Academic Publishers

Gedeputeerde Staten van Noord-Holland. 1982. Discussienota voor de Structuurschets van Noord-Holland. Haarlem (Neth.)

Geerse, Andries. 1993. Centro histórico de Santos. Masters thesis. Faculty of Architecture TU Delft

Gehl, Jan. 1971. Livet mellem husene. Kopenhagen(Denmark): Arkitektens Forlag (Leven tussen huizen. Zutphen (Neth.): De Walburg Pers)

Giere, Ronald. 1999. "Using Models to Represent Reality." . In: Model-based Reasoning in Scientific Discovery, edited by Lorenzo Magnani, Nancy Nersessian & Paul Thagard; pp41-58. New York (N.Y.): Kluwer Academic/Plenum Publishers

Goeverden, K. van; J. Schrijver & A. van den Broek. 1998. "Nieuwe vervoersystemen: Staalkaarten vervoervraag- en aanbod." In Colloquium Vervoersplanologisch Speurwerk 1998: Sturen met structuren. Delft (Neth.): CVS

Gooding, David. 1996. "Creative Rationality: Towards an abductive model of scientific change." *Philosophica*: 103-123

Govers, Bas; Peter van der Ham & Fons van Reisen. 1998. "Sturen met infrastructuur: op zoek naar samenhang tussen ruimte en rail in de Zuidvleugel." In: Colloquium Vervoersplanologisch Speurwerk 1998: Sturen met structuren; pp.6-23. Delft (Neth.): CVS

Graaff, Erik de & Rob Cowdroy. 1997. "Theory and Practice of Educational Innovation; Introduction of Problem-Based Learning in Architecture." *International Journal of Engineering Education* (3): 166-174

Graaff, Erik de & Anette Kolmos. In press. Characteristics of problem-based learning. Accepted for publication in the *International Journal of Engineering Education*

Graafland, Arie. 2001. "Contemporary design research: A material practice." In: Research by Design,

International Conference Faculty of Architeture Delft University of Technology in co operation with the EAAE/AEEA, november 1-3 2000, Proceedings A, edited by Marieke van Ouwerkerk and Jürgen Rosemann; pp.17-23. Delft (Neth.): Delft University Press

Groot, A.D.de. (1961) 1968. Methodologie; Grondslagen van onderzoek en denken in de gedragswetenschappen, 4th print. Den Haag: Mouton & Co

Gruen, V. 1965. The Heart of our Cities, the urban crisis: diagnosis and cure. London: Thames and Hudson

Gunsteren, L. A. van. 2001. " Architectural design: Skill, Science or Religion." In: Research by Design, International Conference Faculty of Architecture Delft University of Technology in co operation with the EAAE/AEEA, November 1-3 2000, Proceedings B, edited by Anja Langenhuizen, Marieke van Ouwerkerk & Jürgen Rosemann; pp.143-149. Delft (Neth.): Delft University Press

Hamel, Ronald. 1990. Over het denken van de architect; een cognitief-psychologische beschrijving van het ontwerpproces bij architecten." (A cognitive psychological description of the architectural design process). PhD Thesis. Amsterdam: AHA Books

Hanson, Norwood R. 1958. Patterns of Discovery, an inquiry into the conceptual foundations of science. Cambridge (UK): Cambridge University Press

Harsema, Harry. Undated (about 2000). "Tussen functionele ordening en formeel ontwerp." In: De Kern van de Stedebouw in het perspectief van de 21ste eeuw, edited by Maarten Ettema et al.; katern 5. Published by *Blauwe Kamer*

Harvey, David. 1973. Explanation in Geography. London: Edward Arnold (Publishers)

Heeling, Jan. (1981) 2001. "Stedebouw als formele ordening." In: Jan Heeling over Stedebouw, edited by Henco Bekkering & John Westrik; pp.13-44. Delft (Neth.): Delft University Press

Heeling, Jan. 1998. "Een zoektocht naar de grondslagen van de stedenbouwkunde." In: Stedelijke Transformaties, edited by E. Hulsbergen, H. Meyer & M. Paasman; pp.11-36. Delft (Neth.): Delft University Press

Heide, Henk ter & Danny Wijnbelt. 1994. Tussen kennen en kunnen; Over de verbinding van onderzoek en ruimtelijk ontwerp. Nederlandse Geografische Studies/Netherlands Geografical Studies 182. Utrecht/ Den Haag (Neth.): Koninklijk Nederlands Aardrijkskundig Genootschap/Faculteit Ruimtelijke Planningswetenschappen Universiteit Utrecht/Rijksplanologische Dienst

Heimans, A. 1965. Bebouwingsdichtheid en grondgebruik voor de woningbouw in stadsuitbreidingen. PhD Thesis. Den Haag (Neth.): Ten Hagen

Herngreen, Rik. 1991. "Kwaliteit is geen optelsom van sectorale belangen." *Blauwe Kamer* (1): 15-21.

Hertzberger, Herman. 2002. "Creating Space of thought." In: Ways to Study and Research - Urban, Architectural and Technical Design, edited by T.M. de Jong & D.J.M. van der Voordt; pp.389-398. Delft (Neth.): Delft University Press

Heynen, Hilde. 1990. "Fragmentatie in de periferie; De 'tapijtmetropool' van Willem-Jan Neutelings." *Archis* (3): 16-21

Hillier, Bill; John Musgrove & Pat O'Sullivan. 1972. "Knowledge and Design." In: Environmental Design: Research and Practice; Proceedings of the EDRA 3/AR 8 conference 1972 edited by William J. Mitchell; pp.29-3-1/14. Los Angeles: University of California

Hillier, Bill & Julienne Hanson. 1984. The Social Logic of Space. Cambridge (UK): Cambridge University Press

Hillier, Bill & Alan Penn. 1991. Is dense civilisation possible?: Or the shape of cities in the 21st century. London: The Bartlett, University College London

Hodgson P.E. 1979. "Presuppositions and Limits of Science." In: The Structure and Development of Science, edited by Gerard Radnitzky & Gunnar Andersson; pp. 133-147. Boston Studies in the Philosophy of Science no 59. Dordrecht (Neth.): D.Reidel Publishing Compagny.

Hoeven, Frank van der. 1999. "De dictatuur van de infrastructuur." *Atlantis* (November) (Faculty of Architecture): 42-46.

Huisman, Patricia. 1996. Kennis gewogen - Analyse van sociaal-wetenschappelijk denken: kritiek en aanwijzingen. PhD Thesis. Assen (Neth.): Van Gorcum

Hulsbergen, Edward D. 1992. Positie en Ruimte, Kwetsbare groepen in de stad: denkbeelden en feiten. PhD Thesis. Delft (Neth.): Publikatieburo Bouwkunde

Hulsbergen, E; H. Meyer & M. Paasman (editors). 1998. Stedelijke Transformaties. Delft (Neth.): Delft University Press

Hulsbergen, Edward & Pity van der Schaaf. 2002. "Ex Ante Research." In Ways to Study and Research - Urban, Architectural and Technical Design, edited by T.M. de Jong & D.J.M. van der Voordt; pp.159-162. Delft (Neth.) Delft University Press

Hulsbergen, Edward. 2003. "De kat en de brij." *Atlantis* (Januari): 10-14

Ihde, Ron. 1991. Instrumental Realism - the interface between philosophy of science and philosophy of technology. Bloomington and Indianapolis: Indiana University Press

Jacobs, Jane. 1961. The Death and Life of Great American Cities. New York (N.Y.): Random House

Jacobs, M. 1990. Stedebouwkundige Luchtkastelen. Masters thesis. Faculty of Architecture TU Delft

Jacobs, M. 2000. Multinodal Urban Structures, a comparative analysis and strategies for design. PhD Thesis. Delft (Neth.): Delft University Press

Janis, Irving L. 1972. Victims of Groupthink. Boston (USA): Houghton Mifflin Company

Jansen, Jeroen; Kees Machielse & Gert Vogel. Undated (about 2000). "Het Vergeten Knooppunt; over de Relatie Dagindeling en het concept Netwerkstad." Nota in opdracht van de Rijks-Planologische Dienst. Den Haag (Neth.)

Jong, R. de & Frits Schipper. 1987. "Heuristiek en het twee-contexten onderscheid in de wetenschapsfilosofie." *Wijsgerig Perspectief* : 144-149

Jong, T.M. de. 1978. Milieudifferentiatie; een fundamenteel onderzoek. PhD Thesis TU Delft

Jong, Taeke de. 1992. Kleine Methodologie voor Ontwerpend Onderzoek. Meppel (Neth.): Boom

Jong, T.M. de. 1994. Populatie en habitat van mensen. Monograph Milieu/SOM 24. Delft (Neth.) Faculty of Architecture TU Delft

Jong, T. M. de. 2002a. "The scientific role of architecture." In: The Architecture Annual 2000-2001; Delft University of Technology, edited by A. Graafland et al. Rotterdam: 010 Publishers

Jong, T.M. de. 2002b. "Designing in a determined context." In: Ways to Study and Research - Urban, Architectural and Technical Design, edited by T.M. de Jong & D.J.M. van der Voordt; pp.443-449. Delft (Neth.): Delft University Press

Jong, Taeke de & Leen van Duin. 2002. "Design research." In Ways to Study and Research - Urban, Architectural and Technical Design, edited by T.M. de Jong & D.J.M. van der Voordt; pp.89-94. Delft (Neth.): Delft University Press

Jong, T.M. de; R. Moens & C.v.d Akker. 2002. Grondgebied, Ecologie en Techniek. Schaalgelede

Stadsecologie voor Ontwerpers. Internal publication Faculty of Architecture TU Delft.

Jong, Taeke de & Martin Paasman. 1998. Het Metropolitaine Debat - een vocabulaire voor besluitvorming over de kaart van Nederland. Zoetermeer (Neth.): Stichting Milieu en Stedelijke Ontwikkeling (MESO)

Jong, T.M. de & C.M. Ravesloot. 1995. Beeldkwaliteitsplan Stadsdeel 'De Baarsjes' Amsterdam. Zoetermeer (Neth.): Stichting Milieu en Stedelijke Ontwikkeling (MESO)

Jong, Taeke de & Jürgen Rosemann. 2002. "Naming components and concepts." In: Ways to Study and Research - Urban, Architectural and Technical Design, edited by T.M. de Jong & D.J.M. van der Voordt; pp.35-42. Delft (Neth.): Delft University Press

Jong, Taeke de & Theo van der Voordt (editors). 2002a. Ways to Study and Research - Urban, Architectural and Technical Design. Delft (Neth.): Delft University Press

Jong, Taeke de & Theo van der Voordt. 2002b. "Criteria for scientific study and design." In: Ways to Study and Research - Urban, Architectural and Technical Design, edited by T.M. de Jong & D.J.M. van der Voordt; pp. 19-30. Delft (Neth.): Delft University Press

Jonge, H. de. 1986. "Ontwerpend Onderzoeken." *De Architect* (oktober): 42-43.

Klaasen, Ina. 1974. Het gebied rond Aigle, Canton Vaud, Zwitserland - een landschappelijke studie. Masters thesis. Universiteit van Amsterdam

Klaasen I. 1985. "Ruimtelijke Ordening en emancipatie." *Stedebouw en Volkshuisvesting* (12): 532-539

Klaasen, Ina (editor). 1993. Het Stromende Stadsgewest; plananalyse derde Eo-Wijersprijsvraag. Delft (Neth.): Publicatiebureau Bouwkunde

Klaasen, Ina. 1996. "Al het mogelijke." In: Taeke de Jong & opponenten, Essays over variatie. Monograph Milieu 100; pp.105-108. Delft (Neth.): Publicatiebureau Bouwkunde

Klaasen, I.T. 2000a. Valkuilen bij stedebouwkundig ontwerpen: het verwarren van model en werkelijkheid. Monograph Milieu/SBK 72. Delft (Neth.): Faculty of Architecture TU Delft

Klaasen, I.T. 2000b. "The functional/spatial composition." In: Composition and Analysis, edited by C. Steenbergen et al.; pp.62-66. Bussum: Thoth Publishers

Klaasen, I.T & M. Jacobs. 1999. "Relative location value based on accessibility: application of a useful concept in designing urban regions." *Landscape and Urban Planning* : 21-35.

Klaasen, Ina & Beeno Radema. 1985. "Ruimtelijke struktuurmodellen: een aanpak voor stedelijke en regionale struktuurplanning." In: Planologische Diskussiebijdragen 1985; pp.721-735. Delft (Neth.): Delftse Uitgeversmij

Klaasen, I.T. & M.Scholten. 1998. "Railsystemen in autowijken, een problematische structuuraanpassing: het geval Amstelveen." In: Colloquium Vervoersplanologisch Speurwerk 1998: Sturen met structuren; pp. 691-704. Delft (Neth.): CVS

Klaasen, I. T. & J. H. van der Want. 1988. "Kernzaken en randverschijnselen - lokatiekeuze WHC's Amsterdam en Rotterdam functioneel-ruimtelijk geanalyseerd." *Stedebouw en Volkshuisvesting* (9): 315-323.

Kleefmann, F. 1984. Planning als zoekinstrument. Planologische verkenningen, deel 5. Den Haag (Neth.): VUGA-Uitgeverij

Koertge, Noretta. 1978. "Towards a New Theory of Scientific Inquiry." In: Progress and Rationality in Science, conference, Kronberg, July1975, selected papers, edited by G. Radnitzky & G. Andersson (Volume LV111 of Boston Studies in the Philosophy of Science); pp. 253-278. Dordrecht (Neth.): D. Reidel Publishing Company.

Koningsveld, Herman van. 1976. Het verschijnsel wetenschap. Meppel (Neth.): Boom

Kortlandt, F. H. H. 1997. "Alle talen van de wereld." In: *NRC-Handelsblad*, Science Supplement, 21-6-1997.

Krabbendam, Ph. 2001. "The Cook, the Pudding and the Seasons." In: Research by Design, International Conference Faculty of Architecture Delft University of Technology in co operation with the EAAE/AEEA, November 1-3 2000, Proceedings B, edited by Anja Langenhuizen, Marieke van Ouwerkerk & Jürgen Rosemann; pp.198-203. Delft (Neth.): Delft University Press

Krauss, Lawrence. 1994. Het geheim van de Natuurkunde. Amsterdam: Contact

Kuhn, Thomas. (1959) 1991. "The essential tension: tradition and innovation on scientific research." In: The Third University of Utah Conference on the Identification of Scientific Talent, edited by C.W.Taylor. Salt Lake City (USA): University of Utah Press. Reprinted 1991 in: Richard Boyd, Richard Philip Gasper & J.D. Trout: The Philosophy of Science; pp. 139-147. Cambridge (Mass., USA): MIT Press

Kuhn, Thomas. (1962) 1970. The Structure of Scientific Revolutions (2nd enlarged ed. 1970). Chicago: University of Chicago Press

Kuhn, Thomas. 1970. "Reflections on my Critics." In: Criticism and the Growth of Knowledge, edited by Imre Lakatos & Alan Musgrave; pp.231-278. Cambridge (UK): Cambridge University Press

Kuipers, A. 1961. "Model and Insight." In: The concept and the role of the model in mathematics and natural and social sciences, edited by H. Freudenthal.; pp.125-132. Dordrecht (Neth.): D. Reidel Publishing Company

Kusiak, Loek. 1989. "Gezondheidszorg duldt geen planologische bemoeials." *ROM, Tijdschrift voor Ruimtelijke Ordening en Milieubeheer* (8/9): 10-13.

Lakatos, I. 1970. "Falsification and the Methodology of Scientific Research programmes." In: Criticism and the Growth of Knowledge, edited by Imre lakatos & Alan Musgrave; pp.91-196. Cambridge (UK): Cambridge University Press

Lakatos, Imre. 1976. Proofs and Refutations - The Logic of Mathematical Discovery (edited by John Worrall and Elie Zahar). Cambridge (UK): Cambridge University Press

Lakatos, I. 1978. The Methodology of Scientific Research Programmes (edited by J.Worrall and G.Currie). Cambridge (UK): Cambridge University Press

Lakatos, Imre. 1999. "Lectures on Scientific Method." In: For and Against Method - Imre Lakatos and Paul Feyerabend, edited by Matteo Motterlini; pp. 19-112. Chicago (USA): The University of Chicago Press

Lang, Jon. 1987. Creating Architectural Theory; The Role of the Behavioral Sciences in Environmental Design. New York (N.Y.): Van Nostrand Reinhold Company

Langenhuizen, Anja; Marieke van Ouwerkerk & Jürgen Roseman (editors). 2001. Research by Design, International Conference Faculty of Architecture Delft University of Technology in co operation with the EAAE/AEEA, November 1-3 2000, Proceedings B. Delft (Neth.): Delft University Press

Laudan, Larry. (1981) 1991. "A Confutation of Convergent Realism." In: Philosophy of Science Vol.48: pp. 19-48. Reprinted 1991 in: The Philosophy of Science, edited by Richard Boyd, Philip Gasper & J.D. Trout; pp.221-245. Cambridge (Mass., USA): MIT Press

Lawson, Bryan. 1990. How Designers Think - The Design Process Demystified. Oxford (UK): Butterworth Architecture

Leclercq, Els. 1999. The New Urbanism, een alternatief voor stedelijke uitbreidingen in Nederland. Masters thesis. Faculty of Architecture TU Delft

Lee, Colin. 1973. Models in Planning. Oxford: Pergamon Press

Leupen, Bernard. 2002. "Concept and Type." In: Ways to Study and Research - Urban, Architectural and Technical Design, edited by T.M. de Jong & D.J.M. van der Voordt; pp.107-116. Delft (Neth.): Delft University Press

Levinson. 1999. "Het Noorden kwijt - Taal bepaalt ons ruimtelijk oriëntatievermogen." In: *NRC-Handelsblad* Science Supplement 18-12-99

Linden, G. 1997. "Verstedelijking, vervoerplanologische concepten en ontwerpmethodologie." In: Verstedelijking en Vervoersplanologische Concepten, edited by H.J.Ebels & F.le Clercq; pp.180-187. Amsterdam: AME/Universiteit van Amsterdam

Lohuizen, Th. K. 1948. De eenheid van het stedebouwkundig werk. Inaugural address. TU Delft

Luyten, J. & B. Hoefnagel. 1995. Het oog van de wetenschapsfilosoof; Visies op wetenschap en techniek. Amsterdam/Meppel (Neth.): Boom

Lynch, Kevin. (1958) 1990. "A theory of urban form." In: City Sense and City Design, Writings and Projects of Kevin Lynch, edited by Tridib Banerjee & Michael Southworth; pp.355-378. Cambridge (Mass., USA): MIT Press

Lynch, Kevin. (1960) 1992. The image of the city. Cambridge (Mass., USA): MIT Press

Lynch, Kevin. (1961) 1990. "The pattern of the Metropolis." *Daedalus* (1): 79-98. Reprinted 1990 in: City Sense and City Design, Writings and Projects of Kevin Lynch, edited by Tridib Banerjee and Michael Southworth; pp. 47-64. Cambridge (MA/USA): MIT Press

Lynch, Kevin. 1972. What time Is This Place? Cambridge (Mass., USA): MIT Press

Lynch, Kevin. 1976. Managing the Sense of a Region. Cambridge (Mass., USA): MIT Press

Lynch, Kevin. 1981. A Theory of Good City Form. Cambridge (Mass., USA): MIT Press

Lynch, Kevin. (1985) 1990. "Reconsidering The Image of the City." In: Cities of the Mind, edited by L.Rodwin & R.Hollister; New York: Plenum. Reprinted 1990 in: City Sense and City Design, Writings and Projects of Kevin Lynch, edited by Tridib Banerjee & Michael Southworth; pp.247-256. Cambridge (Mass., USA): MIT Press

Lynch, Kevin. 1990. City Sense and City Design, Writings and Projects Of Kevin Lynch, edited by Tridib Banerjee & Michael Southworth; pp.65-86. Cambridge (Mass., USA): MIT Press

Lynch, Kevin. (Undated) 1990. "The Visual Shape of the Shapeless Metropolis." Reprinted 1990 in: City Sense and City Design, Writings and Projects Of Kevin Lynch, edited by Tridib Banerjee & Michael Southworth; pp.65-86. Cambridge (Mass., USA): MIT Press

Magee, Bryan. 1973. Popper. London: Wm. Collins & Co Ltd

Magnani, Lorenzo. 1999. "Model-based Creative Abduction." In: Model-based Reasoning in Scientific Discovery, edited by Lorenzo Magnani, Nancy Nersessian & Paul Thagard; pp.219-238. New York (N.Y.): Kluwer Academic/Plenum Publishers

Magnani, Lorenzo. 2001. Abduction, Reason and Science - Processes of Discovery and Explanation. New York (N.Y.): Kluwer Academic/ Plenum Publishers

Meadows, Dennis. 1972. Rapport van de Club van Rome. Utrecht (Neth.): Uitgeverij Het Spectrum N.V.

Meheus, Joke. 1999. "Model-based Reasoning in Creative Processes." In: Model-based Reasoning in Scientific Discovery, edited by Lorenzo Magnani, Nancy Nersessian & Paul Thagard; pp.199-218. New York (N.Y.): Kluwer Academic/Plenum Publishers

Meulenbelt, Karin. 1991. De uitstralingseffecten van het Stadhuis-Muziektheater (Stopera). *Rooilijn (2)* : 38-44

Mey, Margot, G. 1994. Het stedelijk mozaiek (The urban mosaic; preferences of households as guidelines for the design of urban settlements). PhD Thesis. Faculty of Architecture TU Delft

Mey, Margot G. 1996. Tijd-ruimtelijke dynamiek en stedelijke inrichtingen. Delft (Neth.): Delft University Press

Mey, M.G. & H.ter Heide. 1997. "Towards spatiotemporal planning: practicable analysis of day-to-day paths through space and time." *Environment and Planning B: Planning and Design*: 709-723.

Meyer, Han. 2002. "Plan analysis." In: Ways to Study and Research - Urban, Architectural and Technical Design, edited by T.M.de Jong & D.J.M. van der Voordt; pp.125-136. Delft (Neth.): Delft University Press

Meyer, Han; Jan Heeling; John Westrik & Eugene Sauren. 2000. "The composition of the town plan." In: Architectural Design and Research: Composition, Education, Analysis, edited by Clemens Steenbergen et al; pp.32-35. Bussum (Neth): Thoth Publishers

Mill, John Stuart. (1859) 1991. On Liberty And Other Essays. Edited by John Gray in 1991. Oxford (UK): Oxford University Press

Ministerie van Volkshuisvesting en Ruimtelijke Ordening (VRO). 1977. Samenvatting Globaal Ecologisch Model (GEM). Studierapporten Rijksplanologische Dienst 5.3.B. Den Haag (Neth.)

Ministerie van Volkshuisvesting, Ruimtelijke Ordening en Milieu (VROM). 1996. Randstad en Groene Hart. Den Haag: Sdu uitgevers

Modder, Jaap. 2002. "De '80-kilometer-stad' zit zonder regie." *Building Business*(4): 67

Monestiroli, Antonio. 2001. " Research by Design." In: Research by Design, International Conference Faculty of Architecture Delft University of Technology in co operation with the EAAE/AEEA, November 1-3 2000, Proceedings A, edited by Marieke van Ouwerkerk & Jürgen Rosemann; pp.41- 46. Delft (Neth.): Delft University Press

Muller, Wim. 1990. Vormgeven - ordening en betekenisgeving. Utrecht (Neth.): Lemma

Nersessian, Nancy. 1999. "Model based reasoning in Conceptual Change." In: Model-Based Reasoning in Scientific Discovery, edited by Lorenzo Magnani, Nancy Nersessian & Paul Thagard; pp.5-22. New York (N.Y.): Kluwer Academic/ Plenum Publishers

Niiniluoto, Ilkka. 1999. "Abduction and Geometrical Analysis. Notes on Charles S.Peirce and Edgar Allan Poe." In: Model-based Reasoning in Scientific Discovery, edited by Lorenzo Magnani, Nancy Nersessian & Paul Thagard; pp. 239-254. New York (N.Y.) Kluwer Academic/Plenum Publishers

Nio, Ivan & Arnold Reijndorp. 1997. Groeten uit Zoetermeer- stedebouw in discussie. Rotterdam: NAI Uitgevers

Ouwehand, Andre; Kees Fortuin; Maarten Davelaar & Reinout Kleinhand. 2001. Contourenschets 'sociale wijkvisie. Nota in opdracht van het Ministerie van Volkshuisvesting, Ruimtelijke Ordening en Milieubeheer. Den Haag (Neth.)

Ouwerkerk , Marieke van & Jürgen Rosemann (editors). 2001. Research by Design - International Conference Faculty of Architecture Delft University of Technology in co operation with the EAAE/AEEA, November 1-3 2000, Proceedings A. Delft (Neth.): Delft University Press.

Palmboom, Frits. (1987) 1990. Rotterdam, verstedelijkt landschap. 2nd revised edition. Rotterdam: Uitgeverij 010

Pasveer, Erik. 1991. "Reconstructies van een onvoltooide toekomst." *POLIS* (Faculty of Architecture TU Delft) : 5-10.

Peursen, C. A van. 1986. Filosofie van de wetenschappen. Leiden: Martinus Nijhoff

Peursen, C.A. van. 1987. "Heuristiek: een historische inleiding." *Wijsgerig Perspectief* : 130-133.

Peursen, C. A. van. 1994. Na het postmodernisme; van metafysica tot filosofisch surrealisme. Kampen (Neth.): Kok Agora

Popper, Karl R. (1959) 1968. The Logic of Scientific Discovery. London: Hutchinson & Co. Reprinted New York (N.Y.): Harper & Row Publishers Inc.

Popper, Karl. (1962) 1968. Conjectures and Refutations: the growth of scientific knowledge. New York (N.Y.): Basic Books. Reprinted New York (N.Y.): Harper & Row Publishers Inc.

Popper, Karl R. 1972. Objective Knowledge - an Evolutionary Approach. Oxford (UK): The Clarendon Press

Popper, Karl. 1976. Unended Quest – An Intellectual Autobiography. Revised edition. Glasgow (G B): Fontana/Collins

Punter, John & Matthew Carmona. 1997. The Design Dimension of Planning - Theory, Content and Best Practice for Design Policies. London: Chapman & Hall

Putnam, Hillary. (1974) 1991. "The Corroboration of Theories." In: The Philosophy of Karl Popper, edited by P.A. Schilpp. Illinois (USA): La Salle. Reprinted 1991 in: the Philosophy of Science, edited by Richard Boyd, Philip Gasper & J. D. Trout; pp.121-137. Cambridge (Mass., USA): MIT Press

Quine, W.V. 1995. From Stimulus to Science. Cambridge (MA, USA): Harvard University Press.

Radder, Hans. 1996. In and About the world: Philosophical Studies of Science and Technology. New York (N.Y.): Albany State University of New York Press

Radnitzky, Gerard. 1979. "Justifying a Theory versus giving Good Reasons for preferring a theory." In: The Structure and the Development of Science, edited by Gerard Radnitzky & Gunnar Andersson; pp. 213-256. Dordrecht (Neth.): D. Reidel Publishing Compagny

Rambhajam, Soesma & Ron Zijp. 2002. Sixxxhavengebied.; Masters thesis. Faculty of Architecture TU Delft

Rapoport, Amos. 1969. "Facts and Models." In: Design Methods in Architecture, edited by G.Broadbent & A.Ward; pp.136-146. London: Lund Humphries

Rapoport, Amos. 1976. "Sociocultural Aspects of Man-Environment Studies." In: The Mutual Interaction of People and their Built Environment, edited by Amos Rapoport; pp.7-35. Den Haag: Mouton Publishers

Rapoport, Amos. 1977. Human Aspects of Urban Form. New York (N.Y.): Pergamon Press

Rescher, Nicholas. 1976. Plausible Reasoning; An Introduction to the Theory and Practice of Plausibilistic Inference. Assen/Amsterdam (Neth.): Van Gorcum

Reuser, Bart & Martijn Schenk. 2000. "Het gelaagde land, het aanzien van Nederland in 2030." In: Deltametropool - Tijd als instrument van ordening, edited by B.Eijking; pp.40-45. Delft (Neth.): Delft University Press

Rijpma, Jelle. 1991. "Stedebouwkundig ontwerpen." *POLIS* (Faculty of Architecture TUDelft): 11-14.

Rijpma, Jelle & Ina Klaasen. 1991. "Over stedebouwkunde." *Stedebouw en Volkshuisvesting* (1): 3.

Risselada, Max. 1993. Plannenmap: het ontwerp van het grote woonhuis. Internal publication Faculty of Architecture TU Delft

Rodermond, Janny. 1997. "Stedenbouw in de houdgreep – Een discipline ingeklemd tussen politiek, cultuur en economie." In: Essays ter gelegenheid van de honderdste geboortedag van Cor van Eesteren, edited by Herman Moscoviter; pp.23-30. Amsterdam: BNSP/EFL

Rooij, R.M. 1999. "Coherent multinodal couplings in the urban web for succesful cities." In: Five Years 'Crossroads of Theory and Practice, edited by P.H.L. Bovy; Proceedings Part 1: 5th TRAIL Annual Congress 1999 (Den Haag 1-12-1999); Delft (Neth.): The Netherlands TRAIL Research School

Rooij, R.M.. The Mobile City. The planning and design of the Network City from a mobility point of view. PhD Thesis. TRAIL Thesis Series. To be published

Roozenburg, N.F.M & J.Eekels. 1991. Produktontwerpen, Structuur en Methoden. Utrecht (Neth.): Lemma

Rosemann, Jürgen . 2001. "The Conditions of Research by Design in Practice." In Research by Design, International Conference Faculty of Architecture Delft University of Technology in co operation with the EAAE/AEEA, November 1-3 2000, Proceedings A, edited by Marieke Ouwerkerk & Jürgen Rosemann; pp.63-68. Delft (Neth.): Delft University Press

Rosenau, Helen. 1983. The Ideal City, it's architectural evolution in Europe. London: Methuen & Co.Ltd

Saane, Peter van. 1991. "Openbare Ruimte." *Blauwe Kamer* (1): 40-42

Sachs, Oliver. 1995. An Anthropologist on Mars. New York (N.Y.): Alfred A. Knopf

Salingaros, Nikos. 1998. "Theory of the Urban Web." *Journal of Urban Design* (3): 53-71

Salingaros, Nikos. 1999. "Urban Space and its Information Field." *Journal of Urban Design* (1): 29-49

Salingaros, Nikos. 2001. "Fractals in the New Architecture." www.archimagazine.com/afrattae.htm (04-2003).

Salingaros, Nikos. 2003. "Connecting the Fractal City." Keynote speech, 5th Biennial of towns and town planners in Europe. Barcelona. Http://applied.math.utsa.edu/Xsalingar/connecting.html -05-2003

Sarlemijn, A. 1993. "Designs are cultural alloys, STeMPJE in design methodology." In: Design Methodology and Relationships with Science, edited by M.J.de Vries, N.Cross & D.P.Grant; Nato ASI Series D: Behavioural and Social Sciences Vol.71; pp.191-248. Dordrecht (Neth.): Kluwer Academic Publishers

Schafer, A & D.Victor. 1997. "The Past and Future of Global Mobility." *Scientific American* (Oct): 36-39.

Scholten, Michiel. 1992. KAN KAN, een struktuurvisie voor het stedelijk knooppunt Arnhem-Nijmegen. Masters thesis. Faculty of Architecture TU Delft

Scholten, Michiel. 1996. Opstappen. Ruimtelijke randvoorwaarden voor de inrichting van Metrostationsgebieden. Internal publication Faculty of Architecture TU Delft.

Schomberg, R. von. 1991. "Wat is er controversieel aan een wetenschappelijke controverse? De omgang met wetenschap in het beleid." *Filosofie & Praktijk* (2): 57 - 69.

Schrijnen, Joost. 1995. Manifest - Tijd voor Stedebouw, Landschapsarchitectuur en Infrastructuurontwerp. Uitgave ter gelegenheid van het 60-jarig bestaan van de BNS (Amsterdam).

Schurch, Thomas W. 1999. "Reconsidering Urban Design: Thoughts about Definition and Status as a Field or Profession." *Journal of Urban Design* (1): 5-27.

Smit, Annet Jantien. 2002. "The American Dream is changing." *Blauwe Kamer* (3): 57

Smook, Rutger. 1984. Binnensteden veranderen. PhD Thesis. Zutphen (Neth): De Walburg Pers

Soest, Jan Paul van, et al. 1988. De werkelijkheid van het model. Stichting voor Publieksvoorlichting over Wetenschap en Techniek. Bloemendaal (Neth.): Aramith Uitgevers

Spek, Stefan C. van der. 2003. Connectors, The Way beyond Transferring. PhD Thesis. Trail Thesis Series T2003/1; The Netherlands TRAIL Research School. Delft (Neth.): Delft University Press

Spillers, W.R & S.L.Newsome. 1993. "Engineering Design, Conceptual Design, and Design Theory: A Report." In: Design Methodology and Relationships with Science, edited by M.J.de Vries, N.Cross & D.P.Grant; pp.103-114. Nato ASI Series D: Behavioural and Social Sciences Vol.71. Dordrecht (Neth.): Kluwer Academic Publishers

Stearns, Forrest W. & Tom Montag (editors). 1974. The Urban Ecosystem - A Holistic Approach. Stroudsburg (Pennsylvania, USA): Dowden, Hutchinson & Ross, Inc.

Steenhuis, Marinke. 2000. "Markerwaard." *Blauwe Kamer* (3): 30

Steiss, Alan Walter. 1974. Models for the Analysis and Planning of Urban Systems. Lexington (Mass., USA): D.C.Heath and Compagny

Suárez, Mauricio. 1999. "Theories, Models, and Representations." In: Model-based Reasoning in Scientific Discovery, edited by Lorenzo Magnani, Nancy Nersessian & Paul Thagard; pp.75-84. New York (N.Y.): Kluwer Academic/Plenum Publishers

Teerink, Sef. 2000. Een Provinciaal Omgevingsplan voor Zuid Holland? Een onderzoek naar integrale ruimtelijke planning. Masters thesis. Faculty of Architecture TU Delft

Thagard, P. & D.Croft. 1999. "Scientific Discovery and Technological Innovation." In: Model-based Reasoning in Scientific Discovery, edited by Lorenzo Magnani, Nancy Nersessian & Paul Thagard; pp.125-138. New York (N.Y.): Kluwer Academic/Plenum Publishers

The Open University. 1974. The 'Conflict Thesis' and Cosmology. Block 1, unit 3 of: Science and Belief: from Copernicus to Darwin. Milton Keynes (UK): The Open University Press

Thieme, J.C.; D.J.M. van der Voordt & H.B.R. van Wegen. 1989. Effekten van Grootschalige Ingrepen. Een programmeringsstudie; OSPA werkstuk nr.13. Delft (Neth.): Faculty of Architecture

Thüsh, M. 1993. Almere, uitgeslapen stad. Masters thesis. Delft (Neth.): Faculty of Architecture TU Delft

Toorn, Willem van. 1995. "Jargon: Bomen". Blauwe Kamer/Profiel (3): 7

Toulmin, Stephen. 2001. Return to Reason. Cambridge (Mass., USA): Harvard University Press

Trancik, Roger. 1986. Finding Lost Space. New York (N.Y.): Van Nostrand Reinhold

Urbach, Peter. 1978. "The Objective Promise of a Research Programma." In: Progress and Rationality in Science, conference, Kronberg July 1975, selected papers; pp.99-113. Dordrecht: D. Reidel Publishers

Urhahn, G. B. & M. Bobic. 1994. A Pattern Image. (2nd edition 2000). Bussum (Neth.): Thoth Publishers

Valk, Arnold van der. 1990. Het levenswerk van Th.K.van Lohuizen 1890-1956 – De eenheid van het stedebouwkundige werk. Delft (Neth.): Delft University Press

Vance, J. E. 1977. This Scene of Man: The Role and Structure of the City in the Geography of Western Civilisation. New York (N.Y.): Harper and Row

Veen, Arthur W.L. 1976. Schudden voor gebruik, een bijdrage aan de grondslagdiscussie in de fysische geografie. Inaugural address. Groningen: H.D. Tjeenk Willink BV

Verheyen, Fons. 2002. Het schijnbaar onmogelijke en omgaan met twijfel. Inaugural address. Delft (Neth.): Faculty of Architecture TU Delft

Verpaalen, Pepijn. 2001. Netwerkregio - De netwerkstad als stedelijke regio. Masters thesis. Faculty of Architecture TU Delft

Vidakovic, V. 1988. De Ruimte voor de Tijd. Den Haag/Amsterdam: Rijksplanologische Dienst/Gemeente Amsterdam

Viro-werkgroep. 1992. "De Dubbelstad: een kwestie van kiezen of delen." *Stedebouw en Volkshuisvesting*: 39-42

Vitruvius Pollio, Marcus. (About 25 BC)
- 1999a. De architectura / Ten books on architecture., Translation and commentary by Ingrid D. Rowland and Thomas Noble Howe. Cambridge (UK): Cambridge University Press
- 1999b. De architectura libri decem/Handboek Bouwkunde. Translated by Ton Peters. Amsterdam: Atheneum Polak & Van Gennep

Vogelij, J. C. 1984. "Stedebouwkundig ontwerpen." *Stedebouw en Volkshuisvesting* (5): 210-221.

Voort, R. Th. van der & K. Doevendans. 1984. "Conceptuele stedebouw." *Stedebouw en Volkshuisvesting* (1): 3-14.

Vries, Gerard de. 1984. De ontwikkeling van wetenschap - een inleiding in de wetenschapsfilosofie. Groningen (Neth.): Wolters - Noordhof

Vries, M.J. de; N. Cross & D.P. Grant (editors). 1993. Design Methodology and Relationships with Science. Nato ASI Series D: Behavioural and Social Sciences Vol.71. Dordrecht (Neth.): Kluwer Academic Publishers

Vries, M.J. de. 1993. "Design methodology and relationships with science: introduction." In: Design Methodology and Relationships with Science, edited by M.J.de Vries, N.Cross & D.P.Grant; Nato ASI Series D: Behavioural and Social Sciences Vol.71; pp.1-14. Dordrecht (Neth.): Kluwer Academic Publishers

Vroon, Piet. 1995. Tranen van de krokodil. Baarn (Neth.): Ambo

Vught, F. van & J.van Doorn. 1976. "Toekomstonderzoek en forecasting." *Intermediair* 51: December 17

Walen, Janette D. & Ed F. Nozeman. 1985. "Evaluatie van een ziekenhuisverplaatsing." *Stedebouw en Volkshuisvesting* (September): 383-390.

Weeber, Carel & Wouter Vanstiphout. 1998. Het wilde wonen. Rotterdam: Uitgeverij 010

Weide, A van der; C. M. Steenbergen & A. Homan. 2001. "Highrise-Belvedère." In: Onderzoeksatelier Buitenplaats - (ont)spanningsveld, edited by E. van der Kooij.; pp. 32-54. Delft (Neth.): Delft University Press

Westrik, John. 1989. "De toepasbaarheid van stedebouwkundige ontwerpmethoden." In: Stedebouwkundige ontwerpmethoden, edited by John Westrik & Hans Büchi; pp.59-78. Delft (Neth.): Publicatiebureau Bouwkunde

Westrik, J. 1993.: Ontwerpopgaven in de Stad. Reader. Internal publication Faculty of Architecture, TU Delft

Westrik, John. 2002. "Urban Design Methods." In: Ways to Study and Research - Urban, Architectural and Technical Design, edited by T.M.de Jong & D.J.M. van der Voordt; pp. 433-442. Delft (Neth.) Delft University Press

White, William H. 1988. Rediscovering the City Center. New York (N.Y.): Doubleday.

Wijnen, D. M. P. 2002. Bereikbaarheid beleven, Leefbaarheid bereiken - Structuur van de openbare ruimte Rotterdam; Masters thesis. Faculty of Architecture TU Delft

Wilde, Rein de. 1987a. "Verklaren in de sociale wetenschappen." In: Wetenschapsleer, edited by M. Korthals; pp.115-135. Heerlen (Neth.): Open Universiteit

Wilde, Rein de. 1987b. “De relativiteit van sociaal-wetenschappelijke kennis.” In: Wetenschapsleer, edited by M. Korthals; pp.137-154. Heerlen (Neth.): Open Universiteit

Zandvoort, H. 1987. “De ontwikkelingen van theorieën: onderzoeksprogramma's.” In: Wetenschapsleer, edited by M. Korthals; pp.41-58. Heerlen (Neth.): Open Universiteit

Zimmerman, Gerd. 2001. “La Gaya Scienza.” In: Research by Design, International Conference Faculty of Architecture Delft University of Technology in co operation with the EAAE/AEEA, november 1-3 2000, Proceedings A, edited by Marieke van Ouwerkerk & Jürgen Rosemann; pp.56-59. Delft (Neth.): Delft University Press

Zoete, Paul. 1997. Stedelijke knooppunten: virtueel beleid voor een virtuele werkelijkheid.; PhD Thesis. Amsterdam: Thesis Publishers

Zonneveld, Wil. 1991. Conceptvorming in de Ruimtelijke Planning. Deel A. Patronen en Processen. PhD Thesis. Amsterdam: PDI-Universiteit van Amsterdam

Author Index

Subject Index

Acknowledgements

My interest in both spatial structures and in science and its philosophical aspects dates from my student years in Amsterdam. The same goes for my interest in the application of scientific knowledge. I was fortunate in having the late Prof.Dr.Ir.A.P.A.Vink, who shared my interests, as my supervisor on the way to my *doctoraal examen* in Physical Geography. I owe him.

My appointment as lecturer in urban and regional design meant a switch from natural spatial structures to man-made spatial structures. Supervising this switch was Prof.Ir.N.A.de Boer. I owe him even more. But Niek of course wasn't the only one who taught me the ins and outs of urban & regional design; both colleagues and students did as well. The one person from those early years I must mention here is Ir.B.Radema. Beeno, you'll recognize quite a few of your ideas in this book.

From the late 1980's until half way through the 1990's new sources of inspiration were Prof.Dr.Ir.T.M.de Jong, and my then postgraduate students Marc Jacobs, Michiel Scholten, Miranda Thüsh, Maarten Witberg, Andries Geerse and some others who will come across their names in the list of references. Without them this book could not have been written.

My supervisor Prof.Dr.P.Drewe, my co supervisor Dr.E.de Graaff, Dr.E.D.Hulsbergen, Ir.I.Kriens, Dr.Ir.M.Jacobs, Prof.Ir.H.Beunderman, Drs.B.S.van Schuppen en Drs.T.van Velzen I thank for the work climate they created for me, for their moral support and for comments on some chapters of this book. Victor Joseph, Bob de Wit and Ernst Damen I thank for, respectively, the translation, the drawing of some of the figures and, *pars pro toto,* the maintenance of my computer - the irregularity of their working hours fortunately matched mine.

Finally my close friends: I owe it to you that I was able to get started on this project.

Ina Klaasen
September 15, 2003